Secularism or Democracy?

IMISCOE **(International Migration, Integration and Social Cohesion)**

IMISCOE is a European Commission-funded Network of Excellence of more than 350 scientists from various research institutes that specialise in migration and integration issues in Europe. These researchers, who come from all branches of the economic and social sciences, the humanities and law, implement an integrated, multidisciplinary and internationally comparative research programme that focuses on Europe's migration and integration challenges.

Within the programme, existing research is integrated and new research lines are developed to address issues crucial to European-level policymaking and provide a theory-based design to implement new research.

The publication programme of IMISCOE is based on five distinct publication profiles, designed to make its research and results available to scientists, policymakers and the public at large. High-quality manuscripts written by – or in cooperation with – IMISCOE members are published in these five series. An editorial committee coordinates the review process of the manuscripts. The five series are:
1. Joint Studies
2. Research
3. Dissertations
4. Reports
5. Textbooks

More information on the network can be found at: www.imiscoe.org.

IMISCOE **Research** includes publications resulting from research of IMISCOE members, such as research monographs and edited volumes.

Secularism or Democracy?

Associational Governance of Religious Diversity

Veit Bader

IMISCOE Research

AMSTERDAM UNIVERSITY PRESS

Cover illustration: This section of tiles, entitled 'Tres Culturas', composes a panel in one of the many murals found in Frigiliana. Like others tiles seen in the villages of Andalusia's Axarquía region, it memorialises the settlement, resistance and eventual massacre of the Moriscos after the Reconquista. Photo by Veit Bader.

Cover design: Studio Jan de Boer BNO, Amsterdam
Layout: The DocWorkers, Almere

ISBN 978 90 5356 999 3
NUR 741 / 763

© Veit Bader / Amsterdam University Press 2007

Summary contents

Preface

Introduction Contested religious pluralism

PART I MODERN STATES AND RELIGIONS, SOCIOLOGICAL AND
HISTORICAL CONSIDERATIONS: SETTING THE STAGE

1 Secularisation and separation? Institutional diversity of
religious governance

PART II RECONCEPTUALISING PRINCIPLES AND MAKING POLITICAL
PHILOSOPHY FIT FOR THE TASK OF ACCOMMODATING
RELIGIOUS DIVERSITY

2 Contextualising morality: moral minimalism, relational
neutrality, fairness as even-handedness

3 Priority for liberal democracy or secularism? Why I am not
a secularist

PART III DILEMMAS AND LIMITS OF ACCOMMODATION, PRINCIPLES
AND CASES: APPLYING MORAL MINIMALISM

4 Religious freedoms and other human rights, moral
conundrums and hard cases

5 Relational neutrality and even-handedness towards
religions: softer cases and symbolic issues

Detailed contents

Preface

This book on the governance of religious diversity is written from a methodologically areligious perspective that is characteristic of sociology and political philosophy. However, it seems appropriate to start with a personal 'confession': in a traditional sense, I am *religiös unmusikalisch* – to use Max Weber's famous phrase. I also do not feel the need to stylise my attraction or even my awe for complexity, diversity and contingency – the postmodern versions of traditional poly- or pantheism – into an 'immanentist counter-metaphysics'. As an *observer*, on the one hand, I am bewildered by the unnameable atrocities that have been and are still being committed in the name of monotheisms and its secular counterparts such as National Socialism or Marxism-Leninism, as well as in the name of polytheisms – *suum cuique* originally meant *Jedem seine Hekatomben* – and its secular counterparts, such as rivalling nationalisms. On the other hand, I acknowledge that much praiseworthy good has been and is still being done by committed religious and non-religious believers in symbolic universes of all kinds. As political theorists and citizens, we clearly have to counterbalance the polytheistic praise of diversity with the monotheistic guarantees of equality, as is so nicely phrased in the slogan: all different, all equal. As people trying to live meaningful lives, we may eventually learn to resist the temptations of all integrated, coherent and all-embracing symbolic universes, whether religious or secular (the sacralisation of the world in secularist and scientistic ideologies). Eventually, we might be able to live with finitude, mortality, contingency and diversity without trying to fill the empty space left by traditional religions and positive metaphysics with old or new substitutes like pantheism or an immanentist positive metaphysics – praising 'god in nature's endless and incredible complexity and beauty' – aestheticism, or old or new versions of negative theology or negative dialectics, even if 'pianissimo' (as the most privatised and 'subjectified' varieties of this old desire) or some 'horizontal transcendentalism' (the unnameable 'Other' in all of us). We can live without a 'future for such illusions' and without repeating heroically that 'God is Dead' or being condemned to an abyss of 'materialism', 'egotism', 'individualism', 'consumerism', 'decisionism' or what have you. In short, we might, eventually, become mature.

This already suggests that I defend religious diversity and its associational governance not for religious or perfectionist reasons as an ethically preferable way of life but for moderately anti-perfectionist moral reasons of justice. My hope is that individuals – religious or secular or those beyond the religious/secular divide – may be able to realise their divergent individual and collective life projects under conditions of peace, toleration and secure basic needs and rights for all, conditions that are fair, i.e. not too unequal for the respective minorities.

I would like to express my thanks for comments by participants and, particularly for written comments on theses for the book or on articles or earlier versions of chapters presented at the following conferences, symposia or workshops:

- 'Recasting European and Canadian History' (ENCS Conference, Bremen, 18-21 May 2000; Erik Fossum);
- 'Should We Institutionalize Religious Pluralism and, if so, How?' (Amsterdam, 30 June 2001; particularly Paul Hirst, Tariq Modood, Heiner Bielefeldt);
- 'Ethno-Religious Cultures, Identities and Political Philosophy. Contextualised Morality: Problems and Prospects' (Amsterdam, 2-5 July 2002; David Hollinger);
- 'Public Religion and Secular Democracy' (IMISCOE B6 workshop, Amsterdam 26-28 May 2005; Michael Minkenberg);
- 'Religion and Multicultural Citizenship' (Sydney, 11-13 July), and
- many meetings in my department at the University of Amsterdam and the Dutch Research School of Practical Philosophy (Hent de Vries, Ruth Sonderegger, Bart van Leeuwen, Sawitri Saharso, Michiel Leezenberg, Karel van der Leeuw).

For detailed written comments on some chapters of the many drafts of the manuscript, I am indebted to Rainer Bauböck, Joe Carens, Jac Christis, Geoff Levey, Marcel Maussen, Rob Reich and Lucas Swaine.

Last but not least, my friends and colleagues Ewald Engelen, Ton Korver, Pieter Pekelharing and Luuk Wijmans from Amsterdam, and Frank Cunningham and Will Kymlicka from Canada have commented on all of the chapters in the first long draft (and some also on many chapters in the later drafts) and helped me to drastically shorten the manuscript. Words cannot express my gratefulness for the time and energy they spent in their close readings and for the sophistication of their comments, criticisms and suggestions of all sorts. For reasons of space, I am unable to refer in detail to any of those whose elucidations, annotations, and proposals to either elaborate or delete, so much helped me to improve my text. All remaining errors and shortcomings are mine.

Many thanks also to Ewald, Pieter, Ton, and Ulla for their encouragement and moral support during the long and difficult journey of writing, rewriting and trimming the manuscript, particularly during those times when I was losing my confidence.

My thanks also to the Dutch Science Foundation (NWO) for a grant (*'onderwijsvrijstellingssubsidie'*) in the first semester of 2004-2005 and for a grant for the English editing, to Ron Salfrais for editing, and also to Ottho Heldring for taking over one of my courses in the first semester of 2005-06, which allowed me to finish the manuscript.

Many core ideas of the book have already been published in articles on religious and cultural diversity, multiculturalism, institutional pluralism and associative democracy in journals or volumes but the texts have been substantively rewritten, integrated and also slightly revised during my research and writing of the book. My morally minimalist position that slowly developed during the later 1990s became particularly more determined and outspoken. In addition, I gave more weight to the libertarian element in the combination of libertarian, democratic and egalitarian perspectives, which, since the late 1980s, led me to call my position a 'libertarian, democratic socialism', an oxymoron in the ears of traditional philosophers and politicians.

Introduction: Contested religious pluralism

Until the 1990s, the view that religious pluralism had caused deep troubles for centuries but has now ceased to create structural problems for political practice and political theory in modern state societies was absolutely predominant in politics, political philosophy and the sociology of religion after the Second World War. Religiously motivated or legitimised wars and civil wars were 'far behind us'. The principle of religious tolerance is widely recognised, and the institutions and practices of toleration are deeply rooted. Established churches no longer have the power and authority they once did. Moreover, in many of these societies, the differentiation of religion from economy, politics, science and education is a major part of their organising schemes and constitutions. Religious convictions are matters of private decisions, and competing religious organisations do not interfere in politics, having lost or given up their public or political roles. Liberal, democratic, republican, socialist, feminist or otherwise 'progressive' political parties share the assumption that modern states are 'secular' states that require a strict constitutional, legal, administrative, political and cultural separation of state from organised religions. In normative theory, particularly in political philosophy, there has been wide and deep agreement on principles of tolerance and religious freedoms, i.e. that liberal-democratic regimes should be neutral with regard to religions, that politics should be 'secular' in their justifications and effects, and that religious organisations and convictions should only be allowed to play a role in 'private' life or in civil society. In predominant theories of modern societies as well as in the sociology of religion, it was also taken for granted that modern state societies are 'secularised', and that this requires a complete separation of religion from all other functionally differentiated social systems and organisations, particularly from the political system and the state.

This predominant view of the relationship between religion and state could easily acknowledge that things are still different in pre-modern and modernising state societies in the 'rest of the world'. Although its core assumptions were never left unchallenged even in the West, the predominant view has only fairly recently started to show more serious cracks. The thesis that religious beliefs and practices would inevitably decline, based on evidence in Western Europe, clearly does not hold for the US and 'the Rest'. The thesis that all religious concerns and worries will only be limited to and pertain to the private realm is contradicted by their recent widespread presence in the public realm. Currently, conservative and fundamentalist religions as well as progressive religions are re-politicising 'private' relations and re-normativising the economic and political spheres. The thesis that modern societies would require a 'strict separation' of organised religions and politics is even incompatible with existing patterns in the US and France. It is clearly at odds with the continuing huge institutional diversity in other Western countries and in the 'rest' of the world.

This counterevidence, which has been gathered and presented by critical sociology and the history of religions for quite a while now, has gained at least some recognition in politics because considerable numbers of immigrants contributed to make lively ethno-religious diversity increasingly visible since the 1960s. The politics of multiculturalism tried to accommodate ethno-national diversity in different countries in divergent ways. Here, they contributed to some pluralisation of public cultures and also to a reconsideration by critical liberals and postmodernists of basic assumptions of standard liberalism in political philosophy, such as principles of 'difference-blind' state neutrality and of unitary citizenship. The relationship between religion and politics, however, was largely neglected in the literature on multiculturalism. This was the case, despite the fact that new religious minorities have been making increasingly politicised claims, starting with the demand for practical accommodation of their religious practices (codes of dress, prayer, diets, slaughtering and burial) by way of exemptions. These demands then went on to include some autonomy in organised societal spheres (like non-governmental religious schools or religious instruction in governmental schools), demanding that states pluralise education, the media, public cultures and symbols of national identity. Finally, the most demanding include some form of group representation and participation in the political process. In this way, religious issues became central political issues again, and most states with liberal-democratic constitutions started to accommodate claims that could mobilise moral and legal support by referring to legally binding rights such as freedom of religion, equal treatment and anti-discrimination. Both the political demands and grievances of religious minorities and the responses by governments have been influenced by widely diverging regimes of governance of religious diversity. However, at least for a short while, it seemed as if increased religious diversity – and even new forms of institutionalisation of religious pluralism – could be seen not only in a dramatised and negative way, i.e. as a threat to peace, security, stability, cohesion, toleration and democracy, but also as an opportunity and a promise. These practical developments also eventually entered political theory in the 1990s and it looked as if the standard assumptions of the predominant view might lose force and could be contained.

All of this has dramatically changed since 9/11 and the 'war against (Islamist) terrorism', or so it seems. Religion is certainly now again right in the centre of politics in this declared clash of civilisations. The predictable result seems to be that (generally) liberal policies of accommodation are increasingly under pressure, but particularly those aiming to pluralise public cultures and symbols and especially institutions. At the same time, intentionally or unintentionally, declared religious divides have deepened at the international level.

Old constellations and battle lines in Europe from the 16th and 17th centuries have been revitalised and 'Enlightenment' rationalists and evangelists of an aggressive secularism venture to present themselves as the only reasonable people fighting both fundamentalist and conservative religionists as well as the 'progressive liberal' multiculturalists and postmodernists. In addition, they present their preferred institutional option – a fully secularised state together with a 'strict' separation of state and politics from completely privatised religions – as the only reasonable solution to preventing religious warfare and guaranteeing peace, security, toleration and democracy. The more simple-minded adherents of these views propose that 'all the world has to become America' or try to export 'the French model of *laïcité*' as the alternative to 'Anglo-Saxon' liberal multiculturalism and to 'neo-corporatist' European religious regimes. The more sophisticated voices continue to remind their compatriots that they themselves do not live up to these ideals and constitutional promises but they try to sell the same utopia.

I strongly believe that these are the wrong constellations, the wrong alternatives and the wrong battle lines being raised *in politics*. In this book, I argue for a third way, defending two major political claims. First, policies of liberal accommodation of religious and cultural diversity are a better alternative than both the old and new republican or liberal policies of assimilation and the unlimited toleration of religious and cultural practices incompatible with the hard core of liberal-democratic constitutions. Second, democratic institutional pluralism and associative democracy in particular provides better institutional opportunities to the realisation of peace, toleration and core principles of liberal democratic constitutions than, on the one hand, the strict separation of organised religions from a presumed 'religion-blind' and strictly 'neutral' state defended by standard liberalism and republicanism and, on the other hand, the religious (neo-)corporatism (illiberal and anti-democratic institutional pluralism and rigid 'pillarisation') defended by traditionalist and orthodox religious organisations and leaders.

Before going into details, I would like to present the briefest outline ever of what associative democracy means for the governance of religious diversity, its differences with idealised American denominationalism and neo-corporatist European regimes of selective cooperation included.

Associative democracy (AD) rejects constitutional establishment. It supports the legal, administrative and political recognition of organised religions. It balances strong guarantees for individual or 'inner' religious freedoms and strong guarantees for associational or 'outer' freedoms of religion and provides maximum accommodation to religious practices, constrained only by minimal morality and basic rights. In addition to tax exemptions for organised religions, it provides public funding for faith-based organisations in all sorts of care and education, given public scrutiny and quality standards. It provides opportunities for these organisations to be even-handedly involved in standard setting and governance of these services. Recognised religions are not only explicitly allowed to play a public role, they should be given specific information rights and corresponding information duties with regard to contested issues on an even-handed basis with other *weltanschaulichen* organisations (based on 'philosophical ways of life'), they should be given rights and opportunities to participate in public fora and hearings, and they should be included in advisory ethical councils.

AD differs from *neo-corporatist European regimes* in four main regards. First, AD criticises the existing varieties of weak and plural constitutional establishment of churches. Then, although acknowledging thresholds for the recognition of organised religions (cooperation is inevitably selective), it requires less demanding and more flexible thresholds to counterbalance the many legal, fiscal and political privileges of the established majority religion(s). Also, it explicitly alleviates the plight of vulnerable minorities (dissenters, women and children) within religious majorities and minorities through external guarantees of their basic rights and free exit. In addition, it provides meaningful exit options and couples recognition and public funding by balancing demanding criteria and associational freedom. Last, in doing so, it helps to counterbalance the strong conservative bias in organisations and leadership of majority and minority religions and helps to develop more open versions of the governance of religious diversity.

Associational governance differs from the ideal model of *American Denominationalism*, which offers no official public recognition of religion and relegates religion to the 'private sphere' or 'civil society'. It claims to prevent any religious impact on 'political society' and the state. Officially, there should be no public financing of religions and of faith-based organisations in social services, care and education. These claims are considerably weakened, however, by the facts that non-establishment and state neutrality cannot prevent but actually serve to mask religious majority bias, and that faith-based organisations, recently also in education, are publicly funded without proper assessment of the dilemmas of recognition, selective cooperation and institutionalisation. Compared to both the neo-corporatist European way and the American ideal-cum-practice, associative democracy is thus an attractive third way.

I also think that *political theory* is still not sufficiently prepared to deal with the increasing (visibility of) religious diversity and, particularly, with the threat of religious-political fundamentalism. American political liberalism has dominated the debates for some time now. It is characterised by a focus on principles and rights, on limitations or exclusion of religious arguments in public debate, a secularist interpretation of liberal-democratic constitutions, and a strictly separationist interpretation of the legitimate relations between organised religions and the state. Postmodernist and traditional communitarian critics have criticised and rejected these 'solutions' but have, at the same time, sacrificed principles such as neutrality, equality and even moderate universalism. We can do better; third ways are possible. Conceptions of a moderate universalism and embedded impartiality provide a better meta-theoretical framework than radical, abstract universalism or radical ethical particularism. Relational state neutrality and fairness as even-handedness are more appropriate meta-legal principles than difference-blindness and fairness as hands-off. And priority for democracy is more appropriate than exclusivist secularism or liberal reason restraints, or so I will try to show.

Yet, in this book, my main task is not critical but constructive, because I am presenting proposals to redesign institutions and policies. Cultural and religious diversity is now widely defended in different varieties of liberal theories of multiculturalism and postmodern theories of identities and becoming. However, institutional pluralism is still fairly underdeveloped or even absent from the agenda. This book is a plea for an institutional and attitudinal turn in political philosophy, political theory and the social sciences. The increasing acknowledgement in recent political philosophy that institutions and contexts are more worthy of attention in analysis than they were assumed to be is stimulated by three core moments combined in contextualised moral theory: the fact of moral pluralism or value pluralism, the recognition of under-determinacy of principles, and the re-evaluation of practical knowledge.

Contextualised moral theory and the proposed institutionalist turn in political philosophy also induce us to rethink the academic division of disciplines because both of them have to draw on a wide variety of studies in the social sciences (most prominently the history and sociology/anthropology of religions, comparative institutional economy, sociology and political science). If there were any space in the academic division of labour for such a border-crossing, multi- and inter-disciplinary endeavour, it would be the field of political theory. This cuts through the institutionalised cleavages between moral and political philosophy (specialising in normative theory) and the social sciences (specialising in rich descriptions, sound explanations and perhaps some modest forecasting). My proposed version of political theory criticises the terrible lack of institutional concreteness that characterises mainstream political philosophy and its terrible lack of historical and comparative knowledge of the 'real world'. In addition, it criticises the hidden normative bias of many social scientists who refuse to spell out their own normative perspectives and commitments. It is only fairly recently that social scientists have taken up the task of a critical evaluation of existing institutions and policies and, more reluctantly, of also engaging in productive and imaginative institutional design. I explicitly try to combine the normative approach of political philosophy with issues of the practical design of institutional arrangements.

Designing new institutional settings of religious pluralism and policies that claim to be more in line with re-conceptualised principles and institutions of liberal democracy and also to be more effective in containing religious fundamentalism is clearly a huge task of stunning complexity. It is plainly impossible to simultaneously deal with meta-theoretical philosophical issues and normative principles, history and comparative analysis of institutions, policies and cases, and institutional design and policy recommendations in depth and in detail. Before I indicate how I intend to order and reduce this complexity, I hasten to say that I am fortunately not the first or only person engaging in such a complex enterprise. I can draw substantially on the work of recent political philosophers such as Joseph Carens, William Galston, Will Kymlicka, Bhikhu Parekh, Jeff Spinner, Michael Walzer, legal theorists such as Marc Galanter, Silvio Ferrari, Michael McConnell, Ayalet Shachar, Gerhard Robbers, and social scientists such as Rainer Bauböck, John Bowen, Joel Fetzer, Matthias Koenig, Michael Minkenberg, Stephen Monsma, Christopher Soper, Nancy Rosenblum, Ulrich Willems and others.

Compared with this developing strand in political theory, my approach shows two specificities that make it fairly original. First, I defend a conception of minimal morality that should be applied and enforced everywhere but which, at the same time, allows maximum accommodation of non-liberal but decent groups within liberal-democratic polities. Unlike other moral minimalists, however, I combine this moral minimum with standards of more demanding – liberal, democratic, egalitarian, pluralist – differentiated moralities that can be and should be applied, depending on groups, issues and contexts in a considered way, as long as they do not infringe upon standards of minimal morality (I call this the 'non-infringement proviso'). In other words, I combine a liberalism or multiculturalism of 'fear' with more demanding ones of hope. Second, I systematically connect emerging discussions of institutional pluralism in political philosophy with a broad social science perspective of governance, distinct from government or governing, that has not yet been applied to problems of ethnic and national minorities in multiculturalism literatures in general, or to problems of religious minorities in particular. The governance of religious diversity has also been widely neglected in the sociology of religions, which has mostly focused on describing and explaining diversity of religious beliefs and practices.

For these reasons, compared with critical political philosophy and legal theory, my approach is more explicitly focused on the governance of religious diversity, and it is also more comparative and institution-centred. Compared with critical social science, I connect the operative normative principles and legally institutionalised norms, which are used in evaluation studies ('grounded normativity'), to moral principles and to divergent ways of grounding them. I hope that my connection of normative and descriptive debates will create some new and unexpected perspectives and perhaps even lead to productive cooperation and learning across disciplinary and national boundaries.

Trying to capture the stunning complexity, instead of neglecting or prematurely reducing it, inevitably implies some superficiality. Doing 'political philosophy in the vernacular' (Kymlicka) means that I cannot extensively discuss issues of meta-ethics and moral philosophy. I also cannot go into critical discussion with sociologists of religion or extensively present the relevant results for my purposes. Space also prevents the presentation and discussion of specific countries or cases in any detail. Instead, I have chosen a broader historical and empirical comparison of many cases, policy fields and countries. However, space and also the limitations of my knowledge and expertise make it impossible to present and critically discuss the respective evidence in detail (I had to cut one third of the original manuscript). In addition, I completely depend on a selection of historical and comparative studies by others and can only hope that I have not ignored relevant sources. In all these regards, my book remains fairly sketchy. I present a broad and general synopsis that needs further critical and constructive elaboration in almost every chapter but my hope is that my synthesis may stimulate this elaboration and thus open new directions for further research.

In addition to these serious limitations, I had to restrict the scope of historical and empirical comparisons to religious diversity within 'Western' states with liberal-democratic constitutions, partly for reasons of

space but also for lack of competence. I have tried in several ways to respond to expected charges of Eurocentrism, Christian or Western bias.
First, my concept of religion and my discussion of secularism and secularisation are explicitly articulated in a way to avoid this bias. Second,
my concept of a threshold of institutional differentiation between religions and states/polities is explicitly critical with regard to theories of
modernisation and modernity modelled after idealised Western societies. Third, I show that non-Western religions have been suppressed
and treated as the 'alien' insiders right from the beginning and are increasingly treated so nowadays. In addition, I often refer to India – the
liberal-democratic state with the richest religious, linguistic and cultural diversity on the globe – in order to counter the dangers of bias. I do
this because this huge laboratory of diversity and institutional pluralism has been widely but still astonishingly neglected by predominant
political philosophy (Bhargava 1998) and also because it may serve as
an interesting constitutional and policy model (Bhargava 2005). I also
think that demonstrating the broad diversity of institutions and policies
even within the West may help to introduce at least a fine modicum of
sensitivity for a start. Finally, heated political debate on religious issues
is currently characteristic of most countries. However, one only finds
really productive debates in political philosophy in a few countries, and
India is certainly one of them. In response to the mounting criticism
of liberal philosophy by philosophers such as Nandy and Madan, one
increasingly finds attempts to re-conceptualise, instead of replacing liberal principles by political philosophers such as Rajeev Bhargava, Akeel
Bilgrami, Tariq Modood, Bhikhu Parekh and Amartya Sen, originating
from the Indian subcontinent, from whom I have learned a lot and
with whom I share some important theoretical and practical insights.

The book is divided into four parts. In part I, I present sociological and
historical considerations for a critical assessment of the twin myths of
secularisation and strict separation of state and religion, which have
dominated theories of modernity and sociology of religion after the
Second World War. By demonstrating their conceptual, theoretical and
empirical flaws, I hope to end the unhappy marriage between 'modern
sociology' – a type of social theory which is based on evolutionary and
structural false necessities – and a liberal political philosophy that only
legitimises the predominant interpretations of the underlying institutional patterns in a few Western countries. Having set the stage in this
way, in part II, I hope to make political philosophy fit for the task of
dealing with religious diversity by re-conceptualising universalism,
neutrality, fairness and, particularly, secularism, by introducing my version of contextualised moral theory, and by defending my conception
of minimal morality and its relation with more demanding liberal, de-

mocratic, egalitarian and pluralistic moralities. In part III, I apply my conception of minimal morality to hard cases, to show that and how maximum accommodation of religious practices has, on the one hand, to be limited by minimal but tough moral and legal constraints. While on the other hand, I apply my conception of differentiated moralities to softer cases, to show that and why states with liberal-democratic constitutions should easily, not grudgingly, accommodate religious practices that do not conflict with the hard core of minimal morality and law. In part IV, I materialise the proposed institutional turn in political theory, preparing the ground for informed institutional and policy recommendations. I take up the indications from earlier chapters that institutionally pluralist arrangements provide better chances for minorities and, at the same time, for increasing the actual degree of relational state neutrality and for finding more fair and even-handed solutions. I discuss different institutional models of democracy and of religious governance and present and defend associative democracy against moral and realist challenges.

In chapter 1, I show why we need a concept of religion freed from its Christian, Protestant bias under conditions of increased presence and visibility of religious diversity both for practical and theoretical reasons and I present a poly-contextual and perspectivist conception. The main part is devoted to a criticism of secularisation and strict separation and the consequences this perspectivist critique has for political theory and practice. From a *sociological perspective*, I try to show that the thesis of an inevitable decline of religious beliefs and practices, derived from Western European countries, conflicts with all of the evidence from the US and the rest of the world. The thesis that all religions change into subjectivised, de-culturalised, individualised and privatised beliefs, following the idealised model of radical Protestantism, is ambiguous and at odds with practices of old and new orthodox religions and with Christian and non-Christian religions going public. The thesis that modern societies require a strict separation of state from religions, drawn from an idealised American model – here the US is not the 'exception' but the norm – is at odds with the actual relationships in all liberal-democratic states and should therefore be replaced by a minimal threshold of institutional, organisational and role differentiation or, in legal terms, the two autonomies of the state from religions and of (organised) religions from the state. Recent states with liberal-democratic constitutions show a huge diversity of regimes of religious government. Some have established state churches that have little power, others are characterised by plural establishment or cooperation between state and officially recognised religions, while only some combine non-establishment with intended strict separation. All states grant religions a special legal status, all finance religions at least indirectly, e.g. by tax exemptions, and all finance faith-based organisations in care either directly or indirectly. Only a tiny minority rejects any public financing of religious schools, but the huge majority (including France and recently the US as well) do so either directly or indirectly. Yet, they do so in widely diverging ways and this bewildering diversity is intensified inside states at different levels of government. Thus, different states (or the same states at different levels) grudgingly accept or reject claims by minorities to accommodate religiously prescribed codes of diet (e.g. kosher, halal), dress (turbans, yarmulkes, head scarves), prayer in public institutions, to pluralise educational curricula and pedagogies, to pluralise public culture and symbols of national identity, and to allow religious exemptions from general laws and regulations. These institutionalised patterns and policy traditions also have an impact on predominant paradigms of jurisdiction. The same human rights are interpreted and balanced in divergent ways and we cannot see convergence into one optimal, let alone morally required, institutional and legal policy model, neither in the European Union nor globally among liberal-democratic states. From the perspective of *liberal-democratic politics and political theory*, the important issues are firstly not whether societies are 'secularised' but whether states are indifferent, i.e. neither 'secular' nor 'religious' but equidistant to both, respecting the two autonomies. Secondly, these issues are which relationships between state and organised religions are the most conducive to the principles and practices of liberal democracy. Instead of propagating 'strict separation' and the principles of strict neutrality and religion-blindness of the state (which may or may not be fine in an ideal world but may be second best or worse in the real world) we may have to re-conceptualise liberal principles (part II) and design alternative regimes of religious governance (part IV).

In chapter 2, I present a substantive, critical re-conceptualisation of those principles of liberal political philosophy that are important for debating the accommodation of religious diversity and its limitations. Moderate universalism and embedded impartiality enable us to avoid the pitfalls of abstract universalism and ethical particularism. A moderately universalist morality under conditions of reasonable pluralism of the good life tends to be a minimalist morality that may be combined with more demanding differentiated standards of liberal, democratic and egalitarian morality. Thinking of deep ethno-religious cultural diversity seriously makes us recognise that polities, including liberal-democratic states, cannot be strictly neutral or 'religion-blind' and cannot guarantee complete cultural equality. Strict neutrality and a conception of justice as 'hands-off' have to be re-conceptualised as relational neutrality and fairness as even-handedness in cultural matters. Finally, four facts have stimulated a shift towards a contextualised theory of morality. First, the fact that not only our conceptions of the good life, but also our moral principles conflict with each other (moral pluralism, distinct from ethical pluralism and moral relativism); second, the fact that our articulations, interpretations and applications of the respective moral principles are indeterminate (under-determinacy of principles); third, the fact that normative reasoning cannot be confined to moral arguments but includes ethical, prudential and realist reasons, often at odds with each other (complexity of practical reason) and, finally, the fact that for the contested arts of interpreting and balancing principles and rights and of weighing moral, ethical, prudential and realist arguments, philosophical armchair reflection and theoretical knowledge is overburdened, reductionist, or indecisive, to say the least (re-evaluation of practical knowledge).

In chapter 3, I present a contextualised discussion of secularism and explain why I am not a secularist. Liberal-democratic states are not 'secular' states but constitutional states, guaranteeing minimal morality and, in addition, standards of liberal-democratic morality, minimally understood. Calling them 'secular' is not terminologically misleading but politically innocent because the 'power of words' or the 'politics of symbolic action' is so strong. This has important but generally neglected historical, structural and strategic disadvantages. Next, I discuss why both first-order 'ethical secularism' and second-order 'political secularism' have to be rejected. I also discuss why an independent political and secular ethics as a foundation of liberal democracy and why the exclusion of religious reasons (exclusivist secularism') or of all 'comprehensive reasons' (Rawlsian 'reason-restraints') from public debate are unfair under conditions of reasonable pluralism, implausible and tendentiously at odds with freedoms of political communication and considered anti-paternalism. In short, I argue that 'secularism' of all sorts – the predominant meta-narrative or knowledge regime – has to be replaced by priority for liberal democracy, which I then defend against foundationalist philosophical challenges and against religious challenges by showing how and under which conditions Christian and other religions have doctrinally, institutionally and attitudinally learned to accept priority for liberal democracy.

Before turning to these institutional and attitudinal aspects explicitly in part IV, I analyse whether and how my plea for moral minimalism and my re-conceptualised principles of relational neutrality and fairness as even-handedness aids in resolving the thorny issues of possibilities and limits to accommodate religious practices in liberal democracies. In chapter 4, I defend maximum accommodation of practices of illiberal and non-democratic but decent religious minorities constrained by the standards of minimal morality, combined with some of the more demanding minimalist standards of liberal-democratic morality in cases where religions vie for public money. First, I address tensions between individual and associational religious freedoms before turning to tensions between religious freedoms and other basic human rights, i.e. 'Associational Freedoms versus Nondiscrimination and Equal Opportunity', 'Modern Criminal law versus the Nomos of certain Ethno-Religious Groups', and 'Religious versus Modern, Civil Family Law'. Divergent balancing of conflicting basic rights (as moral pluralism makes us expect) is the normal business of constitutional courts guided by dominant legal and jurisdictional paradigms that are informed by country-specific regimes of religious governance. Compared with the enormous amount of legal, politico-philosophical and ethical literatures that discuss hard cases, my approach is firstly characterised by an explicit attempt to resist liberal-democratic congruence, and secondly by clearly spelling out that differences between conflicts, issues and groups are important. For example, between illiberal and undemocratic religious groups and those who endorse liberal-democratic morality internally and amongst illiberal minorities between isolationist or retiring minorities (internally decent and externally peaceful), 'totalistic', ultra-orthodox or fundamentalist but peaceful, and violent political fundamentalists. Thirdly, my approach is characterised by a broader spectrum of policy repertoires, compared with autonomy or external state intervention only.

Comparatively softer cases and symbolic issues are addressed in chapter 5, where I discuss different kinds of claims to pragmatic and symbolic accommodation by new religious minorities that clearly do not conflict with liberal-democratic morality. Even if they may require considerable legal and practical accommodation, they should be easier to resolve, particularly if liberal-democratic states and politics were committed (as they should be) to the principles of relational religious neutrality and fairness as even-handedness. Contrary to republican claims, minimal liberal-democratic morality does not require exclusive governmental schools. However, in systems that realise a near-monopoly of governmental schools, the demand to pluralise curricula, pedagogy and the culture of governmental schools is even more pressing than in educational systems that allow for directly public-funded non-governmental religious schools and/or for pluralised religious instruction in governmental schools. Resistance to fair accommodation in all these cases is as characteristic for actual educational policies in all countries as it is morally impermissible, and the same holds for claims to fair exemptions from and fair accommodations of existing rules and practices of public and private administration. Resistance to fair pluralisation of public cultures and symbols of national identity is as widespread and even fiercer, and demands for fair representation of new religious minorities in the political process that would empower them to raise these morally legitimate claims more effectively are rejected out-right by republican and liberal assimilationists.

In chapter 6, I draw the consequences from my criticism of liberal reason restraints and argue for a minimalist conception of civic and de-mocratic virtues (a mixture of attitudes and competencies) that should complement but not replace liberal-democratic principles. Virtues are learned in appropriate institutional settings and interactions, but the high hopes and expectations that associations in civil society would work unambiguously as seedbeds of democratic virtues have to be tem-pered. After this, I focus on institutions directly. I introduce different types of institutional pluralism (political/territorial, social, ascriptive minority pluralism), which can be characterised as 'power-sharing sys-tems' that guarantee divergent units some say in the political process and also meaningful autonomy or self-determination to decide specific issues. I analyse diverging models of democracy and show that associa-tive democracy combines territorial pluralism (multi-layered polities, e.g. federalism) with social pluralism (organised interest representation of classes, professions, clients, consumers) and autonomy and repre-sentation of territorially less or non-concentrated minorities such as gendered minorities and many ethnic and religious minorities. It is more conducive to minorities than all other models of democracy, but it is also much more flexible and open than existing 'corporatist' or 'neo-corporatist' varieties of institutional pluralism. Against this back-ground, I analyse important differences between ethnic and religious diversity, asking whether religion is really as different from ethnicity as is often assumed, and present four different types of incorporation of ethno-religious minorities into democratic polities. In a short compari-son of regimes of institutional pluralism, I try to show that modern de-mocratic polities may even learn important lessons from non-demo-cratic forms of institutional pluralism, particularly from the millet sys-tem in the late Ottoman Empire, which obviously did not live up to the minimal standards of liberal-democratic morality. Recent types of insti-tutional pluralism, such as 'consociational' democracy and 'neo-cor-poratist' interest representation, however, are compatible with modern liberal democracy.

In chapter 7, I connect these discussions more explicitly with the in-corporation of religious diversity. First, I present normative institu-tional and policy models of religious governance and give reasons why I focus exclusively on a comparison of two models, i.e. 'non-constitu-tional religious pluralism' and 'non-establishment combined with pri-vate pluralism'. I then state and defend my claim that a specific version of non-constitutional religious pluralism, associative democracy pro-vides an institutional alternative, a realistic and feasible utopia, to es-cape from the ritualised opposition of idealised American denomina-

tionalism and corporatist varieties of selective cooperation still domi-
nating policy discourses and blocking institutional imagination and
practical experiment. Associative democracy, like all existing varieties
of religious institutional pluralism empowers religions, but – as a moderately libertarian version – is more conducive to old and new religious
minorities and, particularly, to vulnerable minorities within minorities
in the following ways: first, in addition to guaranteeing exit rights, it
provides meaningful exit options. Second, it tries to encourage debate
and discussion inside religious organisations, particularly if they accept
public money and want to be represented in the political process, without overriding meaningful associational autonomy. Third, recognition
and institutionalisation of religions enlarge the possibilities and means
of minimal legitimate state supervision and control. And, last but not
least, associative democracy makes productive use of the idea of differentiated morality, i.e. standards of minimal morality have to protect the
basic needs, interests and rights of all, including vulnerable minorities
within minorities, such as minors and women. Their basic interests require external supervision, control and sanctions (by the liberal state)
without the rough-shot overriding of meaningful associational autonomy in caring for their best interests as evangelists of liberal autonomy
and liberal-democratic congruence propose. These claims are then defended against the charges that associative democracy would be not
conducive to or even undermine individual autonomy, modern democracy and citizenship, and strictly legal and also substantive equal treatment of all religions and 'church autonomy'. Contrary to liberal and republican assimilations, associative democracy recognises the tensions
between moral principles. Instead of heroically propagating tragic
choices or big trade-offs between 'your (individual) rights and your
(collective) culture', its institutions enable better and more sensible
balances.

In chapter 8, I show that a certain minimum amount of institutionalisation is inevitable because the presence of old and new religions
changes mutual expectations, leads to the development of their own
organisations, and also to different varieties of public recognition by
states, whether through legislation, jurisdiction and case law or
through administrative regulation and decisions. Institutionalisation is
a conflictive process, involving promises and risks for religions and
governments. As an illustration of the dilemmas, I compare the patterns of Muslim representative organisations in various European
states and the US, which is characterised by a fairly strong impact of
denominationalism on all new religions, a limited system of selective
cooperation between administrations and religions, and the absence of
state-induced or state-imposed patterns of organisation and representation of religions. In a short evaluation of these patterns, I try to show

that all have to deal with tensions between individual versus associational freedoms of religion, freedoms versus equalities, legal versus more substantive equality, democracy versus efficiency and effectiveness, and the respective trade-offs. No existing pattern, but also no ideal model, can maximise them all. Yet, I also try to show that associative democracy provides better opportunities than American Denominationalism and rigid European 'corporatist' systems of cooperation because it combines voluntarism with a more open, pluralist and flexible system of selective cooperation.

Even if a sensible balance of the moral dilemmas may be achieved, the unintended consequences or the empirical effects of institutionalising religious pluralism may be so serious that non-establishment cum private pluralism may finally be the better alternative. After all, the way to hell is paved with good intentions and realism forbids ruthless experiments with associative democracy. Chapter 9 addresses the most serious realist objections. All forms of religious institutional pluralism (including the most flexible and libertarian ones) are said to induce fixed and rigid religious categorisation by the state, to foster 'fundamentalist' organisations and leaders, to be so rigid and inflexible that they cannot easily adapt to changes in the religious landscape and systematically work against new religious minorities. They are also said to undermine minimal peace by stimulating religious conflicts, to undermine minimal stability, social cohesion and political unity, to undermine habits of toleration and conciliation or minimally required civil and democratic virtues. This is because religious institutional pluralism does not provide for common public institutions and spaces where these virtues can be learned in practice (e.g. common schools, non-communal political parties, everyday interaction in practical life, in workplaces and neighbourhoods). I try to show that associative democracy is the least vulnerable to these objections because it strengthens voluntarism and the cross-cutting of associational ties. In contrast, imposed inclusion into common institutions and enforced assimilation, proposed by liberal or republican critics are indeed prone to producing many of the said counterproductive consequences. Finally, everything depends on contextual variables such as economic growth and distribution, stability of established and broadly accepted liberal-democratic constitutions, democratic culture and practices, the character of minorities and the relationships between majorities and minorities and, last but not least, on volatile external factors such as situations of security emergency. Like all other options, associative democracy has to face serious trade-offs, but it is flexible enough for pragmatic adaptations. It is a realistic utopia developed by democratic experimentalism.

In chapter 10, I turn to education, historically and recently the most contested and conflict-prone area in the relations between governments and religions. Civic republicans, deliberative and social democrats, socialists and laïcists claim that all religious schools in all contexts produce extremism, social fragmentation, increasing inequalities and the erosion of civic virtues and bonds. Using comparative evidence, I try to persuade them that they should at least moderate their charges and reconsider their often favoured option of governmental schooling. In particular, I try to show that there are many cases showing that educational systems that provide fairly equal public funding for religious schools help to guarantee more equal educational opportunities for all children, providing they are appropriately regulated and controlled. Social justice or substantive equality requires public funding in the 'real world' of serious inequalities, or so I want to show. A mixed or pluralist regime of associational governance of education provides better chances to address the difficult tensions between moral principles such as freedoms of education and diversity versus nondiscrimination, equal educational opportunities and also public control of minimal civic and liberal virtues. In addition, it provides better chances of resolving tensions between moral principles and pedagogical aims and also standards of efficiency and effectiveness. I also try to show that the American educational reality deviates from the ideal model, which bans any public financing of religious and other non-governmental schools. American reality allows for practical experimentalism with voucher systems, with charter and magnet schools and other alternatives. However, practical experimentalism is often hindered by predominant dichotomies that distinguish between either state or market and either private or public provision. Such dichotomies are descriptively inadequate, preventing more satisfying solutions in the vein of associational governance to the structural problems that confront all educational systems. Associationalist regimes also promise to be more effective and efficient and allow for the smooth, incremental, piecemeal adaptation and innovation of educational systems.

As you will see, there are many cross-references in this book. To limit the size of these references, it has been decided to work with abbreviations. These are chap. for chapter, sect. for section and para. for paragraph. A cross-reference within this book includes no other text but its abbreviation and numerical correspondence. A cross-reference to another book or publication, however, provides further reference details.

PART I

MODERN STATES AND RELIGIONS, SOCIOLOGICAL
AND HISTORICAL CONSIDERATIONS: SETTING THE
STAGE

1 Secularisation and separation?
Institutional diversity of religious governance

If ever there was a contested concept it must be religion. We all know what it is, we all have opinions about it, and we all judge it. Since we all know something different, our opinions and judgements differ as well. The contributions of social science and philosophy have not really helped in clarifying the issue of 'what we talk about when we talk about religion'. In this chapter, I set out to at least clear the field a little, by focusing on two tenacious misunderstandings in the study of religion and religions. These misunderstandings are 'secularisation' and the 'separation' of state and religion, both the result of some biases that we hope to correct.

First, the Western, Christian, Protestant bias in the concept of religion is erroneous and unfair under conditions of the increased presence and visibility of religious diversity. We need a poly-contextual and perspectivist concept of religion (sect. 1.1).

Second, as this bias has had an impact on definitions and descriptions of secularisation in its cultural, societal and political meanings, I emphasise the distinction between the perspective of religions, sociology, liberal-democratic politics and normative political theory (sect. 1.2). From the perspective of sociology, I try to show that a generalised use of secularisation is counterproductive and should be avoided. The theses of an inevitable decline of religious beliefs and practices, and of an inevitable subjectivation and privatisation, are at odds with empirical evidence. I also refute the hard core of the thesis that 'modern' societies demand a strict or complete functional and institutional separation of states and politics from (organised) religions. The huge diversity in the relationships between societies, politics, culture, state and organised religions is at odds with the myth of strict separation (sect. 1.3). I defend a minimalist threshold of functional, institutional, organisational and role differentiation.

Third, it is important to demonstrate the huge gap between ideal models of strict separation and the actual muddle we live in. That states actually do not do what liberal philosophers and politicians think they should do is not normatively deplorable. From a perspective of grounded normativity in political theory (sect. 1.4), there are defensible grounds for actual practices and institutions. Refuting false evolution-

ary, structural and functional necessities of modernisation theories be-
fits recent developments in institutionalist social sciences, which highlight contingency, path dependency and institutional diversity. Also,
this opens perspectives for practical experimentalism, for imaginative
institutional and policy alternatives, i.e. realistic utopias. This is explored in part IV.

1.1 Religions and religion

The diversity of competing religions belies unilinear conceptions of
evolutionary civilisation, imperialist or Eurocentric definitions and descriptions of religion.

Monotheistic religions compete intensely with each other, as they engage in aggressive missionary and proselytising campaigns. At the
same time, they compete with polytheistic and non-theistic world religions and their export into the West. Increasingly, animistic, spiritual-
ist 'tribal' religions are going global and religious syncretism is rising,
particularly in Latin America and Africa. The situation of a more or
less peaceful coexistence of divergent types of religions visualises religious diversity. The process may be summarised as a development
'from hegemony to pluralism' (Bouma 1999; Martin 1990: viif, 293ff,
1993; Luhmann 2000: 141ff, 341ff).

Within Western Christian or Judeo-Christian state societies, one also
finds competing monotheisms, intensified reactive Protestant fundamentalisms within Christianity, Islam as the old foreign 'enemy' and
the new 'enemy' from within, an import of all types of Eastern world
religions (Hinduism, Buddhism, Zen), new age sects and spirituality,
the increased visibility of native people and their religions, and a massive growth of every possible form of syncretism.[1]

In this context, two characteristics of religions (plurals) prevent the
finding of a common, objective core of a practical and a scientific concept of religion (*singularis*). First, the variety of types or forms of religions is overwhelming.[2] Second, observations of religions are inevitably embedded in competing religious and cultural traditions themselves. There is simply no neutral viewpoint.

In law and jurisdiction, these changes have contributed to a reconsideration of traditional Christian concepts of religion. The development
of the jurisdiction of the US Supreme Court in famous religion cases –
polygamy, flag salute, conscientious objections and other exemptions,
use of drugs – exemplify and illustrate this.[3] Originally, the Court's decisions showed an unreflective and unrestricted bias in favour of the
majority religion of (Protestant) Christianity (e.g. in the famous anti-
polygamy rulings against Mormons) (Galanter 1966: 231ff, 257; Green-

awalt 2000: 206ff). Even when broadened to include Catholicism and Judaism, these favoured concepts of religion were monotheistic or at least theistic (God, Supreme Being), dogmatic (favouring 'derivative theological articulation' over 'religious activity'), belief-centred (discriminating against ritual-centred religions), and content-centred (favouring 'high' or 'civilised' religions over 'low' or 'barbarian' ones). The perspective of the dominant religious majority, implicitly or explicitly endorsed by the Court, was taken as the objective standard. During a long and still continuing process of learning – stimulated by conscientious objection cases (Miller 1985: 363ff; Chambers II 1993; Stanfield II 1993; Eberly 1993) – many parts of this definition have been dropped. In recent cases, the Court has used very broad, ecumenical, permissive and subjective definitions of the religious, focusing on the perspective of the claimant. The practical dangers of such an all-inclusive and subjective definition are so obvious that the Court applies an uneasy mix of criteria such as sincerity, centrality (not to all religions but to the particular religion in question), time and some measure of shared public understanding to prevent the paradoxical results of the new *latitudinarianism*, particularly in exemption cases. Attempts to avoid legal definitions of religion (by explicit legislation and/or jurisdiction) are, however, counterproductive from a liberal rule-of-law perspective because they would only increase the discretion of administrations (sect. 8.4).

The same difficulties of finding a defensible balance between broad definitions of religion that seem to exclude nearly nothing, and more specific definitions that seem to be narrowly linked to particular religions, are characteristic of recent scientific discussions. All attempts to press the enormous diversity of religions into the straitjacket of one 'ontological', 'anthropological' or psychological concept of the 'essence' of religion have failed. Alternative attempts by sociologists of religion are inevitably more abstract and promising. They have to start from reflections on the fact of 'polycontexturality of descriptions of religions' (Luhmann 2000: 352). Competing religions observe and describe each other, and the external descriptions by social scientists (e.g. regarding the 'function of religion') can be neither neutral nor objective (Luhmann 2000: 118); nor can they try to replace them, as a 'Criticism of Religion' and a non-reflective comparative science of religions have attempted for so long. They have to avoid the trap of 'civilisatory progress' (Luhmann 2000: 351f) and its remnants in evolution and societal differentiation, and they have to analyse historically and religion-specific semantic elaborations of the religious code.

In my view, the most promising attempt has been made by Niklas Luhmann, who sees religion as a 'specific system of meaning and communication'. Religious communications – beliefs, discourses and practices – are distinguished from other communications by the use of a specific binary code: transcendent/immanent. The specific reference problem is seen in the 'indeterminability, self-referential recursivity, non-observability of the world and of the observer in the world.' This is answered by religion in a way that guarantees 'the determinability of all meaning against the horizon of indeterminability present in the experience' (2000: 127, 141). A short explication of these highly abstract and – in this brevity – rather cryptic phrases may show some of their comparative advantages.

First, religion is a 'specific' system of communication[4]. It is 'in no way responsible for meaning as such' or synonymous with cultural symbolism, meaning, sense, identity (Geertz, Luckmann) or even with articulated symbolic universes such as ideologies.

Second, Luhmann resists the reaction to dilute the conceptual requirements of religion by (a) subjectivising it (Luckmann 1967) or (b) completely historicising it or dissolving it into cultural practices generally. In the former case, in exact analogy to the jurisdiction of the US Supreme Court, religion dissolves into religious experience or religious intents or the arbitrary claims of believers and practitioners, as art dissolves into what artists declare to be art. In the latter case, genealogists of religions like Asad (2003) or Robertson (1987) and comparative scientists would still have to answer the question: genealogy of what? A practice-centred conception of religion (in the tradition of Pascal) is just as much in danger of losing the specificity of religious practices as are many definitions of religion in cultural anthropology that focus on rites and cults (Durkheim), on attitudes and habits (Mauss, Asad), on *illusio* (Bourdieu 1987) or all commitments of 'ultimate concern' (Tillich), or on functional equivalents like 'civil religion'.

Third, the transcendent/immanent code that distinguishes between the religious and the non-religious avoids semantics such as Durkheim's basic distinction between sacred and profane spheres. It enables Luhmann to demonstrate that the 're-entry of the difference between Immanent and Transcendent into the Immanent (that is the Sacred)' (2000: 127) is only one option that has to compete with the 'idea of transcendence totally without difference' or an 'ultimate meaning without any form' (e.g. in fashionable 'negative theologies' or theories of 'horizontal transcendence'), recently resulting in a 'de-sacralisation of religion' (127, see 146).

Fourth, it keeps the descriptions of the Transcendent (spirits, powers, gods, God, Nirvana, Brahman, Self) open and avoids the exclusions common to monotheistic, theistic, belief-centred and dogmatic conceptions.

Fifth, it is critical of private, subjectivised, belief-centred conceptions that reproduce a mythical ideal of radical Protestantism as an evolutionary end state of religion in (post)modernity, implying if not soliciting a Protestantisation of Catholicism, Orthodox Christianities (but also of Lutheranism, Anglicanism) and of Islam and Hinduism.

Last, it keeps the internal structure of religions open while not privileging de-institutionalised (informal, spontaneous, less hierarchical) and congregational or church-like forms.

The fact that all observations and perspectives, including scientific ones, presuppose observers, interests and problems, and that they are embedded in history, societal and cultural structures. In brief, the considered perspectivism of this concept presupposes 'methodological atheism' or 'a-religiosity' (2000: 278) but does not prevent or relativise scientific truth claims, as is so often the case with postmodernist criticism. For the purposes of this study, I use Luhmann's concept of religion without any further critical discussion.[5] It is fully appropriate for recent conditions of religious diversity in a globalising world. Its considered perspectivism also opens new avenues to discuss secularisation.

1.2 Secularisation

In our times, 'secularisation' has a triple, connected and contested meaning. Culturally, it designates the secularisation of general cognitive and normative cultural frames: views of world, society and man. Socially, it designates a decline of religious beliefs and practices in modern societies. Politically, it refers to a secularisation of state and politics. These distinctions are also of practical importance.

The construction of a 'double dualist system of classification' (Casanova 1994: 15) of the world in pre-modern European Christendom is a good starting point for understanding cultural secularisation. On the one hand, the world was divided between 'this world' and 'the other world'. On the other hand, 'this world' was divided into two heterogeneous realms, 'the religious' and 'the secular' (re-entry), and this 'spatio-structural' dualism was institutionalised throughout society. Cultural secularisation presupposes the validity of the historical meaning of the original concept of 'saecularisatio' in canonical law (Strätz 2004: 782ff and Marramao 1992: 1133f). From the early 19th century on, 'secularisation' was increasingly used to designate the progressive breakdown of the dualist system of categorisation (Zabel 2004: 809-829, and Marramao 1992: 1135-1151). I summarise some of the implicit biases and ambiguities characterising the debate (Casanova 1994; Robertson 1987, 1992; Rooden 1996; Asad 2003) since these have influenced the sociological research on social and political secularisation, the focus of my analysis.

First, concepts, processes and debates show a Christian and Western bias. They do not cover all religions of the world. However, even within the Christian-dominated world, they show a clear Church bias and either neglect or seriously underestimate folk religions or 'paganism'. Eventually, the original Catholic, explicitly anti-Protestant bias was countered by an explicit bias in favour of Protestant or Protestantised, 'subjectivised' or 'individualised' religions. In addition, 'secularisation' has focused on state-church relationships and this original state bias influenced later discussions of religion. Also, discourses on 'secularisation' commonly seduce us to analyse processes from their – real or nostalgically constructed – origins. This origin bias determines the terms of decline, loss, demise and erosion to the detriment of differentiation, gain and productive attempts to conceptualise history from the present or the future.

Second, the *evaluation* of secularisation has been *ambivalent*: its original pejorative meaning has been replaced by more or less positive evaluations.

Finally, in the process of a change in meaning from a legal concept (in canonical law, in church-state law) to a broad, metaphorical, free-floating, cultural and philosophical notion, it no longer has clear boundaries and distinctive power. It became a vague, ambivalent, multi-dimensional term with many and often incompatible meanings. We have to see whether and how sociology has been able to overcome these biases and ambiguities. Against this background, sociologists have a hard time living up to their claims of formulating concepts and theories of secularisation which, as scientific ones, had to be 'secular' (in the sense of not being bound to religion and being methodologically a-religious) without being 'secularist'.

With a few exceptions (de Tocqueville, William James), social scientists have long taken secularisation for granted as a common sense and plain truth. From the 1960s on, this thesis began to be met with skepticism. The concept turned out to be fuzzy and polyvalent, its descriptive content vague and the explanatory theories weak. The empirical evidence hinted at religious change (e.g. privatisation or subjectivisation) (Luckmann 1967), not at decline, loss of significance or of function. The majority of sociologists of religion declared the thesis useless, rejected it and opted for abandoning it (e.g. Martin 1965), to replace it by studies of religious change or by historical and comparative 'genealogies' of religion (Robertson, Asad, Veer). If there is a need to retain a concept of secularisation (Martin 1978, Luhmann 1977, Casanova 1994), one has to specify its meaning and its dimensions, and to analyse these in an analytically separable way. Casanova's distinctions between three different theses and understandings are a useful point of departure: 'secularisation' (i) as decline of religious beliefs and practices, (ii) as individualisation or privatisation of religion, (iii) as functional, institutional, organisational and role differentiation.

In my short discussion, I show that it would be better to drop the decline thesis (para. 1.2.1). We should distinguish between the claims of individualisation, privatisation and subjectivisation. There are good theoretical, empirical and normative reasons to reject both privatisation and subjectivisation and to qualify the individualisation thesis (para. 1.2.2). We also have to carefully circumscribe the differentiation thesis (para. 1.2.3).

1.2.1 Decline of religion(s)?

Some political philosophers believe that a decline of religious beliefs and practices requires a 'secularised' state and politics (sect. 1.3). They are again misguided in taking for granted that 'modern' societies are secularised societies. Sociologists defending the thesis of an inevitable decline of religion in 'modern' societies have usually focused on Western state societies and on Christian churches, denominations and sects. They developed more or less extensive lists of indicators to measure and test the assumed decline, ranging from 'belief' (in God, dogmas) to 'practices' (baptism, weddings and funerals; attendance at services; praying, saying grace before meals and other religious practices 'at home') and to 'institutions' (membership, adherence, identification with the organisation; financial support, relative number of religious professionals, etc). In addition, they studied variations in all of these regards, checking for background variables as generation, class, income, education, sex/gender, ethnicity and urban versus rural residence. They have shown that (Western) European societies are characterised by comparatively high degrees of 'decline' of 'belief/practice' and belonging, notwithstanding the huge variety between the extremes of East Germany (formerly GDR), followed by the Czech Republic, Scandinavian countries and the other extremes of Ireland and Poland (Hervieu-Legér 1996; Crouch 2000; Madeley 2003). Also, we note higher levels of individual religious beliefs: 'unchurching' or 'believing without belonging' (Davie 1996; Willaime 2004: 334f).

Whether subordinate folk religions have declined or prospered is usually not analysed. Judaism, Islam, Hinduism, Buddhism and other 'High religions' inside Western states are often lumped together as 'Other Religions'. Even strong defenders of the decline thesis admit that their development (a consequence of immigration rather than conversions) does not fit into the picture, but they rescue the thesis by claiming that these immigrant religions are 'pre-modern' or 'traditional'. This move is more difficult towards the newly developing 'invisible religions', the 'new age of spirituality' and strong evangelical revivals inside the West that are at odds with the original decline thesis (though their empirical importance should not be overestimated; Bruce 2005 vs. Kendal). On a global scale, the decline thesis so obviously conflicts with the evidence that their defenders have to resort to the crudest version of modernisation theory, declaring the 'Rest' as pre-modern or modernising.

Even if one confines the thesis to mean the decline of Christian church religions in the West, there is still the anomaly of the United States, the most 'modern' country and, paradoxically, also the most Christian and the most religiously diverse. The decline thesis does not cover 'the West' but only Europe. American exceptionalism has been traditionally explained by the absence of an established church and fierce competition among all denominations. Yet, the two predominant views on the consequences of religious diversity for the plausibility of religion are incompatible (Bruce 1992: 172). The first view is that religious pluralism threatens the plausibility of religious belief systems by exposing its human origins and that it makes religious belief a matter of personal choice rather than fate (Berger). The second view claims that it 'strengthens the appeal of religion by ensuring that there is at least one version to suit every taste; by preventing the institution from being compromised by associations with ruling elites, and by forcing suppliers to be more responsive to potential customers.' Instead of trying to reconcile the two views, like Martin and Wilson, Bruce contends that both 'too readily accept that the US is a major anomaly'. If one makes 'legitimate comparisons' – taking smaller regions or states within federal republics or supra-state polities as units – one can show 'that the contrast of stagnant and bankrupt establishment in the old world and vibrant lively dissent in the new is an unhelpful caricature'.

Appropriate comparisons are also important in two other regards. First, what is the point of departure of the assumed decline of religion? The implicit assumption of 'a golden age' of (Christian) religiosity in 'the Middle Ages' (Hornsby-Smith) or in 'past ages' (Wilson 1992: 207) is weak: institutionalised structures and power asymmetries are mainly responsible for 'high religiosity'. Second, if one compares organised religions with contemporary competitors like 'humanist' organisations and secularist counter-organisations (political parties in particular), the decline of the latter 'has been far more severe than anything suffered by the churches. If the contest between religion and secularisation is one between organisations and articulated systems of belief, then religion rules undisturbed. Its 'enemy' is not aggressive laïcism but indifference' (Crouch 2000: 273).

In the face of so much counterevidence and so many counterarguments, a generalised decline thesis is indefensible. The two obvious defence strategies are to immunise the thesis against evidence by granting lots of exemptions – on the globe, in the West, within Europe – or by insisting on long-term tendencies of modernity against 'short-term countertendencies'. A crude and normative modernisation theory then has to shoulder the burden of proof. Instead of replacing the decline thesis with a generalised counter-thesis that religions, like migrants, are 'here to stay' or even that they get 'more rather than less significance' (Robertson 1987: 7; 1992: 4), it is more productive to drop the thesis and focus on the changing forms and types of religions and of religiosity under specific institutional conditions and in specific contexts. Many defenders of the other two understandings of the secularisation thesis seem to accept this.

1.2.2 Individualisation, subjectivisation, and privatisation of religion(s)?

The privatisation thesis is part of the statements on structural change – cultural rationalisation of world- and self-concepts, pluralisation of religious frames, functional differentiation, and individualisation of religious orientations and ways of life (Dobbelaere 1981, Tschannen 1992). The thesis is compatible with the decline thesis and with its anti-thesis, the revival thesis. Its central claim is that beliefs and practices are privatised or – often uneasily synonymous – individualised or subjectivised. The thesis has a dual analytically separate but practically connected meaning (Willaime 2004: 341) First, it refers to the kind of religious belief and practice appropriate under conditions of modernity (or of 'late-' or 'postmodernity'): the individualisation thesis. Second, it claims that organised religions give up or have lost their public roles (the most appropriate meaning of privatisation).

1.2.2.1 'Individualisation' or 'subjectivisation'?

The claim under this heading is that all religions under conditions of 'postmodernity' eventually lose their collective (or cultural and ritual) dimensions and that all of them shift from practice-centred to individual belief-centred religiosity. For example, the global 'neo-Islam des jeunes' (Roy 2002) or French or European Islam (Kepel 1996) is portrayed as 'de-culturalised', disconnected from all common, ritual practices, including ethno-national and territorial ones.[6] Second, it is said that religions become subjectivised 'religions of the heart', focused on 'expression' and 'authenticity' (related to the 'shift' from practice and belief to identity).[7] Third, it is asserted that religious belonging (belief and practice) is ever more voluntary. It is becoming a matter of choice and not of fate.[8] And, finally, it is said that religious belonging today is a contingent individual choice.

Indications of such shifts are seen in the 'Protestantisation' of the Catholic, Orthodox and Christian religions, and in the changes of other 'old' religions like Islam, Judaism, modern Hinduism, on the one hand. This is also the case, on the other hand, in the revival of old religions (e.g. pietism, Methodism and, particularly Pentecostalism; Martin 1990) and the rise of new 'invisible religions of the heart', and in the post-conventional 'new age spirituality'.

Some sobering remarks. First, the selling of Protestantism as 'the' modern Christian religion is misguided. Lutheranism and Episcopal Protestantism do not fit this definition. Second, the idea of a religion that is bare of all collective, social and practical dimensions is an absurdity. All human linguistic and cultural practices are inherently social (all meaning is social, after all, fully 'private' or 'subjective' languages are a non-starter), and belief without a minimum of shared attitudes and practices is a sham.[9] Third, voluntarism is a matter of degree, even under '(post)modern' conditions. The idea that religious beliefs could be completely disentangled from ascriptive (racial, ethnic, national) practices, and also from cultural (e.g. linguistic) practices is a non-realistic utopia even for the most universalist of religions.

The hard core of the thesis is that religious belief and belonging is (both from the perspective of believers and nonbelievers) a contingent, individual decision (the fourth meaning), for two structural reasons. First, the increasing (awareness of) religious diversity shows that belief, practice and belonging are not a matter of natural or supernatural fate but a matter of personal choice, '*une affaire d'option individuelle et non plus évidence collective*' (Hervieu-Léger 1986: 59). Second, as a consequence of functional differentiation of systems and related role differentiation in modern societies, all individual inclusion decisions are seen as contingent.[10]

The question is whether organised religions can adapt to new forms of religiosity or will only survive as a part of modern fundamentalisms.[11] Luhmann is fairly open in this regard and specifies some of the conditions of the former option. Organised religions 'would have to accept the difference of believers, other believers and nonbelievers and to gain possibilities from this difference, from this otherness, to strengthen belief' (317). Like Casanova, Bouma and others, I believe that at least some churches are beginning to learn this lesson. In addition, they self-reflectively resist the temptations of privatised and invisible religions. They are public and go public.

1.2.2.2 Privatisation of religions?

The second meaning of the thesis is that organised religions bend to the private sphere or, like Methodists or Pentecostalists, voluntarily give up any public or direct political roles. This is partly based on the former claim: the response to the structural change in individual religiosity, affecting internal structure and external relations to society and state. As a corollary, it refers to the differentiation thesis. If one understands the thesis as a generalised empirical description, there are four countertendencies.

First, we have the cultural defence thesis: '[w]here culture, identity, and sense of worth are challenged by a source promoting either an alien religion or rampant secularism and that source is negatively valued, secularisation will be inhibited. Religion can provide resources for the defence of a national, local, ethnic, or status-group culture' (Wallis & Bruce 1992: 17f, with Polish, Irish, American examples; see Martin 1978; 1990: 275f).

Second, the closely related cultural transition thesis refers to immigrant groups and, more generally, to disruptions of the way of life of traditional groups through industrialisation and urbanisation: 'Where identity is threatened in the course of major cultural transitions, religion may provide resources for negotiating such transitions or asserting a new claim to a sense of worth' (18).[12]

In both cases, religious beliefs and practices become intensified, and they are certainly not privatised. Collective religious identities serve as markers of cultural difference and as resources for organisation and mobilisation (para. 6.4.1). Here, religious organisations are eminently public and insist on their public visibility. The two cases also demonstrate that individualisation and privatisation can be deciphered as strategies of majorities to assimilate minorities, hidden under the guise of 'neutrality' and 'modernity'. This socio-logic of power asymmetry (Guillaumin 1995, Bader 1998, Juteau 1999) is absent from most of the sociology of secularisation and, less surprisingly, from liberal political philosophy. The cases can be extended, and then cover international relations between states and religious majorities and minorities under conditions of structural asymmetries of power in the global arena (religions and colonialism, imperialism, post-colonialism and 'Islam in the West'), with 'individualisation' and 'privatisation' fulfilling the same or similar functions.[13]

Are these cases exceptions and the tendencies 'countervailing factors, sometimes generated by the same process of modernisation' (Wallis & Bruce 1992: 9) related to pre-modern people or areas, or to problems connected with modernisation and absent 'in the long term' (ibid. 19)? If so, the privatisation thesis, like the decline thesis, is transformed from a descriptive and explanatory into a predictive and prescriptive thesis. This is more obvious in the third case: American exceptionalism. Organised religions in the US are quite public and play an enormous role in politics, both in the conservative and fundamentalist varieties ('moral majority' and the 'neo-con' communitarianism of the Reagan and Bush administrations), and in the more decent variety of 'public religions'. The right-wing variety marks 'a break from recent trends in European Christianity' that has clearly not been anticipated by secularisation theorists.

Fourth, is the development of conservative and fundamentalist Christianity an anti-modern reaction to modern contingency? But then, some non-fundamentalist churches accept contingency and still play important public roles in the US, in Europe[14] and on a global scale. Fragile as this may be, it has not been foreseen and is at odds with the privatisation thesis traditionally understood. To uphold the thesis then implies that there is no escape from the turn of a 'testable and falsifiable empirical theory ... into a prescriptive normative theory of how religious institutions ought to behave in the modern world' (Casanova 1994: 38).

Religious believers and practitioners may thus learn that their decisions are contingent, that they may practice other religions or none, without privatising their religion. They may learn to react to 'commodification' by reflexively stabilising their second-order preferences instead of falling prey to consumerism, hedonism and continuous preference change. Organised religions may learn to develop into modern and public religions. Privatisation is not a structural trend dictated by modernity, but a historical option (Casanova 1994: 39, 215, 222) preferred by pietistic trends and religious individuation, and externally by liberal conceptions of the public sphere. 'De-Privatisation' can be a viable option. Processes of modernisation are more contingent than modernisation theory admits, and modern state societies show more contingency and institutional variety (sect. 1.4) than structuralist and functionalist sociology allow for. My claim is that the differentiation thesis (para. 1.2.3) stimulates a counterfactual and maximalist interpretation of 'strict' or 'complete separation' of state and politics from religion.

1.2.3 Minimal or complete differentiation?

Some minimal threshold of institutional, organisational and role differentiation between religions and other systems, between organised religions and other organisations (specifically the state) is functionally required for modern societies. Religions have given up direct political control[15] over state, society and culture, over 'the' economy, science, arts, law and politics in those parts of the world where they once exercised these powers. They have gained internal and lawful autonomy by the same process. States are relatively autonomous from churches and churches from state control. This is indicated by terms such as 'twin tolerations' (Stepan 2000), or 'two autonomies' (Ferrari 2005). The labels signifying this differentiation – autonomy, control, freedom, non-interference and separation – may differ. As in other cases, however, differentiation is always a matter of degree on a scale from the pole connecting complete 'separation' with some to minimal or no 'separation'.

The minimalist interpretation requires a threshold of differentiation between 'worldly' powers (states, politics and leaders/politicians) and 'spiritual' powers (organised religions and religious leaders/specialists). The differentiation is characteristic for the West and dates from long before modernisation or 'secularisation' as, for example, the protracted *Investiturstreit* in the Holy Roman Empire of German Nations clearly shows. It also characterises non-Western states like the Ottoman, Mughal and Chinese empires (Hirst 2001, Eisenstadt 2000, Asad 2003, Bhargava 1998a: 497f, 511). Two remarks are appropriate.

First, religious toleration – implying limits to the control over religion(s) by states and by religions over states – is not a Western invention. Historically, Christianity has not been tolerant. It eventually learned from its mistakes wherever protracted warfare between intolerant religions/polities could not be won decisively (Bhargava 1998a: 522ff vs. the cultural nonadaptability thesis).

Second, state-church problems and the urgent need to resolve them only emerge in specific traditions, in particular in the Christian religious tradition. This comparative insight is crucial for a sober discussion of recent accusations that Islam knows of no 'separation between State and Church'.[16]

Achieving the minimal or threshold differentiation has mainly been a problem for states in the Christian West. If one wants to call a state that is not controlled by religion a 'secular' state, then 'secularism' – or better 'secularity' – is not specifically Western. Instead, it had to be rather painfully learned in the West.[17] A 'secular' state, then, is increasingly 'indifferent' or 'agnostic' with regard to competing religious, metaphysical and thick moral worldviews: a non-religious state (not anti-religious, atheistic or hostile to religions; see chap. 3.1).[18] Neither the historical emergence nor the existence of such a state requires considerable degrees of cultural or societal secularisation, absent in early modernity, and only developed during the 19th and 20th centuries.

The minimalist version of the differentiation thesis is almost universally accepted. The link of the thesis to secularisation and modern society, however, suggests two more demanding interpretations: either fully autonomous functional systems (or 'spheres', 'fields') such as the religious and the political system and/or fully autonomous organisations (the famous thesis of a complete separation of states and churches) and professionalised roles/activities. Many sociologists overestimate the autonomy of functional systems and organisations and underestimate the institutional variety of these systems. In this regard, it is unfortunate that Luhmann's theory of functional differentiation of social systems also misdescribes the relationship between the political and the religious system, the state and organised religions. The general approach of an autopoetic systems theory allows otherwise.[19]

Upon review, the differentiation thesis promotes a counterfactual and maximalist interpretation of separation and neglects path dependency and institutional variety. The ideology of American separationism as a model of institutional secularisation and of modernised society? The 'idealised' institutional model, not the actual muddle of the US, as the inevitable future for all modern state societies? Even authors who recognise that institutional differentiation is not unilinear and universal are tempted to posit a complete separation of Church and State in the long run as an 'irresistible, structural trend' (Casanova 1994: 213; Minkenberg 2000 and 2003: 11, 15; and, more carefully, Martin. Criticism by Marquand & Nettler 2000: 2 and Fox 2006: 563).

1.2.4 Conclusions

What are we to make of the secularisation thesis? Do we abandon the concept or can we retain it and, if so, in which meaning? For my discussion, it is useful to distinguish three different perspectives (Casanova 1994: 20, Luhmann 2000: 282f): (i) the observations from the perspective of religions (or 'the religious system'), (ii) of sociology, and (iii) of normative political theory.

From the perspective of religion, it is vital to ask 'how religion itself sees its other side' (Luhmann 2000: 282-284) and to describe it as secular or secularised, based on secular communications, given that 'other observers may describe the same states of affairs differently'. Religion and secularisation form an opposition only in a religious context (283). Therefore, the distinction between religious and secular opinions is important for religions but much less so for democratic politics.

From the perspective of sociology, the use of the concept is counterproductive.[20] The argument that we need the term 'secular' to indicate and demarcate 'the narrower area of non-religious social communication' (282) is not convincing. We could simply call it: 'non-religious communication' instead of 'secular communication', a non-religious state (beyond the religious-secular divide) instead of a 'secular state'. Society, economics, science, politics and culture are 'secularised' in different degrees, if observed from the perspective of (totalising) religion. From a sociological view, the same process is better first described in terms of the degrees of institutional, organisational and role differentiation. Second, we currently clearly see that there is no need for an integrating 'meta-narrative' or 'symbolic universe' – whether it is an overarching religious world-view (Crouch 2000: 37f) or a postmodernist 'immanentist metaphysics' (Connolly 2005) or a 'wissenschaftliche

Weltanschauung'. Modern societies and modern conceptions of non-foundational and agonistic democracy can and should leave this centre empty. In addition, modern societies cannot and need not be morally integrated in any traditional sense (Luhmann 1997, Bader 2001e: 134-139).

From the perspective of liberal-democratic politics and normative theory, the important question is not whether society and state are fully secularised or secular and completely separated from religions. First of all, we know that the emerging 'secular', indifferent state has not been a liberal, let alone a democratic state (Hunter 2005). In addition, this indifferent state certainly did not require or presuppose any social or cultural secularisation of beliefs and practices. It rather required the taming of absolutist claims of religions regarding state and law. Next, we all know many examples of recent secular states that violated minimum standards of liberal democracy, and of minimal morality (3.1). Also, the existence of a liberal-democratic state does not require a culturally or socially secularised society, as the example of the US shows. Neither does a culturally and socially highly religious society require a 'religious state', nor does a culturally and socially secularised society require a 'secularist' or 'secular' state. A state that respects and guarantees the two autonomies of state from church(es) and churches from state is enough. The issue is: which forms and degrees of differentiation are compatible or even conducive to the principles and practices of liberal democracy?

The meta-narrative of secularisation is misleading. It should be disconnected from liberalism and democracy (Casanova 2005) and it should be replaced by priority for liberal democracy. Whether a state is secular or not is not decisive. What matters is whether it is decent and liberal-democratic. Whether communications, arguments and opinions are secular or religious is not decisive, but whether they are conducive to an agonistic democratic dialogue.

1.3 Institutional diversity of religious governance in recent Western states

1.3.1 Governance and government of religious diversity

Recent institutional analyses distinguish structured patterns (formations, *Ordnungen*), e.g. regimes of governance and of government. Patterns are constituted by all relevant interactions between economic, social, ethno-national, political, legal, judicial, administrative institutions and (organised) religions. Studies of these patterns analyse mechanisms of action co-ordination (markets, networks, associations, communities, private and public hierarchies), actors (including governments), their organisations, mobilisation and strategies. The perspective of governance is narrower: it excludes markets by focusing on regulation, including mechanisms of action co-ordination and enabling non-market (self-)regulation. The perspective of governmental regulation is narrower still. It focuses on one (internally diversified) actor, i.e. the state, and on action co-ordination by public hierarchy (rules, particularly law and law-like regulations).

A few remarks on religious governance. First, religious competition on 'God's Biggest Supermarket' is important for the chances of religions and for religious diversity. It is not, however, a mode of governance. It is an invisible-hand mechanism of customs, laws, self-regulation within and among competing religions, and of public bodies. Second, religious governance implies some regulatory capacity from outside or above (by private or by semi-public and public hierarchies), or through self-regulation (democratic religious congregations, informal religious networks, associations and communities). Because 'management of religious diversity' (Bouma 1999) is restricted to hierarchy and top-down competencies, governance is the broader and better term. For an analysis of 'governance of religious diversity', public non-state actors and a variety of semi-public and private actors are important. Government, on the other hand, means regulation by public hierarchies – the differentiated state – and their specific means (legal and administrative rules, jurisdiction and – the threat of – force). Policies of deregulation and privatisation induce shifts from government to governance.

The normative implications of these differences will be discussed in part IV. We will see that radical libertarians and individualist liberals trust minimally regulated and fair religious markets; republicans rely on a democratic government of religious diversity; deliberative democrats add strong associations in 'civil society'; and communitarians add strong communities. Only associative democrats use the full spectrum of governance and government and also place a strong emphasis on associational governance. Here, I start with a short summary of cultural and structural pluralism in Europe and its impact on region-specific patterns of religious pluralism (para. 1.3.2) that serves as a background for the analysis of regimes of government in Western states (para. 1.3.3) before drawing lessons for political philosophers (sect. 1.4).

1.3.2 Path-dependent patterns and regimes of religious governance in the West

An analysis of the institutional diversity of religious governance requires an historical sociological approach. It conceptualises 'multiple modernities' (Eisenstadt 2000), in opposition to the classical paradigm of modernisation and secularisation. The relatively contingent and path-dependent outcomes of multiple processes of modernisation (Martin 1978, 1990: 274f, 294f) are initiated by many interdependent causes (modern capitalism, modern states, the Protestant reformation, the modern scientific revolution), and triggered by critical junctures or contingent events: the Reformation; the English Civil War, the American revolution, the French revolution, the Russian revolution, the Dutch revolution, the Scottish and Swiss Reformations, and the distinct developments in Lutheran countries (Brake 2004). The emerging patterns are shaped by pluralism:[21] cultural (the division between main confessions, their characteristics and the different degrees of religious pluralism of the respective confessional-cultural areas), and structural (the typical constellation of state and nation formation).[22]

European *cultural* pluralism has been the result of the Christian synthesis of Jewish and Islamic (the 'internal Others'), Greek Hellenistic and pagan traditions. The division of the Roman Empire into a Western and an Eastern part resulted in a basic division between Western Latin (a Roman Catholic paradigm) and Eastern Greek Christianity (a Byzantine paradigm).[23] The Protestant reformation resulted in a geographical split within Western Christianity between North (Protestant) and South (Catholic). Apart from obvious and well-known doctrinal differences, Protestantism is structurally distinguished from Catholicism by (1) the consideration of law as an *'adiaphoron'*, not necessary for the *'salus animarum'*; (2) the translation of the ecclesiological doctrine of covenant into congregationalism (outspoken in reformed and radical Protestantism) and criticism of hierarchy; (3) 'separation' of church and state, and (4) the clergy is allowed to marry. These distinctions are more pronounced, given the split between Lutheranism and reformed or radical Protestantism. Lutheranism – predominant in the Scandinavian countries and in Northern Germany – is characterised by established churches, a strong identification of church and state, a hierarchically organised 'Episcopal' church, the gospel as 'pray, pray and obey' (Manow 2004). Reformed Protestantism is predominant in Switzerland, the Netherlands, Great Britain, and in the United States, English Canada, Australia and New Zealand. It is characterised by strong anti-*'etatism'* (particularly of the free churches, Dissenters, Calvinists, Baptists, Methodists and Evangelicals compared with the more scholarly circles of traditional congregationalism or Anglicanism), a fairly strict state-church separation, an emphasis on the autonomy of the holy local congregation (churches being conceived as decentralised, local, democratic and Congregationalist, instead of Episcopal), and an emphasis on a strictly individual link between believer and God, together with self-help, individual responsibility, asceticism and a marked 'spiritual egalitarianism'. Eastern Christianity also became divided between a northern, Russian-Orthodox region and southern, Mixed-Orthodox (Greek and Slavonic) and partly Islamic regions.

The resulting pattern of four religious core regions in Europe had a lasting impact on cultural foundations and components of nation building, state-church relations and processes of cultural secularisation. Instead of one unilinear thesis, we get at least two hypotheses of cultural secularisation: (i) 'the more pluralistic organized religion is, the less marked cultural secularization is, and inversely (ii) the more monopolized organized religion is the more pronounced cultural secularization is.' (Spohn 2003a: 273) Pluralising Protestant cultures show weak cultural secularisation; monopolistic religious cultures (Catholic, Orthodox, Islamic) lead to a clerical-anticlerical split (Martin 1978, 1990). Only in the latter countries does one find explicit declarations of a 'secular' state in constitutions (France, Mexico, Turkey; see Markoff & Reagan 1987: 173f).

European *structural* pluralism resulted from the breaking up of the Roman Empire. Four core areas emerged, loosely connected to different epochs of state and nation formation: (i) the Western European zone of early state formation, where the imperial structures of the declining Western Roman Empire lost their impact very early. In the newly created institutional orders of separate political centres, *'ethnies'* were transformed into nations more or less congruent with states. (ii) The Western-Middle European zone with the much later unitarian state formation. There, the continuing impact of the Holy Roman Empire of German nations prevented nation-state unifications until the 19th century, and nations are less congruent with the new states. (iii) The East-Middle European zone, where the impact of Empires continued until far into the 20th century. Peripheral nation building and weak states resulted, with strong tensions between ethnically heterogeneous populations. (iv) In the Eastern European zone, empires and reactive, contractive nation building with strong ethno-national conflict potentials continue into the 21st century.

Sociologists do not agree on how to put these different constituent elements together in a typology of region-specific patterns. A short summary of Martin's influential distinction of the patterns of religious governance in the 'Western world' (1978: 59) neatly demonstrates the lasting institutional diversity of state-church relationships. It helps to understand the normative evaluations and models of political philosophers, so often unreflectively governed by the national settings they happen to live in.

1. The American pattern, characterised by high religious pluralism, low anticlericalism, high cultic participation, high stability of democracy, centre-left political orientation of Catholicism, religiously

toned civil religion, broken church-state nexus, secular school system and non-existent religious parties.

2. The English pattern, characterised by medium religious pluralism, fairly low anticlericalism, fairly low cultic participation, high stability of democracy, centre-left political orientation of Catholicism, religiously toned civil religion, retained church-state nexus, religious and then semi-secular school system and non-existent religious parties.

3. The Scandinavian Pattern, characterised by low religious pluralism, low to medium anticlericalism, very low cultic participation, high stability of democracy, secular civil religion, retained church-state nexus, secular school system with religious fringe and very minor religious parties.

4. The Mixed pattern, characterised by high religious pluralism, fairly low anticlericalism, high cultic participation,[24] high stability of democracy, centre-left political orientation of Catholicism, mixed school system, influential religious parties.

5. The Latin pattern, characterised by very low religious pluralism, very high anticlericalism, high/low cultic participation, low stability of democracy, high communist influence and right of centre political orientation of Catholicism, strained or broken church-state nexus, increasingly secular school system and extensive religious parties.

6. The Right Statist pattern (e.g. Spanish and Portuguese fascism).

7. The Left Statist pattern in 'communist' or 'Marxist-Leninist' countries.

8. The Nationalist Pattern, characterised by churches of nations without a secure state (Poland, Northern Ireland and Israel).[25]

Before drawing some lessons from such a preliminary historical and comparative analysis of various region-specific patterns, we can increase our sensitivity for institutional diversity by focusing on the variety of governmental regimes of religions.

1.3.3 Institutional diversity of Western governmental regimes

States are not monolithic. Aims and strategies vary, and the legislative, judicial and executive branches often follow contradictory policies. The differentiation only increases when comparing federal, state and local levels. Every state thus shows a variety of partly inconsistent institutional arrangements; and actual policies diverge from legal norms.[26] I summarise the eight most important dimensions of the contemporary relationships between states and (organised) religions in Western states. For each dimension, I present two extreme options (dichotomous modelling) and add important intermediate options (gradualist modelling).

1.3.3.1 Constitutional regimes

Written constitutions of liberal democratic states regulate the relations between (organised) religions and the state. In a legal perspective, the choice is between constitutional establishment of one church or non-establishment. Legal establishment can be further subdivided into strong and weak establishment (Robbers 2001).

Close to approaching strong establishment regimes are Greece, Serbia and Israel. Historically speaking, strong establishment has been the point of departure for disestablishment, plural establishment and non-establishment.[27]

Weak establishment means constitutional or legal establishment of one State-Church, and *de jure* and *de facto* religious freedom and pluralism. It is compatible with some administrative recognition of religious pluralism and different degrees of *de facto* institutionalisation of other religions. It may recognise a certain religious pluralisation of the cultural nation; England, Scotland, Norway and Denmark approximate this ideal type.

An intermediate option is plural establishment. As far as I know, constitutional pluralism exists nowadays only in Finland with two state churches (the large Lutheran Church of Finland and the small Orthodox Church of Finland) in a non-denominational state (Ahonen 2000, Heikkilä et al. 1995). It requires the constitutional and/or legal recognition of more than one organised religion. It may aim at administrative and political pluralism with the intention of pluralising the religio-cultural nation. It was discussed as an option in some American states in the late-18th and early-19th centuries.[28] Recently in England, there have been proposals to end the 'unique relationship between the Church of England and the British state so as to create a plural religion-state-link' (Modood 1996: 3).

Non-establishment characterises all of the other Western states – though often only recently through constitutional disestablishments: the Netherlands (1983) and Sweden (2001) – but also Turkey, Mexico and India. Obviously, the Non-Establishment or Constitutional Separation of State and (organised) religions may mean very different and even nearly opposite regulations and policies in constitutional reality.

1.3.3.2 Constitutional reality

An exclusive focus on legal-constitutional regulation clouds the divergent realities we find. States like Germany, the Netherlands, Sweden, Italy and Spain, on the one hand, and France and the US, on the other, are lumped together as non-establishment countries. A first step in

capturing the relevant differences is to distinguish between three patterns commonly used by legal (Robbers 1995, 2000; Ferrari 2002) and
political theorists (Monsma & Soper 1997, Fetzer & Soper 2004): countries with a state or national church; separatist countries; and selective
cooperation countries. We find selective cooperation in Italy, Germany,
Austria, Spain and Portugal (a country like Switzerland is unique in
combining all three patterns on the level of cantons; Mortanges & Tanner 2005). Separatist and selective cooperation countries share constitutional non-establishment yet differ with regard to the legal status of
religious organisations and related aspects (the regulation and financing of faith-based education, care and welfare organisations). It is possible to broaden the relevant dimensions and include a wider latitude
in the respective scales of 'strict separation' (Barbier 1995) versus 'Ver-
flechtung' (Minkenberg 2003), or 'deregulation' versus 'regulation'
(Chaves & Cann 1992) of state and (organised) religions[29]. We also
find combinations with welfare state typologies (Plesner 2001, Manow
2004) or degrees of 'state-ness', and other modes of governance (Ahonen 2000, Koenig 2003: 85ff).

Hence, constitutional and legal non-establishment is definitively not
the same as separation of state from religion (let alone of nation from
religion), neither historically nor structurally. And it is not the same as
a separation of political or civil society from churches and religions. To
illustrate this, constitutional non-establishment or disestablishment in
the US proved compatible with the political and cultural hegemony of
one church and one religion, and with coalitions of churches and religions (Martin 1978; Monsma & Soper 1997; Bader 1999a; McConnell
1992; Eisenach 2000; and Jacobsohn 2000).

1.3.3.3 Legal status of (organised) religions
Organised churches and religious communities are regulated by states.
The (dichotomous) choice is between granting them special status and
treating them like other associations, through 'the law governing associations' (Ferrari 2002: 10).

Under associational law, religious communities can become legal
persons and perform activities like buying and selling goods, conclud-
ing contracts and receiving donations. This has been the situation in
Ireland since 1871 (Casey 1995: 166; McLean 1995: 339), partly also in
France and the US, and, paradoxically, also in the UK.[30]

Granting religious communities special status – as all other European states do – is done in different ways. There are various options
on a scale from minimal to maximal recognition. Religions are regulated by special, favourable, laws; they are granted exemptions in tax
law, labour law and military conscription. They are also accorded legal
privileges (the right to religious instruction in public schools, to receive

public money for the building or maintenance of houses of worship or for religious schools, religious cemeteries, faith-based care and social services, entitlements of access for ministers of religion to military forces, prisons and hospitals). Legal exemptions and privileges are not granted indiscriminately but require registration. Several established churches – e.g. in Sweden until 2001 (Schött 1995: 319ff), Denmark (Dübeck 1995: 45f) and Finland (Heikkilä et al. 1995: 305ff) – are near the maximum pole of legal and financial privileges. Below that maximum, other religions – both majority and minority religions – may also enjoy a high degree of exemption and privilege.

Notwithstanding the separationist ideology in countries like France or the US, all Western states had to recognise religions, their actual (local) administrative practice, and guarantee at least a minimum of special legal treatment in special law, general law, jurisdiction or case law. Even the 'laïcist' systems are less laïcist than (predominantly French and American) ideologists assume.[31] 'Non-recognition' of religions by legislation, courts and administrations exists nowhere. That should have important normative consequences for liberals (sects. 2.4 and 8.4). Legal recognition may take the form of 'Körperschaften öffentlichen Rechts' – as in Germany (Robbers 1995: 66), Belgium (Torfs 1995: 19ff), Luxemburg (Pauly 1995: 217), Austria (Pötz 1995: 257f), for example – or be regulated in bilateral special treatises or concordats, as in Italy (Ferrari 1995). State recognition and regulation of religious communities requires some minimal thresholds in terms of numbers of adherents, duration and stability of religious groups or some minimal degree of organisation. Selective recognition and cooperation can thus be ranked on a 'scale of openness': 'open-universalist', 'pluralist', 'hegemonial' or 'closed' (Messner 1999). All countries that guarantee religions some special status or public recognition are characterised by a pyramidal pattern of privileges and corresponding regulations or controls, with possibly harsh normative dilemmas (Ferrari 2005, chap. 8).

1.3.3.4 Autonomy of churches and religious communities

The organisational expression of the principle of associational freedom of religion is the mirror image of state autonomy vis-à-vis religions: the non-interference of the state in (organised) religions and in their internal affairs (para. 1.2.3, the two autonomies). Religious autonomy issues are complex and various. They include different degrees of church autonomy in matters of faith (doctrine, dogma, teaching), polity (constitution and organisation, legislation, norm formulation, ecclesiastical law, church authority controlling and representing the religious community), and core ministry (of worship, ritual, liturgy; confidential counselling, confession; teaching the faith, education and training of clergy; dissemination of beliefs to others; temporal care for members and others). And they include administration (such as the right to appointment and dismissal from religious office for religious and ministerial employees, for employees or volunteers contributing to religious missions, for lay employees and volunteers; church discipline, membership – entry, exit, expulsion; territorial arrangements of substructures, the establishment and equipping of offices, finance, administration of church property, exemptions from service and labour law, etc.) (Cole Durham Jr. 2001: 697).

We distinguish between non-intervention regulations, which are central to church autonomy, and positive privileges through enabling legal and financial state actions. In the latter case, an increase in substantive autonomy is normally paid for with a loss in formal autonomy or an increase in state regulation and interference.

With regard to the inner domain of faith, doctrine and core ministry, all Western states recognise the religious incompetence of the state, no matter what legal status is granted to churches or religious communities. The relevant legal restrictions concern generally recognised, though divergently interpreted, limits to freedom of communication (such as preaching violence or libel) and of religious practices that seriously infringe on basic human rights of members (chap. 4).

In matters of organisation, polity and administration, the different legal statuses formally and actually matter (Minnerath 2001: 384ff). Formal autonomy seems highest in cases of non-registered, non-recognised, and non-established religions. Legal registration, recognition and establishment presuppose conditions and some controls. State churches that enjoy the highest amount of privileges and powers have been traditionally subjected to strong state interventions and control in matters of faith and doctrine, of organisation, policy and administration. Even today, their autonomy is 'limited to doctrinal affairs' although 'state authorities are less and less willing to interfere with the internal organisation of religious groups and refrain from making full use of the legal powers they have in this field. Generally speaking, the (doctrinal and organisational) autonomy of religious groups is on the rise: the history of the Church of England throughout the 20th century and the recent reform of Church and State relations in Sweden are good examples of the steps taken toward a broader autonomy of religious groups, even in the countries where the bond between Church and State is still very tight' (Ferrari 2002: 9; see Minnerath 2001: 390-393). All Western states respect church autonomy in matters of organisation, polity and administration and treat religions favourably compared to most non-religious organisation by exempting them from requirements of internal democratic structure, from the application of labour law and collective agreements, and from equal treatment and nondiscrimination laws (sect. 4).

1.3.3.5 Financing of religions

If one distinguishes between direct and indirect methods of financing, three options result: (a) neither churches nor religious communities receive any public money, directly or indirectly; (b) some or all of them receive public money indirectly by means of tax exemptions and/or general subsidies or vouchers; (c) in addition, some receive public money directly by payment of salaries or other costs, by direct religion-specific subsidies, or by 'church taxes'.

Interestingly, there is actually no system in which religions depend exclusively on voluntary contributions of their members (without any direct or indirect assistance by state administrations) or on donations (without any specific tax exemptions). Even the most separationist systems like the American and French grant some general, and some religion-specific, tax exemptions.[32]

Hence, in all Western states, some churches or religious communities receive public money at least indirectly, through tax exemptions or favours (land and real estate tax, inheritance tax, donation tax, corporation tax, trade tax, value added tax and other indirect taxes, which is fairly extensive in Italy, see Ferrari 1995: 199ff and in Austria, see Pötz 1995: 272ff), or through general subsidies. We find subsidies for the restoration of churches in the framework of 'heritage' programmes, for city development, or for social and cultural activities (at least so in Anglo-Saxon countries like England, Ireland and the US, see McLean 1995: 347, Casey 1995: 177f, Monsma & Soper 1997).

Indirect financing of specific churches and religious communities is often combined with direct payment of salaries, pensions or other costs by the state – as in Belgium (Torfs 1995: 33), Luxemburg (Pauly 1995: 225) and Denmark (Dübeck 1995: 45f) – with direct subsidies for specific religious communities, with considerable administrative help by state administrations in collecting contributions (misleadingly called 'church taxes'), as in Germany (Robbers 1995: 73f), Austria (Pötz 1995: 272ff), Sweden (Schött 1995: 325) and Finland (Heikkilä 1995: 314), or by modernised versions of church taxes as in Spain (Iban 1995: 117) and Italy (Ferrari 1995: 199ff). The latter are involuntary taxes on every resident taxpayer. However, together with their income tax declarations, taxpayers can decide whether the money goes to a church or to other social or cultural ends.

1.3.3.6 Regulation and financing of faith-based educational institutions

The relevant options in finance range between full through partial and to no public financing. Public money is normally coupled with some public regulation and control: full financing means least autonomy, partial financing increases autonomy and no financing may mean no regulation and control (the extreme case of full autonomy). However, there is no one-to-one relationship between the mode of regulation and control and the mode of financing.

Only Bulgaria, Greece, Italy, most Swiss cantons and, until recently, the US,[33] reject nearly all public financing of private faith-based educational institutions. In Europe, Australia and some Canadian provinces, we find a wide variety of systems of full (Austria, Belgium, Netherlands, England and Wales, and some Canadian provinces) or partial (Scandinavian states, Australia, Germany, Hungary, France, Spain), direct or indirect public financing of various faith-based educational institutions (Glenn & Groof 2002 and chap. 10.5). The actual 'market share' of non-governmental schools ranges from high (roughly 70% of all pupils in the Netherlands and Belgium) to medium (Australia and England and Wales: roughly 30%), France (roughly 20%) to low (United States less than 20%), Finland (9%), Italy (8%), Germany (5%), Switzerland (5%), and Sweden (4%). In addition, one finds considerable variety of public regulation and control in the selection of staff and students, of organisational form, the content of the curriculum and even classes and lessons, the selection of teaching material, didactics, examination, recognition of diplomas, and in public inspection. Most states also acknowledge that some affinity – or at least no public opposition – to the core of the respective religion is a relevant criterion for the hiring and firing of core teaching personnel (not of other administrative personnel), although the area of exemptions from anti-discrimination articles in constitutions and labour law is increasingly circumscribed by law and jurisdiction (sect. 4.3).

Only strict separationists condemn public financing of faith-based education as incompatible with liberal morality. Since actual institutions and practices differ widely from their ideal, they cannot but raise the red flag of revolution in all liberal-democratic states. Yet, they do not (sect. 5.2 and chap. 10).

1.3.3.7 Regulation and financing of religious instruction in public schools

The alternative is whether religious instruction is part of the curriculum of public schools or not (as in France and the United States). In the latter case, extra-curricular religious instruction may still take place in school buildings (free or for rent). In the former case, the following issues have arisen:

Is religious instruction obligatory for all (as in Denmark (Dübeck 1995: 51), Germany, Spain, Ireland until 1970, Austria (Pötz 1995: 265f), Italy (Ferrari 1995: 195f), and the UK), or are there alternatives (non-religious 'ethics' courses as in Quebec, Finland, some German *Länder* (states), *Alsace-Moselle;* no alternatives for Christian but non-confessional instruction in England)? Do we find full opt-out regulations (exemption from both religious and ethics instruction)?[34] If it is not obligatory, what are the regulations for exemption, and how is the use of opt-out regulations treated?

On which educational levels is instruction provided? Is it provided in separate lessons (in most countries) or integrated in the general curriculum (as in Ireland since 1970, where religious teaching is integrated in 'secular' courses)? By which religions and confessions? (If established, such religions obviously have a head start.) Who selects the instructors? (This is usually the respective churches or religious communities, even if the state pays.) Who decides on the curriculum and organises the lessons? (things get muddy if states presume competence in 'non-confessional' Christian instruction – as in England, Norway, Denmark – or introduce 'neutral' courses in 'religious' or 'inter-faith education', or in the history and sociology of world religions). Is there state supervision of the curriculum and the actual lessons in religious instruction? See extensively: Willaime (ed.) 2005; for normative detail: sect. 5.2.

1.3.3.8 Regulation and financing of faith-based care and social service organisations

All Western countries (Monsma & Soper 1997; Minow 2000; Glenn 2000; Esbeck et al. 2004 and Tomasi 2004) finance faith-based care and social service organisations (traditionally and in some countries even today seen as 'charity' institutions) either indirectly (tax exemptions of all kinds and vouchers) or directly (general or specific subsidies). This includes care for children, youngsters, the elderly; the physically, psychically or mentally sick or handicapped (hospitals), the homeless, drug addicts, criminal rehabilitation, plus housing and nutrition of poor and low-income people. It also includes care for 'welfare-to-work' programmes (Monsma & Soper 2006), for community centres, and at times even for other cultural and leisure activities.

The importance of such organisations differs: it is low in social-democratic welfare systems like Sweden, higher in liberal systems like the UK and the US, and highest in conservative-corporatist systems like Germany, Austria and the Netherlands. The same holds for financing. As with schools, public money is normally conditional upon state-wide standards of quality and professionalism, but organisation and provision, including hiring and firing, is an internal affair of churches, religious communities or related authorities. Except for institutions run by orders and congregations, their personnel is normally covered by collective and individual labour law, social security and pensions, and sector-specific collective agreements (if such regulations are in effect). Exemptions from generally binding equal treatment and anti-discrimination norms are usually more circumscribed than in cases of educational institutions. However, Catholic hospitals, for example, are for obvious reasons not only legally allowed to forbid abortion internally, but also to discharge physicians propagating abortion in public.[35] In neo-corporatist regimes, representatives of (umbrella) organisations of religious providers are included in public sector committees or councils for standard setting and supervision.[36] Strict separationists obviously have to condemn all this as incompatible with liberal morality. All others have to confront tensions, trade-offs and problems of regulation, exemptions, standard setting, performance control, and 'neutral' professionalism (sect. 8.3).[37]

1.3.3.9 An emerging European regime of religious governance?

When we combine these different threads, we see diversity of arrangements within and among states, and no convergence – not in the EU and most emphatically not globally.[38]

Broadly speaking, a common European regime of religious governance requires a shared regime of 'governing religions' or a 'common West-European pattern of church and state relations' (Ferrari 2002: 7). Also, it requires convergence of associational, network, communal-cultural and (semi-)private modes of religious governance. Some claim that the former process is already under way. Three main features are discerned: 'the right to religious liberty,' 'the religious incompetence of the state and the autonomy of religious groups,' and 'selective cooperation of states and religious groups' (Ferrari 2002: 7-11).[39] I confine myself to three critical objections.

First, religious liberty indeed demands many moral and legal constraints. The 'coercive isomorphism' by way of 'legal transnationalism' (Koenig 2007) works through binding international covenants, regional human rights regimes and also 'soft law' like the Declaration on the Elimination of all Forms of Intolerance and Discrimination Based on Religion and Belief (1981), the UN Convention on the Protection of the Rights of Migrant Workers (1990), the UN Declaration of the Rights of Persons Belonging to Minorities (1992) and the various activities of the Council of Europe (European Commission Against Racism and Intolerance (ECRI; Doc CRI 1998, 2001) and of the Organisation for Security and Co-operation in Europe (OSCE). However important this is, it does not lead 'to full institutional isomorphism. Rather, it should be conceived in terms of processes of normative pressure and imitation amounting to a successive diffusion of cognitive and normative schemata' (Koenig 2005: 230f). Two more caveats are in place as well. These principles and rights are interpreted differently in 'national' traditions and jurisdictions within the EU (Monsma & Soper 1997, Soper & Fetzer 2007, Bowen 2007). In addition, the emergence and transnational diffusion of a multicultural citizenship model and of pluralistic modes of organisational incorporation may not be as strong, uncontested and irreversible as Koenig and others assume (Bader 2005: 86ff).

Second, it is contested whether something like the institutional model of selective cooperation really emerges ('political transnationalism'). At least some member states (e.g. France) oppose this option and the EU has no regulatory competence to harmonise rules and practices.[40]

Third, the hold of path dependency is stronger than the effects of 'isomorphic change' through the three causal mechanisms of enforcement, imitation and normative pressure.[41] Claims that the 'global transformation of the classical models of nation states subjects the institutional logics of religion-policies ... to a fundamental change' (Koenig 2004: 87) leading, amongst other things, to an increasing convergence of Western European Islam-politics in the 1990s, are not corroborated by actual developments (chap. 5 and sect. 8.5).

In conclusion, different states, different branches of states at different levels do different things. They will continue to do so.

1.4   Lessons for political philosophers

We do need broader and deeper comparative studies of religious governance and government than presently available. Yet, the research summarised above contains important lessons for political philosophers and theorists.

First, 'establishment', its narrow meaning focuses on constitutionally or legally enforced establishment of one or more (state) churches (McConnell 1992: 688; Miller 1985: 44ff). The broad meaning of 'voluntary establishment' (Eisenach 2000, Miller 1985: 267) includes political and cultural predominance, hegemony or 'domination' (Miller 1985: 316) of a specific religion or religions in 'national political theologies' under conditions of constitutional/legal non-establishment or disestablishment (sect. 7.1). Political theory should not exclusively focus on constitutional or legal aspects: establishment versus disestablishment or non-establishment. It should also take into account a broader range of relevant relationships between civil and political society (parties, politics), cultures, nation(s) and (organised) religions. Furthermore, it should recognise different degrees and different forms of actual (administrative, political, cultural) establishment and disestablishment. In addition, it is plain that different roads lead to religious pluralism, and different institutional settings are compatible with or promote religious diversity. Think of US denominationalism (a more or less free religious market and 'non-establishment plus private pluralism') and the mixed pattern of institutional pluralism (selective cooperation) that may develop in the direction of a more democratic and flexible variety of institutional pluralism, to wit associative democracy (chaps. 7 and 8).

Second, modern societies require a threshold of institutional, organisational and role differentiation between state/politics and religions. As we have seen, this is not peculiar to modern Western state societies: 'pre-modern empires' are also characterised by such differentiation. What the latter lack is an explicit statement and recognition of the moral minimum: the two autonomies. To repeat: the two autonomies do not require, at least in the eyes of European and national constitutional courts, constitutional or legal non-establishment or disestablishment. Most European states are characterised by weak constitutional or legal links between state and church(es). Theories of modernisation or functional differentiation, expecting the dissolution of such links, are seriously at odds with empirical evidence. Institutional differentiation between state and church(es) comes not as a package but in degrees.

Third, the moral minimum does not require anything like a 'complete' or 'strict' separation of religions from state/politics. All states with liberal democratic constitutions grant exemptions to religions and at least indirectly finance religious organisations. They are bound to 'define' and 'recognise' religions at least administratively and most states give religions a special legal status. Strict separationists should seriously consider that the liberal rule of law demands limitations on unbound public administrative discretion. Liberals should advocate either judicial appeal (and emerging case law) or explicit legislation (chap. 8). 'Neo-corporatist' states and states that officially engage in selective cooperation between (organised) religions and governments finance faith-based organisations in care, social services and education. But so do separationist constitutions. Even the US – contrary to Fox's claim – are not the 'unique exception' (2006: 559) in realising 'full SRAS' (537). Strict laïcists in France and strict separationists in the US are selectively alarmed about this. They had better investigate the grounds for such practices in the majority of countries with liberal-democratic constitutions. Practical wisdom and grounded normativity would stand to gain.

Fourth, political philosophers favouring strict separationism should be aware that their ideal models – non-establishment, no financing of religions and 'private pluralism' only – differ markedly from the actual muddle both in the case of idealised American Denominationalism and of French laïcité. The construction of such ideal models produces unwarranted simplifications and serious empirical misdescriptions. These models hinder practical learning from and experimentation with alternatives. If philosophers and politicians are unaware of the unavoidable shifts from model to muddle, and propose uninformed institutions, policies and strategies, nothing is won and much is damaged.

Fifth, institutionalised relations between states and (organised) religions are the result of protracted conflicts (e.g. the famous school and cultural wars in the 19th century) between a multitude of actors commanding unequal power resources: religious majorities and minorities, secularists, legislative, judicial and administrative state agencies. Philosophers have been involved as public intellectuals in these battles and have – maybe only very marginally – contributed to shaping the predominant 'public philosophies' and idealised policy paradigms. As we have seen, pluralising Protestant cultures is characterised by weak cultural secularisation and fairly low anticlericalism and more or less strict but religion-friendly neutrality (in the US) or more substantive and positive neutrality amongst intellectual elites (as in Australia, the Netherlands and Germany), whereas monopolistic religious cultures lead to a sharp clerical-anticlerical split and to aggressive secularism amongst intellectual elites, as in the Latin countries (French *laïcité de combat*).

In summary, political philosophers should be more self-reflective. They must recognise the deep and inevitable historical, socio-cultural, political and institutional embeddedness of philosophising itself. There is no naive escape from partisanship. The challenge is to prevent 'universalising the particular', to gain reflective distance from contexts and battles, and to refrain from the pretence of a completely impartial and neutral view from nowhere (chap. 2).

Part II

Reconceptualising principles and making political philosophy fit for the task of accommodating religious diversity

2 Contextualising morality: moral minimalism, relational neutrality, and fairness as even-handedness

Although they do it in various ways, most liberal, republican, feminist and socialist political philosophers defend the core ideals of secularism, state neutrality and strict separation that seem intuitively so plausible in modern, pluralist societies and that have been elaborated in the most sophisticated way by American political philosophers, setting the tone for the international debate. In this chapter, I do not want to re-iterate my earlier criticism of the predominant style of liberal political philosophy[1] but focus on the positive, reconstructive task. I start with a substantive, critical reconceptualisation of overlapping and mutually re-inforcing principles of liberal political philosophy that are important for debating the accommodation of religious diversity and its limita-tions. Moderate universalism and embedded impartiality enable us to avoid the pitfalls of abstract universalism and ethical particularism (sect. 2.1). A moderately universalist morality under conditions of rea-sonable pluralism of the good life tends to be a minimal morality that may be combined with more demanding, differentiated standards of liberal, democratic and egalitarian moralities (sect. 2.2). The upshot of my argument in this section is, first, that there are some basic norma-tive standards for the accommodation of religious diversity that apply to all polities, including liberal-democratic polities, which should con-strain not only the projects of non-liberal regimes but also the project of liberal regimes in ways that conflict with liberal commitments to strong versions of autonomy and equality. Second, there are additional normative standards that apply only to liberal-democratic polities and that should further commitments to autonomy and equality in ways that do not infringe on the standards of moral minimalism. Thinking of deep ethnic and religious cultural diversity seriously makes us recog-nise that polities, including liberal-democratic states, cannot be strictly neutral or 'difference-blind' and cannot guarantee complete cultural equality. Strict neutrality and a conception of justice as 'hands-off' have to be reconceptualised as relational neutrality (sect. 2.3) and fairness as even-handedness in cultural matters (sect. 2.4). Recognising moral pluralism and the complexity of practical reason more seriously re-quires contextualised morality (sect. 2.5) and an institutional and attitu-dinal turn in political theory (sect. 2.6).

2.1 'A view from nowhere' or relativism? Moderate universalism

Postmodern or post-colonial criticism of modernity, secularism and the strict separation as Western, Eurocentric, imperialist notions is associated with a strong criticism of attempts to present principles of liberal morality as universal (Nandy 1998, Madan 1998, Asad 2003, Van de Veer 1998, de Vries & Sullivan 2006). This often goes hand in hand with claims that all versions of universal morality are impossible or, worse, can only universalise particular moralities. This criticism ties in with old and new criticism of moral universalism by conservatives, cultural anthropologists, historians and sociologists of knowledge, and by constructivist and some hermeneutic and pragmatist philosophers. Here, I try to show, in a highly programmatic way, how we can avoid being caught in the trap of either claiming an uncontested universal morality from some 'Archimedian' point or some God's-Eye-View from Nowhere, or resigning oneself to the deep moral relativism of 'anything goes'.

Completely independent, impartial, neutral and objective knowledge is impossible, indeed. All knowledge, both cognitive and normative, is produced or 'constructed', situated, embedded and relational. The presentation of situated, perspectivist knowledge as completely disinterested, neutral, objective and impartial reproduces five fallacies – disinterestedness, pure origin, transparency, cultural imperialism and absolutism – that have been extensively criticised in different traditions of thought.[2] If 'impartiality is the guise that particularity takes to seal bias against exposure' (Minow 1990: 376) or the central ideological mechanism to universalise the particular, and at the same time, to hide this from view, then we seem to be condemned to particularisms of interests and experiences, of disciplinary perspectives, of theoretical knowledge, of culture and history, and this is the conclusion drawn by most postmodernists and other critics. It is my contention that we are not trapped in those dichotomies and wrong choices as soon as we get rid of the misleading idea of 'absoluteness'.[3] We are not forced to sacrifice impartiality, neutrality or objectivity but we have to reconceptualise these normative ideals in order to both criticise their ideological misuse and to save the laudable intuitions not only under ideal conditions but in the real world.

The elaboration of concepts of embedded impartiality (of normative judgements), relational neutrality (of state institutions), and perspectival objectivity (of truth claims) is guided by the following general intuitions.[4]

First, we have to reject reckless 'standpoint logic' based on strong, deterministic accounts of the relation between objective social positions, experiences, interests and chances for a less particularist, more objective knowledge of the world and more impartial moral principles and normative frames. Negatively privileged social positions, indeed, do not guarantee objectivity or impartiality but they stimulate a need to be better informed and to know more about causes of structural inequalities (Bader 1991, chap. VI). In addition, they stimulate a need for fairer and less particularist normative frames, and their movements and fights serve as carriers for more universalist interpretations of moral principles like liberty and equality.[5]

Second, it is certainly not easy to avoid the perspectives and rivalries of academic disciplines but we can translate their languages, compare their perspectives, criticise their imperialisms, and reject their untenable claims.

Third, theorists in general, and philosophers in particular, have difficulties in fighting the temptation of transparency and the accompanying, often unacknowledged devaluation of experience, emotion, virtues and traditions of practical knowledge. Rejecting 'theoreticism' and 'constructivist rationalism', however, does not condemn us to 'anti-theory', to uncritical praise of practical knowledge or of moral intuitions (sect. 3.5). We need higher degrees of self-reflexivity and institutional safeguards designed to prevent strategies of cognitivist rationalism (Scott 1998; Novotny et al. 2001).

Fourth, acknowledging the inevitable cultural embeddedness of our cognitive and normative frames is one thing, opting for strong cultural particularism, moral relativism or polemic ethnocentrism is quite another.[6] For one thing, cultural frames are neither monolithic (they show internal tensions or contradictions, they develop) nor are they neatly isolated (they overlap and compete with other cultural frames). We can also translate and compare (cultures are not incommensurable, incomparable or incompatible). Acknowledging that even our definitions of basic needs, basic capabilities or rights are inevitably culturally framed and that we evaluate resources and rewards differently does not mean that attempts to develop such universal conceptions and theories of morality would be inconsistent or circular right from the start. It does mean, however, that these concepts have to be fully sensitive regarding cultural differences and structural inequalities, and that these theories have to be minimalist versions of universalism (sect. 2.2). Again, higher degrees of self-reflexivity and openness are very much stimulated by the powerful presence of other voices and by institutional requirements making such intercultural or inter-religious dialogue fairer, even under non-ideal conditions.

These are the claims of a gradational theory of perspectival objectivity, relational neutrality and embedded impartiality. Some parts are better developed than others. However, to my knowledge, the whole has never been worked out satisfactorily. Recognising these fallacies and increasing self-reflexivity are necessary but obviously not sufficient conditions.[7] Conceptions of a 'negotiated' universalism (Bilgrami 1998: 393-399) or Bhikhu Parekh's defence of a non-rationalistic, intercultural dialogue or, more precisely, poly-logue (2000; 2005: 24; Renteln 2004; Sen 2004: 319ff; 2005) insist more clearly on the presence of the voices of all relevant actual stakeholders in order to prevent unchallenged imperialist claims of particular social groups, disciplines, 'reasons' and cultures to universalise the particular.[8]

Explicitly dialogical conceptions of embedded impartiality or justice and perspectival objectivity that are currently gaining in prominence in philosophy have to be supplemented by a variety of internal and external legal and institutional conditions that stimulate and sustain the weak ethics of science and help to achieve higher degrees of self-reflexivity, self-criticism, and modesty. 'Strongly Contextualized Knowledge' in an 'age of uncertainty' (Novotny et al. 2001) stimulates imaginative institutional design for 'Re-Thinking Science'. Rethinking Morality from the perspective of a gradational, moderately universalist, embedded impartiality motivates a shift towards a more minimalist conception of morality (sect. 2.2), an explicitly relational conception of neutrality of state and politics (sect. 2.3), and a reconceptualisation of fairness in cultural matters (sect. 2.4). Compared with recent attempts to contextualise sciences, we may have even stronger reasons to contextualise morality (sect. 2.5).

2.2 Moral minimalism and differentiated moral standards

After the Second World War, demanding theories of egalitarian-liberal morality or justice were elaborated that require a more or less radical egalitarian distribution of a more or less complete list of primary goods either among citizens of states or globally. This *liberalism of hope in the centres* clearly reflects economic growth, remarkable rises in absolute standards of living for all, even some modest decrease in relative inequalities, as well as the absence of actual warfare, fairly high degrees of safety and security. For some time now, one can find indications of a shift from ideal theories of what equality would optimally or maximally require towards more minimalist satisfying theories (Shue 1980; Cunningham 1987; Beitz 1989: 117f; Bader 2005d), from guaranteeing welfare to 'preventing malfare' (Hacker-Cordon 2003), from a liberalism of hope to a new 'liberalism of fear' (Shklar, Margalit, Ignatieff, Levy), a 'liberalism of peaceful existence' (Gray) or a 'tolerable liberalism' (M. Williams) rescuing important insights of old proto-liberals of fear (Hobbes, Pufendorf).

Practically, this shift reflects the end of the golden age of postwar capitalism, a growing disappointment with the rhetoric of human rights,
particularly with the fact that the corresponding duties have been im-
perfectly allocated, a clearer recognition of the urgency of the fight
against absolute poverty, increasing inequality and blatant violations of
basic rights to security and safety by wars, civil wars and ethnic cleansings in the 'Rest-of-the-World' and, more recently, also by perceived or
actual security threats in the centres.

Theoretically, this shift is motivated by a clearer recognition of two
main difficulties of ideal theories. First, equality dissipates into conflicting equalities (legal, economic, social, political, cultural; formal/proce-
dural or material/substantive; equality of resources or welfare or status), the list of primary goods became longer and longer, and problems
of comparing, weighing and measuring them could no longer be neglected. Even supposing culturally homogenous societies, egalitarian-
liberal theories became more complex, allowing for many sub-optimal
solutions instead of the one-best solution. In addition, disagreement
among liberal egalitarians has been mushrooming. Second, in culturally diverse societies, under conditions of reasonable pluralism, one
can no longer neglect the fact that all fields or spheres of justice, all resources and rewards, all primary goods, all needs and even all basic
rights are always divergently interpreted and that each of these cultural
meanings has direct and indirect consequences for their relative evaluation and importance. Theories that claim to be neutral with regard
to the competing versions of a good life have to be sensitive not to impose predominant cultural interpretations, neither inside states nor
globally, not to fall prey to cultural imperialism.

For both problems, moral minimalism and satisfying, threshold or
sufficiency theories seem to provide better, more sensible solutions. In
recent discussions on global justice, theories of basic needs or basic
rights (Shue 1980, Elfstrøm 1990, Jones 1999)[9] and of minimal but
strong global obligations[10] are gaining ground. In recent multiculturalism discussions, the emphatic praise of a perfectionist ideal of rich cultural diversity is losing ground to sober justice-based theories in general, and to a multiculturalism of fear in particular which tries to guarantee basic needs for all instead of requiring a more demanding
egalitarian liberal morality. Here, I focus on the latter and discuss
some problems of 'substantive minimalism' (Cohen 2004) regarding
the contested content of the moral minimum.[11]

The content of a minimal universal morality is not uncontested, it is
not fixed or pre-given in nature, it is historically developing and even
basic needs are always articulated from within particular cultural traditions. Yet, 'at a sufficiently fundamental level ... we should expect conceptions of need to converge' (Miller 1995: 75; see Walzer 1994; 1995:

193; Miller 2006, chap. 7). In terms of basic rights, the essential core *in our times* would clearly not only comprise basic rights to security (life, liberty, bodily integrity and protection against violence) but also basic rights to subsistence and, in addition, rights to basic education and basic healthcare, a certain minimum of due-process rights, freedom of conscience, toleration, minimal though not fully 'equal' respect and, maybe, even to some minimal though not fully equal representation for all those affected from political decisions (Tasioulas 2002). The longer the list of basic rights (e.g. Ingram 2004), the less basic and the more culturally sensitive and contested they become. The same is obviously true for the demanding, long list of capabilities elaborated by Sen and, particularly, by Nussbaum (2000, chap. 1) on the basis of respective international or regional human rights regimes.

For my purposes, it is crucial to distinguish more clearly than usual between four different tiers of morality: (i) minimal morality and rights; (ii) the more demanding minimal morality of liberal-democratic constitutional states, adding political freedoms, political equality and political autonomy and equal respect (modern nondiscrimination) to the more minimalist concept of agency characteristic for all morality;

Table 2.1   *Differentiated morality*

Minimal morality	Liberal-democratic morality	More egalitarian morality	Comprehensive moral liberalism
Basic rights to security and subsistence	Equal civic and political rights	Equal socio-economic and fair cultural rights and opportunities	Specific way of a good life
Rights to life, liberty, bodily integrity, protection against violence	Equal legal rights Free and equal active and passive voting rights	Policies of redistribution: taking socio-economic and political equality of opportunity more serious	Leading an autonomous, self-chosen and transparent life free of illusions
Rights to basic subsistence, basic education, basic healthcare	Freedoms of political communication	Affirmative action policies	
Minimal due process rights	Modern (negative) nondiscrimination rights (equal respect)	Policies of cultural even-handedness	
Minimal respect			
Collective and individual toleration (freedom of conscience)			
Agency and legal autonomy	**Political autonomy**	**Substantive autonomy** Range of meaningful socio-economic and cultural options	**Rational revisability**

(iii) the more demanding egalitarian morality of substantively more equal chances; and (iv) the most demanding morality of comprehensive liberalism with its core values of autonomy as 'rational revisability'[12] (see Table 2.1 on page 72).

I cannot discuss in detail here which specified legal rights from the canon of rights in the respective international or regional human rights covenants and treatises or national constitutions (and in which interpretations) belong to the minimum core of any morality.[13] My interpretation is more extensive and demanding than a strict minimum that is limited to protection against 'death or irreparable physical harm' (Renteln 2004: 19) or 'severe physical abuse or worse' (Lustgarten 1983: 91). However, it is obviously more restrictive than the minimum standards advocated by Parekh (2000) and Poulter (1998: 20ff), entailing not only the long list of international and European human rights but also thicker 'shared values', understood in an institutional sense' (24) as the operative values of British society. It is also much more restrictive than the long list of civil, political, socio-economic and cultural rights in human rights declarations and treatises. Yet, it contains not only 'negative' liberties but also essential 'positive rights' (Shue 1980; Koenig 2003: 122; Cohen 2004).[14]

Two issues in my preliminary distinction between minimal and minimal liberal-democratic morality are particularly contested. First, in my interpretation, minimal morality requires minimal but not necessarily 'equal respect and concern' (Dworkin 1977: 180-183) in the modern liberal-democratic interpretation of nondiscrimination. This allows me to discuss whether dissenting non-liberal but decent minorities should be forced to comply with modern nondiscrimination inside liberal-democratic polities and, if so, in which fields and contexts. For example, they would certainly not in families and churches, but also not without due consideration and within limits in faith-based organisations in care and education (sect. 4.3 and chap. 10). Second, the soft requirement of decent (though not fully) equal representation for all those affected by political decisions (Cohen 2004: 25ff; Rawls 1999) – that decent people and, in an analogy, decent minorities need not have a constitution with equal democratic citizenship – has been extensively criticised. However, it allows a considered, stepwise, morally and prudentially convincing argumentation of the conditions and institutional contexts of the imposition of democracy, both in international relations and within liberal-democratic polities.[15] Both claims should be made plausible in the substantive discussions of relevant cases in chaps. 4, 5 and 10. In addition, it should be stressed that my plea for minimal morality is thoroughly context-sensitive. It does not apply in all contexts or fields and only with regard to certain types of moral problems, particularly those of ethno-religious pluralism, whereas more demanding standards can be defended for other types of problems and contexts. Furthermore, it has to be stressed that the burden of proof should rest with those who claim exemptions from general laws and regulations in liberal-democratic states (e.g. from general labour law, from works council or democratic corporate governance regulations).

Before discussing the advantages and problems of moral minimalism (para. 2.2.3), it seems wise to exemplify its meanings and implications in a short discussion of two hotly contested issues: autonomy and/or toleration (para. 2.2.1), and liberalism and/or democracy (para. 2.2.2).

2.2.1 Autonomy or toleration

Autonomy (the last line in table 2.1) is clearly a central liberal value but its contested and ambiguous meanings range from maximalist, thick concepts to minimalist, thin concepts.[16]

i.   Autonomy as self-creation or authorship of an original, unique self. This non-conformist, ethical, not moral individualism is opposed to all communal ties, attachments, affiliations and obligations. It ranges from clearly anti-egalitarian and anti-democratic elitism (Nietzsche) to more moderate versions of 'self-enacting individuality' (Flathman 1998: 83) to Foucauldian and postmodernist 'arts of the self' and Unger's context-smashing individuals in his 'super-liberalism' (critically: Bader 1991a).

ii. Kantian moral autonomy as an unconditional requirement of reason, severed from all emotions and worldly passions.

iii. Explicitly weaker versions of individual or personal moral autonomy as 'self-determination' that are consistent with communal ties and with 'relational views of the self, with social embeddedness' (Reich 2002: 106). They are characterised by a combination of three core elements, which may be disconnected in other, less demanding conceptions: (a) procedural external independence: no outside person or force controls/manipulates a person's destiny (vs. external, social and political obstacles); (b) internal psychic independence: individuals should not be hindered by internal obstacles to exercise the capacity for autonomy; (c) capacity to reflect, potentially revise or reject inherited, chosen or unchosen practices and ends, commitments, values, desires and beliefs: 'rational revisability'. This combined ideal is defended in different versions[17], depending on the weight that is put on degrees and ways of exercising autonomy and on the divergent ways in which the tension between 'respecting autonomy' that 'counsels against paternalism' and 'exercising autonomy' that 'potentially favours paternalism' (Reich 2002: 108ff) is balanced.[18] Compared with the first two versions, this is clearly a more 'minimalist autonomy' compatible with decisive commitments 'to obedience to traditions, or to rules, or to a ruler', to nonliberal communities (Reich 2002: 102). However, this depends and is conditional on 'how one adheres' (109): all three conditions – external and internal independence and rational revisability – have to be met. In this regard, the self-determination conception of autonomy presupposes and is based on a split-level view of the self or person: the 'second order' volitions, preferences, needs or the second-order self is able to reflect on, control, reject or revise the first-order ones.

iv. Still weaker and more minimalist conceptions of political autonomy that require capacities and exercise of rational revisability only from citizens but not from persons in their non-political lives, as developed by Rawls (1993, 1999; Kukathas 2003: 16; Swaine 2006: 59f) and all deliberative democrats.

v. Even more minimalist conceptions of political autonomy and of legal autonomy that drop the requirement and certainly the legal imposition of (high degrees of) exercising the capacity of rational revisability and focus on respecting individual autonomy. Such respect presupposes only a minimum or threshold of individual autonomy (e.g. 'maturity') – it is a matter of on/off – whereas the exercise of autonomy is always a matter of degree. It is implied in concepts of responsibility in private and criminal law and in legal concepts of political autonomy that guarantee procedural independence against external controls, also against the paternalism under the guise of demanding conceptions of exercising reasonability, critical scrutiny and revisability in Rawlsian political liberalism and more modest recent varieties of deliberative democracy. In addition, respect of autonomy does not only concern individual but also associational or collective autonomy, which is often bluntly overruled by prophets of demanding notions of exercising high degrees of individual autonomy in the more emphatic liberal tradition who do not even recognise serious tensions between individual and collective autonomy and the difficulties to find reasonable balances.[19] This is the main reason why critics like Galston and Kukathas argue for dropping the autonomy language altogether and replacing it by tolerance or toleration.

vi. All traditions, even those that do not have explicit concepts of individual legal autonomy and responsibility share basic notions of minimalist individual agency (vs. conceptions of individuals as cultural dupes or being governed completely by external and internal 'powers'; see critically: Saharso 1999, 2006; Honig 1999: 39).

Most liberal-democratic political philosophers agree that the first two concepts are unacceptable because they are illiberal or anti-democratic, or too demanding, exacting, rarefied or utopian. They seriously disagree, however, on three issues. First, whether conceptions of personal moral autonomy and also political autonomy that are linked to the demanding notion of rational revisability even in their minimalist versions are not too demanding and comprehensive to be imposed (by law and threat of enforcement) on those not sharing the split-level conception of the self and the clearly non-neutral demands of external and internal independence, and rational revisability. Second, whether the distinction between moral and political autonomy can be consistently argued for and whether it can resolve the problems, as defenders of political liberalism think, or not, as critics like Kymlicka and others contend. Third, whether defenders of more minimalist concepts of legal and political autonomy and agency, disconnected from the rational revisability requirement, do not sacrifice too much on the altars of accommodation of cultural diversity in their attempts to gain the most universal agreement possible.

Regarding the first question, it is obvious that more emphatic concepts of moral (iii) and political autonomy (iv) tend to be more particularist, both in a global context and inside the West. They have been increasingly and rightly criticised for imposing limitations on toleration and accommodation that are too strict, as well as for requiring overly perfectionistic educational demands.[20] In turn, the minimalist concepts of agency of all human beings (vi) and of individual legal autonomy (v) are presupposed in international covenants and in constitutions and are also broadly shared nowadays.[21] Regarding the second question, rational revisability – both in the more demanding concept of moral autonomy (iii) and in the more minimalist political autonomy (iv) – is a laudable political ideal that I share. However, compliance with high degrees of capability and exercise cannot be enforced, legally or otherwise. It should be promoted by other ways and means and one should be careful not to undermine the more minimalist moral requirements of legal and political autonomy (v). In other words, one should respect a non-infringement proviso (see below).[22] Regarding the third question, I agree with critics like Kymlicka (2002: 235ff) that the attempt of political liberals to distinguish between moral and political rational revisability fails in the end because the split between citizens and private individuals is implausible and spillover effects are inevitable. But I do have two caveats: one should be more aware of, and one should try to minimise these spillover effects (Tomasi 2002, see sect. 7.3 with Rosenblum 1998); and one should carefully avoid the danger that criticism of the rational revisability conceptions extends into and sacrifices the sober notion of political autonomy (v) or the guarantees of the related political rights and anti-paternalism.

Finally, all conceptions of individual autonomy, whether maximalist or minimalist, should always be combined with the other side of the autonomy coin, the socio-economic, institutional and cultural environments, circumstances or contexts rightly highlighted by Raz, Kymlicka and many others. Substantive autonomy requires the guarantee of a certain minimum of basic security and a certain minimal range of meaningful cultural options – in terms of 'quality and variety' (Reich 2002: 105; 2006) not only of quantity – in order to transform choices that are legally allowed into real possibilities. Exit rights (implied in v) have to be complemented by real, meaningful exit options (para. 7.3.2: associative democracy and regime pluralism). Real exit increases rational revisability and demanding personal autonomy much more – by policies of capacitation – than futile attempts to impose higher degrees of building up and exercising capacities.

As we have seen, critics of demanding exercise-of-rational-revisability concepts and of the related infringement of collective autonomy have proposed *replacing autonomy with tolerance* or toleration. However, here again, one finds contested, ambiguous, minimalist and more demanding, maximalist concepts. Here, I focus on *principles and rights of tolerance,* on collective and individual tolerance (individual freedom of conscience and of expression), not on the related discussion of *attitudes/ virtues* and *institutional regimes* of toleration (sect. 6.1). Both collective and individual tolerance have been learned in situations where protracted religious warfare did not lead to decisive victories and where collective tolerance did not entail individual freedom of conscience (apostasy, conversion, proselytising and heresy)[23]. This individual tolerance was learned, first strategically and later morally, when state makers and political elites saw that the use of state force to change convictions may be counterproductive, and when believers and religious elites accepted the view that religious convictions, exactly because they are so deep, should not be imposed from the outside, from above, by force, but freely endorsed from the inside.[24] Collective tolerance (and related non-liberal regimes of toleration) are pure 'permission conceptions' (Forst 2006: 6). Here, freedom and domination, inclusion and exclusion, recognition and disrespect have been mixed and defined by the authority alone. Permission conceptions have only slowly and inconsistently been replaced by 'respect conceptions',[25] demanding a fuller and more secure recognition of individual freedom of conscience and, eventually also, that democratic citizens respect each other as legal and political equals, following a logic of emancipation rather than toleration (Forst 2006: 12).

In line with my argument above, the moral minimum recently implies a sober respect conception of individual tolerance, incompatible with any ban on or persecution of changing or renouncing one's religion.[26] However, it also has to address serious tensions between collective and individual freedoms of religion so often neglected by emphatic prophets of individual autonomy. It also requires a minimal disposition to tolerate and respect the rights of others. However, one should carefully avoid adding demanding notions such as openness, curiosity, enthusiastic endorsement of difference, or harmonious respect to this minimalist 'gritting teeth tolerance' and to this 'agonistic respect'.

2.2.2 Liberalism and/or democracy: democratic temptations

As we know, liberal and democratic principles and rights conflict with each other and these conflicts cannot be resolved by claiming some deep, foundational *'Gleichursprünglichkeit'* (Habermas 1992) of private and public autonomy (Bader 1993). The eventual compromise of a liberal-democratic morality (Table 2.1, row 2) is more demanding and thicker than minimal morality. In addition to due process rights and minimal but not necessarily equal respect, it requires modern nondiscrimination rights generally and equal political rights that involve a threshold capacity of political autonomy (v). All mature members of a polity have to be treated as free and equal citizens with equal political rights and duties, irrespective of class, status, education, 'race', sex, gender, ethnicity and religion. In voting, their ballots have to count equally. In democratic decision-making, 'error has the same rights as truth' (*anti-paternalism proviso*) and, in enacting the obligations of citizenship, eventually have to overrule competing obligations of faith as well as other competing deep obligations (*priority for democracy*). Even if one rejects the full-blooded 'rational revisability' conception of political autonomy (iv), these rights and institutions cannot be completely neutral or anti-perfectionist. For four reasons, however, democrats are tempted to develop more demanding, thicker and more perfectionist notions.

First, democracy's egalitarian drive: Compared with 'due respect' and equality before the law, political equality tends to a more substantive notion of equality, particularly if one does not focus exclusively on formally equal political rights but asks for more equal actual political chances (table 2.1, row 3) – as all more participatory democrats do – requiring at least a modicum of socio-economic equality, e.g. the effective guarantee of a minimum income.[27]

Second, democracy's deliberative drive: Democracy – like modern private and criminal law – requires a minimum of personal agency and responsibility but political autonomy is often claimed to be much thicker than legal autonomy. It is assumed that individuals are able to make their own free choices. Less aggregative, more deliberative conceptions of democracy[28] demand that these choices be reasonable in all of the three core elements of 'rational revisability' discussed above, and that persons are able and willing to distance themselves from their particularist interests. The stronger democracy's deliberative drive, the more difficult the not very plausible distinction between political (iv) and moral personal autonomy (iii) becomes.

Third, the drive towards liberal-democratic congruence: Even the thinnest liberal conceptions of democracy – centred on principles and rights – cannot do without a certain minimum of civic and democratic duties, virtues and good practices in order to make democracy a stable and working system of political decision-making. Virtues and good practices are embedded in liberal-democratic cultures and habitualised in individual attitudes or ethos. Although non-perfectionist defenders of democracy are at pains to distinguish civic and democratic 'public' virtues and practices from more comprehensive ones that are characteristic of competing 'private' ways of a good life, such an attitudinal bifurcation in a public and a private personality is, as already stated, implausible and unfeasible. The longer the list of civic and democratic virtues becomes, and the stronger the required democratic ethos is made,[29] the more it becomes obvious that liberal democracy itself is a *contested* way of the good life.

A fourth difficulty is related to democracy's majoritarian drive that has to be tempered in 'modern' democracy by liberal anti-majoritarian devices such as guaranteeing basic individual rights, constitutional protection of minorities, and liberal exemptions and accommodations, highlighted by liberal and particularly by libertarian conceptions of representative democracy. Stronger conceptions of democracy have more difficulties in resisting this majoritarian drive; they are tempted to transgress these constitutional borders, to require democratic congruence deep down in all associations thereby transforming democracy into a full-blooded way of the good life.[30]

The first two more demanding conceptions (the egalitarian and participatory ones) are legitimate if they do not violate the non-infringement proviso (clearly not only Schumpeterian minimalism is compatible with democratic constitutions), but the next two (congruence and majoritarianism) are incompatible with the liberal side of liberal democracy.

2.2.3 Moral minimalism's problems

Some of the advantages of moral minimalism seem obvious. Its standards are more robust, can mobilise more support, and are easier to enforce. Hence, thin but strong minimal morality combines fairly universal support with important strategic reasons. Higher sensitivity to relevant cultural differences is built in. Claims to exemptions by countries or by ethno-religious minorities inside liberal-democratic polities can be treated more easily and fairly without violating basic needs or interests of individuals or minority groups within minorities (sects. 4.3 and 4.5 plus sects. 7.3 and 7.4). Yet, moral minimalism is plagued by four serious theoretical and practical problems.

First, does accepting moral minimalism include that different kinds of higher, more demanding standards are not morally required but only permissible and laudable requirements of justice (Walzer 1995: 293), that they are political standards that democratic polities are free to decide on by consent or majority and to legally impose upon citizens and residents (Føllesdal 1997; Shapiro 1999)? Or should we argue for a 'differentiated morality' (Engelen 2003; Bader 2005d)? In that case, one would have to distinguish between standards of minimal morality that have to be applied globally and should be made binding legal obligations in all countries where this is not yet achieved due to inadequate or lacking legislation and jurisdiction, and more demanding moralities that may or may not be legislated.[31]

Second, and more important than this terminological problem, is the question of whether moral minimalism would more or less inevitably lead to the levelling down of existing higher standards instead of ratcheting up lower ones (Caney 2001: 115f vs. 'satisfying cosmopolitanism'). This is the core of liberal-democratic opposition against exemptions for non-liberal ethno-religious minorities (chaps. 4, 7 and 10).[32] In addition: is moral minimalism sufficient to make it secure and stable? The persuasive force of these charges depends on the assumption that people's actions are governed and constrained only or mainly – and much more strongly – by moral obligations and that, without this moral backing, political and legal obligations would inevitably be weak. I argue for differentiated moral standards because I share moderate versions of this charge. More demanding standards of minimal liberal-democratic morality or of stronger substantive egalitarian morality are not weakened by minimalism, except on the assumption that people live up to higher standards only if these are backed by legal obligations and sanctions.[33]

Third, substantive minimalism is not only important for purely prudential or strategic reasons, as is often claimed. Even the core values of minimalism: life, liberty and peace are important moral values in themselves that cannot be taken for granted. Situations of war, civil war and emergency dramatically remind us of this old insight of a 'liberalism of fear'.[34] Even if you are convinced, as I am, that there is no context-independent hierarchy or lexical ordering of principles and rights,[35] it is plain that these core values gain elemental priority in situations of emergency. Is minimalism, then, 'the most we can hope for' (Ignatieff 2004: 173; McConnell 2001: 7f)? I agree with Williams (2005) and Cohen that 'minimalism may be more than we should ever reasonably expect. But hope is not the same as expectation. And minimalism draws the boundaries of hope too narrowly' (2004: 2) because, firstly, it neglects the counterproductive effects of self-reinforcing mutual fear, distrust and strategic action (the dynamics of escalation of conflicts: Bader 1991: 348-355). Liberals – not old and new conservatives – have good reason 'to fear fear itself' (Shklar). Secondly, not all situations are situations of escalating emergencies. In more normal situations, we need not confine ourselves to guarantee the 'smaller values' of moral minimalism, of living together (Bhargava 1998: 509ff)[36] but can promote some greater values of 'living together well' and the respective more demanding moralities of liberal-democracy (adding the fuller set of nondiscrimination rights and political rights) and of more egalitarian justice (adding substantive equality), and even more comprehensive liberal morality and morality of pluralism that I myself all endorse. And we have good reasons to hope that their guarantee and successful gradual realisation may contribute to prevent emergencies of security and subsistence and make minimalism more stable.

Fourth, such hope is reasonable only if greater values and more demanding moral standards are promoted in the right way – that is by voluntary means such as persuasion, interest, good practical examples and 'seduction' instead of imposing them by legal sanctions backed by (threat of) violence[37] and enforced cultural assimilation (sect. 7.3). In other words, more demanding moralities should not infringe upon smaller values and moral minimalism.[38] I call this the *non-infringement proviso*, which has so often been violated in old crusades under the banner of Religious Truth or Western Civilisation and now again in recent crusades under the flag of 'Freedom and Democracy' globally and of 'Autonomy and Free Choice' inside states. Minimalism serves as a crucial brake against sacrificing ordinary values like toleration. 'Giving deliberative priority to peace-as-social-concord' instead of measuring practices against the demanding 'standards of equality and autonomy first, and then asking whether or not it should be suppressed' may, indeed, lead to a 'more creative', 'more humane and less doctrinary liberalism – in short: a tolerable liberalism' (Williams 2005: 38 and 40). This is the main reason why I start from moral minimalism, instead of from a maximalist, comprehensive liberal morality like Joseph Raz. Minimalist morality should be enforceable and sanctioned by (the threat of) legal violence. Compliance with minimal liberal-democratic morality may be enforced and sanctioned inside liberal-democratic polities in some contexts but it is obviously urgent to try to persuade (by argument and by good example) decent but non-liberal and non-democratic minorities before using force. In addition, one should make room for exemptions and accommodations for those minorities who are 'theocrats' but grudgingly accept the minimal rules of law and democracy in the polity (sect. 7.3 and Swaine 2006, chap. 4).[39]

2.3   Moderate anti-perfectionism and relational neutrality

The principle of state neutrality has been introduced fairly recently in constitutional debates and liberal political philosophy, mainly in the US, serving many purposes and provoking heated and continuing debates. I will shortly present my reasons why I think that strict neutrality is misleading both in the justificatory and in the consequentialist sense, and that neutrality as 'benign neglect' is a dangerous myth with regard to both ethno-national and religious diversity.

Liberal political philosophers defend justificatory neutrality of state institutions and policies, and constitutional lawyers think that liberal-democratic constitutions require a neutral or 'secular purpose'. If 'liberal neutrality' expresses the principle that the state should 'not justify its actions on the basis of the intrinsic superiority or inferiority of conceptions of the good life', "neutrality' may not be the best word' (Kymlicka 2002: 217). This is because a liberal state should not be morally neutral regarding all and every way of life but only with regard to those that are 'justice-respecting' or compatible with minimal morality. Justifications should be at least moderately 'anti-perfectionist'. Neutrality is also often combined with a specific method of justification that seduces to 'abstract away' all cultural diversity and particularism instead of sensitively taking into account these cultural frameworks in deliberations and negotiations on impartial principles, as a perspective of embedded impartiality and relational neutrality requires.

Most liberal philosophers acknowledge that state policies cannot be strictly neutral in their consequences, particularly in their indirect, long-term effects, and that state institutions, rules and policies have unintended but foreseeable unequal and harmful, direct effects for some reasonable comprehensive doctrines and ways of a good life. Yet, they often seem to think that this would not be a moral problem, even if it could be avoided without seriously infringing on morally legitimate and compelling state interests.[40] Constitutional lawyers tend to be more sensitive than bluntly anti-consequentialist philosophers. 'Difference-blind' justifications, principles, rules, institutions and policies, which are systematically correlated with structural inequalities and outcomes, are incompatible with widely shared moral intuitions and any responsive moral theory.

The idea that the liberal state should benignly neglect ethno-cultural and religious diversity is certainly stronger than the requirement that it should be moderately anti-perfectionist. In the US, 'neutrality' has been introduced as a second-order principle to guide interpretations of the Non-Establishment and Free Exercise clauses of the First Amendment. As in all other cases,[41] 'blindness' or 'benign neglect' of religious diversity can only result in presumed neutrality hiding actual bias in favour of religious majorities (Galanter 1966, 1998; HLR Note 1987; Thiemann 1996; Laycock 1997; Tomasi 2001, 2004). It is a remarkable sign of the intuitive strength of this second-order principle that even critics of the supposed ethno-national neutrality of the state share it when it comes to religion. Kymlicka is rightly known for his astute criticism of the myth of ethno-national state neutrality (1995, 2002, chap. 8). He rejects the usual 'analogy between religion and (ethnic or national) culture' as 'flawed' (1997: 21). The 'idea that liberal-democratic states (or "civic nations") are indifferent to ethno-cultural identities is manifestly false. The religion model is altogether misleading.' (2002: 345). Yet, he accepts that benign neglect, blindness, strict neutrality towards religious diversity and also strict separation of organised religions and state/politics are correct descriptions or at least adequate normative principles without any further scrutiny.[42] 'It is possible for a state not to have an established church. But the state cannot help but give at least partial establishment to a culture.' (1997: 27) There should be a 'firm' or 'strict separation of church and state' (2002: 344) and a corresponding 'depoliticization of religious identities' (1997: 21).

Non-establishment in the US (initially only at the federal level) did not prevent but served to hide political, social and cultural establishment of majority religions, as is plain from many historical and sociological studies.[43] Constitutional non-establishment has only been the first stage in a continuing and unfinished process compatible with de facto political, social, cultural and symbolic establishment of Protestant Christianity. The second religious disestablishment eventually led to a higher degree of actual relational neutrality of the state, and though less so, also of American society, politics and culture from Evangelical Protestantism as its historical civil religion. This was the result of challenges by competing, organised minority religions, first by Roman Catholicism, and then followed by Jewish minorities. The emerging 'non-christological theism' or 'Judeo-Christian deism' has been contested by Black Muslim churches and new sects, though largely without success. Political life inside 'Godland' and American foreign policy (the 'chosen country', the 'chosen people') is still dominated by Christianity. Whether a third, moral disestablishment can be discerned and where this would leave American civil religion is very much contested.[44] During this long, chequered history, the American state has

certainly not been neutral, neither in purpose/intent nor in the direct
or indirect effects of educational, social and welfare policies. The myth
of strict neutrality neglects this continuing history (Minow 2000). It is
also unmasked by the continuing presence of legal privileges such as
congressional and military chaplains paid from public funds, tax exemptions, exemptions from military service or from combat duties,
state officials swearing belief in God, prayers in the Supreme Court
and US congress, 'In God We Trust' on US currency, etc. (HLR Note
1987).

Neither neutrality nor the famous 'wall of separation'[45], let alone 'secularism', can be found in the text of the American Constitution or any
other international covenant. They have been invoked by judges and
constitutional theorists as second-order guides to provide more coherent interpretations of the two religion clauses. Critics of the US Supreme Court's record have characterised the questionable logic and
contradictory opinions of the decisions[46] as 'perplexing', 'bizarre', 'fatu-
ous', 'a hodgepodge' and 'judicial meandering'.[47] Changing majorities
and minorities of justices grouped around divergent positions such as
'separationist, 'secular purpose', 'strict neutrality', 'symbolic accommodation',[48] 'strict neutrality', 'nondiscriminatory neutrality' and 'benevolent neutrality' paradigms.[49] It seems, however, that conflicts are only
repeated on a meta-level instead of achieving agreement or more consistent rulings.

Still, these debates teach some lessons: first, there is no such thing
as an unproblematic neutral, let alone secular purpose, particularly not
if achieved by abstracting from or neglecting the competing perspectives.[50] Second, the 'benign neglect' of direct effects of 'neutral state
policies' reproduces constitutional or legal fictions of blindness. 'Benign neglect' is incompatible with impartiality and both legal and substantively equal treatment, particularly under conditions of an expanding regulatory and provisional role of the welfare state.[51] Third, for fear
of unequal and discriminatory treatment of other religious and of non-
religious people, 'strict neutrality' in cultural and symbolic matters
would require the stripping of all cultural practices and symbols of
their particularist ethno-religious origins and meanings, a literally impossible claim. The new notion of fairness as even-handedness (sect.
2.4) has emerged from these constitutional debates, particularly from
'symbolic accommodation'.[52]

That benign neglect results in the reproduction of mythical histories
and deceiving actual descriptions should not come as a surprise. Yet it
might still be a valuable *normative or prescriptive device*. However, in the
real world, under conditions of structural and cultural inequalities, 'benign neglect' can never achieve nor even approach but actually hinders

fair and equal treatment of minorities or impartial judgement. Examples from jurisdiction, administration and legislation may show this.

By itself, the perennial repetition of the norm that judges should rule impartially – symbolised by *iustitia* with the veil – has never prevented biased jurisdiction on the basis of class, sex, gender, race, ethnicity, nationalism or religion. To achieve higher degrees of impartiality, listening to the voices of all parties is a first but insufficient step. This must be complemented by institutional and policy devices that increase the capacity of sensitive listening by pluralising the judiciary.[53] Only by a fair representation of relevant minorities may the laudable normative goal of impartial justice become more than an ideological veil hiding from view the predominant bias in the interpretation and application of universal, neutral and difference-blind rules.

The same holds true for the different departments of government (executive powers). The laudable normative ideal of neutral state administration may be realised to a higher degree by a difference- and inequality-sensitive politicisation of administration in a framework of 'separation of administration and politics' (Jörges 1999). Now, a fair representation of relevant minorities becomes more important as the discretionary powers increase (higher civil servants), and the more the boundaries between making and applying the rules become blurred (Hoekema et al. 1988).

That 'benign neglect' works counterproductively for achieving higher degrees of impartiality and neutrality is broadly acknowledged nowadays when it comes to rule-making by legislation. The old liberal ideas that members of parliament deliberate and decide on the common good without intermediaries such as political parties would be the optimal setting to guarantee the neutrality of the state is still with us in legal fictions. These fictions of the free mandate require MPs to be accountable only to their own consciences, cut loose from all interest groups, perspectives and negotiations. However, they have been replaced by pluralist, political party democracy, which is based on the insight that higher degrees of relational neutrality can only be achieved if one takes explicitly into account the experiences, perspectives and, last but not least, the organised voices of all those whose interests are affected and at stake – their own voices and those of their representatives, not those of benign paternalist pretending to speak for them – and also that deliberations cannot be cut loose from negotiations. The general arguments in favour of moderate universalism are here translated into widely diverging institutional devices of collective political decision-making (e.g. normative models of 'democratic justice' and 'deliberative democracy') or more broadly into negotiations cum deliberations among all those relevantly affected by collective decision-making about standards, their application and control in different societal fields ('associative democracy').[54]

The upshot of all these measures is that higher degrees of actual state neutrality under conditions of structural and cultural background inequalities cannot be achieved by 'benign neglect' of differences and inequalities, but only by explicit recognition and sensitivity to relevant differences, including ethno-national and religious ones, and by appropriate ways of voice, listening and some say (muscle) for the respective minorities. One possible interpretation of this is that 'strict neutrality' can still be conceived of as a morally required aim or goal, a regulative idea, a normative vanishing point that may never be completely realised even in an ideal world. Trying to realise this difference-blind aim, however, would require difference-sensitive means, strategies or policies.[55] A competing interpretation doubts that difference-blind aims themselves would be morally required, even if unachievable. In order to clarify this issue, we have to spell out more clearly what 'differences' may mean.

2.4 Fairness as even-handedness

'Differences' have played a very ambiguous role in critical ethnic and racial studies, critical legal studies, critical feminism and multiculturalism. In my view (Bader 2005e, 2006b), differences signify three crucially distinct phenomena that also have an impact on appropriate normative ideals.

First, differences are often meant to indicate structural inequalities of positions and of allocations (Bader & Benschop 1989), e.g. legal inequalities or economic, social, political inequalities even under conditions of strict legal equality. The appropriate ideal that guides fights and policies against structural inequalities is a universalist principle of justice, which Carens has coined 'fairness-as-hands-off'. This requires that class- or elite-descent and ascriptive categorisations should not have any impact on the distribution of resources and rewards, and we also think that cultural ways of life should not matter either, except in cases where a clearly demonstrable link exists with individual performances and ambitions, under the condition that cultures would be fairly freely chosen. Here, we should 'regard people abstractly, taking into account only generic human interests' (Carens 1997: 817), treat individuals as equal human beings with equal basic needs or rights, equal claims to essential natural and societal resources, not as being categorised or belonging to particular categories or groups. International and constitutional anti-discrimination law is an increasingly adequate legal articulation and specification of this ideal. Cultural differences, self-definitions and identity claims should not count, and a difference-blind ideal, goal or aim is just right.

Second, cultural inequalities between respective majorities and minorities, which may continue to exist even after serious legal and political inequalities have eventually been overcome (e.g. rich 'middlemen minorities' or rich national minorities) or even under conditions of rough complex equality. Brian Barry and other egalitarian liberals neglect cultural inequalities completely or reject that they would pose problems of justice, although they themselves inconsistently invoke such arguments in their defence of nation-states. The appropriate principle of justice that should guide minority protection and liberal accommodation cannot be fairness-as-hands-off, however.

Third, cultural differences or cultural diversity under conditions in which severe structural and cultural inequalities are absent. In 'ideally fair' or 'just societies', justice would obviously be silent. If one distinguishes between both structural and cultural inequalities and diversity or differences, 'difference' is not the problem but inequalities, at least for all justice-based theories. In this ideal world, racist, ethnicist, sexist, genderist, religious and nationalist inequalities would cease to exist and there would be no reason for affirmative action, multiculturalism or minority protection policies. Many universalist cosmopolitans seem to think that in such a 'gender-free society' (Okin 1989: 171) gender, ethnic, national and religious differences would also lose their meaning and impact on habits, life-styles, ways of life, patterns of interaction and distinction, and that the appropriate utopia would be a 'difference-blind' society. From a perspective of justice, we may leave this issue to be discussed and resolved by happier people in some imaginable future, although this overly abstract, rigid and individualistic view seems to be at odds with the equally held opinion that an ideally just society should allow a broad variety of collectively lived and organised cultural diversity.

Fairness-as-hands-off cannot be conceived as an appropriate principle in matters of culture and the symbolisation of collective identities because it neglects the inevitable partiality of all cultures, public cultures of liberal-democratic states included. For a start, it 'is a very radical ideal. It is hard to know what space would be left for ordinary politics on this account ... apart from libertarians, most of those advocating liberal neutrality do not run up the red flag of revolution' (Carens 1997: 819). The history of particular ethno-national and religious cultures is inevitably inscribed in public spaces, times, cultures and symbols of all liberal polities, however 'thin' or 'civic' they may be:

> No society can therefore totally avoid being biased against some of the practices of, and thus discriminating against, its cultural

minorities. Its identity limits its capacity for fairness, and to ask it to be indiscriminately tolerant in the name of fairness to minorities is to be unfair to it. If our concept of fairness does not take into account the demands of communal identity, it becomes abstract, impracticable, politically irrelevant, and a source of much avoidable guilt (Parekh 1995: 8).

In the end, strict neutrality and fairness as hands-off would literally strip people of their histories, languages, public holidays based on religion, public monuments, rituals and symbols of national identity, public dress codes, history and literature lessons in public education, etc. (Bader 1997b: 793-796). The result would be the fiction of a 'naked public square'. Even in an ideal world, this is not only impossible, it is also neither morally required nor desirable. A more appropriate reformulation of justice in this regard is fairness-as-even-handedness, stating that in order:

> (t)o treat people fairly, we must regard them concretely, with as much knowledge as we can obtain about who they are and what they care about. This approach requires immersion rather than abstraction... The guiding idea of evenhandedness is that what fairness entails is a sensitive balancing of competing claims for recognition and support in matters of culture and identity. Instead of trying to abstract from particularity, we should embrace it, but in a way that is fair to all the different particularities. Now, being fair does not mean that every cultural claim and identity will be given equal weight, but rather that each will be given appropriate weight under the circumstances and given a commitment to equal respect for all. History matters, numbers matter, the relative importance of the claim to those who present it matters, and so do many other considerations (Carens 1997: 818; 2000: 8ff).[56]

To sum up, both second-order principles of 'strict neutrality' and 'fairness-as-hands-off' with regard to ethno-religious inequalities and differences try to articulate important moral intuitions but do so in the wrong way. Strict neutrality should not be sacrificed in favour of outright particularism but replaced by moderate anti-perfectionism and relational neutrality which – under conditions of serious cultural inequalities – are better able to realise the intuition that constitutions, laws, institutions, policies and administration should be ethno-culturally and religiously as neutral as possible. Fairness-as-hands-off is appropriate for fighting structural inequalities. Fairness-as-even-handedness is appropriate for fighting unfair treatment of cultural minorities in matters of public culture, where strict neutrality is impossible and total equal treatment is not only unachievable but also counterproductive and unfair to majorities. It helps to guide the difficult arts of balancing involved in claims to accommodation (chap. 5). Both second-order principles point directly towards an explicitly contextualised morality.[57]

2.5 Contextualised morality

Arguments like these have stimulated a contextual turn in political theories of immigration and the incorporation of minorities (Walzer, Kymlicka, Carens, Parekh, Bauböck, Rosenblum, Greenawalt, Spinner-Halev) and more generally in theories of justice (Shapiro 1999; Hacker-Cordon 2003). Arguments for moderate universalism, relational neutrality and even-handedness are complemented by three main reasons that inspire a more general contextual approach in political philosophy: moral pluralism, under-determinacy of principles, and the complexity of practical reason and judgement.

Reasonable pluralism of the Good is now broadly accepted, however it remains seriously contested as to whether this 'ethical' pluralism (in the Habermasian sense) also implies pluralism of the Right (moral pluralism) and, if so, which version. It is safe to say that the predominant Rawlsian and Habermasian theories still reject the basic statements of moral pluralists that, even within a shared 'thin', liberal-democratic or purely political conception of justice: 1. basic rights often contradict each other, and so do our moral principles (most famously: equality vs. liberty); 2. we have independent and good reasons or grounds for affirming these conflicting principles; 3. we are unable to bring them into a context-independent lexical order or hierarchy; 4. we have to weigh and balance these conflicting principles, and 5. the implied difficult moral trade-offs cannot be resolved in a context-independent way (Galston 2002; Bader & Engelen 2003; Galanter 1998: 260ff; Fogelin 2003: 42f, 56ff).

In a way, the recognition of the under-determinacy of principles is part and parcel of any reasonable moral theory. General and inevitably abstract moral principles have to be specified to be applicable in various contexts and cases. Yet, it is increasingly acknowledged that under-determinacy goes deeper. Not only is the application context-dependent,[58] so are our articulations and interpretations of the moral principles themselves (Thiemann 1996: 87, Wolterstorff 1997: 174). We have to refer back to cases to clarify the meaning of abstract formulations (Carens 2004a), our interpretations are embedded in and shaped by institutional contexts (Unger 1983), and our articulation of principles themselves cannot be fully separated from general (cultural, linguistic) frameworks inevitably embedded in historical, societal and cultural contexts (sect. 2.1). Even in one and the same general framework and context, egalitarian liberals in modern Western societies reasonably disagree on what justice requires, and we cannot even understand their deep moral disagreement without citing the often implicit institutional shaping of liberty and equality and the preferred institutional translations or redesigns. The fact of under-determinacy and the resulting moral disagreement has led to the striking shift towards deliberative democracy in the Post-Rawlsian tradition (e.g. Gutmann & Thompson 1996; Bohman 1997). If moral philosophers continue to seriously disagree on what justice requires, on constitutional essentials, if there seems to be no single best answer,[59] we should shift our focus to public deliberation and democratic decision-making and also question our conceptions of reasons and deliberation (Bader 2007c; see sect. 3.5).

Moral philosophy may exclusively specialise in moral reasons and arguments, but political philosophy has to deal with the complexity of practical reason and judgement. Normative arguments include not only moral oughts (what we owe to humanity), ethical-political oughts (what we should do as members of specific communities, e.g. 'nation-states'), prudential oughts (requiring us to do what is in our well-informed, rational, long-term interests), and realistic oughts ('ought implies can') (Bader 1995a: 215ff). Evidently, these requirements conflict with each other and it is increasingly acknowledged that there is no clear, context-independent formula for weighing and balancing them, even if one agrees on a lexical ordering, e.g. that – all things considered – moral arguments should trump ethical-political and prudential ones.

Together, the trio of moral pluralism, under-determinacy and complexity of practical reason also impact our concept of normative knowledge. For the difficult arts of interpreting and balancing competing principles and reasons, numbers matter, power asymmetries matter, history matters, constitutional, political, socio-economic and cultural contexts matter, and consequences matter (Goodin & Tilly (eds.) 2006 for the social sciences). Philosophical armchair reflection is overburdened, reductionist or indecisive, to say the least. Contextual approaches require a re-evaluation of practical knowledge or insider wisdom and of judgement and action. Criticism on the limits of theoretical knowledge is not monopolised by the conservatives, spanning from Burke to Oakshott, it is also shared by liberals like Polanyi and Hayeck, communitarians like MacIntyre or Walzer, anti-theorists like Bernard Williams, and also by Scott (1998), Schön (1983), by republicans and democratic pragmatists like Dewey, Barber, Putnam, Shapiro and egalitarian liberal contextualists like Carens (2004a) and myself (1997, 2003a).

That contexts, institutions and practical knowledge matter is one of the most cherished wisdoms of strong contextualist critics of even moderate universalist moral and political philosophy. In turn, all varieties of strong contextualism have been rightly criticised for easily accepting status quo institutions (including all morally indefensible structural inequalities and power asymmetries) and uncritically reproducing insider wisdom and morally despicable intuitions.[60] If contexts also matter for moderate universalists, they cannot be decisive.

I cannot here discuss different varieties of contextual political philosophy in order to distinguish morally acceptable from illegitimate ones depending on questions like where, in which regards, and how contexts matter (Bader & Saharso 2004: 111ff).[61] In my view, the important dividing line among contextual approaches runs between strong (conservative or postmodern) and moderate contextualists. I refute strong contextualism on all levels. Moderate universalism criticises strong moral particularism and relativism in general, the distrust of general, abstract principles even within given contexts in particular, and the exaggeration of the problem of under-determinacy. Moderate contextualists allow for context-transcending principles but insist we relate principles to different contexts and cases to explain and develop their meaning. Principles like liberty or equality, though abstract and in need of specification are not indeterminate but under-determined: they may not exactly state what is positively required but clearly exclude any serious lack of freedom (e.g. slavery) or serious inequality in whatever contexts. In this regard, all moderate or reasonable contextual or semi-contextual approaches (Shapiro 1999: 5 and 24) have to avoid the dangers of unchecked particularism (classism, racism, sexism, elitism and nationalist power asymmetries). Strong contextualists reject theoretical criticism of moral intuitions and practical knowledge, whereas moderate contextualists criticise the often elitist bias of inside knowledge and insist on a continuous back and forth between (internally contested) moral intuitions in a wide variety of contexts and cases, on the one hand, and theoretical or reconstructive criticism, on the other hand. In brief, they insist on a wide, reflexive disequilibrium (Carens 2000: 4; 2004a: 122f). There may be no one single right practical judgement and one best institutional setting, but this does not mean that existing contextual judgements and institutions would all be morally permissible or the ones that would best fit.

Clearly, depending on the levels and ways in which contexts enter theorising, there can be a wide range of moderate contextual approaches: some more modest, others more demanding, some more universalist and others more particularist. However, they are all more or less explicitly comparative and historical. At this point, the contextualist turn in political philosophy ties into the recent institutionalist turn in the social sciences. As political philosophers 'in the vernacular' (Kymlicka 2001) increasingly combine normative analysis with empirical descriptions and explanations (crucially depending on social sciences), recent social scientists develop institutionally rich diachronic and synchronic comparative studies, and also engage in policy and institutional evaluation studies, inquiring into good fits and best practices. This 'grounded normativity' could be fruitfully combined with explicit normative analysis by political philosophers who specialise in this business. Both might help to stimulate institutional imagination and policy learning.

2.6   A plea for an institutionalist turn

If taken seriously, moderate universalism, relational neutrality, fairness as even-handedness, moral pluralism, under-determinacy, the multi-layered character of normative social reality (principles, institutions, cultures/virtues, and practices) and the complexity of practical reason require a contextualised theory of morality, combined with an institutional turn in political philosophy and theory (Bader & Engelen 2003).[62] Our interpretations and applications of moral principles and rights such as religious freedom(s) are massively influenced by respective predominant institutional regimes of religious governance in different countries, by legal paradigms and traditions of jurisdiction and administration, and so are our arts of balancing and trading off conflicting principles such as individual and associational religious freedoms. Obviously, institutions and practices of religious governance have to balance moral, ethico-political, prudential and realistic requirements. Institutions and traditions of judgement and policies in different countries do not follow abstract blueprints of secularism, strict separation of state and (organised) religions and strict neutrality, for example, even in countries where these may be the predominant models or ideologies. Philosophers may criticise this as inevitable but deplorable deviations from what would be morally required in an ideal world. Or they may learn from these practical, often very pragmatic ways of doing things that there are no optimal models that fit all contexts (certainly not the 'blueprints' designed by armchair theorists), that we might find practical ways of dealing with trade-offs that differ from the tragic, big trade-offs and 'sacrifices' in grand theory, that practical experimentalism may also develop innovative new institutions and policies that may be broadened and deepened by institutionally sensitive theorising, that institutional pluralism also provides better chances for realistic, reasonable utopianism (Bader & Engelen 2003: 391-395) in the field of religious governance and policies.

3 Priority for liberal democracy or secularism? Why I am not a secularist

Liberal political philosophers have defended three closely related second-order principles that should guide discussions about the governance of religious diversity. These are secularism, strict separationism and strict neutrality. In chapter 2, I have tried to show why we should reconceptualise neutrality as relational neutrality and why this is important.

Now I would like to turn to a critical discussion of normative secularism. In chapter 1, I elaborated a poly-contextual and perspectivist concept of secularisation. From the perspective of religions, it is perfectly legitimate to describe their other side as secular, a secular world based on secular communications. From the perspective of sociology, a generalised use of the concept turned out to be counterproductive. From the perspectives of liberal-democratic politics and normative political theory, the important question is not whether societies or cultures are increasingly 'secularised' (we can agonistically bracket these questions) or whether state and politics are 'strictly separated' from religions, but whether they are compatible with or conducive to minimal morality or minimal liberal-democratic morality. In this chapter, I argue that liberal-democrats and liberal political philosophers need not and should not be secularists. This is an important consideration because secularism in all its meanings is the paramount meta-narrative or the predominant knowledge regime in many countries, and because words are so powerful (Beckford 1987: 26).

In debating secularism in political philosophy, Rajeev Bhargava (1998) has convincingly argued that one should firstly distinguish between the level of institutions and practical politics and their justifications and secondly between first- and second-order justifications.

At the level of *institutions and politics*, the disputes are concerned with questions of whether liberal states and politics are or should be 'secular' at all and, if so, what this would require, e.g. the guarantee of the two autonomies, the exclusion of religious reasons from public debate, or the strict separation of state/politics from religions. I reject the terminology of secularism in this regard for four main reasons. Firstly, because emerging modern states may or may not have been 'secular' – in the sense of respecting the relative autonomy of state from religion(s) and of religions from the state – but they have not been liberal, let alone democratic. Secondly, some Western states and politics in the last century were certainly 'secular' but violated not only minimal standards of liberal-democratic morality but even of minimalist morality, including the twin tolerations. In both these regards, I defend a highly contextualised interpretation (sect. 3.1). This is the first and most important reason why I am not a secularist. Here, I disagree conceptually and theoretically with the efforts of Taylor, Bhargava, Connolly and others to work out alternative conceptions of secularism (Bhargava 1998: 2, 488, 513) instead of seeking an alternative to secularism. Thirdly, minimal liberal democratic morality does not require (but is actually incompatible with) the exclusion of religious reasons from public debate and, fourthly, liberal-democratic constitutions do not or should not require a strict wall of separation between 'secular' state/politics and religions.

Whether one calls liberal-democratic states/politics secular or – as I prefer – either relationally neutral or indifferent (i.e. beyond the 'religious-secular' divide, equidistant from both) or just liberal-democratic, is not an innocent terminological dispute, because words are powerful in politics and theory. If one calls them secular, one has to justify this or one has to explain 'why secularism?' or 'what is secularism for?' (Bhargava 1998: 10, 486ff). Secularism, indeed, is not a self-explanatory value. Justifications have to refer to the values promoted by these institutions and policies. *First-order justifications* mention important substantive values like autonomy, equality, democracy and leading a full-fledged transparent life (ethical secularism), less perfectionist political values of liberal democracy (political secularism), or 'arguments from ordinary life' and the 'smaller' values of moral minimalism, such as the prevention of sectarian warfare (civic peace), toleration, aversion of unbearable suffering and degradation of life. I reject ethical secularism and also the ambiguous and misleading concept of 'political secularism' (sect. 3.2). This is the second reason why I am not a secularist.

Second-order justifications refer to higher order values or procedural foundations. I reject the exclusive foundation of the morality of liberal democracy by independent, secular political ethics and also by a version of an overlapping consensus that still excludes religious reasons and foundations in one way or another (sect. 3.3). This is the third reason why I am not a secularist. Here, I share the basic arguments with Taylor, Bhargava and Connolly against the inherent unfairness and the paradoxical character of ethical secularism. However, I also mobilise them against 'political secularism', against an exclusivist independent 'secular' political ethics, and against remnants of exclusivist secularism in a Rawlsian overlapping consensus.

In section 3.4, I explain my interpretation of the core aspects of Priority for Liberal Democracy – an extensive interpretation of the freedoms of political communication and of its anti-paternalism – in opposition to all versions of exclusivist secularism before defending this interpretation against philosophical foundationalism (sect. 3.5) and against religious challenges (sects. 3.6 and 3.7).

3.1 Contextualising secularism: should liberal-democratic states be secular and, if so, in which sense?

Any minimally decent state has to live up to the requirements of the minimal morality set out in chapter 2. A threshold of institutional differentiation of state and religions, the two autonomies of state from religions and religions from state, is a crucial part of minimal morality. Bhargava has lucidly expressed this core idea:

> A clash of great ideals and ultimate values 'has the potential of depriving people of leading even a minimally decent existence, an ordinary life. To secure an ordinary life, protect basic this-worldly goods, all ultimate ideals must be expunged from the affairs of the state, whose sole business is to procure for everyone minimum standards of decent living. On any account, ultimate ideals are definitionally constitutive of religious worldviews. It follows that religion too must be separated from the affairs of the state. The separation of religion from politics is required in order to avert unbearable suffering and degradation of life. In particular, loss of life and liberty is evil and must not be taken away from anyone no matter to which religious community he belongs' (1998: 490f).

The two autonomies, together with individual and collective religious tolerance, have to be guaranteed by all minimally decent states, not only by Western states. Confining myself to Western states, the following historical and structural arguments are important for debates on whether and, if so, why this minimum should be called 'secular', e.g. 'secularized legal and political institutions' (Hunter 2005), a minimalist 'politico-legal secularism', or 'political secularism' (Ferrari 2005, Bhargava 1998, 2005).

3.1.1 Historical contextualisation

In European history (the constellation of hierarchically organised, competing Christian religions and emerging sovereign states that both claimed supreme jurisdiction over the same domains, para. 1.2.3), the equation of public and political and, much later, of liberal and democratic with secular has been understandable. In the 16th and 17th centuries, state sovereignty, due process and collective and individual tolerance had to be fought for. This was first done in battles against defenders of absolutist or fundamentalist religions and established churches. Later on, they had to be defended against those 'common ground' theorists of freedom of religion and conscience who, like Locke, explicitly or implicitly limited these freedoms to the variety of conflicting Christian denominations, not extending their arguments into a principled defence of freedom of conscience for all religious believers. In a context in which the enemies of a general freedom of conscience (as of most other liberal and democratic principles and rights) were absolutist religions, minimal or public morality appeared as secular morality. A religious or theological defence of the public morality of liberal democracy, so prominent later among the Founding Fathers in the US, seemed unthinkable. Hence, its true and exclusive defenders seemed to be secular philosophers developing 'independent political ethics'. These battle lines have been very much sharpened in the school and cultural wars during the 19th century and the protracted resistance of the Catholic Church against liberalism and democracy, a fact that helps explain *laïcité de combat* and the explicitly secular character of the French state and constitution. A liberal and democratic state seemed to inevitably be a secular state, at least in the minimal sense of guaranteeing the 'two autonomies' that had to be defended mainly against religious threats.

The emergence or historical origin of the indifferent state may have been possible in some contexts only as a secularist state, and aggressive secularist ideologies and policies may have been necessary to pave the way for a non-religious polity. Only good historical counter-factual thought experiments could teach us whether an indifferent state could also have otherwise emerged in France or Turkey. Yet it is important to insist (and a theory of multiple modernities shows this) that this is exactly what actually happened in other contexts such as in the US. In addition, an alternative to the strongly secularist and monolithic theories of state sovereignty (Bodin, Hobbes, Pufendorf) has been available (e.g. the explicitly pluralist theory of Althusius). Anyway, here (as in other cases), the conditions for the origin of a social configuration need not be, and are not the same as, the conditions for its existence and further development.[1]

Emergent modern states, however, increasingly realised state sovereignty and state indifference against rival religious and secular claims long before they became liberal and eventually also democratic. Morally speaking, liberal and democratic states have to be indifferent states, but not all indifferent states have been liberal or democratic. If one

wants to call emergent states 'secular' states in their opposition to absolutist religions and strong established churches (and, from the perspective of religions, this is an adequate terminology in this context), then
one also has to indicate that this minimalist version of 'politico-legal
secularism' should be clearly distinguished from more demanding notions of liberal or democratic political secularism. ('Political secularism'
is quite ambiguous in this respect: see sect. 3.2.) The idea of a secular
state – one might then better say: of the 'secularity' of the state, distinguished from secularism (Glenn & Groof 2002a: 107) – is a (minimalist) moral ideal, not – as Hunter 2005 and Saunders 2005 think – a
strategic bare *modus vivendi*. It has been historically violated more often
than not by 'secular modernizing states'. 'Subjects' were not legally
treated as equals even long before (some) became citizens and also for
a long time after, and states certainly did not show the required religious indifference but continually engaged in religious homogenisation
policies. One should also not forget that this indifferent state did not
presuppose any meaningful societal or cultural secularisation of beliefs
and practices that only developed in Western Europe in the second half
of the 20th century. It rather required the taming of the claims by absolutist or totalistic religions to control state and the law (para. 1.2.4).

During the 20th century, this context changed.[2] The minimalist morality of decent and of liberal-democratic polities increasingly needed to
be defended against 'secular' totalitarian states, not only against fascist
(e.g. Nazi Germany) and 'socialist' regimes (e.g. the USSR), and
against Third World authoritarian regimes, such as Cambodia, Iraq
and autocratic secularist Arab states[3] but also against secular totalitarian ideologies like Marxism-Leninism, Stalinism, Maoism (MELSM),
against the atrocities of chauvinist aggressions, of ethnic cleansings
and the related racist and ethnicist ideologies. These 'secularist nightmares' have been as serious as the threat by explicitly theocratic regimes such as the Islamic Republic of Iran or the Taliban regime in Afghanistan.

Recently, the context has changed once again since the terrorist attacks by political Islamicists and the 'war against terrorism' led by the
fundamentalist neo-conservatives of the Bush administration in the
name of 'freedom and democracy'. Religious fundamentalism in politics, particularly after the demise of fascist and communist regimes
and ideologies, seems to be the real danger, and this partly explains the
astonishing re-emergence of radical Enlightenment philosophers and
their interventions in public debates. Still, the important issue is not
whether states/politics are secular but whether they are decent or liberal-democratic.[4]

3.1.2 Structural contextualisation: different kinds of threats

This historical sketch already suggests that there are different kinds of religious and secular threats to liberal democracy, and that 'secularism' terminology may only be an appropriate response in some regards. It is important to distinguish these threats before getting into a meaningful discussion of their seriousness and of adequate strategies to address them.

Only in opposition to old and new religious threats by fundamentalists, intending to replace state indifference or state autonomy with a theocratic regime, does the insistence on the secular character of law and the state make sense. The liberal-democratic state has to be a nonreligious state, respecting the two autonomies plus individual and collective tolerance and its 'secular' or, better, indifferent character has to be defended against recent religious fundamentalists in politics (religious leaders, movements and organisations), whether they are Protestant, Catholic, Orthodox, Islamic or Hindu. These threats also have to be credible and serious, and much depends on whether states are fairly well-established liberal-democratic polities, more or less authoritarian and illiberal regimes, or regimes in transition to liberal democracy (sect. 9.8), which also may help explain different degrees of the credibility and danger of Islamicism in different countries. The situation in countries with Muslim majorities is clearly different from countries in which Muslims (of all kinds) are a comparatively small minority (all Western states).[5] There are also important differences among states with Muslim majorities, e.g. Saudi Arabia, Pakistan or Algeria compared with Malaysia, Indonesia and Turkey.[6]

Liberal-democratic polities also have to be defended against different kinds of secularist threats. First, civil strife and civil war do not only arise from the ultimate values and zealot-like passions of competing absolutist religions but also from competing ultimate racist, ethno-centrist, chauvinist values and from secularist, totalitarian ideologies like fascism or other versions of 'national socialism', which, once in power, massively violated any decent morality however minimally conceived, as indicated above. Racist, ethnocentrist and chauvinist threats to decent and liberal-democratic morality have historically often been massively intertwined with religious threats and the respective homogenisation policies. The appropriate concepts and measures in fighting them cannot invoke the 'secular' character of state and politics because this is exactly how they understand themselves. Instead, one has to apply the standards of minimal and of liberal-democratic morality.

Second, the secularist threat emerging from certain scientistic ideologies meant to replace religious symbolic universes and totalitarian regimes by the utopia of a full-scale 'scientific religion' (Saint Simon) or an explicitly anti-religious 'scientific' or 'materialist', all-embracing *Weltanschuung* (Marxism-Leninism) and ruthless attempts to install totalitarian regimes in states that called themselves 'really existing socialist countries'. Most of these 'secularist regimes of the Left' (Martin) have intentionally violated even minimalist notions of religious autonomy. They have also violated any morality, however minimally understood.

In both cases, it is clearly counterproductive to appeal to the 'secular' character of the state, because all these ideologies have been explicitly secularist and anti-religious. Here, the appropriate opposition is not between 'religious' and 'secular' state/politics, but between absolutely immoral secular states/politics and minimally decent or liberal-democratic morality and politics. A 'secular' state and 'secular policies' are not appropriate measures for fighting these secularist nightmares so characteristic of large parts of the 20th century in the West as well as for other states in the rest of the contemporary world. Secularism cannot be the solution because it is part of the problem. The remedy in all cases is a minimally decent state.

Third, secularist violations of the two autonomies are also characteristic for philosophical criticism of religion in two prominent historical versions. Radical Enlightenment philosophers have respected freedom of individual conscience, but they have been, and still are, tempted to neglect or undermine associational freedoms of religion and collective toleration. In addition, outright elitist philosophical critics of religion in the Nietzschean tradition also reject the principles and practices of liberal democracy.

Last, another but less well-known secularist threat to liberal democracy emerges from the regimes and ideologies of scientism, professionalism and bureaucratic administration. This threat of expertocracy does not come from attempts to replace religions by competing, all-embracing scientistic symbolic universes, as in the second case, but from more specialised and field-specific ideologies and practices. It has been analysed in critical science studies, in critical sociology of professions and of private and public administration or management but is rarely addressed in debates on secularism (see, however, Minow 2000). Experts of all sorts (e.g. professionals in education, (health)care, social work) are tempted, and are in a structural position to present their internally contested views, diagnoses and therapies as modern, universal, objective and neutral truths. Expertocracy does not directly threaten the two autonomies and individual and collective tolerance, but it is a long-term, 'silent' threat to democracy, intimately connected with 'modernity' and internally opposed to all religion.

In the cases of enlightened radicals, elitist philosophers and expertocrats, the respective threats to liberal democracy are less nightmarish. Yet, in defending the priority of liberal democracy against all kinds of

secularist threats (and the respective elites, movements and organisations), the appeal to the 'secular' character of the state or to 'political
secularism' is not helpful and counterproductive because secularism is
again part of the problem.[7]

Distinguishing and demonstrating the different kinds of threats is
one thing, stating that all threats would pose equal threats (let alone
equating or identifying expertocracy with the Nazi regime), or getting
into debates on whether recent religious fundamentalism would be
more or less threatening than expertocracy, is quite another. For my
limited purposes, I will not even attempt to answer the difficult questions of whether – in the medium and long term – the combined
threats to liberal democracy from bureaucracy, scientism, expertocracy
and professionalism are more serious than the short-term threats from
religious fundamentalism in politics. The latter are clearly visible, loud
and increasingly violent and terrorist. However, they may also be interpreted as dramatic but short-term reactions to ruthless policies aiming
to 'modernise' societies and 'democratise' states from above and/or
from the outside, inimical to decent respect and liberal policies of accommodation. They need not be inherent phenomena of alternative
transitions to democracy. They may fade away in the medium or long
term, whereas the former are silent, highly invisible, non-violent and
routine, but intimately connected to all versions of modern societies
and all varieties of liberal-democratic polities. I can confine myself to
the fairly obvious statement that both dangers are serious and both
have to be addressed equally. Secularist terminology, however, tends to
make the latter invisible.

3.1.3 Societal and cultural secularisation and strategic issues

In addition to this historical and structural contextualisation of secularism, it may help to gain more distance if we discuss the 'secular' character of the state with regard to different degrees of societal and cultural secularisation and also with regard to strategic issues, because both
arguments can be mobilised in defending 'political secularism'.

It is contested whether, and if so how, different degrees of societal
and cultural secularisation and the respective knowledge regimes of secularism should have consequences for debating 'political secularism'.
We have already seen that the emergent proto-liberal, indifferent state
did not require or presuppose any 'secularisation' of society and culture. Recently, most Western European states, Canada and Australia
show much higher degrees of social and cultural 'secularisation' than
the US.[8] Two contrasting consequences could be drawn from this fact.
First, following the logic of important threats and enemies, the US
would – in the face of conservative religious majorities and evangelical

fundamentalism – require a secularist defence of liberal democracy, and this is exactly what the majority of American liberal political philosophers are arguing for. In Europe, however, given the predominance of liberal and increasingly illiberal secularism, it would be important to criticise the knowledge regime of secularism in all its varieties. This would be a contextualised and strategic reading of my own proposal. Second, one could argue that higher degrees of societal and cultural secularisation in Europe would also require that state and politics should be more 'secular', and this is exactly what 'Enlightenment radicals' are asking for. They claim that liberal-democratic morality and principles are not only public but also 'secular', and that the secularist majority preferences should be imposed on all religions, but particularly on religious minorities by assimilation politics.

Though at odds with each other, both arguments are untenable and illegitimate because they are incompatible with religious freedoms and the reasonable pluralism of the Good Life. The minimalist notion of a non-religious or indifferent state does not depend on, and should be completely disentangled from, contested secularisation of society and culture. The highly religious American and Polish societies do not require a 'religious' state (or a radically secular one), nor do highly 'secularised' Dutch and Czech societies require a 'secular' state. However, all require an indifferent, relationally neutral state, equidistant to both religious and secular worldviews and practices.

Finally, there may be strategic arguments for and against secularism in two different contexts. First, in a situation of (post-)imperialism or (post-)colonialism, as in Turkey or India. Turkish secularism has been aggressively elitist and intolerant right from the start (Koningsveld 2004; WRR 2004) and it may be that Kemalist, ruthlessly secularist modernisation policies have been a precondition for the recent development of liberal democracy, as they may or may not have been in France or other modernising European states (Al-Azm 2004 asks this historically troubling question). Paradoxically, the political fundamentalism of Muslim parties contributed to making Ataturk's fairly authoritarian, illiberal and 'regulated' secular republic eventually more liberal and democratic (sect. 3.6). The term 'secular state' does not appear in the Indian Constitution itself (Smith 1998: 193), and Nehru's insistence on the secular character of the Indian constitution and state in order to guarantee toleration may have had some serious, unintended medium- and long-term consequences. Under colonial circumstances, 'the secular state created its opposite, a society in which religion had more rather than less political consequences, one of which being a decline of tolerance of religious difference'.[9] At least it proved to be difficult to defend secularism in a way that cannot be easily accused of prolonging 'Western' colonialism and modernisation. Yet, in criticising the meta-

narrative of secularism from the perspective of priority for liberal democracy in these situations in which religious fundamentalists also criticise secularism (as anti-secularist Hindu agitation does in India or
fundamentalist Muslim agitation does in Turkey), one may end up
with weird coalitions of strange bedfellows in the fundamentalist
camp. And the same may happen in the second, much different context of well-established Western liberal democracies like England or
France (anti-secularist Muslim agitation).[10] In my view, however, defending the liberal and democratic character of law and state in terms
of what they are (i.e. priority for liberal democracy) enables us to avoid
at least some of the counterproductive consequences of secularism terminology indicated above: unintentionally creating anti-secularist religious opposition (parties) amongst moderate religions as in India.[11] It
also allows us to select the right friends and to build up the right coalitions in the current confrontations of religion in politics, by using the
appropriate reasons and terminology. The right kind of division is not
between secular and religious convictions but between fanaticisms of
both kinds (whether secularist or religious) and liberal, democratic and
pluralist views on the other side. Hence, avoiding the meta-narrative of
secularism altogether may also be strategically wise. Unfortunately, it
also cannot guarantee that one is liberated from the entrenched 'secular vs. anti-secular' dichotomy and it cannot prevent that, in defending
the religiously indifferent or agnostic but not 'anti-religious' or 'atheistic' state, one is accused of either religious fundamentalism or anti-secularism by secularist or of 'modernist or (post-)colonial secularism' by
fundamentalists and postmodernists.

The upshot of this discussion is that the meta-narrative of secularism is not really helpful in analysing the threats to minimal and to liberal-democratic morality and states/politics. Even minimally understood 'political secularism' has to cover too many important, diverging
and potentially conflicting aspects: the tensions between guaranteeing
the autonomy of the state from religions and the autonomy of religions
from the state (sect. 8.6), the tensions between individual and collective tolerance (chap. 4), and the tensions between liberalism and democracy.

3.2   First-order justifications: ethical and political secularism?

In his discussion of the various substantive values that are meant to
justify divergent conceptions of 'separation' between religions and state
institutions and policies, Bhargava (1998: 494) has presented the most
fine-grained attempt to distinguish different conceptions of secularism
along three analytically distinct but interrelated axes: first, whether the

justifying values are perfectionist (as in ethical secularism) or anti-perfectionist (as in political secularism), second, whether religious reasons are excluded (as in exclusivist secularism) or included (as in inclusive secularism); third, whether justifications focus exclusively on procedures (as in 'ultra-proceduralist secularism') or on substantive values or ultimate ideals (as in 'hyper-substantive secularism' (1998: 514f)). The most basic and important axis is the first one.

Political philosophers distinguish between strong perfectionist and more or less moderate anti-perfectionist substantive values. Perfectionist values prescribe a specific ethical way of a good life, whereas anti-perfectionist values are those politico-moral principles required for a just life in a minimally moral or in a more demanding liberal-democratic polity. The distinction between the 'ethical' Good and the 'moral' Right may not be watertight (sect. 2.2). In addition, it may turn out that strictly anti-perfectionist political conceptions of justice may not be available or may even be impossible, which is the reason why I have defended 'moderate' anti-perfectionism (sect. 2.3). Still, some such distinction is crucial at least in societies characterised by reasonable pluralism, i.e. under conditions of co-existing but conflicting and incompatible cultural and religious varieties of the good life.

The relevant substantive values (Bhargava 1998: 8, 489ff) can be ranked along this axis on a scale from strong perfectionist and also particularist values to more or less moderate anti-perfectionist and also universalist values (sect. 2.2). We have seen that 'autonomy as self-creation' and 'rational revisability' (the strong individualist and perfectionist value of comprehensive liberalism) are strongly secularist. This *ethical secularism* sees religions as illusions, requires the strictest possible separation of state and religions, and also the strict exclusion of religious reasons from public debate. This secularism is a parochial, individualist liberal, purely Western project. In addition, it seems incompatible with religious freedoms. All other moralities and connected conceptions of political and legal autonomy and agency are less perfectionist, particularly if 'political autonomy' is freed from rational revisibility requirements and defended in a way that recognises and tries to minimise inevitable spillover effects into more comprehensive personal autonomy. They have better chances to be globally accepted and can less easily be accused of being exclusively Western. They are frequently called *political secularism* or 'politico-legal secularism' but then the notion of political secularism has quite diverging meanings. Broadly speaking, political secularists would have to specify which moralities (and the related set of civic and political right and institutions) they want to defend: (i) Basic rights to security, including minimal due process, respect, collective and individual toleration (freedom of conscience), and the two autonomies of the indifferent state (the 'politico-legal secularism' of Hunter) or, additionally, also basic rights to subsistence. This option excludes institutions and practices incompatible with *minimal morality*. (ii) Equal civic and political rights and modern nondiscrimination rights ('political secularism' proper that serves as a misleading proxy for *liberal democracy*, excluding decent but non-liberal institutions and practices). (iii) More *egalitarian* morality and rights and also thicker concepts of political autonomy that still allow for competing thick ethico-religious ways of a good life and are therefore often also subsumed under 'political secularism' (excluding libertarianism, thin liberal democracy).[12]

In view of this ambiguity and complexity of 'political secularism', it seems preferable to drop the concept and rather focus on the respective substantive content of the options. However, if one uses the notion, one should distinguish as clearly as possible between these options and explicitly argue for one's choices instead of reproducing the often unrecognised shifts from more minimal to more maximal conceptions so common in recent debates. In section 2.2, I tried to show that more demanding options of 'political secularism' are tolerable only if they are promoted in the right way, yet this *non-infringement proviso* is massively violated by advocates of great secular or religious values in politics and also by many philosophical 'political secularists'.

3.3   Second-order justifications: secular, independent political ethics?

That ethical or comprehensive secularism unfairly privileges secular over religious values and ways of life is the strong conviction of theologically motivated critics of political liberalism in the US like Levinson, Carter, Herberg, Neuhaus, Wolterstorff and Thiemann, and anti-Western critics of secularism in India (like Nandy, Madan) and in Muslim countries. In England, similar complaints have been raised by Anglican, Jewish, Catholic and Muslim opponents of secularism and 'strict separation'. Writing from a Jewish perspective, Sylvia Rothschild fears most:

> (a) purportedly neutral secularism, for there is nothing so dogmatic as that which is dogmatically neutral, and secularism, far from being open to all, closes the many diverse doors to the communities of faith. As I read it, the secular mode is merely another point on the spectrum of religious expression, but one which has no understanding of and which makes no allowances for, other modes of religious expression. On the other hand,

pluralism can, and does, flow from religious vision (in Modood 1996: 56).

The real question then is 'just how do we organise ourselves so that the many voices can be heard, so that one dominant culture doesn't impose itself on us all?' (1996: 58).

If a 'secular' morality cannot be fair, we seem to be caught in a trap, forced to choose between two equally miserable imperialisms. On the one hand, we have 'mono-dominant and triumphant secularism' (Rothschild) and an 'out-and-out (or fundamentalist) secularism, which, in its late twentieth century manifestation, is a climate inimical to any religion' (Rosser-Owen, in Modood 1996: 84). On the other hand, we have 'troubling triumphalism ... by those who believed religion had a monopoly on moral concerns' (Phillips 1996: 27) and the affiliated anti-secularism. Anne Phillips has tried to resolve this dilemma by pointing out that:

> (s)ecularism occupies a dual location in this kind of debate. Those who do not follow any of the world's religions are, by definition, secular in their beliefs; when secularism speaks on behalf of these nonbelievers, it speaks on a par with the spokespeople for Anglicans, Catholics, Muslims or Jews. But secularism also presents itself as the solution after all other voices have spoken, for in arguing for a separation between church and state, it promises to protect the beliefs and the practices of each from the pressures to go along with what any others believe. This looks suspiciously like a sleight of hand, and that's the worry: that the even-handed accommodation of all turns out to be particularly attuned to one.

As so many others, she tries to defend secular public morality on a meta-level as:

> (the) only approach that can even approximate equality of treatment between those who hold different beliefs ... the interests of democratic equality cannot be well served by practices that privilege one church over the others, nor can they be well served by practices that privilege religious values over secular ones, nor – and this is the difficult one – can they be well served by practices that privilege secular values over religious beliefs. The difficulty remains that any way of formulating this puts it in the framework of a secular solution, and some will regard this as diminishing the significance of religion. But the secular separation of church from state is still the closest we can get to

parity of treatment ... Equality is one of the crucial principles of
a modern democracy, and for this reason (even excluding all the
others), the secular solution is the only one I could defend (27f,
as if 'parity' or 'equality' would by definition be 'secular'; see
Audi 1989, 1992).

Here, it seems to me that secularism occupies a triple location: as comprehensive 'ethical secularism', as more or less thin 'political secularism' which claims to offer a fair solution, and as a secularist foundation
of political secularism. Whether secularism can be fair to different religious as well as non-religious people, whether political secularism (often also called 'second-order secularism', to distinguish it from ethical
secularism) may be able to avoid this apparent paradox also depends
on how the latter is grounded.

Second-order justifications refer to the methods or procedures of
foundation. Three methods gained prominence in recent discussions
that 'center around deeper grounds for the separation of state from religion' (Bhargava 1998: 8): the secular independent political ethics
mode, the common ground strategy, and the overlapping consensus
method.[13]

The independent political ethics mode (developed most prominently
by Grotius, Bayle,[14] Spinoza and Kant, and recently defended by Audi
and Habermas) requires full agreement on 'secular' political principles
and on the grounds for justification that have to be secular and rational, e.g. *more geometrico*, contractualist, (quasi-)transcendental. This
most outspoken secularist foundation has obvious problems in dealing
with deep reasonable disagreement amongst such foundations. It cannot consistently be decoupled from more comprehensive ethical secularism (moral autonomy, demanding rationality/reasonableness). Also,
it requires the exclusion of religious reasons from public debates, and
it is associated with 'strict neutrality', 'strict separation' and privatisation of religion. Historically, it has had severe difficulties in coming to
terms with increasing religious diversity. It may turn out to be 'rather
"Christian" in spirit (Taylor 1998: 33f), particularly if some atheists,
suspicious of religious believers as potential traitors 'push farther the
process of making religion irrelevant in the public sphere', engaging in
'*Kulturkampf*' (36). This has been and will continue to be perceived as
unfair:

> What the unbelieving 'secularist' sees as a necessary policing of
> the boundary of a common independent public sphere, will of-
> ten be perceived by the religious as a gratuitous extrusion of reli-
> gion in the name of a rival metaphysical belief. What to one side

is a more strict consistent application of the principles of neutrality is seen by the other side as partisanship (36).

In addition, in non-Western societies, it will be perceived as an imperialist import of 'Western' secularism. The Common Ground Strategy
(Pufendorf, Locke, Leibniz, and in the 20th century, most prominently
Mahatma Ghandi or Hans Küng) to justify the political principles can
be seen as its religious sister. It 'leans on all existing religions' (Bhargava 1998: 8) and aims at a 'state which is even-handed between religious communities, equidistant from them, rather than one where religious reasons play no overt role' (Taylor 1998: 35). Historically, it assumes that everyone shares some religious grounds 'even if these are
rather general' like non-denominational Christianity, Biblical theism, or
post-Enlightenment deism. The original model can be extended to new
non-European contexts to also include Islam, Hinduism, Buddhism
and other religions.[15] However, the model has two inherent weak-
nesses. First, the common ground is still religious, excluding non-religious grounds. In 'today's diversified societies, the only thing we can
hope to share is a purely political ethic, not its embedding in some religious view' (37), however broadly conceived. Second, the common
ground strategy tends to treat religious reasons within traditions as given and fixed, to neglect internal dissent and, most importantly, focuses only an some minimal common denominator instead of opening
existing reasons for comparative and normative debate (Cohen 2004;
Miller 2006, chap. 7).
   Both the independent secular ethics and the common religious
ground foundations require a deeper consensus on second-order justification that seems to be either unavailable, or imposed and unfair and,
in addition, at odds with reasonable pluralism. We need a third mode
'equidistant from – or perhaps a hybrid between – the two others'. A
moderately understood Overlapping Consensus 'lifts the requirement
of a commonly held foundation. It aims only at universal acceptance of
certain political principles (this is hard enough to attain). But it recog-
nizes from the outset that there cannot be a universally agreed basis
for these, independent or religious' (Taylor 1998: 38). Rawls has spelled
out the basic characteristics of this method: it is 'political, not metaphysical', it is 'non-foundational' or un-foundational – it does not depend
on agreement on one comprehensive doctrine of the good life, be it secular or religious, but thrives on diverging reasons that back its political principles.[16] Rawls himself has also initiated a process in which the
overlapping consensus has increasingly been freed from secularist
remnants by softening the requirements of rational constructivism and
contractualism, by accepting that his conception of justice as fairness
is one in a 'family of reasonable political conceptions' (1999: 141), by

resisting to identify 'public' with 'secular' reason and, most ambiguously, by softening but not abandoning the exclusion of religious reasons from public debate (Bader 2007c).[17]

Post-Rawlsian deliberative democrats have spelled out some of these
important developments more clearly. To the degree that this is
achieved, the overlapping consensus provides a mode of 'deliberation
cum negotiation' that 'can be usefully followed – we should better say,
re-invented – almost anywhere' (Taylor 1998: 38). However, because
the consensus requirements are moderated and exclusivist secularism
is dropped, it is better to give it a new name: moderately agonistic democracy, characterised by the absence of liberal reason-restraints and
of consensus requirements, by deliberations cum negotiations, by unrestricted freedoms of communication, and by an inclusive multi- or
poly-logue (sect. 3.5).

Reviewing the discussion in the first three sections, I hope to have
made the following points plausible; in reverse order:

First, only a weak version of an overlapping consensus and moderately agonistic democracy, but certainly not an independent political
ethics, can resolve the apparent paradox of second-order secularism so
aptly phrased by Phillips and Taylor. Without deep foundations, it may
still provide a fair and fairly stable ground for minimally moral and for
liberal-democratic polities.

Second, first-order 'political secularism' has been too ambiguous a
notion. It also turned out to be misleading to call principles or values
of decent or liberal-democratic polities 'secular' and, most importantly
– because the rejection of ethical secularism and political secularism
may only concern political philosophers – to call these states and their
constitutions 'secular' instead of indifferent or liberal-democratic – because these are core issues in recent practical politics.

Third, the terminological confusion of liberal and democratic or public with secular is misleading for three main reasons, particularly in a
context in which religions increasingly have learned 'to bracket the
truth-question' or to resolve their 'fundamentalist dilemma' (Casanova
1994: 165; Müller 2005: 36ff).

i.   It seduces us into conceptualising the justificatory non-neutrality of
     liberal democracy in terms of secular versus religious arguments or
     foundations. The main question is not, however, whether argu-
     ments are secular or religious, but whether or not they are compati-
     ble with and/or support minimally moral or liberal-democratic poli-
     ties.

ii. It neglects the possibility and existence of principled religious or
     theological foundations of morality and institutions of liberal de-
     mocracy in general, and of a principled, non-exclusive right to free-

dom of conscience in particular. It also excludes the possibility of public reason in theological and religious arguments. It thus unfairly discriminates against those theologians and religions defending liberal democracy (Thiemann 1996: 131ff; Bader 2007d).

iii. It directs our criticism of absolutism or fundamentalism in politics in a one-sided and myopic manner against religious or theological fundamentalism and thus tends to neglect all secular threats to liberal democracy discussed above, even if they may be more dangerous in the long run.

If one agrees with these statements, then it would clearly not be enough to criticise 'ethical' or 'strong secularism', as most political theorists do who think seriously about these issues. It would also be necessary to explicitly criticise 'second order secularism' (Phillips 1996: 27f; Rosenblum 2000: 15, 18; Keane 2000), 'weak' or 'inclusive and religiously sensitive secularism' (Parekh 2000: 335), 'moderate secularism' (Modood 2001, 2003, 2005), 'political secularism' (Bhargava 1998, 2005; Bielefeldt 2001) or 'laïcication de laïcité' (Baubérot 1990; Willaime 2004). One should not call the overlapping consensus a 'secular mode' (Taylor 1998: 48), nor, most importantly, should one call decent and liberal-democratic states 'secular states' (Müller 2005: 37), or defend 'strict separationism'.

The more sensitive defenders of secularism referred to here try to keep the institutional form of secularism flexible and open and refuse to identify 'a separation' (Phillips, quoted above) or 'the separation' of church and state (Bhargava above) with the ideology of the 'wall' of separation.[18] In para 1.3.3, we have seen that various church-state relations are deemed compatible with the two autonomies and with individual and collective toleration, at least by constitutional lawyers. Strict separation does not even exist in the US or France. 'Secularism' as strict separationism seems clearly not to be required by decent and liberal-democratic morality and polities. This is an additional reason for defending the priority for liberal democracy instead of ever more confusing secularisms of all sorts.

3.4 Priority for liberal democracy

The philosophical meaning of priority for democracy is a radicalisation of the idea of a really freestanding conception of political justice. Principles and practices of decent and liberal-democratic polities are more important than the whole variety of conflicting philosophical or religious foundations, mainly because all foundational theories are at least as contested as our ordinary understanding of these principles and practices. It may even be worse: 'we may be burdened with a bunch of rotten theories intended to justify what are really a set of wonderful practices and institutions', as Yack (1986) put it. Fortunately, the validity of minimal morality does not depend upon the truth of competing moral theories of basic needs, interests and rights, and the same holds for principles, institutions, virtues and practices of liberal democracy. In this sense, priority for democracy implies a considered commitment to non-foundationalism (sect. 3.5) that may also be described as 'philosophical shallowness' (Hunter 2005) or 'epistemological and moral abstemiousness' (Geuss 2002: 333). I have already explained that minimalist morality, as morality, cannot and should not be 'neutral' because it has to exclude immoral institutions and actions. I explained why even the most minimalist version of liberal-democratic morality cannot be fully anti-perfectionist because it requires a threshold of political autonomy, individual responsibility and civic and political virtues. Certain religious virtues may be incompatible with the latter, but so are certain secular virtues and *ethoi*. Moderate democratic anti-perfectionism cuts both ways, so to speak.

Focusing now on the democratic aspect of liberal-democratic morality, two minimally understood characteristics of democracy are important for explaining the meaning of 'priority of democracy'. First, a specific conception (together with the accompanying rights and institutions) of democratic debate: public arena and freedoms of political communication. Second, a specific egalitarian, non-paternalistic mode of decision-making, requiring that all defenders of 'absolute' religious and secular truths have to solve their fundamentalist dilemma. Both presuppose the general characteristic of democratic politics: politics with non-violent means, i.e. without the threat or actual use of physical force within the framework of a monopoly of the legal use of violence characteristic for modern states.[19]

3.4.1 Freedoms of political communication

Democratic debate requires and in turn strengthens a public arena in which the divergent opinions and proposals can be published, exchanged, discussed, negotiated and transformed, and in which new ones can emerge. Political philosophers have tended to present idealised models of bottom-up democratic deliberation in one unified public arena, guided by public reason strictly separated from negotiations and power asymmetries.[20] Democratic constitutions are more sober in this regard. They do not, and cannot, guarantee the absence of power asymmetries and the exclusive 'use of public reason'. However, they guarantee crucial preconditions for actual democratic debate, the freedoms of political communication, i.e. freedom of opinion, of information, of print and other media of mass communication, of assembly, propaganda and demonstration, of association or organisation, and of petitions and hearings. It is a common understanding among constitutional lawyers that these freedoms do not, and should not, discriminate between secular and religious opinions. The public arena must be the place where the contest between all opinions or voices takes place, whether religious or secular. In this perspective, it is really astonishing that philosophers of political liberalism – pretending to articulate the public or political morality of liberal democracies – have presented, and tenaciously defended, issue constraints, content constraints and reasonableness constraints solely for religious reasons and arguments. Content constraints for religious arguments are incompatible with any informed legal understanding of the freedoms of political communication. Also, restrictive interpretations of opinions as emphatic 'reasons' are at least at odds with an extensive interpretation of these freedoms that is crucial for lively democratic debate, which is the cornerstone of deliberative, stronger or more empowering conceptions of democracy. The US Supreme Court, for instance, does not restrict political communication to 'verbal' communication (let alone to 'reasonable opinions') but explicitly includes 'emotional-expressive' and 'symbolic communication'.[21]

Freedoms of political communication, like all other human rights, are not absolute. However, at least from a democratic perspective, the two relevant restrictions have to be circumscribed as neatly as possible. In addition, and in our context most importantly, they have to apply equally to religious and secular opinions. First, the traditional arguments for banning or prohibiting speech – like 'advocacy, clear and present danger, bad tendency, obscenity, and libel' – have to be very critically scrutinised because they are under serious pressure, particularly in emergency situations, as we are painfully reminded nowadays. In my view, only demonstrable 'clear and present danger' serves as a legitimate candidate. If such public order or civic peace constraints and maybe other 'compelling public interests' apply to religious speech, they should apply exactly in the same way to secular speech. Second, free speech may conflict with other important human rights, most prominently with nondiscrimination. As in the first case (call for violent action), discriminatory 'speech' is action and its freedom is limited by other constitutional rights and by criminal law, however different the balance of these two important but conflicting rights may legitimately be drawn, as contextualised theory makes us expect. Again, 'religious hate speech' should not be treated differently than 'secular hate speech'.[22]

3.4.2 Anti-paternalist decision-making

Whatever else political autonomy and equality may require, in its modern, liberal-democratic variety, it minimally requires that all opinions and voices eventually have to count equally as votes[23] when it comes to final decision-making. This applies even if paternalistic elites, maybe for the best of reasons, think that they are uninformed, misinformed, false, morally wrong or disgusting, etc. This specific egalitarian, anti-paternalistic mode of decision-making[24] requires that all defenders of 'absolute truths', whether religious or secular (e.g. philosophical or 'scientistic') have to learn how to resolve their respective fundamentalist dilemma. In traditional terms, they have to learn that popes, ayatollahs, philosophers and scientific experts are not allowed to be kings. If anything at all is eventually sovereign, it has to be *vox populi*, i.e. the interests and opinions as perceived and articulated by the people themselves. Another way of saying this is that 'error has the same rights as truth'.[25] Fundamentalist (interpreters of) religions have to learn to stem the temptation towards theocracy, and all kinds of professionals or scientific experts have to stem the temptation towards expertocracy. Again, it is crucial to understand and phrase the conflict between political absolutisms of all sorts and priority for democracy, not in terms of religious fundamentalism versus secularism (as it is so often done not only by aggressive secularists and political philosophers), but also by reformist theologians in the Islamic tradition.[26]

All religions (lay believers and practitioners as well as elites and organisations) eventually have to learn to accept priority for democracy. In section 3.6, I summarise whether religions find their own ways to solve the fundamentalist dilemma under liberal-democratic conditions and, if so, how.

If this is clear for religions, it is less well known and often forgotten that the same holds for all types of secular truths. While many modern religions and churches struggled to resolve this dilemma, many prominent modern philosophers have not even addressed it properly. This is evident for some of the recently fashionable, prominent 'continental' philosophers like Nietzsche, Schmitt and Heidegger. To a much lesser degree, many Anglo-Saxon liberal moral philosophers are also guilty of such an elitist 'conquest of democratic politics' (Barber 1988). The history of modern social science is also rife with scientistic ideology, from Saint-Simon's scientistic religion and Marxist-Leninist 'scientific socialism' via 'scientific racism' to the recent conquests of democratic politics by neo-classical economic ideology. In addition, the practices of many scientists and professions (e.g. technicians, medical practitioners, architects, city planners, economists, developmentalists, deep ecologists, pedagogues, therapists, sociologists and judges) are rife with illegitimate scientocracy or expertocracy (Scott 1998). All of them still have to learn that in democratic deliberation and decision-making, their 'truths' are no more than opinions among others.

One might say that religions are particularly prone to theocracy because belief, particularly Revealed Belief, would be grounded in transcendent sources, would be 'absolute' and beyond any doubt or, in modern language, would be stabilised against countervailing arguments and evidence,[27] whereas philosophy and modern sciences and professions, in particular, would be inherently connected with democracy, mainly for two reasons: (i) because they acknowledge that all knowledge, including all religious knowledge, is man-made or 'constructed' and (ii) because the almost universal acknowledgement that humans can err, that all our knowledge, including all philosophical or scientific truth, is not 'absolute' but fallible. Such a widespread view, however, would first of all reproduce an Irenic picture of the modern sciences, professions in particular, clearly at odds with actual practices. Philosophers, scientists and professionals learn to become self-critical not only and not mainly by respective *ethoi* (e.g. Popperian falsification) but by competition, rivalry and institutional conditions under which others try to falsify their claims and criticise their practices (sect. 2.1). Second, it would continue to underestimate institutional and practical dimensions of learning democracy and, third, it would underestimate the degree to which modern religious believers and theologians came to terms with contingency and also criticise earthly representatives of divine or transcendent powers as fallible.

3.5   Philosophical foundationalism or priority for democracy?

Sophisticated modern political philosophers who fully accept the fallibility of all human thinking in science and philosophy are still hampered by secularist remnants in two ways. First, they have difficulties in accepting (or are openly opposed to) the idea of a freestanding public morality and 'un-foundationalism' and, second, they hold on to one or another version of 'exclusivist secularism'.

In many regards, philosophers are the heirs of theologians, particularly when it comes to the 'need for security', the quest for certainty, truth and deep foundations – so one-sidedly used in charges against all religions (Marshall 1993: 852ff; see critically McConnell 1992: 738f). They too, for long, had difficulties in not falling prey to the temptation of 'truth-power' or becoming a 'philosopher-king' that has accompanied the history of philosophy since Plato. Analogous to theocracy, one could coin this 'philosophocracy'. Coping with contingency, living with uncertainty and bracketing truth claims when it comes to democratic decision-making has not been easy for philosophers generally, even for moral and political philosophers. Modern American pragmatists have been the first to have thoroughly and convincingly done so, [28] but the priority for democracy must still be defended against recent philosophical imperialists.

As stated above, the basic and most fundamental insight of a priority for democracy is that the validity of basic rights does not depend upon the truth claims of competing theories of rights, like natural rights theories, deontological contractarian theories, consequentialist theories and needs theories. Nor does the validity of democratic institutions and practices depend on competing theories of democracy. This priority of rights over theories of rights, or of democracy over theories of democracy, is based on two arguments. First, foundational philosophical theories are not only fallible in principle but also actually deeply contested – and will continue to be so for the foreseeable future – whereas the amount of agreement on basic rights even globally seems to be much higher. Second, like Henry Shue, I am convinced that 'practice now is far ahead of theory' (1995: 27).

> The idea of rights ... responds to common moral intuitions and accepted political principles ... human rights are not the work of philosophers, but of politicians and citizens, and philosophers have only begun to try to build conceptual justifications for them. The international expression of rights themselves claim no philosophical foundation, nor do they reflect any clear philosophical assumptions. (Louis Henkin 1990: 6, quoted in Shue 1995: 27).

Philosophy in general, but also political philosophy, is often in the rearguard.

The fear that, without solid or rock-bottom philosophical groundings, basic rights and democracy would be unstable and shaky continues to motivate generations of philosophers to come up with deep foundations. The 'high' guarantees by God, Natural Rights and *lumen naturale* from the theological traditions have now been replaced by Ratio, Reason or Language, by transcendental (from Kant to Apel or Gewirth), quasi-transcendental or universal-pragmatist (Habermas) strategies in order to guarantee equality, freedom, autonomy and consensus or agreement deep down, i.e. in the 'nature' of human nature, reason, or speech.[29] Even if these philosophers clearly criticise the philosopher-king temptation, as for instance Habermas does by distinguishing between the roles of citizens and philosophers, they stick to the idea that rights and democracy can only be stable if we also agree on their deep foundations. For this reason, they do not grasp the spirit of, or explicitly disagree with, the radicalised Rawlsian idea of a freestanding, non-foundationalist conception of public morality and political justice and its preferred method of an overlapping consensus freed from its constructivist and exclusivist remnants.[30]

Alluding to Lefort (1999: 49f), non-foundationalism can be seen as a philosophical stimulus of modern democracy as an open project helping to prevent the political form of a society from being seen as the realisation of a transcendent vision. The public articulation of religious pluralism and the rejection of 'ultimate philosophical foundations' may both have a constitutive function, keeping the space of ultimate symbolic foundation empty or open (Koenig 2003: 224; Willems 2003: 314, 318). As is easily seen if one considers Richard Rorty's position, non-foundationalism in itself, however, is not a guarantee of – in Rorty's own words – the priority for democracy. Rorty along with most postmodernists is tempted to foresee justificatory non-foundationalism, or better anti-foundationalism, for moral relativism.[31] In addition, Rorty (1994) joins standard political liberals in all of the essential substantive issues at stake: exclusivist secularism, privatisation of religion, secularist suspicion of all religions, and even secularist myopias with regard to secularist intolerance (Bader 1999a: 625f). Clearly, non-foundationalism does not prevent aggressive secularism nor does it guarantee that all voices 'are put on a par with everybody else's voices' (Rorty 1997: 4). Rothschilds' question: 'how do we organize ourselves so that the many voices can be heard (1996: 58 quoted above) is still on the table and Taylor's recommendation: 'Let people subscribe for whatever reasons they find compelling, only let them subscribe' (1998: 52) still has to be defended against exclusivist secularism.

Most liberal political philosophers, however, do not trust the institutional and procedural modes of liberal democracy to provide enough stability and legitimacy. They see a need to restrict the contents and kinds of reasons in public deliberation by excluding religious reasons that seem particularly dangerous. I briefly summarise my criticism of exclusivism (Bader 1999a) by focusing on Rawls for two reasons. First and foremost, he has eventually been forced to distinguish clearly between 'public reason' and 'secular reason and secular values' (1999: 143). His version of public-restraint arguments, in opposition to Audi, Macedo and many others, is fairer than secularist exclusivism because it applies to all non-public reasons equally, whether religious or secular. Second, in four consecutive steps, it became ever more inclusivist (Greenawalt 1995, Bader 2007c). The restraints apply only in well-ordered constitutional democracies, not in less or poorly ordered societies; only in fundamental questions (constitutional essentials, basic justice) not for ordinary political issues; mainly or only for judges and executive officials; and not in all forums of deliberation (in the 'domestic sphere' and the 'non-political forum' of civil society) but only in the 'public political forum' (1999: 133).

First, the content restraints on public reason are further weakened because Rawls increasingly sees that the 'content and idea of political justice may vary' (1993: 226) and are contested. Hence, the broader version of political justice, which includes the more demanding principles of equal opportunity and the difference principle, is increasingly restricted to a narrower version of basic rights and needs (Greenawalt 1995: 201f). Second, even regarding this hard core of moral minimalism, Rawls acknowledges tensions among 'many political values that may be weighed differently' (1993: 240). Hence, Rawls sees that the use of public reason results in major disagreements on all levels. The meaning of the restraints becomes emptier because of contested political conceptions, contested ideas of public reason, huge disagreements due to moral pluralism, under-determinacy of interpretation and application of principles, plus the burdens of judgement, which 'always exist and limit the extent of possible agreement.' The standards of reasonableness and rationality, such as consistency, theoretical truth and objective empirical validity are also watered down and not applied rigidly. As a result, the restraints cannot exclude much but are still thought to filter out admissible from inadmissible reasons.

This progressive weakening of the restraints is in itself important, even independent of the validity of mounting criticism that has been directed against the distinction between well-ordered and poorly ordered societies (risk of 'prospective immunisation'); between constitutional essentials and ordinary politics (ideology of an apolitical supreme court); against the idea that one can actually, not ideally, achieve impartiality, neutrality or the common good by bracketing non-public reasons and interest, by insulating them *from* instead of including them *in* deliberations; and against concepts of reason that privilege cognitivist ratio (clearly and propositionally articulated arguments) and discount practical knowledge, emotions and passions (Parekh 2000: 304-313). Homogenous views of public reason (singular) have to be rejected and the multiplicity of perspectives and reasons has to be explicitly recognised. 'Public reason' does not guarantee, and public reasoning does not result in consensus. Reasonable reasons are not reasons we share, or agree with; they should be 'sharable' in the sense that they should be understandable, comprehensible, intelligible or accessible.

These or similar restraints have been introduced by liberal political philosophers in an attempt to regulate, discipline, control or at least guide public reasoning to prevent chaotic, unruly, heated and contentious public debate, and to allow for orderly deliberation and decision-making. Critics propose modest inclusive versions of public reasons (Greenawalt), or more radically inclusive versions (Parekh, Tully, Connolly). They also defend a broadened and pluralised perspective on public reasoning. Two interconnected consequences for mutual understanding, decision-making and democratic legitimacy are of particular interest here.

First, the breakdown of liberal restraints and the acceptance of an explicitly wide and inclusive view of public reasoning do not in themselves lead to chaotic talk or the breakdown of decision-making and democratically legitimate law. Compared with the detached public deliberation proposed by Rawls, modelled after an idealised version of legal and judicial deliberation, public talk will be clearly and healthily more 'anarchic', unruly, lively and passionate, less purified, cleansed, dreary and conservative, and more open for even fundamental challenges. Yet it need not get completely 'out of hand', [32] provided that debaters behave in a civilised way. Not only principles but also (maybe mainly) appropriate attitudes and virtues may help to establish (minimally) orderly and civilised public talk and decision-making. The Rawlsian 'political virtues such as reasonableness and a readiness to honour the (moral) duty of civility' (1993: 224) presuppose such an attitudinal basis. In the end, Gutmann and Thompson's 'principle of reciprocity' also turns out to be less a principle than a virtue: 'uncertainty about the truth of their own position', as opposed to rigidity, dogmatism and arrogance (1996: 77).

Second, we see the cunning of institutional reason at work: participating in public talk under conditions of guaranteed and sanctioned freedoms of political communication and an effective ban on violence eventually imparts some minimally required and attitudinally based virtues of moderation and toleration. In addition, the line between the 'disciplining' of passions by interests (Hirschman) and by morality is as blurred as are strategic and moral motives, negotiations and deliberations. This is increasingly also seen by defenders of deliberative democracy (e.g. Deveaux 2005). Moderately agonistic theories of democracy have to combine plausible accounts of civic and democratic virtues with institutional designs that enable lively and inclusive public debate (para 6.1.2).

3.6 Religions and democracy

In general, for secularist philosophers and politicians and for 'orthodox' religious fundamentalists alike, religion and democracy are incompatible and in deep or fundamental contradiction with each other. This is a very specific, biased presentation of the real 'problem' of 'citizenship ambiguity', which is 'present in any religion that recognises a divine or transcendent normative authority higher than that of earthly institutions' (McConnell 2000: 92). 'Believers inevitably face two sets of loyalties and two sets of obligations': the demands of faith (or of an 'authority outside the common wealth') and the 'obligations of liberal-democratic citizenship' (Rosenblum 2000). One way of presenting this tension is to construct 'conflicting truths of religion and democracy' either moderately (Cunningham 2005) or radically, independent of the type of religions and the conflicting interpretations of them, and also completely independent of the historical context and the types of liberal-democratic states and policies (Bruce 2004: 18). The other interpretation insists: 'much depends on the nature of the religion and of the state' (McConnell 2000: 91), that we cannot talk about a 'fundamental truth' or 'the essence' of religion or specific religions outside history and societies. Political philosophers should resist the temptations to construct some essential, a-historical truth of Christianity or Islam to be found by authoritatively stating or researching its 'original intent'. [33] In addition, they should reject the notion of an essential and radical difference between Christianity and Islam that has become so fashionable nowadays. [34]

If the relationship between religion and democracy is not defined once and for all, if religions are neither inimical nor friendly to liberal democracy by definitional fiat, we have to discuss how, when and under which conditions those (organised) religions, previously inimical, can learn to accept priority for liberal democracy. We can expect that such learning is particularly difficult and urgent for religions that are totalistic or integralistic (subordinating all spheres and aspects of life), are not minimally tolerant with regard to other believers and nonbelievers, are theocratic in the sense that earthly representatives (leaders and/or organisations) of divine revelation claim absolute truth and strict obedience of all (believers and nonbelievers), and are not only missionary-like but aggressive and violent. [35]

We can distinguish three different, connected ways in which these politically fundamentalist religions can and have learned to become minimally moral and have eventually accepted or even actively promoted a priority for liberal democracy: a more practical institutional learning, a practical attitudinal learning and a more theoretical (theological, doctrinal) learning. First, political institutions, at least partly, impose their own logic on religions and stem the temptations of these political-fundamentalist theocracies. For reasons of state, States and Empires induce at least some minimal differentiation of religion and politics, earthly and divine issues, and authorities (para. 1.2.3 and above). Living under institutions of a constitutional liberal democracy in general and participating in multi-party competition in particular contributes to making even these religions more liberal and democratic. Second, practical interactions in everyday life among people of widely divergent religious beliefs and practices teach practices and an ethos of toleration, at least under appropriate or decent regimes of toleration (Walzer 1997). Practical interaction in democratic politics teaches democratic virtues (sects. 6.1 and 9.3-9.6). Third, I am deeply convinced that such institutional and practical learning is at least as important as theoretical learning by scholars – so much highlighted by philosophers – who try to re-interpret or challenge dogmas and to find religious sources and justifications for moral principles of tolerance, personhood, equality and freedom.

Roman Catholic and Orthodox *Christianity* certainly did qualify as politically fundamentalist theocratic religions. At least from the Reformation onwards, the Catholic Church and all other churches, denominations and theologians had to come to terms with internal religious diversity, with the modern state and with emerging liberal-democratic constitutions in a new way. This required some doctrinal learning. In a first step, they learned to see peace, stability and public order not only as strategic or purely prudential values, but also as moral ones (see above). In order to make 'religion peaceable', authors like Grotius and Coornhert started to replace 'dogma and creed with a morality oriented to social peace' (Shah 2000: 125ff; Galston 2002: 24ff). This has not only been a doctrinal learning process ('adiaphora'; priority of tolerance) but also a process in which doctrines became less important than practices of toleration (virtues and cultures). Learning the priority of toleration started to tame fundamentalist theological doctrines and also opened avenues to reformulate parochialist, dogmatic and sectarian conceptions of Christianity as a more universal Christian ethics. But it did not include a priority for liberal democracy.

This only happened in a second step: different radical protestant denominations – Quakers, Baptists, Separatists, Methodists (Handy 1976: 199ff), and also *Remonstranten, Rekkelijken,* and Unitarians (Israel 1995, chaps. 5, 16 and 20)[36] – started to develop conceptions of religion in which liberal democracy explicitly gains priority over denominational truths when it comes to political decision-making or developed denominational truths compatible with democracy, so that the two could not come into conflict. Protestant religions are made compatible with liberal democracy from the inside (Miller 1985; Eisenach 2000; Thiemann 1996).[37]

In a third, much later and still much shakier step, Catholicism learned the same lesson. In the 1880s, conservative Catholic bishops in the US still defended the thesis that the 'ideal situation could only be an established church in a confessional state' (Casanova 1994: 182). The 'Americanists' defending the 'anti-thesis' that 'the principles of the Church are in thorough harmony with the interests of the Republic' could still not 'offer a theological rationale for democracy, freedom of religion, and disestablishment.' Eventually, the Catholic Aggiornamento delivered this rationale before and during the Second Vatican Council.

This theoretical learning process has been massively stimulated by institutional conditions. American Constitutionalism not only reinforced Protestant learning (Madison, Jefferson and Washington were practising Christians), but also had profound transformative effects on the American Catholic Church (Macedo 1997: 65ff).[38] The institutional conditions of multi-party democracy put transformative pressure on Catholic political parties in Europe in the second part of the 19th century. Like the developing Catholic movement and organisations in civil society, in reaction to aggressive secularism, these were originally fundamentalist and openly theocratic, intransigent and intolerant (Kalyvas 1996: 258f). The unintended and paradoxical results were three-fold. First, 'confessional parties proved to be a factor of mass incorporation and democratic consolidation' (Kalyvas 264). Second, the emerging confessional political leaders formed important counter-elites against clerical elites and Church authorities. Third, even the Catholic Church (which ceased to openly combat liberalism and democracy only in 1918 and officially accepted modern democracy only in 1944) came under transformative pressure to liberalise and democratise – to desacralise and declericalise but not to secularise – from the inside. '(D)emocracy in Europe was often expanded and consolidated by its enemies' (264).[39]

To summarise, Christian religions (particularly established churches) have learned to accept the priority for democracy only as a result of protracted conflict. Protestant denominations and free churches living under conditions of an established church had learned this from painful experiences much earlier and more deeply than Established Lutheran, and particularly Catholic and Orthodox Churches. However, under the conditions of liberal-democratic constitutional states, even Churches that think of themselves as 'the depositor of divine truth' (Casanova 1994) eventually learned to accept the notion that, when it comes to public democratic decision-making and voting, error has the same rights as truth instead of 'no rights' (Cohen 2004; Galanter 1966: 289f; Rawls 1993: 60ff; Weithman 1997: 7).

If one clearly sees that learning the priority for democracy 'in the West' has been a rather conflictive, complicated, lengthy and still unfinished process, then a self-critical reflection of this process, 'including all the misunderstandings, polemics, and reforms inevitably involved, would provide an excellent basis for interreligious and intercultural dialogue' (Bielefeldt 2000: 100) as well as for understanding such learning in 'the Rest', particularly for *Islam*. The fashionable statement that Islam would inherently prevent learning the same lessons that Christian churches and denominations eventually and painfully learned is particularly astonishing for the following reasons.

First, when compared to Roman Catholicism and Orthodox Christianity, Islam is far less centrally and hierarchically organised, knows neither Pope nor 'church' and presupposes a direct, immediate and equal relation of all believers to God.

Second, and partly for this reason, the differentiation between polity and religion has been more outspoken in Muslim Empires. This institutional differentiation began as early as the 7th century, starting with the *Umayyad* dynasty, to be later contained by the *Abbasids*, who tried to instrumentalise Islam for reasons of state; it was fully developed in the Western Empire by the *Almoravids* and *Almohads*, continued even into the *Mughal* empire and was again fully developed in the late *Ottoman* empire (Adanir & Faroqhi 2002; Zürcher & van der Linden 2004 and WRR 2004).

Third, decent regimes of toleration (of the three 'religions of the book') and astonishing practices of everyday toleration were developed in *al-Andalus*, and in the Millet system in the late Ottoman Empire, which outstrip everything comparable in the contemporaneous Christian world (Adanir 2000; Mayer 1999: 148).

Fourth, in addition to these practical and institutional aspects which are, to repeat, the most important ones, the 'original' teachings were at least as universal, and the social ethics of Islam are at least as egalitarian as the Christian and clearly more in favour of equality of the sexes (Ahmed 1992: 41, 62f). There is also a long and rich tradition of competing interpretations by schools of legal theorists, theologians and philosophers (Schacht 1982; Peters 1998; Bowen 1998; Esposito & Voll 1996). Some of these theoretical interpretations were fairly radical, e.g. the clear distinction between the *shari'a* and Islamic law (*fiqh*), the interpretation of the *shari'a* as universalist, egalitarian and solidaristic ethics and the 'rationalism' of the *mu'tazila theologians* (9th and 10th centuries, see Leezenberg 2001: 60ff; WRR 2006, chap. 2).

For roughly a century now, this theoretical learning process has clearly been under way again inside Islamic countries and, more recently, among Islamic scholars in different European Countries and North America. Space prevents the presentation or discussion of these complex developments, which include pragmatic reforms in the framework of the *shari'a* (Bielefeldt 2000: 106; Bowen 1998 for many); a critical reconceptualisation of the *shari'a* (An-Na'im 1990; Ahmed 1992 for many); a clear recognition of threshold institutional differentiation or the two autonomies and of individual and collective tolerance, and of Islamic democracy, often misleadingly refered to as 'political secularism in Islam' (Abdarraziq, Zakariya, Mawdudi, Ahmed; see extensively

Abou El Fadl 2001, 2002; WRR 2006: 35-53). Making Islam doctrinally more liberal and democratic takes place both in Muslim countries and in countries receiving considerable numbers of Muslim immigrants and these discourses are increasingly interconnected and have mutual impact on each other (Mandaville 2001, chaps. 3 and 4).

As in the case of Christianity, theoretical and practical learning depend on institutional conditions, most prominently on the presence or absence of liberal-democratic constitutional states. For historically contingent reasons, modern democracies emerged in the West, not in countries with Islamic majorities.[40] According to the Freedom House classification, of the 43 countries that recently show Muslim majorities, only seven can be classified as more or less well-established and stable liberal democracies, but none of them are in Arab countries with their strong patriarchal social orders and political autocracies (Brumberg, Plattner & Diamond 2003; Minkenberg 2007). The institutional pressure towards the democratic transformation of Islam(s) that can be detected in countries like Turkey or Indonesia and, obviously, for Muslim minorities in the West[41] is absent there, and this cannot be explained by 'Islam'. 'If the political circumstances were right' (Ahmed 1992: 229), we could expect and partly see that liberal-democratic institutions do their disciplining work and contribute to make Islam compatible with minimally understood liberal democracy. It is a nice example of the paradoxical nature of the cunning of institutional reason under conditions of multi-party systems that Islamic, politically fundamentalist parties in Turkey (like their confessional sister-parties in Europe) emerged in reaction against (authoritarian and elitist Kemalist) secularism, but learned to profit from and eventually to defend democracy and thus contributed to democratise Turkey.[42]

3.7   Priority for democracy vs. religious challenges

If religions have eventually learned to accept liberal democracy from the inside, it is clearly unfair to reproduce the 'secularist distrust' against all religions as being inherently fundamentalist. Yet, the priority for democracy must not only be defended against exclusivist secularism, it must also be defended against the main religious and theological challenges, which are all either untenable or unfair.

First, the public morality of liberal democracy is said to be impossible or unstable without religion. Religion must have been the 'ultimate guarantor of liberty' for the American Founding Fathers[43] and these statements continue to be repeated to this day, with minor variations. The claim that a non-religious morality would be impossible is so obviously untenable and has been so often convincingly refuted that I refrain from repeating the arguments: morality does not depend on religion, structurally or conceptually.[44] Whether a non-religious public morality can be stable does not depend on religious or secular foundations but on whether religious or non-religious institutions are more creative seedbeds of minimally required civic and liberal-democratic attitudes and virtues (sect. 6.1).

Second, the claim that religion is needed as an antidote to consumerism, egotism, materialism, emotivism or moral decisionism (Parekh 1996: 21, 1998; Wolterstorff 1977: 178f) belongs to the standard repertoire of Catholic and also Muslim criticism of 'Western liberalism or democracy'. It is convincingly refuted by Kulananda 1996: 68, Herrick 1996: 48f, Audi 1989 and many others. Non-religious morality is neither inherently 'utilitarian' or 'materialist' or whatever, nor does the liberal state 'monopolize morality' (Parekh 2000: 328). Modern social and political life also does not in itself encourage consumerism or egotism, although capitalism may do so. In addition, and more importantly, religion is not 'society's conscience and moral sentinel' (1998: 80) nor does it indiscriminately do all the good and beneficial things Parekh claims.

Third, it is argued that religious appeals to a higher divine sovereignty in general, and some forms of religious establishment in particular were needed to prevent unlimited state sovereignty and secularist myths and practices of unlimited politics.[45] Parekh is convinced that religion 'provides a valuable counterweight to the state ... Just as we need opposition parties to check the government of the day, we need powerful non-state institutions to check the statist manner of thinking, including the glorification of the state' (1996: 21). This argument is retained and expanded in his later book:

> The modern state is abstracted from society and tends to become bureaucratic and remote. While this has enabled it to rise above social, ethnic, religious and other divisions and institutionalize such great values as equality before the law, liberty and common citizenship, it has also been the source of many of its weaknesses (2000: 329).

The state is 'shallower', external to society, 'incapable of nurturing the moral life of the community'. This argument is unconvincing for three reasons. (i) All 'secular' anti-statists – libertarians, anarchists, liberal anti-majoritarians, liberal and associative democratic pluralists – agree that we urgently need powerful non-state institutions (part IV). Some of them, however, would very much doubt whether religious claims to a 'higher sovereignty' would be helpful in this regard. (ii) All defenders of a 'thin' state also try to demonstrate that and explain why such a state can be fairly 'strong'. That government should be 'external to society', is also defended by all pluralists trying to develop modes of associational governance. Fortunately, it is not the task of any liberal state 'to nurture the moral life of the community'. However, this does not mean that liberal democratic institutions would not be capable of nurturing the minimally required thin public morality and the civic and democratic attitudes and virtues of citizens. (iii) They would rightly be sceptical regarding general claims that 'along with the family, schools, voluntary associations and other social institutions religion plays an important part in sustaining the deeper springs of morality' (2000: 329). Some religions and religious institutions, such as those that have thoroughly learned their anti-fundamentalist lessons and also have liberalised and democratised their own institutions from within, may do this but others clearly do not (Rosenblum 1998; Warren 2001; sect. 6.1).

Fourth, religions are said to provide a necessary counterweight against 'rationalist modernity' (Parekh 2000: 330). In my view, all reasonable reminders of the 'Limits of Reason' are welcome, be they conservative (Oakeshott), liberal (Hayek), pragmatist (Dewey, Putnam) or republican (Barber). Religious critics may join secular critics of statism and of the hubris of constructivist rationalism, but they certainly do not deserve a monopoly or a privileged voice in this choir. Non-religious, self-reflective criticism of the limits of rationality, the state and politics are at least as strong and, in my view, more convincing (Scott 1998: 309ff; 2.5) than prima facie deep religious safeguards. The latter seem to lie beyond any human control and manipulation. However (at least as the bad historical record of their Christian and Islamic versions shows), they have always been tempted to install some earthly representatives of the Supreme Sovereign, pretending to speak with a far higher authority than our human reasons.

Fifth, 'if religion is prone to the vice of fundamentalism, the state is prone to the equally undesirable evil of nationalism' (Parekh 1996: 21; 2000: 328). Religion 'stresses the unity of the human species and challenges the tendency to limit morality to the territorial boundaries of the state' (330). This may be true of some universal salvation religions sometimes, but it is important to stop talking about religion in general terms as Parekh himself clearly recognises 'that religion has often supported aggressive nationalism and horrendous wars' (2000: 328). To get a clearer view of the relationship between religions and nationalism, one would first have to acknowledge the serious tensions between the universal ethical core of some religions like Christianity and Islam and their particularisation into 'national religions'. The particularising trend seems to be much stronger and deeper than Parekh has assumed. Next, one would have to acknowledge the crucial historical role religions have played in the formation of national myths and identity.

Finally, fundamentalist Christian denominations as well as fundamentalist Islamic and Hindu scholars reject not only the real possibility of a truly universal religion but also the universal validity of minimal and of minimal liberal-democratic morality. The claim that the priority for democracy is exclusively a Christian or a 'Western' project is thoughtfully rejected by Ahmed, Bilgrami, Bhargava, Bielefeldt and others: history is not destiny, and historical origin is not decisive for validity claims, particularly if it is not neglected or 'abstracted away' but reflected upon. This rejection is more convincing, if one also criticises the identification of minimal morality or minimal liberal-democratic morality and institutions with 'secular' morality or institutions, as I have tried to show. Religious believers, particularly fundamentalists, also complain that liberal democracy is not really pluralistic, multicultural or 'neutral' with regard to the competing versions of a good life, that it shows a particularist bias towards a specific way of life by favouring demanding concepts of tolerance, autonomy, reason or 'rational revisability' (sect. 2.2), or even individualist self-creation. They rightly recognise that even minimalist liberal-democratic morality cannot and, as all morality, should not be morally 'neutral' and, in addition cannot be strictly culturally neutral or anti-perfectionist, even if one tries to minimise the inevitable spillover effects of legal and political autonomy. [46] Even if one defends maximum accommodation for ultra-orthodox religious practitioners within the constraints of minimal morality, this points to an unavoidable, minimal price to be paid for living under liberal-democratic constitutions. The specific limits of toleration of practices of different religious groups (e.g. of illiberal, anti-democratic ultra-orthodox religions as long as they do not endorse or engage in violence) are further explored in chapter 4.

PART III

DILEMMAS AND LIMITS OF ACCOMMODATION,
PRINCIPLES AND CASES: APPLYING MORAL
MINIMALISM

4 Religious freedoms and other human rights, moral conundrums and hard cases

Religious Freedom is an important moral principle and a basic human right, guaranteed by international law and liberal-democratic constitutions. As all other human rights, it is not an absolute right. It may conflict with other basic human rights, and these tensions and the necessary balancing are not guided by a context-independent 'lexical hierarchy' of basic human rights (Poulter 1998: 98-106; Renteln 2004). Its contested interpretations and appropriate applications (at least in the eyes of moral pluralists) are informed and coloured by the various regimes of religious government in liberal-democratic states. The facts that norms do not form a 'logically coherent system' and that balancings are embedded 'in heterogeneous societal configurations' (Koenig 2003: 151f) create leeway for heterogeneous but morally legitimate practices (para. 1.3.3.2; Parekh 2000).

In this chapter, I discuss these interpretations and tensions, starting with religious freedom itself and the tensions between the negative freedom of religion from state control and interference and the positive freedom to believe and practice (sect. 4.1). Then, I address tensions and actual conflicts between associational or collective religious freedoms and other important civil and political rights, particularly in cases of illiberal and undemocratic religions. In section 4.2, I discuss the relevant distinctions between religious groups, issues and conflicts in this regard. I distinguish between three different hard cases of such conflicts between the *nomos* and practices of such groups and the core requirements of minimal morality and of liberal democratic morality, minimally understood, i.e. conflicts with principles and rights of non-discrimination and equal opportunities (sect. 4.3), with the core of modern criminal law (sect. 4.4), and of modern private personal law, civic marriage and divorce law in particular (sect. 4.5). In chapter 5, I turn from hard cases, characterised by basic-rights conflicts to softer cases that could and should be more easily resolvable, if liberal democracies were to actually live up to their proclaimed principles and rights, and the presumed relational religious neutrality of states and policies. In both chapters, I argue for as much accommodation as is compatible with the standards of moral minimalism (though my standards constrain more than Renteln's 'maximum accommodation' (2004)) or the more demanding but still miminalist standards of liberal-democratic morality. Only in part IV do I also use the more demanding moral standards of egalitarian liberalism and discuss different ways of combining moral minimalism with more demanding liberal and democratic principles. I then hope to show that associative democracy provides more productive and flexible institutional and policy options for finding sensible balances and trade-offs in both hard and soft cases, compared with strict separationism and with other varieties of liberal institutional pluralism and accommodationism.

4.1   Religious freedoms

Religious freedom, like other moral and legal principles, does not exist in a vacuum. Principles and rights have to be balanced with other principles, such as nondiscrimination or equal opportunity (moral pluralism). Moreover, religious freedom itself is a complex, under-determined concept that implies many freedoms. Its interpretation and application is influenced by divergent understandings of the positive, negative or neutral relationship between religions and liberal democracy and by historical facts and societal contexts (contextualised morality). But it is not a situation where anything goes. Interpretations and institutional options have to be compatible with the core of religious freedom.

4.1.1   Religious freedom, religious freedoms

One of the most broadly recognised, carefully phrased and balanced articulations of this core is article 9 of the International Covenant of Civil and Political Rights.[1]

(1) Everyone has the right to freedom of thought, conscience and religion; this right includes freedom to change his religion or belief and freedom, either alone or in community with others and in public or private, to manifest his religion or belief, in worship, teaching, practice and observance. (2) Freedom to manifest one's religion or beliefs shall be subject only to such limitations as are prescribed by law and are necessary in a democratic society in the interests of public safety, for the protection of public order, health or morals, or for the protection of the rights and freedoms of others.

Freedom of religion is clearly 'not an un-differentiated or uni-dimensional concept, but is a constellation of overlapping and sometimes conflicting claims for specific freedoms' (Galanter 1960: 217ff). Galanter presents a contentious, tentative, long but not exhaustive list of the different meanings and dimensions of this core concept, derived from US Supreme Court decisions (218ff):

> Freedom from religious compulsion (including free exit); freedom from persecution or discrimination because of religious beliefs or practice; freedom from state-sponsored religion; freedom from state use of religious standards; freedom to enlist state cooperation in carrying out religious purposes; freedom to obtain (from government) opportunities to implement religious values; freedom from private interference with one's religious beliefs and practices; freedom of religious association and the freedom of association to maintain autonomous internal government; freedom of religious choice; freedom to transmit and implant religious views in the next generation; freedom to express, publish, distribute, and teach religious views; freedom from compelled disclosure of religious views; freedom from governmental restrictions upon activities accorded positive religious significance; freedom from governmental compulsion to perform an act accorded negative religious significance; freedom to define the religious or sacred.

Together, these claims spell out an enormous complexity. Two questions however enable some simplification. They are the traditional and intertwined questions about freedom from (negative) and freedom to (positive freedom) and about whose freedoms are involved (individual, parental and familial, associational).

The freedom to believe, or the freedom of individual conscience and the freedom to practice religion in worship, ritual, teaching and observance (whether collectively or individually, in 'private' or in 'public' spaces), and the freedom of religions from illegitimate state control often conflict. Positive freedom is compatible with aid and may even call for it, whereas negative freedom from illegitimate state control seems to require 'no aid' or 'no interference' (Galanter 1966: 288ff, 1998: 260ff; HLR Note 1987: 1632ff). I first address the issues of negative freedom.

4.1.2 Negative freedoms of religion

Even if one favours an almost exclusively negative interpretation of religious freedoms, as libertarians and classical liberals do, there is clearly a need for some legitimate external control and state intervention. The suffix 'legitimate' control points to the fact that the freedom of religion from the state, as all other freedoms, is morally and legally constrained by two other considerations: first by reference to some public or 'compelling state-interest', such as 'order', 'safety', 'health' and even 'morals' and, second, by the protection of equal rights and liberties of all, believers and nonbelievers. This protection implies layered duties for the liberal-democratic state for three reasons.

First, because negative religious freedom is not only directed against interference by the state (the negative duty of non-interference) but also against all forms of illegitimate interference by other religions and by 'secular' groups and organisations (Shue 1995: 13), the state has the positive duty to protect all religions from such interference (UN Declaration on religious discrimination 1981, Art. 4).

Second, negative religious freedom protects not only individual freedom but also the associational or organisational freedoms of religions[2] that may conflict with each other, particularly where individual religious freedoms of consciousness and expression and especially the freedom to exit religions are threatened by co-believers and organisations. If 'heresy', 'apostasy' and 'conversion' are banned and sanctioned by religious law and organisations, as was the case for centuries in Christianity and still is the case in Islamic law,[3] the liberal-democratic state has at least the difficult positive duty to protect the exit rights of citizens from their 'own' churches or mosques.

Third, collective practices, sanctioned by religious customs, laws (nomos) and authorities may conflict with other important human rights of both members and non-members (sects. 4.3 and 4.5). Every liberal-democratic state has the positive duty to protect the basic rights of all its citizens and residents without unduly overriding associational freedoms.

A minimalist moral evaluation of the various constitutional regimes (para. 1.3.3.1) shows that strong establishment is clearly incompatible with equal negative religious freedoms. Even in its tamed forms, as in Greece, it more or less massively discriminates against other believers and nonbelievers and it allows more or less massive state interference or control of established religions. All other constitutional regimes – explicitly including weak and plural establishment and cooperation regimes – are understood to live up to the minimal moral and legal threshold, in this regard,[4] though they strike a different balance between non-interference and protection of basic rights. Predominantly libertarian separationist regimes, such as in the US, different from French statist separationism, tend to sacrifice protection of basic rights of believers, children in particular, against social pressure and reckless religious leaders to fairly absolute associational autonomy on the assumption of free entry and exit. Pluralist regimes, AD in particular, give more weight to the positive duty of liberal-democratic states to protect vulnerable minorities inside (organised) religions. They too are faced with the problem that this is much more difficult in cases of loosely organised, 'invisible' sects – think of recent examples of (enforced) 'millenarist' suicides – compared with more organised sects such as Bhagwan or Scientology and organised churches. Their policies of public or even legal recognition of (organised) religions, however, add considerable public pressure and scrutiny to make religions behave minimally moral. Yet, it may easily seduce states into transgressing the contested borderlines between legitimate external intervention in order to protect minimally understood basic rights and illegitimate control in attempts to impose more demanding values of liberalism and democracy (chap. 8).

4.1.3 Negative and positive freedoms

The positive freedom to believe and practice needs more than the minimally required liberal scrutiny in order to safeguard individual freedoms. It requires some materially 'equal treatment of religions', either bent on correcting historical inequalities (e.g. for indigenous people or Jews in Germany), preferably by invoking justice-based arguments.

Constitutions, constitutional courts – and also political philosophers and prevailing public opinion – in different countries understand and balance in divergent though never uncontested ways. In the US, the prevailing ideology of strict separationism stresses negative freedoms and non-intervention. Libertarians and radical individualistic liberals deny any positive state duty in this regard, emphasised by an accommodationist reading of the Free Exercise Clause (McConnell 1992; *Sherber v. Verner 1963*). Equal treatment of religions means equality before the law, and the absolute priority of negative individual freedom discounts any more substantive notion of equality. Providing aid to religions should not be the state's business. Only strict, formal neutrality (*Lemon vs. Kurtzman*) and strong separationism is seen as compatible with equality, because all other options are said to be inherently unfair either to other religions or to nonbelievers.[5]

In most other countries, predominant opinion tries to find more sensible balances between negative and positive freedoms. Part 1 of the new constitution of the Netherlands, for example, 'guarantees equal treatment in equal circumstances to all persons. It is clear that, under the Constitution, public authorities in the Netherlands shall be neutral with respect to the various religious and non-religious denominations ... It is clear that once authorities subsidise or support certain activities, religious counterparts cannot be excluded for that reason. Article 1 forbids this.' (Bijsterveld 1994: 207, 211). This interpretation rejects the 'assumption often made in the US that religious organisations have a bias or a distinctive axe to grind, while non-religious secular organisations are neutral. In the Netherlands, secular and religious organisations alike are seen as operating out of certain philosophies or beliefs,' and 'nonreligious organizations are seen not as truly neutral but are yet another *richting*' (Monsma & Soper 1997: 78; see 178 for the German Constitutional Court 1975).

4.1.4 Positive freedoms and equal treatment of religions

In a short criticism of libertarianism and strict separationism, I hope to show that Monsma and Soper are right in stating that this more expansive and balanced understanding of religious freedoms is more appropriate (1997: 202) and allows for more consistent rulings in educational and welfare service issues (McConnell 1992). Tomasi has convincingly shown that 'egalitarian versions of liberalism generate extensive positive religious freedom rights ... Egalitarian liberalism thus requires a far more substantial mixing of church and state than do more minimalist classical conceptions of liberalism.' (2004: 326)

Libertarianism and strict separationism might be seen as maximising equal legal treatment of all religions as well as of all others in an ideal world because a liberal-democratic state would not be allowed to directly or indirectly aid, subsidise or finance any religious or comparable 'secular' cultural institutions or activities. All this would be none of the state's business and should be left to the equal playing field of religious and cultural markets and the healthy working of free competition. This strictly anti-perfectionist conception of justice would, however, maximise equality before the law only if the liberal-democratic state did not privilege specific religions historically in numerous direct and indirect ways, if it actually were the minimalist state demanded by libertarian theory, and if this minimalist state could be completely religiously and culturally neutral.

First, according to the libertarian conception of justice, a policy of strict, formal or legal equal treatment is unfair and harsh in all cases where states have systematically or structurally disadvantaged minority religions or, put slightly differently, where the actual playing field in the religious market has been massively and unfairly shaped by governments. Historically, this has been the case in all monopolistic or oligopolistic religious regimes of governance, either constitutionally (e.g. when constitutional disestablishment has been fairly recent, as in the Netherlands or Sweden), or legally, administratively, politically and materially (as in the US, where non-establishment has been combined with a long history of numerous actual privileges for Protestant churches). The history of all liberal-democratic states is obviously rife with examples of policies that allowed majority religions to build and continue their predominant position. In cases where they continue to exist in clear contradiction to the demands of all liberal conceptions of justice, equality before the law minimally requires that old and new minority religions be treated equally or at least even-handedly. If they have been dismantled only fairly recently after centuries of unfair privileges, libertarian justice surely demands at least some restitution or redress because the preconditions for fair and healthy religious competition have been absent. In practical terms, it is remarkable that these consequences are rarely drawn by libertarian philosophers and politicians.

Second, a minimalist libertarian state would certainly neither provide nor subsidise a whole range of welfare and social services, such as healthcare, care for children, elderly, handicapped or poor. Yet, we have seen (para. 1.3.3.8) that all existing states with liberal-democratic constitutions, including the US and France, do not leave this to markets alone but are massively involved in policies of regulation, subsidies and also provisions that affect the diversity of believers and nonbelievers in many direct and indirect ways (Minow 2000, Tomasi 2004). These are policies that cannot be strictly neutral, either in the justificatory sense of a secular purpose, or with regard to their direct and indirect effects. Libertarians certainly raise the red flag of revolution in theory in this regard (sect. 2.4), but rarely ask what an absolute libertarian policy of state absence, non-regulation and non-subsidy would prescribe for the long and strenuous 'meantime' between now and the realisation of this radical utopia. Equality before the law, in my view, would then mean that we treat service providers, whether public (e.g. state) or associational (e.g. faith-based) equally or even-handedly in terms of direct or indirect financing or subsidies, as is done in different ways and degrees by most liberal-democratic states, including France and the US. If service delivery cannot be strictly culturally/religiously neutral in the real world (sects. 2.3 and 5.3), even defenders of a strictly anti-perfectionist conception of justice should address the question of how it could be made relationally more neutral, particularly if they are in favour of exclusively public or state care.

Third, in the case of care, some culturally and religiously neutral provision may at least be thinkable though not realisable (sect. 5.3); for the provision of education, it is evidently impossible (sects. 5.2 and 10.3).[6] In addition, a liberal-democratic state cannot scrap all religiously contested issues from the agenda of legislation or pretend that laws on stem-cell research, cloning, abortion, genetic modification of food, same-sex marriage and euthanasia, etc. could be just 'secular' or 'neutral'. Radical libertarian and liberal 'hands-off' policies would only try to hide predominant cultural and religious biases from view.

That no liberal-democratic state has followed the advice of strictly anti-perfectionist libertarianism may be seen as an indication of the normal tension between the ideal world (what justice would ideally require) and the real world. It can also be understood as an indication that something is wrong with the ideal, that the utopia itself is not required, desirable or laudable (sect. 2.4). All critics of justice as hands-off and of the libertarian reduction of equality to equality before and in the law have to face difficult trade-offs. These trades-offs are between, on the one hand, negative freedoms and legal equality and, on the other hand, more substantive notions of equality (Bader 1998: 447ff) and justice as even-handedness, both in general and in cases of religious freedoms. If governments directly or indirectly finance religions or if they subsidise welfare and educational provision, they have to answer questions such as: What are religious associations or organisations? Which ones should be recognised? What are the requirements for recognition and subsidies in terms of thresholds and minimal standards? This involves the dangers that the state defines religions and illegitimately intervenes in issues of organisational form and content of religion (public recognition and public money are connected to public scrutiny, see Minow 2000: 1080f.), and that the state continues to privilege old and already publicly recognised majority religion(s). Criticising 'strict separation' obviously implies that the border lines between public and private, between state and religions become more contested and negotiable (Minow 2000). However, border crossings and influence in both directions may be morally illegitimate and intolerable and violate the two autonomies. All liberal accommodationists have to balance the liberties from and the liberties to (Robbins 1987: 135, McConnell 1992: 692ff). They have to take existing inequalities into account and find ways to combine 'involvement' and 'relational neutrality' (sect. 8.6).

4.2 Groups, conflicts and issues

Associational or collective freedoms often contradict individual *negative* religious freedoms as well as other important civil and political rights, particularly in cases of deeply illiberal, anti-democratic, fundamentalist or totalistic religions.

4.2.1 Minorities

For a contextualised theory of morality, it is obvious that differences between minorities make a difference. First, however, one must draw the boundaries; it is a commonly shared intuition that indigenous peoples and tribes should be treated differently than national minorities, immigrant minorities and religious minorities. The minorities-within-minorities dilemma is concerned only with illiberal and undemocratic minorities. It is important to state right from the outset that many recent national, immigrant and religious minorities are not much different from majorities in democratic constitutional states, and that many indigenous peoples were democratic, though not liberal, long before conquering majorities were.

Second, with regard to illiberal and undemocratic minorities, three types[7] seem to require different treatment by liberal-democratic polities: (i) isolationist, 'retiring', internally decent and externally peaceful religious minorities that do not ask for public money and political representation, but just want to be left alone (paradigm cases: Amish, Hutterites). (ii) 'Ambitious', totalistic but peaceful, conservative or 'neo-fundamentalist' religious minorities that ask for public money and strive for public presence, even political hegemony (paradigm case: minority Catholic or Orthodox Churches, neo-conservative Protestants, neo-fundamentalist Muslims). (iii) Modern, illiberal and anti-democratic religious fundamentalists that use all means, including violence, to impose their totalistic, reactively purified religious regimes (paradigm cases: Islamicists and some Protestant, Jewish and Hindu fundamentalists).

In all these cases, liberal democratic polities have to intervene if, and to the degree to which, minorities or majorities seriously harm the most basic needs of their own minorities, children and women in particular. Isolationist religious minorities, however, do not harm the basic needs of others, they do not pose a threat to internal social and political stability, minimally understood, or to external peace and they do not ask for public money or other positive privileges, although they may impede the exit of their members. These three types of arguments may legitimise external interference and stronger scrutiny. Other than these arguments, there are not many good reasons for liberals to interfere with them, if they want to be left alone. The rights of ambitious, totalistic, but peaceful orthodox religions to go public and propagate an illiberal and authoritarian *Heilsstaat* are guaranteed by the freedoms of political communication and only restricted by the same rules holding for all others (para. 3.4.1). Nevertheless, if they vie for and accept public money either directly (subsidies) or indirectly (tax exemptions, vouchers), this gives liberal-democratic polities a special mandate to investigate, and a greater regulatory mandate over their institutions (sects. 7.4 and 10.6). Violent religious fundamentalists not only blatantly violate the basic needs of their members and others; if they are able to do so, they also threaten social and political stability and peace. Even the most minimalist interpretations of no-harm principles and priority for liberal democracy require extremely close public scrutiny and, if prudent, also prohibition and persecution within the confines of the rule of law.

4.2.2 Issues

The predominant cultural practices of illiberal and undemocratic minorities may conflict in numerous ways with a broad and extensive list of human rights of vulnerable minorities: rights to life, bodily integrity, nondiscrimination, due process, property and civil capacity, nationality, political participation, healthcare, education, employment, social security, marriage and so on (Nussbaum 1997, 1999, 2000). Contrary to conservative leaders and 'absolutist Free Exercise' lawyers, associational religious freedom has to be constrained by individual religious freedom and other human rights of members. However, depending on the length of the list and the interpretation of the respective rights (sect. 2.2), this intuitively plausible argument is often misused to impose 'thick' and perfectionist liberal-democratic morality and autonomy under the guise of universalism upon everybody, thus overriding any meaningful associational autonomy with strong policies of liberal and democratic congruence 'all the way down' (Rosenblum 2002: 165). For many reasons, it seems wise to focus on minimalist but strong moral and legal constraints: The longer the list of needs, interests, rights and capabilities, the greater the danger that cultural imperialism (which is incompatible with reasonable pluralism) will be imposed both internally and globally. Hence, I primarily focus on cases where predominant, though internally contested, practices conflict with the basic needs or rights of vulnerable minorities in three legal areas that seem to require different responses from liberal-democratic polities: conflicts of the *nomos* (customs, group laws) with minimal liberal-democratic requirements of nondiscrimination and equal opportunity in labour law (sect. 4.3), with the morally minimalist core of modern criminal law (sect. 4.4), and with the core of modern, state-enforced private personal law, particularly marriage and divorce law (sect. 4.5).

4.2.3 Three theoretical and political options

One can distinguish three prominent ways to deal with these tensions and conflicts in political philosophy and in actual politico-legal strategies.

First, complete deference or 'full autonomy' (Swaine 2001: 320ff) to the *nomos*, to the decision-making and authority of ethno-religious groups is defended by two radically different theoretical and political positions. Radical libertarians like Kukathas (2003) defend complete deference to the *nomos* of religious groups, far-reaching autonomy and an absence of any state intervention or scrutiny, assuming free and informed consent by adults: entry into groups, associations and organisations should be as free as exit. Traditionalist or conservative communitarians (as well as conservative religious leaders and fundamentalist religious politicians) defend absolutist deference and autonomy in a completely opposite way. 'Our' illiberal and anti-democratic religion does not value 'individual autonomy' and 'free choice' at all, or not in the same way that radically individualist modern liberals do.

Second, it took a long time before universalist egalitarian liberals recognised the particularity of nation-state cultures, and also that cultural inequalities pose a normative problem which has to be addressed – as Kymlicka (1995, 2002) has convincingly shown. Nowadays, however, 're-universalizing citizenship' is becoming increasingly prominent among liberal universalists, including feminists, and among republicans and deliberative democrats, as a reaction to undifferentiated theories of cultural group rights and to undifferentiated policies of 'identity' and multiculturalism (Bader 2005, 2006b). Unreconstructed individualists try to avoid the 'apparent dilemma for the modern liberal regime': 'If the government defers to the wishes of the religious group, a vulnerable group of individuals will loose basic rights; if the government commits itself to respecting equal human rights of all individuals, it will stand accused of indifference to the liberty of conscience' (Nussbaum 1997: 98; 2000: 14, 168, 187) or better, the neglect of associational religious freedoms. Many feminists insist on a rigorously individualistic and secularist interpretation of human rights, particularly religious freedoms. They fiercely attack all group rights, particularly any associational or collective autonomy for (organised) religions, and they proscribe all separate codes or systems of religious law, insisting on a uniform civil code, as all individualist liberals do. Brian Barry, the self-declared defender of egalitarian liberal universalism, has also claimed that 'culture is the problem, not the solution' (2001). Such a strictly individualist, secularist and context-insensitive universalism favours radical policies of state-imposed and state-controlled liberal-democratic congruence.

Both absolute accommodationism and external interventionism positions deny that a serious dilemma exists and that one has to balance conflicting claims. Though completely opposed to each other, they share three crucial assumptions (Shachar 2001). (i) They tend to reproduce a mythical image of culture as static, isolated, homogeneous and uncontested, either with an apologetic or a critical intent. (ii) They either neglect injustice inside minorities or they neglect cultural inequalities between majorities and minorities: only structural inequalities are sometimes seen as unjust, while cultural inequalities do not enter the cognitive and normative frameworks of authors like Barry at all. Both approaches solve the dilemma of multicultural accommodation by declaring it nonexistent. (iii) In practical terms, they confront vulnerable individuals and minorities within minorities with a simplistic, tragic choice: 'your culture or your rights' (Shachar 2001: 90). For conceptual, theoretical and practical reasons, both options are counterproductive (Robbins 1987: 148; Beckford 1993: 131-133; Rosenblum 1998: 79, 2000: 166). The first option reduces the requirement of even minimally understood compatibility with human rights and with more demanding priority for liberal democracy practically to zero. The second option tries to impose thick notions of liberal autonomy and democracy in a self-contradictory way on all associations: 'liberal and democratic congruence' through and through (Galston 2002: 9).

Third, this leaves us with a more attractive approach: 'Liberal-democratic accommodationism'. Broadly understood, this accepts that there is a problem and that there is a need to balance individual autonomy and individual freedoms with associational freedoms, with multi-layered collective autonomy and with other human rights. As I see it, these authors share three important insights.

One, there is a real dilemma to be addressed, though the nature of this dilemma may be contested. Some authors try to show that it should not be seen as a conflict of moral principles – as 'competing equality claims' (Phillips 2005: 118ff, 122), or as a 'rights conflict' (Moore 2005: 274) – but rather, one concerning more pragmatic and political conflicts of interests, power, positions or identity. Also claimed is the fact that such conflicts allow easier negotiations, practical deliberations, compromise and contextual ways of resolution (Deveaux 2005, Eisenberg 2005), particularly if one listens to the internal voices of minorities within minorities. Yet, these authors accept that they may be confronted with hard strategic dilemmas (Phillips 2005; Reitman 2005). This attempt to redefine the tension or even to harmonise conflicting rights (Holder 2005: 294) may be laudable. In many regards, it is also productive: Not all cases are hard cases, we indeed do not need to understand rights as shooting guns; we should not be trapped by strategies of reactive ethnicisation or culturalisation presenting pure, homogenous, essentialist, static and uncontested cultures in conflict. Others, however, insist that there are times when we have to deal with conflicting moral principles and rights and also with conflicting, incompatible cultural practices (Mahajan 2005: 98; Okin 2005). As a moral pluralist, I am convinced that conflicts of moral principles and rights are the normal stuff of liberal morality and practical judgement even in the absence of any deep cultural or religious diversity. These conflicts – e.g. between individual and associational autonomy – are more serious if they are over-determined by more or less deeply conflicting predominant cultural practices. We cannot reduce all tensions to strategic dilemmas or soft cases.

Two, it is also fairly uncontroversial that minorities that not only politically but internally more or less explicitly accept principles and practices of liberal democracy are not the problem. Instead, the problem lies with more or less deeply illiberal and anti-democratic minorities like anti-modern, totalistic, conservative or orthodox religions of either the isolationist/retiring variety (Spinner-Halev 2000; Swaine 2005) or of the more aggressive, ambitious, politically fundamentalist variety.

Three, most authors who think seriously about the problem also accept that there are 'no easy answers' (Okin 2005) applicable to all minorities within minorities in all contexts.

Within this broad range of agreements, however, liberal accommodationists seriously and reasonably disagree about the scope and interpretation of appropriate principles and their balancing and about adequate institutions and policies. The varieties of liberal accommodationism (sect. 7.2) include moderate civil libertarians (Rosenblum), liberal democrats, liberal communitarians (Selznick 1992: 288), communitarian liberals (Etzioni 1996: 191), structural accommodationists (Glendon, McConnell), associative democrats and other varieties of democratic institutional pluralism as Galston's liberal pluralism (2002: 10, 36f) or Shachar's joint governance approaches.

4.3 Associational freedoms versus nondiscrimination and equal opportunities

Predominant practices of illiberal and undemocratic ethno-religious minorities (and majorities!) often conflict with minimally understood principles of nondiscrimination and equal opportunity. Both the US Supreme Court and many European courts have dealt extensively with cases of church property, internal decision-making procedures and authority, appropriate forms and degrees of public accountability and scrutiny, in which associational freedoms conflict with the rights of nondiscrimination and equal opportunities of members and outsiders as clients or employees.

All courts have been at least hesitant to interfere with church autonomy (paras. 1.3.3.6-1.3.3.8) but the US Supreme Court has been particularly reluctant in this regard. Its decisions have been guided by a mixture of libertarian assumptions, Free Exercise, and of a suspicion of all state intervention in the 'private' sphere. In cases of property disputes, this has resulted in unconditional deference to ecclesiastical law, decision procedures and practices as interpreted by church authority. This rule has not been upheld in cases of tax exemptions and subsidies for churches and faith-based service institutions not living up to anti-discrimination rules in labour and employment, to minimal educational, health and social service standards, or to rules of financial accountability. Here, the tension between the principles of church autonomy and nondiscrimination and equal opportunity is so evident that it is difficult for Courts to neglect. Contextualised morality and responsive law require that the respective principles are stated clearly, that their tensions are recognised, and that criteria and rules are elaborated to guide contextual moral and legal judgement in cases of racist, genderist and religious discrimination inside, or exclusion from religious and faith-based organisations. 'Certain social values such as equal opportunity and racial nondiscrimination are now viewed as partly enforceable by the state on institutions linked to churches' (Robbins 1987: 141, 148). The enforcement is based on the assumption of the public trust theory that accepting public money gives the state a special mandate to investigate, and a greater regulatory mandate. Even so, the extent, degree and type of regulation and interference are hotly contested.[8] In such matters, the following arguments have to be taken seriously.

4.3.1 Nondiscrimination and the shield of privacy

Racist, sexist, genderist and all other ascriptive discriminations are now widely perceived as morally wrong and proscribed by international, constitutional and criminal law. Yet it is also widely accepted that ascriptive exclusion and discrimination – however morally wrong – have to be legally tolerated in some cases, depending on the goals of associations (broadly understood) and the degree of voluntariness of membership.

'Miscegenation laws' should be banned (Hollinger 2003a) but 'ethno-racial self-segregation' in partner selection, marriage and family life is legally allowed. Intimate relationships should be treated differently to strictly private clubs, pubs and discos, churches and faith-based non-profit organisations, profit organisations, political parties, neighbourhoods and public places. Racist and genderist exclusions from 'close interpersonal relations, such as love, family, friendship, and primary group attachments' (Warren 2000: 129) cannot effectively be prevented by law. Policies of legal inclusion would be extremely difficult and mostly counterproductive. Exclusions also seem to be prima facie legally more legitimate: 'their associational fabric ought to be, and usually is, jealously guarded. This is necessarily so, since intimate associations are all too easily disrupted by external political or economic pressures' (Warren 2000: 129f). Even if one criticises the traditional 'private-public' dichotomy that always serves to hide structural power asymmetries within 'private' families and associations[9] as well as in 'private' capitalist corporations from view, one should be sensible with regard to legal protections of intimate relations. The unavoidable side effect of a morally permissible or maybe even required shield of intimacy is the protection of ascriptive discriminations to a certain degree. Protection of intimacy has been traditionally guaranteed by protection of 'the private'. Criticism of this standard ideology of privacy, however, does not resolve the tensions between the need to legally protect familial and associational autonomy and the discriminatory and exclusionary effects of such protections. The traditional shield of privacy loses its *prima facie* legitimacy the farther associational goals and practices are removed from intimacy. Defining some goals and activities as 'private' does not close but opens the debates in which a whole series of arguments are important. First, are the exclusions connected to the core of practices as defined by the association? The exclusion of heterosexuals from gay discos may be legitimate, but exclusion of blacks from gay discos, and the exclusion of women from the *Jaycees* is not. (Sincere) religious belief may be a legitimate criterion for selection by religious and faith-based organisations (FBOs) and orthodox religious political parties[10] but FBOs 'must obey federal laws prohibiting discrimination on the basis of race, colour, national origin, gender, age, and disability' (Esbeck 2004).[11] Second, do the exclusions protect minorities or majorities? For example, the exclusion of straight people from gay discos may be more legitimate than the exclusion of gays from hetero discos. In all these debates, one has to state the principle of nondiscrimination explicitly and in general before discussing whether exemptions may be morally and legally acceptable. In addition, the burden of proof should clearly rest on those churches and faith-based organisations asking for exemptions, e.g. from collective labour agreements, particularly in cases of overexploitation of personnel legitimised by 'charity'. Unfortunately, very little general guidance in theoretical literature is available (see, however, Warren 2000: 127).

4.3.2 Religious versus economic organisations

Religious core organisations (in the Christian tradition: churches) may be treated differently than faith-based organisations, and FBOs (such as schools, universities, (health)care institutions, social services and welfare institutions) should be treated differently than profit organisations sailing under the flag of religions. This is to prevent an imperialistic use of the Free Exercise Clause protecting 'all manner of enterprises (e.g. of the Unification Church, Scientology in the US or the latter in Germany – V.B.) with the shield of the First Amendment'. Otherwise, we would be 'equating freedom of worship with the right to pursue profitable activities without public accountability' (Robbins

1987: 148). Two problems, however, are fairly difficult to resolve in this regard: first, not all religious traditions have 'churches' and, in addition, the degree of institutional differentiation between worship, education, healthcare and social services may often be minimal or absent, as in ethnic minority churches (Penninx & Schovers 2000) or mosques which, particularly in non-Muslim countries, fulfil many social service functions. Second, distinctions between 'religious', religious-related and 'purely economic' activities and institutions are contested because a clear, agreed-upon, 'objective' definition of religion is not available, and purely 'subjective' definitions are too easy to manipulate strategically (sect. 1.1).

4.3.3 Central versus peripheral activities to faith

Even within religious core organisations, it is important to distinguish between issues, creeds and practices that define the very core of religions versus more or less purely administrative and fiscal issues. Liberals do not really contest that it is none of the state's business to legally interfere with definition and decision-making in matters of belief. Yet beliefs and practices, 'opinions and actions' are very much interrelated. Sexist and genderist discrimination is still part of the predominant orthodox understanding of Catholicism, conservative Protestantism and Islam, and the exclusion of Blacks is claimed to be central to some racist Protestant churches (e.g. the American Presbyterian Southern Church) as well as to Dade Christian schools (*Brown v. Dade Christian Schools*).

Ascriptive exclusion can then be legally defended[12] because 'control over membership' is crucial to the viability, and 'compelled association *is* a threat to the viability of groups whose liberty is grounded in voluntary association and fellowship. Religious liberty means individuals are not forced to join or prevented from leaving groups; *Dade* introduces a third element – freedom from compelled association. The ruling compelling a church school to admit unwelcome members is the very definition of loss of self-government' (Rosenblum 1998: 98; similar: Shachar 2001; Smith 1998: 203 for India).

If ascriptive discrimination inside religious organisations is directly and not just accidentally connected with core beliefs and practices, it can also be defended in a similar way. If the Catholic church, according to its own established decision-making procedures and authorities, rejects the possibility of female priesthood, just as some Anglican churches reject the possibility of gay bishops, the state should not legally impose nondiscrimination legislation upon the churches even if feminist Catholics or liberal Anglicans demand such legal action. If churches, following their established procedures, do not allow women or gays as members or excommunicate them if they 'come out' – as they have done and still do with dissenters – the state cannot legally forbid them from doing this without overruling and completely eroding associational autonomy.[13]

By analogy, if faith-based organisations (such as schools or hospitals) require that their core personnel, teachers and medical staff adhere to (or at least do not oppose) the religious core, and also that they do not 'come out' as gays or lesbians, the state should not legally impose non-discrimination or Equal Opportunity in Employment acts.[14] Yet, the shield of protection of associational freedoms does not cover a faith-based selection of administrative personnel, janitors, students or patients. Quasi-automatically covering all work and employment in faith-based organisations should not be allowed. Employment as a janitor is different. The burden of proof, again, rests plainly on FBOs and the requirement to demonstrate that discriminatory employment practices are religiously based does not threaten the viability of groups (Rosenblum 2000: 174-179).[15]

4.3.4 Unduly disadvantaging outsiders

Exclusion from FBOs implies disadvantages and unequal opportunities for outsiders, as (potential) employees and as customers or clients. The severity of these disadvantages clearly depends on the available alternatives for the excluded, influenced by issues such as: are these organisations big or small? Are they oligopsonists or even near monopsonists on specific (occupational and/or geographic) labour markets (as the Mormons in Utah)? Are they oligopolists or monopolists in service provision (e.g. Catholic schools or hospitals in some small cities or rural areas)?[16] Are they organisations of religious minorities or religious majorities? A context-sensitive balance between the principles of associational autonomy and of equal opportunity clearly has to take these issues into account: the more serious the disadvantages for excluded outsiders, the more pressing is the application of equal opportunity legislation or, alternatively, the public guarantee of non-religious service provision.

4.3.5 Dangers of public scrutiny and financing

Public recognition of religions in general (para. 1.3.3.3) and indirect and direct financing in particular (para. 1.3.3.5), do not provide harmless benefits because the price is comparatively greater governmental control and public scrutiny. Accepting public money gives the state a morally and legitimately special mandate to investigate and a greater regulatory mandate over these organisations. This is in accordance with the assumptions of the public trust theory underwritten by AD. A specific danger is always involved here. One of the explicit aims of tax exemptions, for instance, is 'encouraging diverse, indeed often sharply conflicting, activities and viewpoints... Far from representing an effort to reinforce any perceived 'common community conscience', the provision of tax exemptions to non-profit groups is one indispensable means of limiting the influence of governmental orthodoxy on important areas of community life' (Justice Powell, quoted in Kelley 1987: 121). The paramount danger of public scrutiny and interference, however, is that conformity to norms and standards is required that are actually secularist or majority biased, but presented as public, neutral or 'purely professional' (Minow 2000: 1090f; sects. 5.2 and 5.3). This danger is particularly great if norms and standards are exclusively set and interpreted by state agencies, such as the US Internal Revenue Service (IRS) or state school or hospital inspections that exclude a broad variety of service providers (including FBOs) from discussions of appropriate standards, their implementation and control, as proposed by AD (sect. 10.6 for education). In addition, one has to recognise that new religious minorities are particularly dependent upon such exemptions and subsidies, and that they are particularly vulnerable to interference (Robbins 1987: 145).

Particularly thorny issues arise in political systems where political parties are partly publicly financed in cases when orthodox religious parties think of sex and gender discrimination as part of their reading of the Bible and core belief. The radical Calvinist SGP in the Netherlands, for example, excludes women from normal membership, but for the rest accepts the liberal-democratic rules of the game and does not advocate theocracy or a return to weak or strong establishment. On the one hand, the American practice that treats parties legally as private organisations that should not and do not receive public money implies that private money and Big Business have an inevitable but most unwelcome influence on programmes, candidate selection, campaigning and so on. However, on the other hand, American state authorities also do not interfere with the programme, internal structure and decision-making in accordance with an extensive interpretation of freedoms of political communication. In many European countries, political parties are treated as public and also as partly publicly financed bodies. With public money come the opportunities and dangers of public scrutiny. Governments not only prosecute and forbid racist parties but also parties that do not follow their conceptions of '*wehrhafte Demokratie*' in their programmes and internal structure (BVerfGE; KPD and SRP cases). They may also be tempted to use subsidies as levers for change, and emancipation movements campaign for intervention in the internal decision-making structure and for the withdrawal of subsidies for parties. This happened in the recent case of the *Clara Wichman Institute et al. vs. the SGP and the State*. The High Court in The Hague (7 September 2005) declared the Dutch state guilty of violating the women's rights treaty and other international covenants because it did nothing to end discrimination of women within the SGP and even aided the party by providing subsidies.

The following arguments are important. First, the normative and, to a certain degree, also empirical functions of political parties differ from those of churches and FBOs. Parties are supposed to articulate interests and programmatic politics, to educate their members and elites as well as citizens, to mobilise them, increase political participation, select MPs and political elites, whereas FBOs are meant to provide services. In this sense, parties are more directly 'public' and more central to the functioning of liberal democracies. Second, this implies that the traditional 'shield of privacy' grows weaker and weaker, and that application of nondiscrimination is more legitimate for parties than for FBOs, and for FBOs than for 'churches'. Yet, political parties are particularly protected by freedoms of political association and an extensive interpretation of other freedoms of political communication (para. 3.4.1). The state has no business interfering in their internal organisation or decision-making structure (members are mature adults, their freedom of entry and exit is much higher than in religious communities or associations), let alone in their programmes and policy proposals. Third, with public money comes public control, but one should be wary of slippery slope arguments legitimised by reference to the public trust theory. They should be handled with care, and one must always look for the least invasive methods of public regulation and control. In our case, the legitimacy of public scrutiny and intervention is much higher for FBOs than for churches (minimal qualitative standards of service delivery, dependent clients), and higher for educational institutions than care institutions (because of 'educating future citizens'). However, it is much lower for political parties. Their addressees are mature, independent citizens who are supposed to be able to listen to highly contested, even 'weird' or obnoxious positions and to make up their own minds in forming their opinions and voting. Fourth, a liberal state certainly should not publicly finance propaganda incompatible with equal respect and nondiscrimination. In the case of FBOs, public financing does not concern propaganda of sex discrimination but tolerates some inevitable spillover connected with service delivery. In this regard, the decision by the Dutch Court to cut part of the public subsidies to the SGP – such as the scientific bureau and public relations but not eliminating subsidies for MPs and assistance – seems legitimate to me because it is limited and compatible with the principle of equal treatment of all parties in parliament without any censorship of their opinions.

For all these reasons, differences between churches, FBOs, parties and profit organisations, between core beliefs/practices and more peripheral ones, between activities and functions central to faith and lay activities, more peripherally related and non-related secular ones, discrimination of insiders and outsiders are important and worthy of attention. To argue that the state should refrain from legal intervention in core organisations and activities obviously does not imply that illiberal and non-democratic religions should be protected from public criticism. Nor does it imply that the liberal state should not interfere by less invasive but still relatively strong means, such as refusing to grant tax exemptions or subsidies, or to withdraw them under certain conditions, making exit options less costly, and maybe even stimulating dissension. Public authorities can listen to dissenters and give them some say in all of the cases in which church authorities request public assistance, public money or other privileges. Guaranteeing meaningful associational autonomy surely does not exempt religions or FBOs from the burden of proof, from public criticism or scrutiny. The farther one moves from religious core organisations and core activities, the weaker the shield of 'Free Exercise' should be and the more legitimate the legal imposition of nondiscrimination and equal opportunity legislation becomes. In addition, it is more legitimate that the standards and procedures of public scrutiny become more demanding.

4.4 Modern criminal law versus nomos of certain ethno-religious groups

Religiously legitimised practices of caste, bondage, slavery and not guaranteeing legally equal civil and political status for ascriptive minorities are surely incompatible with the most minimalist interpretations of modern freedom, equality and liberal morality (sect. 2.2). Practices such as *sati* (immolation of widows following their husband's death), domestic violence, stranger rape, marital rape, sexual abuse, genital mutilation, honour killing and severe corporal punishments without due process or enforced collective suicide are incompatible with any minimalist morality that protects the most basic rights to life, bodily integrity and due process guaranteed by international law (ICPR arts. 6.1, 7 and 9.1, 14.1, 15.1), liberal-democratic constitutions, and modern criminal and due process law. Cases in which specific ethno-religious practices as interpreted by orthodox or fundamentalist organisations and leaders and by absolutist Free Exercise lawyers conflict with this core of moral and legal minimalism are particularly serious and rightly dramatised by feminist and secularist individualist liberals.

These practices are proscribed by a minimalist understanding of universal morality, both globally and within liberal-democratic polities.[17] According to their own constitutions, liberal-democratic states have the duty to protect individual believers and vulnerable minorities within minorities against their 'own' religious group, associations, leaders and religious courts. Group autonomy can never be allowed to shield these practices. Public opinion and liberal-democratic polities should try to convince minorities to change them, and jurisdictions have to prosecute and punish perpetrators. Principles and practices of minimal and minimalist liberal-democratic morality are surely strong enough to legitimise public scrutiny and interference from the outside (by public opinion, by state jurisdiction, by international courts) in order to sanction such practices effectively.[18]

Given the broad agreement on these crucial limits to toleration and on the necessity of external intervention, three sobering remarks seem appropriate.

First, even core principles and rights, such as bodily integrity that are fairly universally shared, can be understood and interpreted in divergent ways in deeply different religio-cultural traditions. Are certain forms of corporal punishment regularly used by Indian tribes in Columbia to be understood as 'torture'?[19] How should the death penalty or long-term isolated imprisonment/detention ('isolation-torture') be understood in this regard? Are all forms of female circumcision to be understood and prosecuted as genital mutilation (as *infibulation or pharaonic* circumcision certainly is)? Is the removal of the tip of the clitoris a harmless version of 'piercing' (Sheleff 2000: 354-374; Parekh 2000: 275ff)?[20] Should even male circumcision be banned and prosecuted? Instead of imposing 'modern' and 'Western' interpretations without even listening to other interpretations, the universalist pretensions of basic rights are made more plausible and convincing in processes of intercultural or trans-cultural dialogue and negotiation by which 'our' understandings and interpretations can achieve higher degrees of relational ethno-religious neutrality.

Second, most 'modern' criminal codes are rife with ethno-religious particularism, which is hardly required by a relationally universal morality or is permissible in a truly culturally and religiously diverse society. Legal proscriptions of homosexuality in general or same-sex partnerships/marriages in particular – still the rule in most liberal democracies – are a clear case in point. In my view, the same is true for the hypocritical proscription of all varieties of polygamy.[21] This already serves as a reminder that the 'minimal requirements of modern criminal law' are still contested and in flux, and that moral learning processes are open and unfinished.

Third, modern Western societies and cultures are still deeply marked by discrimination and exclusion of 'races', women, homosexuals and minority religions. There is no reason for the self-congratulatory stance and the double standards that so often characterise these discussions. For example, domestic violence is certainly not confined to Jewish, Muslim or Hindu traditions but also a human stain in actual Christian and secular families (Okin 1997, 2002; Williams & Carens 1998). It took a very long time and protracted struggles by the respective minorities before 'we' came to see and evaluate these practices as morally illegitimate, and this learning process is still unfinished and shaky.

Although it is plain that liberal-democratic constitutions pose clear limitations to the accommodation of these practices (this is what the priority for liberal democracy or 'liberal-democratic' accommodation and 'liberal multiculturalism' indicate), it is far from clear how, i.e. by which institutions and policies, the basic human rights of vulnerable minorities inside minorities can be best and most effectively protected (sect. 7.3).

4.5   Religious versus civic marriage and divorce law

Modern marriage and divorce law is based on two moral principles: equality between the spouses and free consent – free entry (no marriage under duress) and free exit (*favor divortii*). The Catholic Church, and to a lesser degree, Protestant churches have been strongly opposed to both, and also rejected religious intermarriages for centuries. It took a very long time before 'equality and liberty' really transformed family law in Western states during the last century. In our days, cases in which customs and religious family law conflict with modern family law mainly involve Hindu, Muslim and Jewish family law.[22] As stated, the dilemma is clear: religious family law plays a crucial role in the reproduction of the *nomos* of groups (particularly control over membership and the role of women). However, at the same time, it sanctions the legal and practical discrimination of women. The dilemma is practically recognised in international private law: Dutch judges having to decide cases of divorce, alimony, custody and visiting rights of Moroccan or mixed-nationality couples regularly applied the legal rules of the *Muddawwana*, which were incompatible with Dutch marriage and divorce law, until family law in Morocco was eventually changed in 2003. The judges declared marriages concluded in Morocco that would be invalid in the Netherlands as legitimate, they declared polygamous marriages as legal, they accepted unilateral divorces where the wife had explicitly or tacitly agreed or at least appeased, etc.[23]

Such practical, area-specific and circumscribed forms of legal pluralism are vehemently rejected by liberal individualists and feminists,
who insist on a uniform civil code.[24] In 1997, Martha Nussbaum argued that 'religious liberty is a right of individuals' and 'liberals should
emphasize this individualistic concept' (1997: 125). Any group rights,
even in the case of national minorities, are rejected (126ff), all forms of
legal pluralism are declined as a 'medieval idea' (124). In 2000, she
implicitly criticised her own position in trying to find a productive middle ground between 'secular humanist feminism' (174-187) and 'traditionalist feminism' (2000: 176ff). She now remains 'neutral about establishment' (208, 210ff) and allows for some legal pluralism in personal law, particularly in cases of minority religions (212ff for Muslims
in India), but she still virtually rejects all associational religious freedoms (188-190, 226).[25]

In a much deeper and theoretically more sophisticated way, Ayelet
Shachar has tried to achieve a balance between the protection of vulnerable individuals and groups inside religious minorities against minority organisations and leaders – the dangers of 'the religious particularist model' (2000: 213ff) – and outside protection of vulnerable religious
minorities against religious majorities, secularists and 'their' state –
the dangers of 'the secular absolutist model' (209ff). How to deal with
the 'paradox of multicultural vulnerability' (Shachar 1998: 289, 2000:
65) and avoid the 'perils of multicultural accommodation' (Shachar
1998: 285ff) in family and divorce law? Drawing on distinctions between religious and economic activities already mentioned in tax exemption and subsidy cases, she distinguishes between the 'demarcating functions' of family law (crucial for the internal reproduction of the
nomos of the group) and its 'distributive functions.'[26] In her 'intersec-
tionist' or 'transformative joint governance approach,' she proposes to
delegate jurisdiction about the demarcating functions to inside courts
of religious groups and reserves jurisdiction about property matters to
state courts, explicitly permitting inputs 'from two legal systems – a
group's essential traditions and the state's laws – to resolve a single dispute (e.g. the *Martinez* case – V.B.)' (1998: 299).[27] Compared to conflicts with the core of criminal law, in these cases interference from the
outside can be much more limited and the space for legitimate group
autonomy can be much broader, without neglecting the basic rights of
women.[28]

Before turning to the discussion of 'softer cases', let me summarise
that, even in these hard cases, the actual policy repertoire is broader
than the choice between external sanctions by the state and full autonomy. I propose combining different policy repertoires such as leaving
minorities alone as much as possible; using external legal intervention
only to protect the basic needs and rights of individuals and vulnerable

minorities within minorities; applying stricter standards of public scrutiny and external control in cases where minorities ask for legal support, subsidies or other privileges from the state. The choice of appropriate policies clearly depends upon the type of minority, the issue-specific conflicts of predominant practices with decent or liberal-democratic morality and law, the specific goals of associations, and the degree of voluntariness and vulnerability of minorities (part IV).

5 Relational neutrality and even-handedness towards religions: softer cases and symbolic issues

5.1 Practical and symbolic accommodation: claims, resistance and policy responses

Only some ethno-religious practices of non-liberal minorities conflict with the core of minimal morality, or of minimal liberal-democratic morality. The broad variety of practices, which do not involve such conflicts (even if they require considerable accommodation) should be easier to resolve, particularly if liberal-democratic states were committed (as they should be) to the principles of relational religious neutrality and fairness as even-handedness (Bader 1997b: 790ff). This is why I speak of softer cases. Nevertheless, accommodation will encounter numerous practical difficulties because administrations and majorities may not be committed to these principles and may try to use all possible means to resist cultural changes, and also for four deeper reasons.

First, the laws of the country (*lex fori*) have been deeply moulded by ethno-religious practices of the predominant majority. Accommodating new claims may involve considerable legal challenges that liberal-democratic polities should accept, instead of requiring that minorities obey an unspecified and immunised law of the land as a minimal condition for 'integration'. Existing legal rules and practices should be scrutinised for morally intolerable ethno-religious bias and we can expect many instances of outdated ethnocentrist and denominationalist bias, as in the cases of feminist and anti-racist legal scrutiny that have exposed mountains of formerly unrecognised sexism and racism incompatible with equality and neutrality (sect. 2.3). This may be less so in constitutional rights and legal rules of private or tort law but more in interpretations of unspecified general norms – such as 'public order' and 'equity and decency' (*contra bonos mores*, Bovens 1993: 171) – and in the rich web of administrative rulings and practices in many fields.

Second, the institutional arrangements of particular liberal-democratic polities cannot be deduced from universal principles. They are deeply (and to a certain degree, also morally legitimately) embedded in the history of predominant ethno-religious majorities (Bader 1997b: 784f). Fairness for old and new minorities does not require 'undoing' this history or getting rid of all these particularisms, but sensitively and even-handedly accommodating institutions to provide fair chances for minorities.

Third, the public or political culture of liberal democracy does not exist in the abstract either but is morally legitimately embedded in the ethno-religious culture of majorities. Fairness as even-handedness requires sensitive accommodations.

Last, dominant ethnicity, religion and ruling versions of the history of a polity are inevitably inscribed in its national political identity, as is obvious in inter-'national' relations. Due to the influx of migrants with different ethno-religious cultures, this also became visible and dramatised again inside polities, not only in countries with a predominant ethno-religious self-conception of national identity but also in countries with a predominant civic or political self-conception (Koenig 2003, Fetzer & Soper 2005). This explains why more or less purely symbolic issues such as wearing *hijabs*, turbans, crosses and the architectural styles of mosques are so hotly contested and why resistance to symbolic accommodation is so fierce, although in principle accommodation of dress codes and pluralisation of public cultures and symbols should be fairly easy because no conflict with liberal-democratic morality is involved and also no costly redistribution is required.

In matters of institutions, political culture and political identity then, the borderlines between legitimate and illegitimate majority particularism are difficult to draw and there is no prima facie evidence of what fair or even-handed accommodation requires in each case.

If one combines these moral difficulties with a theoretical analysis of the demandingness of typical claims for public recognition by ethno-religious minorities and the expected resistance they meet, it is easier to understand why these softer cases often turn out to be hard in various liberal-democratic states as well. Following Koenig (2003: 159-162; 2004: 92ff), I distinguish four overlapping types of claims. First, claims that challenge the legitimacy of political symbols of national identity and ask freedoms for the public articulation of different identities e.g. toleration of religious dress in public (sect. 5.4). Second, minorities claim autonomy in some organised societal spheres, such as private religious schools or some free spaces in public education (para. 5.2.1.2). Both are claims to mere toleration (exemptions and some autonomy) that do not challenge predominant practices and symbols. Thirdly, we have more demanding claims to 'respect tolerance', aimed at a recombination of the central symbols of national identity, like new religious holidays or inclusive blasphemy laws (sect. 5.4) and at pluralising public education (paras. 5.2.1.1 and 5.2.2) or other organisations (sect. 5.3). Fourthly, we have claims for equal chances in the political centre to participate in defining and making society and politics in a way that religious interests, identities and convictions are not excluded (sect. 5.5). The latter claims demand changes in public culture, political institutions, collective political identity definitions and national symbols, and can be expected to meet fiercer resistance (Bauböck 2002; Dassetto 2000 and R. Smith 2003).

5.2   Education and religious diversity

Raising and educating children are the most important ways to transmit religious practices and identities and thereby to perpetuate religious communities. For this reason, religious family law (sect. 4.5) and religious education belong to the most hotly contested issues in modern states. Religious communities and parents, as well as modern state makers and liberal democrats, are intensely concerned with education, and their interests and strategies continue to clash. State makers are concerned with creating and guaranteeing the minimum provision of knowledge and skills required for developing modern societies, such as writing, reading and arithmetic (the 3 R's) and the sciences. In addition, they have (maybe mainly) also been concerned with the production of loyal subjects for the developing nation-state and only much later with the creation of liberal-democratic citizens. Together with armies, schools have been used as crucial anvils of enforced assimilation, intended to eradicate linguistic, ethno-national, religious minority practices and local, parochial and particularist identities. In addition, these three requirements – the societal requirements of 'modernity', the political requirements of 'democracy', and the requirements of 'national unity and identity' – have always been presented as inseparable (e.g. 'one national language') and 'secular' necessities,[1] both in general and with regard to education. Ethno-national and religious minorities may not (have good reasons to) resist teaching basic skills and minimal democracy but they certainly (have good reasons to) resist 'national' and 'secularist' education, which turns schools into instruments of predominant ethnic, national and religious majorities. Properly understood, liberal-democratic morality is incompatible with these practices and liberal democrats have eventually learned that they have been and still are unjustly treating old and new minorities.[2]

   Liberal morality in cultural matters minimally requires making governmental education less majority-biased, less ethno-centred and denomination-centred, more civil/political in order to correct historical cultural injustices with regard to old minorities and create more even-handed chances for new ethnic and religious minorities. However, making governmental education more civil/political does not mean making it culturally 'neutral' because democratic institutions and cultures/virtues are inevitably coloured by particular histories and ethno-religious cultural traditions. Teaching democratic principles, institutions and ethos, therefore, cannot be neutral in two regards. First, old and new ethno-religious minorities have to accept that schools are obliged to teach minimal morality and minimal liberal-democratic morality and virtues (sect. 2.2 and para. 6.1.3.2). Second, they also have to accept that this teaching cannot be done in a way that provides totally equal cultural chances for all, as the myth of fairness as hands-off promises (sect. 2.4).

The history of education in all liberal-democratic countries presents two conundrums because, in practice, minimalist morality is obviously intertwined with maximalist majority bias. First, some illiberal religious minorities may hide their morally illegitimate opposition to teaching minimal liberal democracy behind morally legitimate attacks against religious majority bias of governmental education. This can be studied in the Catholic opposition to predominantly Protestant public education in the US (Handy 1976: 179ff; Miller 1985: 261ff; Laycock 1997; Eisenach 2000; McConnell 2002: 105-118), in the UK, in the opposition of Catholics and Protestants to 'secularist' education (Kalyvas 1996), in recent Muslim opposition to predominantly Christian education in the UK or Germany and 'secularist' public education in France (Koenig 2003, Fetzer & Soper 2005). Second, state administration and professional teacher associations can mask their opposition to critical scrutiny and change of the illegitimate majority bias behind the modernist or liberal myth of neutrality. As all republicans, they may also drastically overestimate the permissible particularism of national education.

Empirically speaking, the great majority of old and new religious minorities in recent Western states do not reject the teaching of the 3 R's, of minimal morality or of minimally understood liberal democracy, although there may be legitimate disagreement about the exact content of these minimal requirements. However, some minorities did and still do, and the respective hard cases have been given so much attention that legal theorists and political philosophers may have lost sight of the practically more urgent issues.[3]

The core issue is how to make education culturally and religiously fairer. I briefly discuss minimally understood liberal moral requirements, bracketing questions like what would be morally and politically desirable from a thicker liberal-democratic view and how to best organise education, issues on which libertarians, liberals, democrats, republicans or associative democrats deeply and reasonably disagree (chap. 10). Here, I focus on matters of curriculum content (para. 5.2.1), on pedagogy and cultures of work and organisation (para. 5.2.2) and on more purely symbolic issues (sect. 5.4). After centuries of struggle, old religious minorities have negotiated institutional settlements and accommodations they have learned to live with or are even content with. New religious minorities recently challenge, and also engage in a renegotiation of these settlements and accommodations, or demand the same rights and treatment as older religions according to the predominant national religious regimes. I discuss 'Muslims in Europe' because of their growing importance in the religious landscape and because of the perceived threats by this traditional 'Other' of the 'Christian Occident'.

5.2.1 Content of education, curricular pluralisation

The content or curriculum of education cannot and need not be completely culturally neutral. The predominant language of teaching has to be the officially recognised language(s). Except in cases of post-colonial migrants, this does not include the languages of immigrants. The literary canon is inevitably and morally legitimately nationally biased; even wide and hotly contested multicultural accommodation does not mean that one could teach world literature without a particular perspective. To some degree, dominant history teaching inevitably excludes the histories of newcomers and the perspectives of other states and nations. Yet, it also commonly excludes the perspectives of most internal minorities (subjugated ethnic, national and religious minorities, sexes, classes and earlier migrants). Rewriting history is as politically contested (*Historiker-Streite*) as rewriting history textbooks. However, even wide and deep accommodation and sensitivity cannot mean that it would be feasible to teach world history from all perspectives. It is also morally legitimate to restrict the perspectives of teaching the history of a particular polity to those whose interests have historically been at stake. Yet, the selection of content and perspective is not completely open or arbitrary. The 'Whig' history of dominant, winning majorities and 'their' state is not only cognitively truncated, it is also morally wrong.[4]

Predominant religion(s) permeate the subjects of teaching history, literature, the arts and civic schooling.[5] They also have a massive impact on teaching religion in religious education classes as opposed to religious instruction classes. Again, it is absolutely impossible to teach all historical and existing religions from all perspectives or from a presumed neutral or simply 'objective' perspective;[6] it is also not morally required. In addition, it is a bad idea (proposed by those secularists who share the feeling that no 'objectivity' is possible with regard to religion) to exclude religious education for this reason from the official curriculum, as is actually the case in many countries. In my view, teaching religion is not qualitatively different from teaching literature, arts or history. For all these subjects, fairness cannot imply fully equal treatment, let alone 'hands-off' neutrality. However, relational neutrality and even-handedness minimally require first that old minorities and losers are not neglected and old injustices are not ignored, let alone reproduced and, second, that new minorities are treated fairly. This includes listening to their voices, which criticise majority bias under the guise of neutrality and secularism,[7] giving them a comparable voice, some say, and fairly equal treatment in all regimes of religious governance that attempt to do this for old religions. Here, as elsewhere, the involvement of counter-experts of ethno-religious minorities in discussing the content of education, standard setting and examinations, etc. helps to unmask unrecognised majority bias (Murphy 2004: 264) and contributes to make education in history, literature, the arts, civics and religions more religiously even-handed and fair. Fairness is thus not monologically declared once and for all (by 'neutral' experts) and/ or imposed by states/majorities but continually renegotiated in a dialogical way (sect. 2.4). All parties involved in this process learn that it is difficult to find fair, sensible, context-specific and feasible compromises.

Understandably, Muslim minorities in the West are primarily concerned with religious education and religious instruction because the majority bias of national educational systems is most visible here. Institutionalised regimes of religious government in Europe with regard to religious education and instruction vary greatly (para. 1.3.3.7), and so do Muslims' claims.

5.2.1.1 Religious education and instruction in governmental schools
Space prevents the discussion of cases that demonstrate the morally illegitimate resistance by educational administration and professional teacher associations,[8] as well as practices of accommodation. Instead, I draw some lessons from comparative evidence regarding religious education and instruction in governmental schools.

First, as can be expected, accommodation is more easy and pragmatic at local levels, as the case of England shows. Although the Education Act of 1944 did not explicitly state that religious education and instruction had to be Christian, this was predominantly the case until the 1960s. 'We speak of religious education, but we mean Christian education'.[9] However, from then on, more attention was paid in syllabi to other religions, partly because representatives of Muslim organisations got seats in the Agreed Syllabus Conferences. In the 1970s, official multi-religious syllabi appeared, thus shifting the balance from religious (i.e. Christian) instruction towards general religious education (Swann Committee 1985). Fierce conservative Christian opposition to these developments eventually succeeded at the national level and the Education Act of 1988 specified that the majority of the acts of collective worship in governmental schools were to be 'wholly or mainly of a broadly Christian character', that 'any agreed syllabus shall reflect the fact that the religious traditions in Great Britain are in the main Christian', and that in religious education the content 'devoted to Christianity in the syllabus should predominate' (DES 1994: 16). According to Fetzer and Soper, however, 'despite the language of the 1988 act, schools have not sought to impose the Christian faith on non-Christian students' (2005: 39). Hence, local accommodation contributed to making majority bias more explicit, at least symbolically, in national legislation, where the Christian identity of the nation is (perceived to be) threatened. However, this did not really prevent flexible, pragmatic accommodation at the local level.

Second, even if no purely 'objective' teaching of religions is possible and the boundaries between religious instruction and education are difficult to draw, they should be more clearly distinguished instead of explicitly blurred as they are in England (Harris 2004: 108f; Gorard 2004: 133ff), Norway (Glenn & Groof 2002: 404-411) and Denmark (Glenn & Groof 2002: 195). Relationally as neutrally and even-handedly as possible religious education classes (informed by comparative history, sociology and anthropology of religions) should be part of the obligatory curriculum of all schools, whether public, semi-public or private. In general, but particularly in contexts of continuing or even increasing internal and global religious diversity, it makes no sense to educate students who are illiterate with regard to other religions. It is pedagogically dubious and morally murky to trust that explicit instruction in one religion as an intended or unintended side-effect serves the purposes of religious education.

Third, if religious instruction were separated from the burden of having to teach religions even-handedly, it would be much easier to answer endless controversial questions: should religious instruction be given in governmental schools? If so, how? Or, should such instruction be totally forbidden, as is the case in France, the US and Switzerland? If religious education were provided evenhandedly, then the arguments against religious instruction in governmental schools seems to be much stronger. Yet, if it is provided as an option in addition to the obligatory curriculum, the moral minimum requires that it should be provided for all religions if enough parents/students ask for it. If religious instruction is made obligatory, as in Germany and Austria, it is additionally evident that meaningful, nondiscriminatory alternative courses in ethics have to be provided for nonbelievers, rather than allowing them to forego attending courses altogether.[10]

Fourth, the case against acts of collective worship in public schools is much stronger because it is hard or impossible to make them really ecumenical for all religious practitioners,[11] and because optional non-participation risks more or less serious social discrimination.[12]

Last, pragmatic piecemeal accommodation to the legitimate wishes of religious minorities as in Britain, is still preferable to no accommodation at all, as in French public schools, where religion is declared a private matter and even multicultural accommodation of curricula of public schools has been extremely slow and half-hearted (Koenig 2003, Fetzer & Soper 2005; Schiffauer et al. 2004; see, however, Willaime 2006 for recent attempts). It seems that open and fair accommodation of governmental education is empirically and also morally related to demands for separate religious schools: the lower the degree of accommodation, the higher the actual demand and the more legitimate the claims (particularly in educational systems that allow) for public funding of religious schools, and vice versa.[13] The logic of this relationship has also been stated by the British Commission for Racial Equality: 'We would estimate ... that the demand for voluntary status would substantially diminish if existing state provision offered and delivered ... schools with a genuine, active commitment to multicultural (and multi-religious! – V.B.), anti-racist and nondiscriminatory education including facilities to meet needs for prayer, diet and dress requirements, as well as particular and organizational matters...' (CRE 1990: 20, quoted in Rath et al. 1996: 227). The commission clearly underestimated the difficulties in 'offer(ing) generous tolerance of religious practices in state schools'.[14] However, even if this could eventually be realised, it does not follow that religious instruction and eventually also public financing of religious schools or even religious schools in general should be banned, as the Swann report proposed (Koenig 2003: 171).

5.2.1.2 Publicly financed non-governmental religious schools

Minimal liberal morality is silent with regard to different possible ways of pluralising education in general, religious education in particular. Furthermore, contextualised theory suggests that there is no one best, context-independent way of doing it. For example, governmental schools only; allowing 'private' but not publicly funded education; or a mixture of governmental and publicly financed schools on a religious or non-religious basis (chap. 10). Bracketing for the moment the question of whether liberal-democratic states are legally obliged to allow non-governmental education at all (as all liberal-democratic states do) and, if so, whether non-governmental education should not only be indirectly but also directly publicly financed under specified conditions (as nearly all liberal-democratic states – except Bulgaria, Greece, Italy and the US until recently – do), where majority religious schools are recognised and publicly financed, minimal morality and equality before the law require a fair and even-handed treatment of minority religious schools and an end to predominant legal and administrative discrimination, which characterises the practice of non-accommodation or grudging accommodation in countries like France, Britain and Germany.

France has an intricate system of direct and indirect public funding of private schools, attended by roughly 16-20 per cent of all students, 90 per cent of which are Catholic (more than 7.8 per cent of all schools) but consistently resists the financing of Muslim schools (Fetzer & Soper 2005: 85-87). Britain also has a system of state funding of non-governmental religious, voluntary-aided (VA) and voluntary-controlled (VC) schools, overwhelmingly Anglican and Roman Catholic, educating 'nearly a third of all primary school children (29 per cent) and 15 per cent of all secondary pupils. Thirty-five per cent of all primary schools and 15 per cent of all secondary schools are church-related' (Fetzer & Soper 2005: 44; Harris 2004: 93ff). Muslims began establishing their own schools in the late 1970s and the early 1980s (by 2000, 66 Muslim schools were listed, and by 2001, 99 schools, all privately funded). Starting in the early 1980s, some Muslims schools applied for state funding. These applications were turned down on different occasions (Rath et al. 224ff for this painful story, in which the secretary of state claimed that the refusal had nothing to do with the schools being Islamic). Besides the usual administrative barriers, the now well-known ideological reasons were mobilised by the Labour party, the Swann report 1985 ('not in the long-term interest' of ethnoreligious minorities and their children) and by a host of secular and teachers associations all concerned about perceived 'sectarian threat', 'racial' segregation, 'social disaster' and national 'disintegration'.[15] Although the High Court ruled in 1992 that the treatment was 'manifestly unfair' and the Labour government approved the first Muslim state primary school in 1997 and recommended expanding both the number of 'church' schools and their diversity (Green Paper *Schools: Building on Success*, 2001: 48), only two Muslim schools were approved as 'grant-maintained schools' (directly financed by the Ministry of Education) in 2001, compared with the more than 4,700 Church of England and 2,000 Roman Catholic schools, the same number as in Germany, where only 4 per cent of children attend private schools (Fetzer & Soper 2005: 116). Compared with the situation in the Netherlands (full public financing of *bijzondere scholen* – nongovernmental schools on a religious or special pedagogical basis), where 46 Muslim schools are recognised and funded, the conclusion that 'in the end, then, Muslims in Britain were able to use the existing pattern of gradual accommodation of newly arrived religious groups to gain state funding for their schools' (Fetzer & Soper 2005: 46) seems overly optimistic.

This may serve as a first indication that aggressive secularist regimes, such as France, do not live up to the liberal moral minimum because they perform poorly in pluralising the content of education in governmental schools and also do not allow religious instruction. At the same time, they also bluntly discriminate regarding their funding practices between religious schools of old majorities and new minorities. Regimes of institutional pluralism (in Fetzer and Soper's terms: weak or multiple religious establishment) may eventually provide fairer funding and better chances to make the content of public education more neutral because religious minorities have a stake in discussing and determining the content and standards, instead of simply declaring existing curricula of 'secular' governmental schools to be neutral.[16]

5.2.2 Pedagogy and educational cultures

Neither the content nor the pedagogy and organisation of education can be just 'neutral', as modern professional teachers organisations often claim. It is plain that ways of seeing, doing and organising education are deeply culturally impregnated, even apart from religious diversity. Long after 'black pedagogy' was overcome, governmental schools were – and in part still are – dominated by traditional authoritarian, teacher-centred, learning-by-listening pedagogy, attacked by reform pedagogues like Pestalozzi, Steiner, Dalton, Montessori and more radically by Dewey and others. These people tried (in various ways) to replace traditional learning by more student-centred, learning-by-doing pedagogy and by more democratic ways of organising education, giving vitally affected students and parents some say. Non-religious parents, maturing students and obviously religious communities also have strong, morally legitimate pedagogic preferences. Educational systems that do not impose 'one republican model of governmental schools fits all' but allow for publicly funded non-governmental schools under specified conditions seem to have far better chances of responding to these legitimate needs, though trade-offs between pluralism and democracy have to be tackled (sect. 10.1).

As in all cases, there are moral limits to acceptable pedagogies. *Minimal morality* requires that basic needs of students not be violated (e.g. limits to allowable forms of corporal punishment, if any (Harris 2004: 113 for the *Campbell* case), treating students with decent respect and at least learning about equal respect, nondiscrimination and non-repression. It goes without saying that all schools have to live up to the moral minimum and that a liberal-democratic polity has a vital interest in educating democratic citizens as well. The latter legitimises mandatory education for all boys and girls for a minimum number of years, to be democratically decided, although circumscribed exemptions may be tolerable for isolationist or nomadic or otherwise mobile minorities and for home schooling. Imposing liberal-democratic pedagogies on schools to teach *civic-democratic minimalism* is certainly more legitimate than imposing liberal democracy on families. However, it is clearly more contested than the bare moral minimum; it is also very difficult to implement and to control, both in governmental and non-governmental schools. Publicly financed Catholic schools have eventually learned to live up to decent and equal respect and Muslims schools under conditions of public scrutiny have also learned this lesson or will eventually do so.[17]

The great majority of Muslims in Western countries neither oppose teaching of basic skills nor the teaching of liberal democracy. Instead, they have raised two fairly moderate claims of religious accommodation.

First, in state schools, they have asked for the introduction of *halal* food, space for prayer and accommodation for religious holidays for Muslim teachers and students. Moreover, they have raised complaints against girls participating in mixed gender gym classes, and against mixed swimming lessons in particular. They have been opposed neither to the equal chances and equal treatment of girls in education nor to co-education in general. Liberal-democratic morality certainly does not require mixed gender physical education classes or boys and girls sleeping in the same room during overnight field trips, and these demands have eventually been pragmatically accommodated in countries like Britain, Germany, the Netherlands, Canada and the US, though not in France (Fetzer & Soper 2005: 42, 84f, 115f). Liberal-democratic morality, however, requires the accommodation of religious food codes, holidays, room for prayers and dress codes (sects. 5.3 and 5.4).

Second, even if governmental schools eventually accommodate Muslim religious activities in all these regards, Muslim organisations still have legitimate reasons for demanding separate Muslim schools because they think that they create a more comfortable learning environment, stimulating better educational achievements (Fetzer & Soper 2005: 44f for the Bradford Muslim's girl school; see chap. 10 for comparative evidence), and because 'Islam is the ethos of the school, not just a religious education lesson half an hour a week' (Hewitt 2001, quoted in Fetzer & Soper: 2003: 45). This claim should also be accommodated in all educational systems that have publicly funded non-governmental religious schools.

5.3   Pragmatic accommodation of religious minority practices

The practices of new religious minorities guaranteed by religious free-doms place existing regimes of religious accommodation under pressure and involve a variety of practical problems. Pragmatic accommodation is morally required in many areas, in private and public organisations and spaces, involving many issues. It is generally influenced by predominant 'philosophies' or discourses of accommodation or assimilation, and it is moulded by the nation-state's specific regimes of governance of religious diversity.

Inside production and service organisations (in the broadest sense; whether private, semi-private or public), religious minorities claim to make room for practices governed by religious law on food (kosher, halal), dress (turbans, skull-caps, headscarves) and prayer that they perceive as obligatory. Liberal-democratic morality requires some flexible accommodation, involving common problems that have to be resolved: contested and negotiated thresholds (minimal numbers of employees or clients and users for schools, houses of worship, hospitals), flexible adaptation of work rules and schedules,[18] creating special prayer rooms or making existing ones ecumenical, adapting buildings (changing the geographical direction of washrooms) and – most importantly and the most difficult to resolve – some adaptations in cultures of work and organisation.[19] Profit-making organisations under conditions of increased ethno-religious diversity have adapted to these requirements mainly for reasons of efficiency and effectiveness, and programmes and practices of 'managing cultural diversity' are gaining momentum or are at least a managerial hype now in many countries and sectors. Resolving problems of thresholds, time schedules, reconstructing buildings and, particularly, changing cultures of work and organisation in a fair and sensitive way is much harder and more difficult than the symbolically dramatised issue of dress codes, which would in principle allow fairly easy adaptation without (great) monetary cost. Still, public attention has mainly focused on the latter.

Uniforms are imposed for three distinct albeit overlapping reasons: they may be functionally required, they are thought to symbolise impartiality, and they may serve to symbolise (national) identity. Obligatory dress codes can be accommodated if they are required for functional reasons such as safety, hygiene or making functionaries recognisable. Turbans or hijabs for nurses in care institutions and hospitals and, maybe even for intensive care personnel and surgeons in the required white or green or blue colours, can be as hygienic and functional (Parekh 2000: 243-248). If school uniforms, e.g. in Britain, are required for the purpose of fighting social-class distinctions among students, religious headdress like the *hijab* in the colours of the uniform would clearly serve the purpose, though *burkhas* or *chadors* should be banned because they prevent the open communication in classes, as is functionally required (Fetzer & Soper 2005: 41; Parekh 2000, Dutch *Commissie Gelijke Behandeling* – Equal treatment Commission – 2005). If no uniforms are required for teachers, then the reasons for banning a *hijab* cannot be 'functional'.[20] If wearing a uniform in private security services, in police and military forces is required to make policemen or soldiers recognisable, sensitive adaptations of headdress are in principle easy (Sikh turbans in the colours of the uniform of the Canadian RCMP, *hijabs* in the colours of the British or Dutch police force uniforms, Parekh 2000: 243ff). Cases in which uniforms are meant to symbolise neutrality or impartiality, e.g. for judges or clerks, are trickier but even here productive adaptations are possible.[21] Resistance to any sensible adaptations in all cases, as in France, cannot be convincingly grounded in functional requirements or in the requirements of symbolising neutrality or impartiality. Quite to the contrary, it stems from the dramatised need to symbolise national identity (sect. 5.4).

Accommodating ethno-religious diversity within organisations often also requires a sensible and fair interpretation of, or changes to, the rules and practices of *public administrations*. This is particularly true when religious minorities claim space for buildings for separate religious institutions, such as schools, care and healthcare institutions, cemeteries and houses of worship, whether publicly funded or not. All these initiatives require the opportunities to buy property and building permits, which are more (in most European countries) or less (in the US) strictly publicly regulated. Local public administration can facilitate or more or less massively hinder religious minorities by not selling or not allowing the sale of property, by setting parking and traffic requirements, by urban planning, by architectural 'style' requirements, and so on. Obviously, there is a need for mutual adaptation and dialogue; negotiations are unavoidable, and negotiations and deliberations take some time. Comparative research on the building of churches, temples and mosques, however, has abundantly demonstrated unfair, discriminatory treatment of religious minorities (Muslims in particular) in all European countries. In addition, there are remarkable differences between European countries as well as remarkable local differences within countries.[22]

The degree of legalisation of administrative practices varies between countries. However, in all of the countries, the accommodation of religious minority practices requires at least some legal exemptions, adaptations or change. Sikhs require and get exemptions from wearing motorcycle helmets; in New York, Jews are exempted from parking requirements on the Sabbath, Jews and Muslims require exemptions from Sunday closing laws and from laws forbidding their practices of ritual slaughter (Ferrari & Bradney 2000; Bleckler-Bergeaud 2007), while Hindus and Parsis require exemptions from legal regulations of burials and cemeteries, etc.[23] These claims are morally and legally grounded in the 'free exercise' of religion and in the equal treatment of minority religions. Eventually, however, they are accommodated in most liberal states but often very slowly and against massive administrative resistance. Some claims, however, require adaptations or changes of laws as well.

In my view, minimal liberal-democratic morality does not determine whether countries should have special laws against religious hate speech – explicitly prohibiting as unconstitutional the incitement to 'religious hatred or intolerance', e.g. in Cyprus (1960), Yugoslavia (1963), and India, or in blasphemy laws (the Netherlands, the UK) – or whether this should be covered by general anti-discrimination laws.[24] Countries do have a choice here, but if it is included in general anti-discrimination laws, this has to be done in an explicit and outspoken way.[25] If there are special laws, then they have the moral and legal obligation to include minority religions in this protection against religious hate speech superficially legitimated by freedoms of speech.[26] Resistance to doing so is clearly motivated by religious majority bias inscribed in national law and national identity definitions. Countries, at least in my view, are morally free to change their legal regimes, but not at a time and in a way that is clearly discriminatory towards minority religions.[27] Countries are also free to balance tensions between freedoms of political communication (including free speech and free media expression) and anti-discrimination (in this case, protection against religious hate speech) in different ways. However, these balances are morally constrained by minimal thresholds guaranteeing both rights instead of guaranteeing an unlimited 'right to insult', as has become recently fashionable in the Netherlands and Denmark.

5.4 Highly or purely symbolic issues

The history of particular ethnicities and religions is inscribed in practices and symbols of 'national' identity, such as calendars, Sundays, public holidays, street names, public monuments and architectural styles, public rituals and ceremonies, oaths, anthems, flags, national heroes and, as we have already seen, styles of uniforms and education etc. (Parekh 1995: 8, 2000: 235ff; Carens 2000; Bader 1997b: 793ff). Pragmatic accommodation to claims by new religious minorities in the cases we have discussed above may involve difficult adaptations of practices and also financial cost, but resistance has been mostly motivated by the unavoidable 'symbolic costs' (Dassetto 2000: 39). This becomes more obvious in cases of more demanding claims to changing the symbols of national identity, where little financial cost would be involved in the fair accommodation required by freedoms of religion and by principles of relational neutrality and fairness as even-handedness.

Christian Sundays and religious festivals are not simply different from Jewish, Muslim or Hindu equivalents. They have been made official, legally binding public holidays. Claims for exemptions for minorities are moderate claims and accommodating them (as required by any meaningful interpretation of religious freedoms) does not change the religious bias of the rules and symbols of the national centre. Does 're-ligious state neutrality', then, require getting rid of all religious legal festivals and holidays, as all consistent secularists should demand? Or, would it even require getting rid of all legally prescribed days off, as a radical principle of neutrality and a principle of justice as hands-off would suggest? This is what is proposed by radical neo-liberal defenders of a 24-hour, seven-day week and 52-week year economy. Or should we decide on having Sundays, Saturdays or Fridays in referenda or parliamentary majority decisions to be held every 10 years to reflect the changing vitality of religions? Or should we introduce a balanced (annual or per decade) rotation scheme? This seems to be a fairly silly idea because we would all be worse off in the end (Carens 2000: 12). Are dominant religious majorities, then, simply free to impose their rules and practices insensitively on old and new minorities? This clearly collides with minimum standards of fairness. If no cultural and religious 'neutrality' is possible and no complete or strict equality can be achieved for all religions, fairness as even-handedness indicates ways out of such dilemmas. Fairness respects the historically inevitable and symbolically sensitive impact of predominant religious majorities on legally prescribed Sundays and accommodates symbolic claims by new religious minorities. One way to achieve this is to legally prescribe one of the holiest days of prominent new religious minorities as a day off (e.g. the *Id ul-Adha*) either in addition to existing Christian holy days such as Christmas, Easter or Whitsun, or – clearly more demanding and contested – in exchange for one of these or one of the many other Christian festivals.[28] An alternative to avoid unfairness regarding smaller new minorities would be a kind of ecumenical feast for all religions, in addition to or in redefining one of the Christian festivals[29] Yet, this would provoke contested debates on the date and new allegations of unfairness by convinced secularists who might defend a 'day of the republic' as the only legitimate public holiday. India sensibly combines these two alternatives by instituting the major religious festivals of publicly recognised larger religions as public holidays and, in addition, by offering smaller religions optional religious holidays.[30]

All Western states embedded in the Christian tradition have considerable difficulties in accommodating such demands by new minority religions to pluralise the symbols of national identity. However, some, like Poland, are clearly more reluctant than others, depending on the degree to which religious traditions have been and still are constitutive for national identity definitions and symbols. [31] Fairness in an ethno-religious diverse society has to find sensitive balances between two conflicting, equally legitimate demands, as demonstrated by Parekh for England:

> Like all other societies Britain has a distinct history, traditions, way of life, and so forth, and hence a specific character that makes it the society it is and distinguishes it from others. Among other things it is profoundly shaped by Christianity ... Since Britain cannot shed its cultural skin, to deny the Christian component of its identity in the name of granting equal status to all its religions is unjust (because it denies the bulk of its citizens their history).' But it 'now has a sizeable number of religious minorities with their own distinct histories and traditions ... The minorities are an equal and integral part of British society, and deserve not only equal religious and other rights but also an official acknowledgement of their presence in both the symbols of the state and the dominant definition of national identity.' (1996: 19). 'The only way to reconcile these two demands is both to accept the privileged status of Christianity *and* to give public recognition to other religions. Christianity may therefore rightly remain the central part of British collective identity, provided that other religions receive adequate though not necessarily equal recognition in the institutions, rituals and ceremonies of the state (20).

As we have seen above, England has serious difficulties with changing its blasphemy law and pluralising the interpretation of the Establishment of the Anglican Church, although this might eventually and grudgingly happen.[32] Weak establishment, as well as plural establishment and non-constitutional pluralism, clearly allows some pluralisation of the symbols of the political centre, though not without resistance.

Ironically, at least one version of 'strict separationism' (non-establishment and private pluralism), i.e. the French republican as the most outspoken secularist of all Western states, is fairly inimical to such pluralisation as the rejection to pluralise holy days and, in particular, the debate and eventual ban of the *foulard* '*dans les écoles, collèges et lycées publics*' clearly demonstrate.[33] The Conseil d'État ruled on November 27, 1989 that the wearing of symbols, including the hijab, is 'not in itself incompatible with the principle of *laïcité* since this display constitutes one's exercise of the liberty of expression and the right to indicate one's religious beliefs'.[34] This liberty however does not extend to symbols that 'by their ostentatious or protesting character... disturb the order or normal functioning of public services'. Five years later, this ambiguous guidance was reaffirmed by minister Bayrou. As a result, the situation on the ground varied dramatically from no objections against wearing the hijab to expulsion of Muslim students for refusing to remove it, depending on the orientation of the particular principal. 'The overall result ... is that since 1989 many Muslim girls and young women in France have been deprived of a normal public education' (Fetzer & Soper 2005: 80). However, despite 'passionate media and political debates, perhaps half of the judges in these cases have overruled the principal and reinstated the student. This has been especially so since the Conseil d'État ruled in 1997 that the hijab is not in itself 'ostentatious' (81).

In 2003, the 'commission de réflexion sur l'application du principe de *laïcité*, the Stasi commission, advised banning the hijab as an ostentatious symbol from *'les écoles, collèges et lycées publics'*. This advice has been included in a law proposal by the government (*'Project de loi encadrant, en application du principe de laïcité* etc.') and also by the Conseil d'État (22 January 2004). On 10 February 2004, French parliament made it a binding law with 494 votes against 36, provoking a heated international debate and fierce criticism mainly by Anglo-Saxon lawyers and public intellectuals.

The main reasons for changing law and policies were initially to overcome the inherent ambiguity and the resulting diversity of decisions characterising the previous situation and, secondly, to overcome claimed changes in practices of wearing *hijab*. The Stasi commission claimed that wearing *hijab* has increasingly been imposed by force or social pressure (by parents, peers and fundamentalist groups) and that the state has a constitutional obligation to protect the freedom of Muslim girls not to wear *hijab*. Distinct from commentators who celebrate the law 'as a legitimate and affirmative expression of French *laïcité* even in an ideal world (Carens 2004),[35] Weil claims that conflicting freedoms regrettably had to be 'balanced'. This balance means the freedom of conscience and expression for those who voluntary choose to wear *hijab* and the freedom of minors from being forced to wear *hijab*. Weil acknowledges that the law makes some Muslim children choose between dressing in a way that they regard as religiously obligatory and receiving a free public education, but defends this with two arguments. First and generally, freedom of religion has to be balanced against other, maybe more important, human rights, like equality between the sexes that gained more prominence since the 1999 revision of French Basic Law, or protection against violence, particularly against minors. Secondly and specifically, by reference to contested facts on different forms of social pressure, 'from insults to violence'. Weil is convinced that the law conforms with European Human Rights and points to the ruling of the ECHR that recognised the right of Turkey to ban the scarf from universities.[36] In addition, he is convinced that the proportionality requirement has also been fulfilled. I agree with the most important moral and prudential points of criticism raised by Carens (2004) against both the law and Weil's defence.

First, the balancing of competing rights is wrongly described. In this case, the right to individual religious freedom does not conflict with a 'right not to wear *hijab*' because there is no legal obligation to wear *hijab* in the first place. The conflicting right in question is the right of all, but particularly of vulnerable minors, not to be physically coerced against their own will.

Second, if some girls are forced to wear *hijab* against their will, the 'solution to that is for the state to protect them from coercion,[37] not to impose its own coercion on others. A general ban on *hijab* for all to prevent some from being coerced is the moral equivalent of (the American) practice of detaining people who belong to certain ethnic and religious groups because they think some members of those groups may be dangerous'. If the intention is not only to protect girls against physical violence but against all kinds of social pressures 'that children often feel from their parents and their communities ... then it is a much more problematic basis for restricting freedom of conscience'.

Third, an unintended side effect of the law is that it imposes choices on some Muslim girls 'between dressing in a way that they regard as religiously obligatory and receiving a free public education'. The law clearly violates the basic right of girls to equal educational chances, a basic need and right that should be protected by the state, particularly if sex and gender equality figures more prominently now in its own revised Basic Law. I have rejected the argument that a serious conflict of basic rights would be involved in this case. However, even if one would accept this argument, the law would clearly strike the morally wrong balance because it leads 'to greater restrictions on the freedom of the very girls it is designed to protect' (Carens 2004). This is particularly severe because, as we have seen, the French state still does not finance private Muslim schools that might provide an alternative way to satisfy this basic need. Weil's argument that 'in the French system, religious pupils – Catholics, Protestants, Jews – can go to religious schools... subsidized by the state' is hypocritical because the 'need to have some Muslim schools' may not have frightened the Stasi commission but has still not been realised.[38] Putting some of the other recommendations into practice – more respect for *halal* food, or pluralising the content of public education – would still not resolve this dilemma.

Fourth, the law is not only unjust, it is also unwise. I address only two unintended consequences that are important for prudential evaluations. The law has to treat all 'ostensible signs' of all religions equally, banning not only *hijabs*, but also turbans, *yarmulkes* and ostentatious crosses, although it is clearly intended only against Muslim symbols. This has raised opposition from all of the affected religions as a further indication that the French 'secular' state infringes upon basic religious freedoms. In addition, many fear that – contrary to the goal of reinforcing a 'moderate Muslim majority' – the law will strengthen Muslim fundamentalism in France. It may still be too early to judge whether this is true. However, if it is 'likely that Muslims in France will not experience this law as a form of reaching out' (Carens 2004), this is a particularly serious consequence because it undermines an implementation '*dans un ésprit de dialogue et de médiation*' (Weil 2004).

Fifth, the law does not demonstrate the new openness to diversity that is claimed to characterise *laïcité plurielle* because most other recommendations of the Stasi commission, particularly those with regard to changes in public holy days, have been dropped without producing an outcry by the proponents of new republican assimilationism.

In the end, *laïcité plurielle, positive, de gestion* (Willaime 2004: 328ff) seems to be more of the same old aggressive *laïcité de combat* that is still predominant among French teacher's unions, French feminists, philosophers and political theorists. The path-dependent pattern of state-religion relationships in France largely explains why *laïcité* has been invoked as a substitute for, and an inversion of its nationalised, 'Gallican' Catholicism[39]. It also explains why the 'neutrality' of public education has been (and still is) the most contested field in debates and policies, although recommendations (by the Stasi commission, by Weil and others) to ban 'ostentatious signs' also in universities, hospitals and so on demonstrate the inherent 'logic' to 'neutralize' all public spaces – 'the naked public square' – known from American debates and practices.

5.5   Representation in the political process

Resistance to the pluralisation of public culture and of symbols of national identity is considerable in all existing regimes of governance of religious diversity because the centre of the nation-state is at stake. Resistance may be particularly strong as a reaction against a perceived threat of pluralisation of cultures and of shifting and overlapping identities in the course of immigration, in addition to perceived threats that

already characterise our age of simultaneous devolution and trans-na-
tionalisation. Politically speaking, it unfortunately does not really help
then if one shows (Bader 2001, 2001d) that identity in general does
not follow the logic of zero-sum games, as is often assumed, and that
most rituals, ceremonies and symbols of national identity are not
'pure', reaching back for centuries, but were invented towards the end
of the 19th century (Hobsbawm, Ringer).

In a comparative perspective, it is important to note that – contrary
to the predominant ideology – the two prominent varieties of strict separationism, i.e. France and the US, do not seem to realise higher degrees of actual pluralisation than religious institutional pluralism.
Strict neutrality and full cultural and symbolic equality in these matters
is neither achievable nor desirable. Relational neutrality and fairness as
even-handedness require imaginative adaptations[40] that may finally be
easier to achieve by pluralising existing religious symbols of national
identity. The ideology of strict neutrality makes the recognition of majority bias more difficult and also works against smooth and pragmatic
accommodation, as the comparison between France and Britain
shows.[41]

The main reason why cultural and symbolic accommodation to
claims by religious minorities seems to be eventually easier in religious
institutional pluralism is the same as why accommodation in general
is easier. Institutional pluralism not only respects associational freedoms of religion explicitly, it also creates opportunities for public recognition of religions, for some forms of representation of recognised religions in the political process, and for a variety of forms of cooperation
between religious organisations and government and administration.
Hence, it accommodates the second demanding claim by religious
minorities for fair chances of representation in the political centre in
order to participate in the 'defining and making of society and politics'.
Policies of cultural and symbolic pluralisation are stronger if backed by
policies of institutional pluralism, and the same is obviously true for
all the other exemptions and pragmatic accommodations claimed by
new religious minorities. Inclusion of religious minorities and their organised political presence in debates, negotiations, deliberations and
compromising makes all the difference.

In contrast, strict separationism is inimical to public recognition and
to all forms of representation of religions in the political process, sometimes even also in public debate. Yet, the irony of the French version is
that it turns out to be completely inconsistent: eventually, it is inimical
only to 'autonomous' forms of collective, public interest representation
of religious minorities that are not under strict state control. The various attempts by French governments to create a national representative body of French Muslims, which was finally inaugurated in 2003

under the name *Conseil Français du Culte Musulman (CFCM)* show this dramatically (sect. 8.5). Such state intervention in religious affairs, characteristic for the French republican, 'post-Jacobin' model of assimilation is unthinkable in the liberal American model.[42] French governments, instead, seem to be imitating the religion-politics of Turkey (Diyanet) that has long been criticised by the EU, precisely at a time when the Turkish government seems to be moving in the other direction.[43]

PART IV

INSTITUTIONAL MODELS OF DEMOCRACY AND
RELIGIOUS GOVERNANCE: ASSOCIATIVE DEMOCRACY

Let us take stock. In chapter 4, the moral constraints of religious freedoms and of the accommodation of religious practices have been discussed. Parental or associational freedoms and church autonomy should not trump the basic interests and rights of children, women, dissenters or other internal minorities (sect. 2.2). Violations should be sanctioned by 'external' state intervention, although this is not the only relevant policy. Where church autonomy conflicts with principles and laws of nondiscrimination and equal opportunities, I applied the more demanding, though still minimalist liberal-democratic standards. The same standards guided my debate on relational neutrality and even-handedness (chap. 5).

The first aim of part IV is to highlight the advantages of my conception of differentiated morality. Demanding moral standards of 'autonomy' and 'toleration' (sect. 2.2) cannot be imposed. Instead, persuasion and good practical examples may convince conservative, peaceful fundamentalist religions to voluntarily re-interpret their own best interests. Associative democracy provides good institutional and policy opportunities to combine the protection of basic needs and rights of all, and the protection of minimal liberal-democratic standards, as well as for accommodating divergent religious practices. Furthermore, it may inspire non-liberal minorities to consider more demanding liberal, democratic, and egalitarian moral standards (chap. 7).

The second aim of part IV is to shift the focus from principles, issues and cases towards institutions (sect. 3.5). In chapters 4 and 5, we have seen that the interpretation, application and balancing of conflicting moral principles and legal rights lean on regimes of religious governance and normative policy models. A contextualised theory of morality (sect. 2.5) confronts us with difficult trade-offs and policy dilemmas. There is no 'one size fits all' institutional and policy model. We found many instances of religiously pluralist institutions that provide better chances for religious neutrality of states and policies and fairer and even-handed solutions to accommodating legitimate claims by new religious minorities.

Contrary to the ideology of strict separationism, the review of the variety of regimes of religious governance in constitutional democracies (sect. 1.3) showed that all states reserve a special legal status for (organised) religions, finance them directly or indirectly, and recognise them 'publicly'. In other words, all liberal-democratic regimes (not only the selective cooperation models) show a certain degree of religious institutional pluralism. This is not a sad, yet inevitable deviation from 'model' to 'muddle'. It is a first indication of the normative advantages, the practical wisdom of religious institutional pluralism. This clears the ground for my claims on behalf of associative democracy (AD). It is better than religious corporatism and the clumsy mix of ideological

denial and practical accommodation in France and the US. Education
is an important example (chap. 10). Egalitarian liberals are well advised
to stop their resistance to direct public financing of FBOs in education,
or so I want to show. AD provides an institutional alternative, a Third
Way, a realistic and feasible utopia to escape from the ritualised opposition of strict separation versus corporatism.

As a backdrop to my analysis of relevant normative models of religious governance in chapter 7, chapter 6 combines a general analysis
of institutional models of democracy and the incorporation of minorities with a discussion of non-democratic and democratic institutional
pluralism. Both chapters emphasise the claim that religious associative
democracy provides commendable institutional and policy solutions for
balancing competing moral principles and normative standards of feasibility and effectiveness. In chapter 8, I analyse the dilemmas of institutionalisation, focusing on Islam in Europe and on the US. Again, the
trade-offs between Church autonomy, the equal treatment of religions
and efficiency and effectiveness are best resolved under AD.

The stage is then set for the analysis of the realistic objections to
AD, echoing earlier debates on affirmative action and multiculturalism
(chap. 9). The idea is that AD is a flexible framework for finding sensitive balances and viable trade-offs between competing normative standards. Finally, chapter 10 illustrates the promise of AD in the organisation and governance of education in culturally diverse societies.

6 Moderately agonistic democracy, democratic institutional pluralism, associative democracy and the incorporation of minorities

I defended moral minimalism and minimal liberal-democratic morality against the temptations of democratic maximalism (para. 2.2.2) and indicated a progressive shift from principles and reason restraints towards virtues and institutions. Now, I defend a minimalist threshold of civic and democratic virtues (sect. 6.1). Then, I elaborate the opportunities in institutional pluralism for religious minorities. I discuss different degrees and types of institutional pluralism and compare institutional models of democracy (sect. 6.2) before introducing the general characteristics of associative democracy (sect. 6.3). In section 6.4, I analyse the differences between ethnic and religious diversity and present different models of incorporation of ethno-religious minorities into democratic polities. I end with a comparison of different non-democratic and democratic regimes of institutional pluralism (sect. 6.5).

6.1 Moderately agonistic democracy: virtues and institutions

Liberal reason restraints eventually became more modest and abstract, excluding less and less (sect. 3.5). Instead of trying to defend progressively softer versions of this restraint strategy, I prefer to disconnect the Rawlsian link between the 'limits of reasons' and the virtue of 'civility'. Continuing, moral, cognitive and evidential disagreement among reasonable people is the normal state of affairs. We should try to tell the 'whole truth', as we see it, on whatever topic and whenever and wherever it makes sense, accept that others do the same on an equal footing, use understandable language and discuss issues in a civilised manner. If we cannot and need not hope for a consensus in common sense, in the sciences, and in moral and political philosophy, then we had better focus on civilised and decent ways of living with disagreement. Civic and democratic culture, attitudes or habits, ethos or virtues and traditions of good judgement and practice become crucial; the 'discipline of public reason' is complemented with the discipline of attitudes and the discipline of democratic institutions and practices.

Recently, we have noticed a shift towards virtue ethics, often combined with conservative or traditionalist criticisms (Anscombe, Oakshott and MacIntyre) of 'modern' or 'liberal morality', or, alternatively, with 'postmodern' criticism as in the emerging tradition inspired by the work of Foucault (Connolly 1995, 1999, 2005). [1] The idea is to replace morality with ethos, and principles and rights with virtues and/or duties. Because I think that these replacement strategies are unnecessary and counterproductive, I follow the line of authors in the liberal tradition (Galston, Macedo, Kymlicka and Barber), who defend a productive complementarity of morality and ethos, principles and virtues, rights and duties.

6.1.1 Civic and democratic virtues: why minimalism?

It is increasingly acknowledged that liberal-democratic states are not viable, self-reproducing, let alone flourishing constitutional democracies if they are dependent upon principles, rights and institutions alone. They also presuppose a threshold or a modicum of virtuous citizens (Kymlicka 2002: 287ff). [2]

To begin with, liberal-democratic virtues are more specific than general political virtues (courage, law-abidingness, and loyalty) and 'executive' virtues like initiative, independence, resolve, persuasiveness, diligence and patience (Galston 1991: 221). Liberal-democratic virtues[3] are compatible with reasonable cultural and religious diversity and competing conceptions of the Good Life. They do not prescribe but allow stronger, more participatory conceptions of democracy and the related virtues. They contain only those virtues needed for the smooth reproduction of liberal-democratic polities. They presuppose general competencies or 'skills' (e.g. reading, talking, understanding and interpreting) and minimal 'intellectual virtues' (Murphy 2004: 247, 257f) but cannot be reduced to cognitive skills and commitments.

Civic culture and virtues point to minimally moral or liberal aspects of rule of law, civic rights and the respective duties. Democratic culture and virtues refer to the democratic part of the liberal-democratic compromise. Before defending civic minimalism, I present a long and rough list, an often uneasy mix of competencies and dispositions (attitudes or habitualised motivations), of generic civic-democratic virtues and the virtues of citizens.

The generic liberal-democratic virtues can be grouped into analytically distinct clusters (the respective competencies and dispositions overlap and do not need to be neatly separated).

First, a disposition of habitualised 'self-discipline' (Connolly 2005: 69) and a commitment to refrain from violence and resolve disputes and conflicts through public debate and peaceful decision-making. The corresponding virtues are civility (opposed to torture, cruelty and brutality), moderation or (permission) toleration (Galston 1991: 228; Warren 2001: 73), trustworthiness (Rosenblum 1998) and a sense of 'minimalist justice'. These are basic ingredients for any decent polity, liberal-democratic or otherwise.

Second, a disposition and commitment to discern the equal rights of others, and the restraint to tolerate and respect them. The corresponding virtues of (respect) toleration (sect. 2.2) and mutuality are basic virtues for any liberal-democratic polity. They are linked to basic democratic principles, such as equal liberties, equal respect and concern and the corresponding duties of reciprocity (Rawls 1993: 217, 253; Gutmann & Thompson 1996; Macedo 1991: 265ff and 273; Barber 1984: 189; Galston 1991: 222; Bauböck 1994: 313). The virtue of toleration can be interpreted in a minimalist but crucial way as 'gritted teeth tolerance of some things you hate' (Connolly 2005: 69), and respect can be seen as 'agonistic respect' (2005: 72; 2000: 614; 1995: 191, 234f) or 'agonistic reciprocity' 'between two contending constituencies, each of which has gained a fair amount of recognition and power in the existing order,' instead of more demanding and maximalist interpretations such as 'mutual recognition', 'openness and curiosity', or even 'enthusiastic endorsement of difference'[4] and harmonious conceptions of respect.

Third, we have the related, more demanding 'deliberative virtues' or 'self-governing reflective capacities', such as 'self-esteem, self-criticism, and experimentation' with regard to public debate.[5] Minimally understood liberal democracy does not require people to participate in public debates but if they do, some minimal capacity and commitment of self-criticism is required. More demanding versions would insist that virtues like 'comparative contestability' of our own 'fundamental perspectives' (Connolly 2004: 611; 1999: 8, 39, 186; 1995: 191) are required for a vibrant pluralist debate.

Fourth, deliberative democrats and defenders of an ethos of pluralism add a more demanding habitualised commitment and corresponding virtues (like a willingness to engage in public debate, a willingness to listen to 'strange and even obnoxious' views), and to engage in persuading others. Again, there are more minimal (Galston 1991: 227) and more demanding versions of these virtues, like Barber's 'mutualistic art of listening' (1984: 174ff; see 182ff), Gutmann and Thompson's virtues like 'civic integrity' and 'civic magnanimity' (1996: 79ff), and Connolly's virtues of 'reflective engagement' (2005: 73, 83; 1995: 5f, 9, 36, 39, 186), 'relational modesty', 'reciprocal forbearance', and 'critical responsiveness'.

Fifth, the capacity and commitment to narrow the gap between liberal-democratic principles and practices: a virtue required to deal productively with the under-determinacy of principles (Galston 1991: 227).

Last, in addition to these input- and throughput-oriented virtues, output-oriented virtues (accepting majority decisions and accepting the time limits and process costs of democratic procedures) are required. Nonetheless, they are blatantly absent from most discussions among political philosophers.

In addition to these generic civic and democratic virtues, citizens should be able to evaluate candidates for office and their performances critically (stressed by conservatives and 'realistic' democrats) and they should be able and willing to at least minimally participate in politics. The participation ladder ranges from the minimal moral or political duty to vote during elections, to participation in public debate on many levels, membership and or leading positions in political parties, representative and administrative public bodies, and so on. Libertarian and liberal theories of democracy require a bare minimum of participation, whereas all of the more 'voice-centred' theories urge more demanding, clearly less anti-perfectionist virtues of participation in talk and action.

This is a very long list (Warren 2001: 73) of ever more demanding and perfectionist civic, democratic and even 'interculturalist' virtues. For my purpose, three arguments are crucial: anti-perfectionism, the relation between regimes and virtues, and how virtues are acquired.

So, what about anti-perfectionism? Demanding democratic and inter-culturalist virtues are at odds with anti-perfectionist virtues. The latter, however, are needed to gain some agreement amongst defenders of competing comprehensive doctrines and ways of life. In para. 2.2.2, I discussed the tension between moral minimalism and democracy's drive towards congruence. Moral minimalism urges us to keep the list of virtues as sober and short as possible. It is urgent to distinguish the minimal virtues required for the functioning of minimally decent polities; the virtues required for the functioning of minimally understood liberal-democracies; the morally laudable political virtues (from the perspective of realising democracy as a prominent or even paramount aspect of a Good Life), and conducive to the 'flourishing' of democratic polities; and the virtues of 'inter-culturalism' or 'pluralism'.

Aggregative, vote-centred theories of democracy are content with the bare minimum of citizenship virtues. Deliberative, voice- and action-centred theories require thicker concepts of democratic political culture, habits and virtues, and of virtues of participation in particular. Deliberative democrats focus on the cluster of deliberative virtues of citizens and also try to pluralise public debate by including gender, ethno-national and religious diversity.[6] Strong democrats more outspokenly complement speech with judgement and action of citizens (Barber 1984: 177f, 209ff) and try to empower citizens through direct democratic political institutions. In addition, proponents of empowered democracy (Unger 1987; Fung & Wright 2003) argue that socio-economic and institutional empowerment is a precondition for a well-functioning political democracy. Empowering citizens includes proposals to include all affected stakeholders. Proponents of associative democracy share and further elaborate the emphasis on the inclusion of relevant stakeholders in speech, decision-making and implementation. They differ in their respective emphasis on 'deliberation' and 'consensus' (Cohen & Rogers: Cohen; Cohen & Sabel), as opposed to compromise, negotiation cum deliberation (Zeitlin 2005) and agonistic speech. They also differ in their emphasis on strong political participation compared to a voluntarist and minimalist conception and a more flexible and sober relationship between voice and exit (Hirst 2001; Bader 2005). Finally, they differ in the hope (e.g. Rosenblum 1998, Warren 2001) placed on associations as seedbeds of democratic virtues (para. 6.1.2). Appropriate regimes of toleration or liberal democracy (rules of the game and institutions) are more important than virtues. Simply put, the better the regimes the fewer virtues that are required: citizens need not be heroes. For liberal-democratic polities in normal conditions, a threshold of civic democratic virtues, maybe combined with some more demanding political virtues, seems enough. Instead of requiring, teaching or even imposing the full set of demanding virtues, it may suffice that only some people are more virtuous, given that all live up to the required minimal threshold. The hard question is whether this will do in emergency conditions when regimes are threatened (sect. 9.8).

Finally, how are virtues acquired? Although learning competencies or skills through formal teaching in schools may be hard enough and require 'learning by doing', teaching the right kinds of attitudes, dispositions, commitments (forming the character of people) is even harder. In addition to learning by doing and the right kinds of everyday interactions, it requires the right kind of 'family' and primary socialisation.

6.1.2 Seedbeds of liberal-democratic virtues

Virtuous citizens do not fall from heaven, nor are they the inevitable side effect of 'shared' principles. They also do not flow quasi-automatically from living in appropriate institutional settings (as many happy institutionalists believe). Institutionalists are right to stress that institutions have more structuring power than principles or virtues in the medium or long term, and that policies to change institutions are more important and feasible than moral pedagogy.[7]

Still, virtues have to be learned and acquired. This can be achieved in four different and overlapping ways. Primary socialisation and intentional schooling come first by inculcating the appropriate virtues and through participation in appropriate practices. Second, learning democracy by doing, i.e. by participating in democratic (political) institutions. Third, learning civic and democratic virtues by participating in the many associations of 'civil society'. Fourth, learning civic and democratic virtues through everyday interaction with demographically widely heterogeneous people (class, gender, age, colour, ethnic and religious origin) in organisations and, particularly, in public spaces (neighbourhoods, cities). Here, I proceed from the assumption that the second road is the most promising since families and schools, as well as civil associations and work organisations create democratic virtues only if they actually practice democracy internally. I only address the third and fourth ways here: most democratic theorists interested in civic-democratic virtues inject high hopes in these 'schools of democracy' or 'seedbeds of virtue'.

Many contend that, in a vibrant civil society, participation in various voluntary associations is an important seedbed of civic and democratic virtues.[8] Rosenblum (1998; 2002: 148f, 163ff) has criticised the liberal, communitarian, deliberative and associative democratic assumptions about the effects of associational life on the moral dispositions of members personally and the consequences for liberal democracy. Neither the optimistic liberal expectations about associations as schools of civic virtues and simplistic transmission belt models of civil society, nor its opposite (the widespread pessimism in the tradition of Rousseau and Madison about associations as a dangerous threat to liberal democracy and a seedbed of particularist vices) are theoretically plausible or empirically corroborated. Rosenblum convincingly shows that the 'moral valence of group life is indeterminate' and that 'no general theory of the moral uses of pluralism' (1998: 17) can be expected. She rightly warns about the 'liberal democratic logic of congruence' (36ff), particularly by legal enforcement, as if the prime purpose of associations would be to produce virtuous citizens.

In the present context, her insight that associations, indifferent or even adverse to liberal public culture, can actually have beneficial moral effects is important. By containing vices, these associations are a kind of safety valve, and they help develop basic virtues like self-control, cooperation, trust, generosity and civility.[9] The argument is convincingly extended to workplaces, where demographically diverse people are bound to work together. 'Even hierarchically organised, non-union workplaces can foster social ties and civic skills that are essential in a diverse democratic society' (Estlund 2003: 137). Whether associations help to develop civic virtues depends on many factors (the kind of associations, the ease of exit and the goods provided, etc. See Warren 2001, tables 5.1, 6.1 and 6.3; see also Fung 2003). We cannot draw general conclusions, although some of Rosenblum's expectations are indeed corroborated: most associations contribute to the learning of self-restraint and civility.

Many sociologists and political theorists contend that moderation, self-restraint, trustworthiness and toleration are learned by regular and continuing everyday interacting with widely 'heterogeneous' people (the fourth way) in all types of organisations – (public or private) schools, armies, profit or non-profit organisations for goods and services – and, particularly, in public spaces (neighbourhoods, cities).[10] Even this simple 'contact hypothesis' must be qualified. Whether the effects of interaction are beneficial depends partly on the voluntariness of interaction and on contextual variables such as (the absence of) threats, (patterns of) discrimination, socio-economic inequalities and negative-sum games (sects. 9.4 to 9.6). Everyday interaction in global cities or mixed neighbourhoods, for example, certainly involves contacts among strangers and fosters conscious awareness of the 'other', but it does not automatically encourage toleration and political openness to the stranger's views and claims.[11]

In summary, principles, rights and procedures are not enough to guarantee decent or liberal-democratic polities, and institutions, associations and everyday interactions do not automatically generate the appropriate and minimally required virtues. Virtues have to be learned by moving back and forth between practices, institutions and principles, and between 'moral pedagogy' and appropriate institutions. In addition, appropriate institutions and interactions for learning depend on crucial contextual conditions: even democratic institutions breed democratic virtues only if these conditions are not too inimical.

6.2 Institutional models of democracy: degrees and types of institutional pluralism

Political equality, political liberty, political autonomy and participation are the operative principles of all modern types of democracy. As principles, they do not determine specific institutional forms of democracies. Actual institutional types and normative models of democracy – e.g. libertarian, liberal, deliberative, republican, strong, empowered, associative democracy (Cunningham 2003; Engelen & Sie 2004: 28-34) – are usually mixed to combine different options. These emerge along four axes: (i) aggregative or vote-centric (libertarian and classical liberal democracy) versus deliberative or voice-centred models (deliberative democracy); (ii) representative versus direct democracy; (iii) institutionally monist versus pluralist democracy; (iv) purely civic-political versus thick ethno-religious democracy. Modern liberal democracies are compatible with different degrees of deliberation and participation, although all have to be minimally aggregative and anti-paternalist; they are all representative, although they allow for ingredients of direct democracy; they all have to be civic-political, although they show considerable variety in actual relational neutrality; and they show much variety in the degree of institutional pluralism. For my discussion of the relationship between religious diversity and democratic polities, the third and fourth axes are crucial. In this section, I distinguish institutional models on the basis of different degrees and types of institutional pluralism. In sections 6.4 and 6.5, I add and integrate the fourth axis.

Existing democratic polities show various degrees of institutional pluralism. That has been convincingly demonstrated by comparative research in political science (cf. Lijphart's, 1984, ideal typical distinction between majoritarian and consensus models or Schmidt's, 2006, comparison of simple and compound polities). All majority-restraining elements – executive power sharing (coalition governments); separation of powers, balanced bi-cameralism, multi-party system, multi-dimensional party system, proportional representation, territorial federalism and decentralisation, written constitution, some 'separation' of state and church, of state and society, of public and private – are devices of political pluralism. Predictably, these are opposed by majoritarian and institutionally monistic thinkers, but their ideal model does not even exist in the quite majoritarian 'Westminster' democracy.

Mapping the diversity of institutionally plural arrangements requires a general definition of institutional pluralism. Broadly understood, Institutional Pluralism (IP) is defined by a combination of two core characteristics: (i) the existing plurality or diversity of categories, groups, organisations or political units, formally recognised and integrated into the political process of problem definition, deliberation, decision alternatives and decision-making, implementation and control.[12] (ii) a fair amount of actual decentralisation. If institutionally pluralist designs imply hierarchical subordination of units, these units should have a fair amount of de facto autonomy or 'self-determination' (whether formalised and constitutionalised or not) to decide specific issues.

All institutionally pluralist arrangements can thus be characterised as power-sharing systems. The power of states (public hierarchies), of private property and of management ('private hierarchies') must be divided, delegated and delimited. This requires a conceptual break with notions of absolute, unlimited, undivided sovereignty and property, and a theoretical break with monistic, unitarian or simply majoritarian normative strategies.[13]

The vast and complex range of practices of IP can be divided into three basic types, according to three major, analytically distinct arenas of representation: political/territorial, social/functional, and minority pluralism.

First, political/territorial pluralism: power-sharing systems in territory-bound units like Lijphart's 'consensus-democracies', given the hypothetical condition that ethno-religious or national pluralism and social/functional pluralism are absent.

Second, social/functional pluralism: the representation of classes, professions, elites, producers, consumers and clients in the political process in different societal fields and organisations such as firms, schools and hospitals at different levels (e.g. sectoral, regional, national and supra-national neo-corporatist councils). Analytically, it is completely distinct from political and from minority or ethno-religious/national pluralism. In practice, it is only possible in combination with political pluralism.

Third, minority pluralism: the main form of institutional representation of ascriptive minorities in different fields and at different levels. This is analytically independent of social/functional and political pluralism, but in practice only possible in combination with political pluralism (see also Safran 2003). When ethno-religious minorities are sufficiently territorially concentrated, this type of pluralism tends to merge with federalist political pluralism. For territorially dispersed ethno-religious minorities and for all other ascriptive minorities, such as women, lesbians and gays, the latter is the only available type of group representation.[14]

Combined with a multi-level approach[15] these types of IP can be graphically represented, as shown in Figure 6.1.

The distinction between *political* and *functional representation* is fairly well established.[16] Territorial representation of national minorities (and their respective models of ethno-national federalism) has a known history as well. However, institutional design and practical experiments with ascriptive minority IP and models of 'tertiary' or 'multicultural' citizenship (Kymlicka 1995) are less known, although they reach back to the early decades of the 20th century ('mixed federations' proposed by Austro-Marxists).[17] Consociational democracy (Lijphart 1984) covers ethnic and national, and also religious groups, associations and organisations. Models and practical experiments with institutional representation of other ascripitive minorities (mainly of women and homosexuals) emerged only recently under the broad and somewhat misleading headings of 'multiculturalism', 'group rights' and the politics of 'difference' or 'identity'.

It is not easy to compare the normative models of democracy, i.e. libertarian, liberal, deliberative, republican, strong, empowered and associative democracy, on their positions on institutional pluralism. Some are unspecified or simply blank. Roughly, the following picture emerges.

All allow a minimum of territorial pluralism, although majoritarian and institutionally monist or 'statist' trends are strongest in republicanism, particularly in French republicanism. Libertarianism and liberalism are less majoritarian and allow for higher degrees of institutional pluralism; they usually insist on a fairly strict separation of state and

Figure 6.1   *Arenas and levels of representation*

Levels / Arenas	Local	Regional/ provincial	State	Supra-state
Political/ territorial pluralism	neighbourhood city (council, administration)	regional legislation, administration and jurisdiction	federal legislation, administration, jurisdiction	EUP, Council, Commission, Committee of the Regions, etc.; Global Institutions
Social/ functional pluralism	firm, hospital, school, university; corporate governance	regional chambers of industry, (neo-) corporatist councils etc.	federal neo-corporatist councils	TNCs, Economic and Social Council of the EU; EGAs
Ascriptive minority pluralism	ethno/religious neighbour-hoods etc.	regional minority institutions, councils etc.	federal institutions of ethno/religious or national minorities	trans-national ethno/ religious communities and institutions

Representations of territorially dispersed ascriptive minorities (such as immigrants, women, homosexuals, elderly) in different societal fields and at different levels

church, state and society, public and private. The implied and neat borderlines get blurred in deliberative and empowered democracy. Associative democracy is explicitly anti-majoritarian and institutionally pluralist in all regards.

Social pluralism is rejected by republicans, libertarians, liberals and also by most deliberative democrats. It is allowed by empowered democracy and it is central to associative democracy.

Ascriptive minority pluralism is again rejected by republicans and by most liberals, although 'liberal nationalism' and 'liberal multiculturalism' create important openings, which is also characteristic for some deliberative and empowered democrats. Associative democracy is most conducive to diverging forms of representation of ethno-national and religious minorities, and creates most opportunities for territorially dispersed minorities.

6.3 Associative democracy

Against this background, it is now time to present a short outline of the core elements of associative democracy (AD) as a flexible, moderately libertarian variety of democratic institutional pluralism (Hirst & Bader in Hirst & Bader 2001; Hirst 1994 for a full elaboration). AD combines all three dimensions of institutional pluralism. While not prescribing definitive, specified institutions of territorial-political pluralism, it does favour as many power-sharing elements as are compatible with the stability and minimal unity of democratic polities (sect. 9.8 for contextual constraints). Compared with other types of democracy, AD is driven by the conviction that all those relevantly affected by collective political decisions are stakeholders, and thus have a say, both for reasons of meaningful democratic representation and in particular for reasons of governmental effectiveness and efficiency. AD favours multi-level government (not restricted to the devolution of powers to states, provinces and municipalities but also beyond 'nation states'). It attempts to keep central government strong and minimal, and restrict government to its core tasks.

The implied 'shifts from government to governance' are stimulated by the institutional design of social pluralism. Social services (education, healthcare and other kinds of care) should be primarily provided by self-governing associations. AD takes full account of the fact of reasonable pluralism and argues that different contents and styles of provision of social services should (be allowed to) go along with different versions of the good life. Services should be public and publicly funded, open to all, but largely non-governmental. Associations should be free to compete with one another for members for the services they provide, and members would bring public funds with them according to a common per capita formula: a voucher system, weighed to correct for serious inequalities, on top of a certain minimum of direct public financing. Therefore, far from there being one welfare state (one bureaucratic formula fits all), there would be as many as citizens wanted to organise, catering to the various lifestyles of individuals and groups, but based on common entitlements. Such organisations would ideally be democratically self-governing (see sect. 7.4 for exemptions). Some might be highly participatory, involving all of the relevant stakeholders (including clients) in their internal decision-making procedures (giving them a voice), others would be more minimalist. However, all of them would have the basic right to elect the governing council, and members would periodically have the option to exit if dissatisfied. Besides traditional neo-corporatists forms of interest representation, associations and their roof organisations play an important role in public standard setting and scrutiny of services and should be flexibly involved in the political process, depending on groups, societal fields and issues.[18]

Associational service provision is a new format, for ethnic and religious groups wanting to set up their own schools, hospitals and institutions to care for children, elderly, handicapped and poor people as well. In this way, AD stimulates minority pluralism, guaranteed by a strong interpretation of associational freedoms and the proposals to represent the interests of different minority groups in the political process. In the same vein, it provides meaningful exit options for minorities within minorities, thus contributing to voluntarism and plural, crosscutting membership in associations.

6.4 Incorporation of ethno-religious diversity

6.4.1 Ethno-religious diversity and state neutrality. Is religious diversity really so different from ethnic diversity?

Normative models of liberal democracy should be relationally neutral. Actual liberal-democratic polities pretend to be neutral. Both, however, vary in the degree of relational state neutrality and may prove either inimical or open to cultural diversity. Modern societies are characterised by various overlapping, field-specific, contested and changing cultural practices: class, elite and occupational cultures; gender and generational cultures; ethnic, religious and national cultures. Here, I address the cluster of ethnic-national and religious cultures, summarising some results of critical sociological and anthropological studies.

For descriptive and prescriptive purposes, one should distinguish ascriptive *categorisation* based on socially defined biological, physiological or phenotypical characteristics (descent, sex, age, skin colour) and on socio-historical characteristics (clustered together in the contested concept of ethnicity, Bader 1995: 63ff; 1997c: 104-117). The respective practices of discrimination, oppression, exploitation and exclusion as well as their ideological legitimisations are not the same. The residual concept of ethnicity masks relevant distinctions among – broadly speaking – 'ethnic minorities'. Indigenous peoples (First Nations), national minorities, ethnic-immigrant minorities, religious minorities, and obviously, gender and social class minorities differ from each other on criteria of historical and continuing injustice (Williams 1998), in degrees of territorial concentration or dispersion, degrees of voluntariness or involuntariness of incorporation into the polity (para. 4.2.1). One size of institutionally pluralist incorporation does not fit all.[19]

Belonging to ascriptive categories or groups is not voluntary. Even critics of liberalism such as Hirst or Rosenblum have difficulties in accounting for the basic fact that freedom of choice is absent, and for its consequences for models of incorporation.[20] Individuals do not choose their associational ties or cultures but are born into and raised within them, and this socialisation 'either through involuntary or nonvoluntary association in groups' (Eisenberg 1995: 171) is partly constitutive of the individual 'in the sense that no self exists apart from these constitutive elements. These attachments are ones that the self can come to understand and reflect on but cannot choose to keep or to discard' (177). Voluntary affiliations 'preserve the individual's autonomy to change her values and dispositions'; non-voluntary affiliations 'one has from birth or are formed in circumstances in which an individual cannot exercise volition'; 'involuntary is an association that the individual actively rejects but, at the same time, cannot avoid because the association is linked to a characteristic that she possesses nonvoluntarily, such as being a woman or Black, and this characteristic influences how she is treated by others'.[21] 'Race, culture, or gender constitute one's self regardless of one's choice in the matter' (179). Three important normative consequences follow.

First, there is no escape from being ascriptively categorised by others, although there are important differences in terms of 'visibility' and inescapability between biologistic ascriptions like sex, 'race', age, handicaps (biology is destiny) and cultural/historical ascriptions (Bader 1998b).

Second, exit rights do not guarantee real exit options when individuals' affiliations and identities are constituted in part by non- or involuntary associational ties that can be too deep to sever.[22] Again, there are important differences between gender, linguistic and religious cultures/habits/identities. Realising exit options from communities can be extremely costly because of (the threat of) ostracism, and even exit from organisations has its price (e.g. weakening minorities politically).

Third, we must be precise in defining ascriptive categories, groups, communities, associations and conflict organisations, and constituencies. *Groups* are constituted by a minimal awareness of the fact of ascriptive categorisation by others – whether they share common cultural practices or not – whereas *communities* are constituted by a certain minimum of shared cultural practices. These may be absent in conflict groups with shared interests to end ascriptive categorisation, discrimination, oppression, exploitation or exclusion (Bader 1995, 2001b). In addition, one may or may not – more or less voluntarily – become or remain a member of an *association or organisation*, but membership talk relating to ascriptive groups is as misleading as it is relating to class. One is categorised by others, one belongs to a class.[23]

Religious diversity (and the formation of religious groups or communities) is now often said to be fundamentally different from ethnic and

national diversity and group formation. In the former case, membership and 'belonging' would be voluntary, based on freedom of choice.
As we have seen, Hollinger opposes the 'application to religious affiliations of the ethnic-minority paradigm' because it leads to institutional
separation and is based on ascriptive instead of voluntary membership.
His proposal to 'apply to ethno-racial affiliations a religious paradigm'
takes for granted that religious affiliation is free (1996: 123f; 2003; see
also Walzer 1997). This, widely shared assumption is empirically untenable. It also has unwelcome, crypto-normative implications.

First, it discards all 'ethnic' religions such as Orthodox Judaism, Hinduism, Shintoism, Confucianism and most 'tribal' religions.[24] Instead,
it (implicitly) favours a highly individualised, subjectivised and de-culturalised conception modelled after an idealised picture of radical Protestantism (para. 1.2.2).

Second and quite generally, religious self-descriptions or identifica-
tions are not freely chosen. One is either born into and raised with religious practices that have an impact upon later choices (e.g. Anabaptism, 'born again', apostasy, heresy or reactive militant atheism), or one
is born into and raised in other religions or non-religious practices that
impact on later choices (e.g. conversion of mature believers). Voluntarism and choice are matters of degree.

Third, categorisation or definitions of religious belonging by others
are surely beyond voluntarism. Belonging to a religious category can
be as ascribed as belonging to 'race', gender, social class, *ethnie* or nation. In this perspective, one cannot choose one's religion as one cannot choose one's ethnie or nation or one's 'race' or sex.[25] Moreover, ascriptive categorisations usually come in clusters and influence, and are
influenced by the predominant cultural patterns of discrimination and
the (political) opportunity structures. Immigrant minorities are racia-
lised or ethnicisised in countries like the UK (making immigrants
from different religions and countries into 'Blacks' or 'Asians') and Sin-
gapore; they are religionised in countries like the Netherlands (making
immigrants from different ethnies – e.g. Moroccans and Berbers – and
countries into 'Muslims').[26]

Fourth, these definitions by others have a paramount impact on self-
definitions, on the formation of groups, communities and collective
identities. They often lead to reactive ethnicisation or religionisation, as
is evident in the development of Islamicist fundamentalism in the
West. Religious groups and religious communities are not just given,
they are created.[27]

Fifth, the emergence and reproduction/transformation of ethnic
communities, defined by a certain minimum of linguistic and ethno-
cultural practices, and of religious communities sharing a certain minimum of religious practices overlap and have an impact on each other,

became indistinguishable in many cases.[28] Upon occasion, however, the theoretical and practical distinction is crucial.[29] The understanding of the overlap between ethnic and religious cleavages and their consequences for conflicts is a case in point (sects. 9.7 and 9.8).

And lastly, diverging regimes of religious governance have a considerable impact on changing religiosity: American denominationalism contributes to making Catholicism, Hinduism and Islam more congregationalist and heightens the degree of voluntary affiliation (Casanova 2005: 24f), and French *laïcité* may or may not lead to a de-ethnicised, de-culturalised and more individualist 'French Islam' (sect. 8.5). The empirical matter is one thing, the normative discussion of pros and cons of different regimes is quite another. Hollinger may be right in his praise of idealised American denominationalism, given that it is clearly distinguished from 'strict separationism'. Again, Casanova argues convincingly that religious pluralism has 'obvious advantages over racial pluralism' because 'under proper constitutional institutionalisation, it is more reconcilable with principled equality and non-hierarchic diversity' (Casanova 2005: 24). Also, the degree of voluntarism is much higher in cases of an 'active, achieved, and reflexive denomination' compared to 'passive, ascribed and nominal affiliation to a religion into which one is born' (25). I discuss the selective affinity of AD and the ideal model of 'denominationalism' (sect. 8.5), without giving in to 'separationism' or the myth of a completely 'neutral' and 'religion-blind' state.[30]

6.4.2 Models of incorporation of minorities into democratic polities

Politics responds in several ways to a perceived increase of ethno-national or religious diversity, whether as a result of immigration or of endogenous developments. If perceived as a threat, the politics of repression and closure or the politics of imposed cultural assimilation are invoked. If perceived as indifferent, politics of toleration (live and let live) ensue. And, if perceived as a valuable resource or as ethically and morally desirable, a politics that actively promotes retention and development of cultural diversity is called for.

Actual states may be based on cultural monism (of the dominant ethnie/nation or religion), reinforced by 'threatening' diversity from within or from abroad. Oligopolistic cultural compacts or regimes may defend themselves against 'threatening newcomers'. In both situations, it is difficult to maintain the myth of cultural neutrality of the state. Finally, states may accommodate new ethno-cultural and religious practices by forging common institutions and practices, adapting their official justifications along the way.

For the purposes of practical evaluation, it is useful to construct a simple, two-dimensional model of types of cultural and institutional incorporation. On the cultural axis, minorities can either be forced to accept, or more or less freely consent to cultural assimilation. Or they may refuse or simply not be allowed to acculturate (cultural pluralism/ diversity).[31] On the institutional axis, minorities can be forcefully included or they may more or less freely seek integration into common institutions (institutional inclusion or institutional monism). Again, they may not be allowed to integrate (coercive exclusion), and they can say no to integration (institutional separation or institutional pluralism). If one cross-tabulates the two axes, one gets four different types of incorporation regimes: (1) inclusion of minorities into unchanged, monist institutions of the dominant majority; (2) institutional separation, and a cultural pluralism based on internal communal assimilation; (3) inclusion in common, ethno-religious relationally neutral institutions (common institutions, which have explicitly been changed to accommodate cultural pluralism/diversity); (4) institutional pluralism and full cultural pluralism.

Figure 6.2 (on page 195) is a slight modification of a figure by Schermerhorn on the conditions of conflict or integration among ethno-religious/national groups (1970: 83).[32] Conflicts result when centripetal strategies of institutional inclusion or cultural assimilation are enforced by majorities and resisted by minorities, if they are able to mobilise enough resources to actually resist. Conflicts also result when centrifugal strategies of enforced institutional separation or rejected cultural assimilation by majorities or states (legally or socially enforced cultural pluralism) are resisted by minorities choosing strategies of full institutional inclusion or relatively free acculturation. The figure highlights not only the main dividing line between (more) inclusionist, monist or 'integrative' (Horowitz) and (more) institutionally pluralist, or 'consociational' arrangements (Lijphart), it also emphasises the distinction between cultural assimilation and cultural pluralism or diversity.

It invites a serious discussion of the conditions and the inherent difficulties of the two realistic utopias (cells 3 and 4) as well as of the transitions to these regimes (sect. 7.2). Such a discussion is better than declaring them to be impossible, or than claiming that legitimate inclusion could solely be achieved in 'post-ethnic' or 'post-national', monist and relationally neutral common institutions – the preferred options of republican assimilationists (Hollinger 1996; Lind 1995; Weil, Schnapper, Kepel) and liberal assimilationists (Brubaker 2004; Joppke & Morawska 2003). Pursuing these lines comes down to neglecting the historical possibility of flexible and open forms of democratic institutional pluralism, vintage associative democracy.[33]

Figure 6.2 *Types of institutional and cultural incorporation of ethno-national mino-rities (polities as example)*

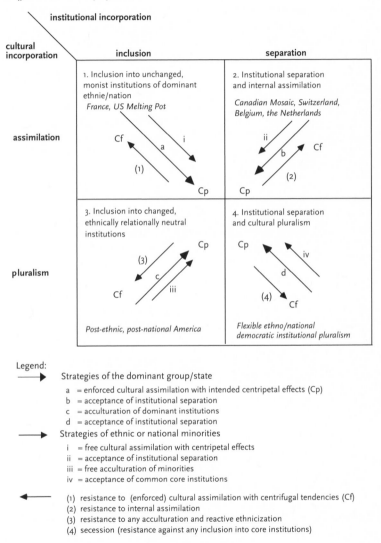

Legend:

⟶   Strategies of the dominant group/state

    a = enforced cultural assimilation with intended centripetal effects (Cp)
    b = acceptance of institutional separation
    c = acculturation of dominant institutions
    d = acceptance of institutional separation

⟶   Strategies of ethnic or national minorities

    i   = free cultural assimilation with centripetal effects
    ii   = acceptance of institutional separation
    iii = free acculturation of minorities
    iv = acceptance of common core institutions

◀⟶   (1) resistance to (enforced) cultural assimilation with centrifugal tendencies (Cf)
    (2) resistance to internal assimilation
    (3) resistance to any acculturation and reactive ethnicization
    (4) secession (resistance against any inclusion into core institutions)

6.5   Regimes of institutional pluralism

6.5.1 Non-democratic institutional pluralism

Historians tell us that, together with modern capitalism, modern (na-tion) states (particularly those following the demotic path from nation to state) have been the biggest cultural homogenisers in world history. These very same nation-states still have enormous difficulties incorporating cultural and institutional pluralism. A short look at the different types of non-democratic ethno-religious and national institutional pluralism may suggest important lessons. Caste and estate systems, multi-ethnic and multinational empires, British and Dutch systems of indirect colonial rule, post-colonial plural and racist apartheid systems deny recognition to or even completely negate the legal, civic and political equality of constituent groups. This is the case both in autocratic forms, where all are subjected to the ruler, and in exclusivist democratic forms, where only dominant majorities have citizenship rights. This is the meaning of non-liberal/non-democratic institutional pluralism, as indicated by the traditional phrase 'separate and unequal'. Even here, we find differences. The more decent forms, like the millet system, may combine high degrees of toleration of cultural and institutional diversity (Sisk 1996: 27f; Rudolph & Rudolph 2000; Rawls 1999).

Recent research challenged the myth of 'Oriental Despotism'[34] and its remnants that figure prominently in discussions of the Ottoman millet system in political philosophy.[35] The myth goes like this:

> Non-Muslim peoples were grouped, for political and fiscal purposes, in several organisations along confessional lines. Their elites were assigned a specific position within the Ottoman ruling system. The status of the Greek Orthodox community, for example, is generally described by reference to the following terms: (i) the Ottoman state was committed to respect the religious status of the members of this specific *millet*; (ii) it recognised juridically the ecclesiastical hierarchy ...; (iii) it granted privileges and immunities to the head of the Church ...; (iv) the Patriarch as the head of the *millet* could exercise a certain degree of civil jurisdiction over the members of this community; (v) the Church enjoyed the right to possess real estate along with the right to extract taxes from the members of the community under its jurisdiction (Adanir 2000: 8).

Adanir and other historians have shown that the reality of the millet system deviated considerably from this model:
i.   Various non-Muslim congregations, particularly Jewish ones, 'evaded being squeezed into clear-cut organisations,' maintaining and reproducing ethno-linguistic cleavages within Jewry.
ii. The model completely neglects the 'importance of communal autonomy on the territorial level as the basic structural element of political integration. Communal autonomy was granted not because communes happened to be religious congregations, but in the first place because they were the smallest administrative units' (Adanir

2000: 9). Territorial local autonomy interfered with religious communal autonomy.

iii. Not only was the 'autonomous communal jurisdiction' limited to religious matters 'relating to culture and family,' it was also further restricted (e.g. inheritance and financial aspects of divorce).

iv. Even religious members of a *millet* had a choice in marriage law between religious and civil jurisdiction.

v. The interpenetration of religious and local autonomy explains the capacity to organise 'large-scale collective action in case of need by overriding confessional divides' (12).

vi. Together, all these aspects explain the fairly cosmopolitan character of cities like Istanbul, Salonika (Mazower 2005), Belgrade, Skopje and Sarajevo in the Ottoman empire (comparable only to *Al Andalus* [Rehrmann 2000, Leggewie 1993]), and incompatible with the prevailing image 'of a compartmentalised society, organised along vertical lines, with minimal intercommunal relationship.' The unprecedented freedom of religion at least partly explains the actual legitimacy of Ottoman rule and its attraction for Protestantism in the Balkans. Compared with the Austro-Hungarian and the Russian empires, and also with all of the contemporary European nation-states, the relational religious neutrality of the Ottoman state was stronger. This idea of relational neutrality was developed even further in the direction of ethno-national and religious neutrality in the second part of the 19th century by the ideology of 'Ottomanism' (Adanir 2000) as a response to the emerging threat of nationalist secession movements in the Balkans. It did not, however, survive the fervour of nationalist mobilisations.[36]

Some important preliminary lessons can be learned from these non-democratic versions of institutional pluralism:

1. If one is primarily interested in institutions (or 'regimes') and practices of toleration, much can be learned from some non-democratic types of institutional pluralism.

2. If one focuses on attitudes or motives of actors explaining practices of toleration, the fairly exclusive focus of liberal philosophers and postmodernists on 'openness, curiosity and enthusiastic endorsement of difference' (Walzer 1997: 10ff) is misleading. 'Resigned acceptance of difference for the sake of peace', 'benign indifference' and 'moral stoicism' (sect. 2.2 and para. 6.1.1) may be more significant. Everyday practices of toleration in intercultural contexts are surely more important than heroic principles and demanding virtues. When it comes to the motives of ruling elites, even the traditional strategic device of imperial rule (*divide et impera*) has led to

fairly stable and tolerant practices and institutions of toleration (see also Horowitz 1991a: 468).

3. Stability and peaceful coexistence are important principles in their own right (sect. 2.2).

4. Some forms of non-democratic institutional pluralism have been more open, flexible and even conducive to practical individual freedoms than traditionally assumed. This prompts the recognition that the astonishing staying power or continuity of cultural and religious diversity under conditions of non-democratic institutional pluralism in the millet system is not solely the result of a forced confinement of individuals into internally autocratic and homogenising community organisations (assumed by Walzer 1997: 69ff and Spinner-Halev 2000: 7, 20, 44). Less stark and exclusive choices between individual autonomy, collective autonomy and cultural survival/flourishing seem possible.

5. Conceptions and practices of a more neutral or even-handed rule and of a more flexible version of IP have at least been envisioned in non-democratic types of institutional pluralism (the combination of 'Ottomanism' and 'millets'). This can stimulate attempts to bridge the divide between neutralist, monist universalism and separationist particularism. The potential transition from the Ottoman or the Austro-Hungarian Empire to democratic institutionally pluralist regimes, recognising full legal and political equality of all citizens, has not been realised.[37] Nevertheless, recent democratic nation states may learn how to become more culturally and institutionally pluralist from non-democratic institutional pluralism.

6.5.2 Democratic institutional pluralism and associative democracy

All modern varieties of social or functional ('neo-corporatist') representation do not replace representative political democracy, they supplement it. Equally, all proposals for ascriptive minority representation and 'multicultural citizenship' are not designed to replace liberal-democratic citizenship. Here also, the principle is that the votes of all citizens – and increasingly also of permanent residents – count equally, irrespective of class, education and ascriptive characteristics. This held for 'pillarised' systems of consociational democracy (cell 2) and it holds even more so for more flexible regimes of democratic institutional pluralism such as associative democracy (cell 4).[38]

Modern liberal democracies are compatible with various degrees of actual relational cultural neutrality. Yet, it took a long time before the normative theories of democracy began to respect 'reasonable pluralism' and its practical consequences. Subscribing to the ideal of a culturally 'neutral' state and politics, their preferred institutional models still differ considerably. Republicans defend the thick version of democracy, embedded in particularist, more or less ethnically and religiously monist cultures. Liberals usually claim that state institutions and policies are (or at least should be completely) neutral. However, they actually use various 'strict separations' and reason restraints to block attempts by different minorities to make them relationally more neutral. Liberal nationalism is caught in a tricky balancing act of maintaining and defending particular national versions of democracy and at the same time, as liberal multiculturalism, allowing for possibilities of institutional representation of different ethno-national minorities. Libertarian claims that the state should be neutral may be more plausible since their proposed thin state and policies are very minimal indeed. Associative democrats share their proposal of a thin state and emphasise that 'thin' and 'strong' are two of a kind. Deliberative democrats and empowered democrats endorse the presence of minorities in public discourse on all issues but are more hesitant than associative democrats when representation in other stages of the political process is at stake.

All four options in Figure 6.2 are clearly compatible with minimally understood liberal democracy, but a first, rough and preliminary moral evaluation shows important differences.

Option 1 – defended by traditional republicans, liberals and liberal assimilationists – is morally unattractive. It goes hand in hand with fairly high degrees of imposed cultural assimilation into predominant majority culture(s), masked by the myth of a culturally neutral state. It promises free individual choice of cultures and ways of the good life but strictly limits cultural expression to private spheres or to 'civil but not political society'. It favours majority culture to the disadvantage of minority cultures. In denying meaningful institutional associative, collective autonomy, it forces a trade-off between individual rights and cultural traditions. Minorities face a tragic choice: 'your rights or your culture'.

Option 2 – defended by corporatists in the Protestant and Catholic tradition – is unattractive for three reasons. First, it confines political participation to elites. Second, it resists cultural assimilation into a predominant majority nation state but allows it for minorities. The hold of minority cultures is counteracted by guaranteed exit rights (but not by real exit options), and neither rights nor options are effectively enforced by state action. Third, 'official' recognition of minorities creates barriers for, and tends to exclude, newcomers. Hence, it does not contribute to a further cultural pluralisation of 'common' national institutions and identities.

Option 3 – an unrealised utopia defended by enlightened republicans such as Hollinger and Lind, and most deliberative and empowered democrats – is attractive if they could shed the hidden remnants of 'old style' assimilationism, now under the cover of 'liberal' or 'republican' assimilation. It would be even more attractive if we were shown how it could be achieved in the 'real' world. Finally, it requires a clear view on the predominant institutions and cultures, and the need for their change in the direction of more relational neutrality.

Option 4 – an unrealised utopia envisioned by some liberal nationals and by associative democrats – is attractive under four conditions. 1. It must be able to cope with institutional rigidities and lockout effects. 2. Toleration and its limits must be spelled out to gain a foothold in minorities within minorities. 3. Exit options must be effectively geared to exit rights in order to increase real choice. 4. AD should be conducive to both elite and rank-and-file participation and seduce minorities into liberalising and democratising their 'communities' from the inside out.

It is my strong conviction that recent designs of associative democratic institutions provide the comparatively best opportunities to achieve these aims. Associationalism has strong roots in Protestant and Catholic varieties of corporatism, which eventually became compatible with liberal democracy[39]. However, its recent libertarian-democratic versions (sketched in sect. 6.3) have never been seriously applied to ethno-religious diversity (Bader 2001b). The remaining chapters of part IV serve to elaborate these claims.

7 Normative models of religious governance: associative democracy, a moral defence

Historical and comparative analysis has shown a huge complexity of regimes of religious governance and a bewildering variety of regimes of governing (organised) religions (sect. 1.3) that is also relevant for a theory of contextualised morality. These empirical regimes are loosely connected with normative policy models, which, for the sake of practical evaluation and institutional design, have to be further reduced into a small set of really relevant options (sect. 7.1). In a short comparison of the relevant models, I try to show why associative democracy provides better institutional and policy options (sect. 7.2). In the rest of this chapter, these moral claims are substantiated in two regards. I try to show why associative democracy is not only compatible with meaningful individual autonomy but actually enhances it (sect. 7.3), and why it is not only compatible with, but also conducive to the flourishing of representative political democracy (sect. 7.4).

7.1 Normative models of religious governance

Normative institutional and policy models of religious governance are not based on inductive generalisations but rather on normative considerations: what institutions and policies ought to look like. Yet they are abstracted or extrapolated from and rather loosely connected with empirical patterns, and these references give the normative discussions some empirical grounding. Like other normative 'models', e.g. the Anglo-Saxon versus the Rhenish model of capitalism, they do not present an accurate description of actual institutional mixes and policies in these countries at different times but they do offer some normative guidelines or 'ideals'. Together with moral and constitutional and legal principles, these policy models inform actual policies either implicitly (as 'operating principles') or explicitly. They also invite thinking about alternative designs. However, even as normative models they are ideals: no actually predominant policy model in any country fits its criteria completely, because there are always rival or competing normative models or highly contested interpretations of the predominant models at work (Monsma & Soper 1997: 10; Lash 2001: 303f; Bader 2007a).

As ideals and policy models, they focus on intended outcomes, and any serious practical evaluation certainly has to take into account unintended consequences; both welcome and unwelcome ones.

Two axes that have been relevant for discussing the diversity of constitutional norms and constitutional reality (paras. 1.3.3.1 and 1.3.3.2) are also crucial for the construction of normative models of religious governance: 'establishment' (starting from constitutional, but adding legal, administrative, political and cultural establishment) and institutionalised monism or pluralism.

Strong constitutional and legal establishment always implies administrative and political monism aimed at religio-national cultural monism, although de facto establishment can obviously only be achieved to a certain degree and with unintended outcomes. Even its recent versions in Greece, Serbia and Israel are incompatible with the 'two autonomies' and with religious freedoms and equal treatment. It is thus at odds with principles of relational neutrality, fairness in all its versions, and priority for democracy. Apart from some Christian and Islamic fundamentalists (particularly in Iran), it is no longer seriously defended as an ideal and for all these reasons it can be excluded from my further evaluation.

Recent versions of weak establishment in Norway, Denmark, England and Scotland are seen as compatible with *de jure* and *de facto* religious freedoms and religious pluralism. It may be compatible with some administrative recognition of religious pluralism and different degrees of *de facto* institutionalisation of other religions, and it may also recognise a certain religious pluralisation of the cultural nation. Recently, it seems to have been defended more for pragmatic or strategic reasons (Parekh 1996) than as a praiseworthy ideal.

Constitutional pluralism or plural establishment, as in Finland, requires the constitutional and/or legal recognition of more than one organised religion. It also seems to be defended not as an ideal, but for pragmatic and strategic reasons to further pluralise weak establishment (Modood 1996).

Non-constitutional pluralism combines constitutional disestablishment (the Netherlands, Sweden) or non-establishment with restricted legal pluralism (e.g. in family law), administrative institutional pluralism (*de jure* and *de facto* institutionalisation of several organised religions), institutionalised political pluralism and the religio-cultural pluralisation of the nation (India, Australia, Belgium, Austria, Germany and Spain approximate non-constitutional selective cooperation). As an ideal, it is explicitly defended by democratic institutional pluralists and, in opposition to existing corporatist varieties, by AD.

Non-Establishment and Private Pluralism require strict constitutional and legal separation of the state from all religions, plus strict administrative and political separation. The model is opposed to legal, administrative and political institutionalisation of religions. The predominant policy models in the US and France use this ideal. However, in both cases, it is crucial to highlight the difference between ideal and actual 'muddle'. The crucial difference with non-constitutional pluralism is that institutional pluralism is strictly relegated to the 'private sphere' of civil society and is not allowed to spill over into political society or the state, particularly not into decision-making. As we have seen, this is the preferred ideal model of most liberals, democrats, socialists, and feminists.

These normative models of religious governance are presented briefly in figure 7.1.

Figure 7.1 *Normative models of religious governance*

	Establishment				
	Constitutional	Legal	Administrative	Political	Cultural
Monism	strong establishment (SE)	legal monism	administrative monism	political monism	religiously monistic nation
Religious Institutional Pluralism (RIP)	weak establishment (WE)	legal monism	some administrative pluralism	restricted political pluralism	hesitantly recognised cultural pluralism
	plural establishment (PE)	legal pluralism	administrative pluralism	political pluralism	recognised cultural pluralism
	non-constitutional pluralism (NOCOP)	restricted legal pluralism	administrative pluralism	political pluralism	recognised cultural pluralism
Strict Separationism	non-establishment and private pluralism (NEPP)	strict legal separation	strict administrative separation	strict political separation	none of the State's business

In my view, the most relevant and promising models that are explicitly defended as ideals are NOCOP and NEPP. Furthermore, the most important dividing lines are between religious institutional pluralism that recognise some forms of selective cooperation (Plessner 2001: 482) between state and organised religions (WE, PE and NOCOP) and strict separationism, on the one hand, and between constitutional establishment (WE and PE) and constitutional non-establishment (NOCOP and NEPP) on the other hand. The former axis may be more important both because constitutional aspects may not be as crucial as legal theorists think (para. 1.3.3.2)[1] and because the administrative, political and cultural aspects of these three varieties of democratic institutional pluralism show an important overlap and they cannot be neatly distinguished from each other.[2]

In my limited practical evaluation, I focus on moral arguments (chap. 7) before comparing examples of the two most relevant models, i.e. NEPP (particularly the differences between France and the US) and NOCOP (European selective cooperation regimes), their dilemmas and possible transitions in order to 'ground' my normative evaluations and my proposal of AD (chaps. 8 to 10).

7.2 Why religious associative democracy? Stating the claims and objections

In my attempt to show why AD provides better institutional and policy options, I proceed in three steps. First, I discuss comparative advantages, shared by all varieties of democratic religious institutional pluralism over NEPP (para. 7.2.1). Next, I try to show how NOCOP, compared with WE and PE, can – and does – better when it comes to responding to criticism by defenders of NEPP, as well as better articulating the principles of priority for democracy, relational neutrality and fairness as even-handedness (para. 7.2.2). Finally, I claim that AD has important advantages over the existing corporatist versions of NOCOP and allows us to escape ritualised choices between either 'structural pluralism' or 'separationism' (para. 7.2.3).

7.2.1 Religious institutional pluralism (selective cooperation) and non-establishment/private pluralism (separationism)

NEPP might seem to be just right in an ideal world, although I have raised some doubts even in this regard (sect. 2.4). NEPP tends to reproduce these inequalities in the real world of historical and structural inequalities between majority and minority religions and of actual religious bias of existing states – cultural/symbolic, political, administrative and even actual legal establishments of predominant religions (Bader 1999a; Eisenach 2000). In addition, NEPP also implies inherent limitations for achieving higher degrees of relational religious neutrality and more even-handed accommodations in many ways.

First, associational freedoms are guaranteed in 'private' or 'civil' society. However, in cases of conflicts with individual religious freedoms, it does not provide a sensible balance. It either systematically favours individual freedoms and tends to overrule associational freedoms or it favours libertarian 'absolutist Free exercise' and does not really guarantee individual freedoms (sects. 4.3 to 4.5).

Second, NEPP one-sidedly emphasises 'negative freedom from' and strictly legal equal treatment of religions. It tends to neglect 'positive freedom to' and more substantive notions of equality or it does not provide a sensible balance (para. 4.1.4). It trusts that free-market governance of religious diversity is just and tends to discount serious historical injustices, which may demand redistributive measures.

Third, it claims to protect religious minorities against assimilatory pressure by religious majorities, often backed or even stimulated by actual states, and it may or may not recognise the importance of collective religious organisations in this regard. The cause of religious diversity is of course in much better shape once it is backed by institutions.[3] Defenders of NEPP agree that states should guarantee religious non-discrimination but neglect or underestimate the importance of public recognition and of enabling state policies even for effective anti-discrimination policies known from affirmative action debates (Bader 1998: 462).

Fourth, NEPP tends to exclude religious reasons from public deliberation (sect. 3.5) by declaring religion to be either private or 'social but not political'. This strategy is unfair for religions in general, but it is also implicitly biased against minority religions because privatisation and individualisation stabilise existing power asymmetries by limiting the possibilities to challenge them effectively in public talk and politics (see para. 1.2.1.2 for this *socio-logic of power asymmetries*). Majorities need not organise and mobilise. They can privately and individually profit from institutionalised advantages and from favourable state policies presented as 'neutral'. Minorities depend on collective action, organisation and mobilisation. They strategically need strong collective identities and public space to effectively challenge unrecognised majority bias of 'neutral' state institutions and policies. The chances of minorities to redress power asymmetries, to challenge secularism bias or majority bias of state institutions and policies are obviously much higher if they have institutionalised and actual opportunities to raise their voices in public, to be listened to (ear), and in one way or another to be included in the political process (muscle, some say). The basic idea of NEPP is that the representation of particular interests and groups should remain constricted to civil society and not spill over into the domain of the state. Of course, interest groups (including churches) may form lobbies and may try to influence political parties and parliaments (and more informally also judges and administration). However, such 'political pluralism' is supposed to prevent or forestall – for fear of mischief of faction – the political institutionalisation of particular interests, not to recognise or formalise it. The famous dichotomies and separations of individual vs. collective, private vs. public, civil society vs. political society, religion vs. state are meant to control the borders. In conditions of structural power asymmetries, they systematically decrease the chances of minorities to have a real impact to make deliberation, legislation and jurisdiction, administrative accommodation and also national culture and public symbols fairer and relationally more neutral.

The various freedoms of religions are complex, under-determined, in tension with each other and with other crucial human rights (sect. 4.1). Their fair and relationally neutral articulation, interpretation, application and the arts of balancing in public deliberation, legislation and courts is not guaranteed by religion-blindness and exclusions of religions as favoured by NEPP, but by giving voice and listening to religious majorities, minorities and minorities within minorities and by sensible modes of representation. Actual religious freedoms for minorities do not fall from heaven. They have to be continuously fought for (Sheleff 2000, chap. 13 on indigenous peoples). Their guarantee should not be left to the law and supreme courts, let alone to political majoritarianism (McConnell 1992: 693, 721f, 728, 734; Monsma & Soper 1997: 200, 209f). Public and political pressure by religious minorities helps remind 'benevolent' religious majorities (including judges) of discriminatory practices. Some form of political or formal recognition provides religions with additional political and legal resources.

Morally legitimate claims for practical accommodation require at least some form of representation (spokespersons, organisations) of religious minorities and some informal 'recognition' by state administrations on different levels at odds with NEPP (sect. 8.1). Public recognition and institutionalised representation of religious minorities that characterise religious institutional pluralism considerably increase the chances of fair accommodations by adding political and legal resources and pressurising supposedly 'neutral' administrations (sects. 5.1 to 5.3).

This may be even truer with regard to claims for even-handed changes in predominant national culture deeply formed by particular religious histories and for sensitive issues of public symbols (sect. 5.4). Representation of religious minorities in the political process in general, and in the political centre in order to participate in the 'defining and making of society and politics' in particular, which is at odds with NEPP, seems to further these transformations (sect. 5.5).

7.2.2 Varieties of Religious Institutional Pluralism (RIP)

By definition, all varieties are favourable for religion(s) and help to fight aggressive secularism and all its remnants in the more 'neutral' or even religion-friendly varieties of NEPP. They are certainly to the advantage of those religions that are publicly recognised and privileged in various ways: old, large, formerly or still weakly established religions.

Whether RIP is also to the advantage of religious minorities is much more questionable. This very much depends on the degrees of openness for smaller, old or new religions or, to put it otherwise, on the degree of actual legal, administrative, political and cultural/symbolic pluralism. In this regard, the varieties of RIP show important differences.

WE clearly shows the signs of earlier strong establishment. To fully express religious pluralism legally and symbolically, it eventually requires either disestablishment or pluralising establishment. Defenders of PE ask for the constitutional establishment of new religion(s) because they take constitutions more seriously, recognising the wrong symbolic message of WE, even if pragmatic and administrative accommodation of new religious minorities can be grudgingly achieved, particularly on local levels.

However, both versions reproduce the inherent disadvantages of constitutionalising religious pluralism. Constitutional law – compared with 'normal' law, executive orders or directives and, particularly, with administrative practice – is (meant to be) fairly rigid and inflexible. It takes a lot of time and qualified majorities to respond properly to changes in the religious landscape. This can only be avoided if one solely constitutionalises the conditions for public recognition of organised religions (e.g. thresholds in terms of time and numbers; recognising moral minimalism), their specific privileges and the mode of representation in the political process instead of naming specific religions in the Constitution.

Disestablishment removes constitutional rigidity, bias towards old majority religions and also some of the limits to openness, but obviously not all non-constitutional barriers inherent in all of the varieties of RIP requiring legal, administrative and judicial recognition of religions. Existing corporatist varieties of NOCOP in Europe still show the stain of old religious cleansings and entrenched privileges for predominant, formerly established religions. Disestablishment or non-establishment (the most adequate constitutional expression of the moral principle of relational religious neutrality of state and politics) does not and cannot in itself guarantee openness to newcomers, high degrees of actual legal, administrative, political and cultural/symbolic pluralism. This can be seen in the perils of public recognition and the practical and symbolic accommodation of Islam in Germany, Italy, Belgium and the Netherlands (sect. 8.5). Publicly recognised religions still defend their privileges, and states are still to varying degrees hostages to entrenched majority religion(s). All this is rightly criticised by defenders of NEPP, such as Hollinger 2003. NOCOP may be favourable for old majority religions but not for new religious minorities (para. 6.5.2 and figure 7.1, cell 2). In addition, it may be bad for minorities within reli-

gious majorities and for religious minorities, and it may also be bad
for liberal democracy.

7.2.3 Varieties of non-constitutional pluralism and associative democracy

AD is the most open and flexible variety of democratic institutional
pluralism (figure 7.1, cell 4) and NOCOP. It promises to combine public recognition and institutionalisation of religious pluralism with flexible adaptation to increased religious diversity that threatens entrenched regimes of religious government, including existing corporatist or 'pillarised' NOCOP (chap. 1, note 1). It is more favourable to
religious minorities and to minorities within organised religions and it
may even be conducive to more demanding conceptions of individual
autonomy, and it is not only compatible with but conducive to liberal
democracy. Like other varieties of RIP, it provides fairly high degrees
of associational autonomy, guaranteed by associational freedoms
(Swaine 2001: 305, 320; Stepan 2000) but promises to overcome the
inherent limitations of non-democratic institutional pluralism, of corporatist institutional pluralism and of NOCOP indicated above. It is a
moderately libertarian version of democratic institutional pluralism
that combines the strengths of institutional or structural pluralism and
of 'civil libertarian liberalism' that it is clearly opposed to old varieties
of structuralist RIP (Rosenblum 2000a).

Rosenblum, however, as so many other liberals and democrats, is
convinced that all varieties of institutional pluralism are incompatible
with 'voluntarism' and 'separationism minimally understood'. She
charges them with trespassing across the voluntarist concern with individual free exercise (2000a: 182f) and with rejecting key elements of
separationism: they inevitably pass the threshold for impermissible establishment of religion and are accused of 'one way protection' (protection of churches from the state only) and 'absolutist Free Exercise' (see
Bader 2003b for criticism). In political philosophy today, it still looks
as if there are only two options that really make a difference: 'structural
pluralism' on the one hand, and 'separationism' or 'civil libertarian liberalism' on the other hand (Rosenblum 2000: 179-183; McConnell
2000: 100ff). Furthermore, it also looks as if these two camps could be
easily associated with traditional political dichotomies of Right/Left or
Conservative/Progressive. Yet, there are more and more interesting options, a fact already clearly indicated by Monsma & Soper 1997. Not
only liberal Protestant believers (Steven Smith, Thiemann, Wolterstorff,
Greenawalt), or liberal Catholics (McConnell, Perry, Glendon, Novak,
Neuhaus, Weigel), not only orthodox Protestants or Catholics, [4] conser-
vationists or perfectionists, not only the religious Right or traditionalist

leaders of ethno-religious minorities defend varieties of religious institutional pluralism but also critical liberals and egalitarians (sect. 7.5).[5]

Before I substantiate my claims in detail, I raise them in a general way to indicate why AD is attractive for minorities within minorities, conducive to higher degrees of voluntarism and autonomy and meaningful democratic participation, compared to both 'structural pluralism' (in many varieties of NOCOP) and 'separationism'.

In opposition to structural pluralism, AD is attractive for minorities within religious minorities for two reasons. First, it strongly protects the basic needs and rights of all individuals against infringements by minority communities, organisations and leaders (as well as against violations by all other agents) by legal sanctions of minimal moral standards (sects. 4.4 and 4.5). Second (like liberalism and libertarianism), AD highlights the crucial importance of voluntarism for minorities within minorities: exit rights have to be guaranteed, and, as far as this is possible, entry should be made more voluntary. In addition, AD also increases' real exit options (sect. 7.3).

Like structural pluralism, AD criticises the liberal congruence that is so characteristic of comprehensive liberal or democratic morality because it is incompatible with meaningful associational autonomy (sect. 4.3). More demanding moral standards of individual autonomy should not be imposed by law and sanctions but by persuasion and by good practical examples. Yet, AD shares the commitment to these more demanding ideals and, compared with libertarianism and liberalism, is actually conducive to higher degrees of individual autonomy and actual freedoms of choice by creating and guaranteeing more appropriate circumstances of choice. First, the range of morally legitimate cultural options will be much broader because the remnants of liberal assimilationism are rejected and higher degrees of cultural and religious diversity can be expected. Compared with libertarianism, religious minorities are in a much better position to reproduce and change their practices on their own terms because, secondly, the range of institutional options in service delivery is much wider. Real choice amongst meaningfully different schools, care institutions, media and so on makes voluntarism more meaningful than 'one model fits all' (sect. 7.4).

Like structural pluralism, AD also criticises democratic congruence. The minimum standards of modern political democracy should not be imposed on the internal life of all associations without due consideration (sect. 4.3). Yet if religious communities or associations vie for public money and particularly if they ask for public recognition and some representation in the political process, it is more legitimate to use higher standards and, at the same time, ensure adequate representation of minorities within minorities. This is a further reason why AD is attrac-

tive for minorities within minorities. AD may not share the high hopes
of many civil society theorists (para. 6.1.2) that associations themselves
work as seedbeds of democratic virtues. It may also be more critical
with regard to emphatic ideals of participation in general but it shares
the demanding ideal of meaningful participation not only in 'politics'
but in everyday life. Also, it provides more opportunities to realise participation of the relevant stakeholders than most other normative models of democracy and particularly than libertarian and neo-liberal de-
fences of parliamentary democracy and capitalist market societies.

All these claims are contested, particularly by defenders of NEPP.
Even if it might be true that AD is less vulnerable to charges against
all varieties of religious institutional pluralism, it might be true that
AD is less conducive for more demanding ideals of autonomy, democratic participation and equal opportunities. And it might be true that
AD is still too closed and rigid compared with the presumed beneficial
effects of the 'free market governance' of religious diversity (the idealised US denominational model (sect. 8.6). However, it can certainly be
more open and flexible than known versions of NOCOP by lowering
the thresholds for smaller and new religious minorities and by com-
pensating for unfair disadvantages.

7.3   Associative democracy and individual autonomy

'There is no point in pluralizing the state only to *create* totalitar-
ianist potentialities and authoritarian practices at the level of associations'

Hirst 1994: 68 (my italics)

AD resists the temptation to legally impose demanding liberal and democratic standards on all associations and proposes the toleration of
non-liberal and non-democratic minorities. To tolerate these practices,
however, is not the same as creating or enhancing them. In this section, I set out to explain that AD is not only compatible with meaningful individual autonomy but that it actually enhances without imposing
it. More substantive autonomy is a matter of degree (freedom of entry
and exit) and it crucially depends on meaningful choices and available
institutional options.

7.3.1 Freedom of entry

Radical libertarians take free and informed consent by adults to enter
groups/associations and free exit rights for granted, but they neglect
the actual degrees of freedom of consent and the actual exit options.

As a moderately libertarian approach, AD can avoid these fictions of voluntariness, which may be harmless only in ideal worlds, while rescuing the attractive features of libertarianism. AD does not only stipulate free entry and exit, but tries to achieve higher actual degrees of freedom. It takes differences in the degrees of voluntariness between and within minorities into account. Children are obviously the most vulnerable category because their freedom of entry is zero, they are the main objects of intergenerational transmission lacking (but progressively gaining in) agency, and they are captive targets incapable of exit (Reich 2005).

Entry into and remaining within minority (and majority) groups is only rarely the result of free and voluntary decisions, as is sometimes the case with religious associations (conversion and Anabaptism), sexual preferences and linguistic groups (e.g. 'coming out', switching gender, or linguistic identities). Most people, however, are either born into or raised in communities. This 'non-voluntary' belonging may be a constitutive element of their cultural practices and self-definitions (para. 6.4.1). People will remain 'members' because they are accustomed to being a part of the group. Belonging becomes 'involuntary' only if exit is legally proscribed or is socially either impossible or extremely difficult. Still, entry and exit are matters of degree, and it is obvious that exit is easier to facilitate than entry.

What, if anything, can AD do to make entry freer? Two of its features may help to soften the harshness of this destiny. First, with regard to minors, they should not be treated as the property of their parents or of their group. Parents and other guardians have to behave as trustees or social stewards of their children (Hirst 1994: 202; Shapiro 1999: 68-84). 'No single agent or group should assume total authority over the lives of children'.[6] AD provides better opportunities to balance the interests of the different relevant stakeholders such as children, parents, minorities, state and international agencies (like UNESCO and ILO), and NGOs. On the one hand, AD recognises the interests of parents and minorities to transmit religious and cultural ways of life to the next generation. These interests are met through the guarantees of parental religious freedoms. However, on the other hand, AD recognises the basic needs and rights of minors: their rights to security (life, liberty, bodily integrity, protection against violence) and to subsistence, and additionally to basic education and basic healthcare.[7] Minors have to be protected from parents, minorities (and majorities!) who neglect their basic interests, and from external agents claiming to represent their 'best' interests. AD criticises both absolutist parental and group freedoms defended by conservative religions – *Mozert v. Hawkins County Board of Education* (versus any 'exposure'), and *Wisconsin v. Yo-*

der – and absolutist state-paternalism overriding parental and group interests.[8]

In this, as in any other case, accepting overlapping authorities provides opportunities for fair and sensible deliberations, negotiations and balances in order to close the under-determinacy gap and find out what the basic rights and interests to healthcare or education include in specific contexts with regard to specific minorities, and by which means and by which external agent(s) they can best be guaranteed. It also increases sensitivity to the fact that morally permissible solutions (e.g. with regard to different forms and degrees of external scrutiny and intervention) may look differently, depending on types of minorities, on the one hand, and different societal contexts, welfare regimes and policy traditions, on the other hand. Even leaving aside minorities, the balance in Sweden (fairly extensive external supervision and intervention by state agencies) is very different from that in the US.[9]

Second, regarding both adults and maturing youngsters, who are gaining agency individually and collectively, AD defends and actually stimulates the pluralisation of membership (para. 7.3.2), promising to increase actual exit options and also the range of freer entry into a whole variety of associations.[10]

7.3.2 Exit

Freedom to exit religions and to change religious belief is part of minimal morality and international law (para. 4.1.1). In cases where religions forbid exit and impose serious sanctions (e.g. corporal punishment or the death penalty, which go far beyond mere expulsion and ostracism), on dissenters, heretics and apostates, liberal states have to guarantee their individual religious freedoms by all prudent means (from persuasion to sanctions). In cases where states back these punishments by law (as is still the case in some Muslim states), supra-state organisations have to try to prevent and sanction these violations of basic rights by all appropriate means. Most people, however, agree that banning punishment and trying to guarantee the formal right to exit is only a necessary but not a sufficient condition for providing and strengthening actual exit rights and exit options. Compared with entry, it is generally much easier to develop policies that stimulate higher degrees of free exit. This is the main reason why Rosenblum (1998: 101, 103), Galston (2002: 55f, 62, 122f) and Hirst focus on the 'real conditions' of freedom of exit. The achievable degrees of freedom of entry will inevitably be lower than those of exit. Actual exit however is difficult. Exit options from indigenous peoples and from totalistic religions are very restricted. First, because exit costs are extremely high[11] as they involve more than identity costs (e.g. the loss of constitutive parts of individual identity for which no ready-made or real alternatives are available, given an individual's psychological make-up) and social costs (e.g. social ostracism and the loss of social relationships and networks). Exit costs may also include high material costs, loss of care and shelter, loss of social and physical security (if social ostracism is combined with disinheritance, loss of employment and social security provided by community-specific institutions).[12] Second, exit is difficult because it requires 'knowledge, capacity, psychological, and fitness conditions' (Galston 2002: 123). A plausible general rule seems to be that the moral requirements of public scrutiny and external protection of vulnerable minorities increase as their actual exit chances reduce (most obvious for minors) or, vice versa, the higher the degrees of free exit, the less need there is to override associational autonomy and the less demanding the standards.

Three features of associative democracy may help to reduce exit costs and thus increase actual exit options.

First, guaranteed access to the means to satisfy basic needs of subsistence and social security. This may be by way of a universal, individualised basic income for all residents (Hirst 1994: 179-184) that may be far less bureaucratic and intrusive than statist welfare arrangements, although AD is compatible with other institutional solutions. Furthermore, it may help to address extreme poverty of minorities within minorities and particularly of children (rightly highlighted by Reich 2005; Shapiro 1999: 105-106), and also of minorities more generally.

Second, open access to a whole variety of public, semi-public, private service providers (education, health and all varieties of care) through a weighed voucher system, combined with direct public financing, creates opportunities for minorities to run their own services in a more egalitarian way. However, such access also increases exit options for individuals into public associations and opens avenues for exiting dissenting minority groups to set up their own services. Yet if they do so, this may again raise exit costs.

Third, the whole institutional design of associative democracy, its specific policies and its public propagation, intentionally and explicitly serves to pluralise membership (Rosenblum 1998), to prevent unwelcome lock-in effects and works indirectly to heighten the degree of voluntary entry and exit. As in Rosenblum's work, AD promotes the 'moral uses of pluralism' – real exit options, overlapping and cross cutting membership in many associations – but not in a direct way by trying to impose 'autonomy', 'choice' and 'free exit' on all minorities. In this regard, one has to clearly distinguish between (i) processes of cultural change and (ii) policies of intentional cultural 'integration' and assimilation of religious minorities into liberal democracies that is so fashionable these days (Bader 2005a).

Living in modern societies in itself has an impact on indigenous peoples and conservative isolationist religions. Even if a liberal state tries to let them live alone as much as possible,[13] they and their children cannot be completely shielded from 'exposure' to the surrounding society and culture that are fairly radically at odds with their own culture. This fact alone inevitably influences their cultural and religious practices, whether they follow fairly radical isolationist strategies[14] or not. It may lead to an unrecognised, slow acculturation or, conversely, to a reactive, intentional purification of their 'traditional' ways of living. In addition, being left alone in a more or less densely legally regulated liberal state inevitably means asking for many exemptions (e.g. from paying taxes, compulsory military or civil service and compulsory education) in order to defend traditional ways of life. Being forced to make use of a modern legal system again has an unintended but unavoidable impact on traditional cultures and religions.[15]

AD even makes such 'tragic choices' (Stoltenberg 1993: 584; Bader 1999a: 616) for all isolationist minorities more pressing by advocating policies intended to make the surrounding society and cultures more open, plural and flexible. Regarding religions, it is common knowledge amongst sociologists that 'non-establishment' in the US, together with intense competition among religions and the permeability of religious associations ('God's biggest supermarket'), has been conducive to congregationalism and higher degrees of voluntarism (1.2; Handy 1976; Miller 1985; Moore 1994; Eisenach 2000; Casanova 2005). It is my contention that AD shares the advantages of this often idealised model of American denominationalism (NEPP) without having to accept its disadvantages.

In summary, AD takes the moral ideal of meaningful individual autonomy more seriously than most libertarians and liberals and obviously than all republicans and strong participatory democrats favouring stronger or softer versions of democratic congruence.

7.4 Associative democracy and (modern) democracy

Liberals and Republicans often claim that AD is either incompatible with (the incompatibility charge) or weak on modern democracy (the weakness charge).

The incompatibility charge means that non-democratic forms of institutional pluralism (whether pre-modern or modern) are incompatible with modern, liberal, representative political party democracy. However, it also suggests the incompatability of those varieties of institutional pluralism that explicitly accept the constitutional framework of modern democracies and do not want to replace, but to supplement, representative democracy based on peoples' sovereignty and principles of political freedom and equality of all citizens irrespective of ascriptive criteria (sect. 6.2). Associative democrats are quite outspoken in this regard (sect. 6.3). The incompatibility charge would only be plausible: 1. if pluralist institutions were to replace, overrule or trump 'peoples sovereignty'; 2. if written constitutions could not be democratically changed (by qualified parliamentary majorities or qualified referenda); 3. if institutions of representative democracy could not be democratically changed; 4. if institutions[16] of federalism, of the representation of organised social interests, or of minorities could not be changed by democratically elected parliaments by specified procedures. This, however, is clearly not the case with existing institutions of neo-corporatism or minority representation and it is certainly not true of AD (Bader 2001a: 36f; 2007b).

The weakness charge – that AD is not (optimally) conducive to the flourishing of parliamentary democracy – is more complex and leads to the intricacies of comparative practical evaluations of different institutional settings of political democracy.[17] Critics of consociationalism, neo-corporatism, multicultural citizenship and multi-level governance claim that these institutions inevitably lead: 1. to the erosion of the 'primacy of (parliamentary) politics'; 2. to the erosion of contentious public debate; 3. to a take-over of politics by bureaucrats and experts; non-representation or under-representation of the new, small, poorly organised and relatively powerless; 4. to informality, lack of transparency and accountability; 5. to overlapping powers and competencies, complexity of layered decision-making and deadlocks. All these issues cannot be discussed here (Bader 2007b). However, a fair evaluation should obviously not compare ideal models (of monist parliamentary democracy) with 'muddle' and it should also focus on the many deficiencies of institutional monism. I bracket these debates and focus instead on a short explication of the possible ways to represent (organised) religions in the political process. In addition, I present the main reasons why and in which way the design of associative democratic institutions may be conducive to the flourishing of political democracy.

7.4.1 Political representation of (organised) religions

In addition to the usual means of political pluralism (voicing organised interests in civil society and lobbying), AD provides for flexible rights and opportunities of representation in the political process for different kinds of minorities, vehemently criticised by most libertarians, political liberals and republicans.[18] The focus of the traditional debates about minority representation, with national minorities and indigenous peoples as exemplary cases, has been on decision-making, implementation and adjudication in the state, i.e. as voice (e.g. guaranteed seats in legislative chambers) and as political muscle (e.g. specified veto powers and power sharing in executive and judicial bodies). These exceptionally strong measures are certainly not appropriate for all minorities, for religions and religious minorities in particular. Almost no one is claiming that minority religions should participate in legislative, executive and adjudicative power sharing at this level, because majority religions generally lost these rights and privileges long ago, and rightly so.[19]

Decision-making, however, is preceded by issue definition, information and the elaboration of decision-making alternatives, which are as important as decision-making itself.[20] In all these regards, religious organisations and minorities together with other groups actually claim a moderate but legitimate role in participation and many states provide for institutional opportunities, which fit perfectly in the institutional design of AD. Their representative organisations are (or should be) given specific information rights and corresponding information duties by state agencies on local, provincial and federal levels (ear).[21] They should be given the rights and opportunities to participate in public forums and obligatory hearings to correct majority bias and aggressive secularism in relation to issue definition (e.g. on morally contested issues such as abortion, euthanasia and genetic engineering). They often are (and should be) included in obligatory advisory religious councils comprising relevant organised religions that can give their opinions on any subjects that interest them (Parekh 2000: 331). This may occur unanimously, in majority and minority opinions, or – together with other relevant stakeholders – in general councils, e.g. 'Ethik Räte' as in Germany (advisory and consultation rights and duties: 'listen to voice'; see 8.5 regarding the EU) . Even reserved seats for publicly recognised religions in legislative committees with a capacity to participate (but not to vote)[22] could be discussed and explored. Measures like these would strengthen religious voices in public deliberation, correct aggressive secularism and strengthen the voices of religious minorities to correct implicit religious majority bias.[23] They would be fully compatible with the freedoms of political communication and also would obviously not cross the threshold of 'establishment'. It should be clear that advice does not include decision-making powers: it should be listened to and taken seriously. However, it may obviously be even regularly overruled with good reasons by decision-making bodies that are elected on the basis of 'one (wo)man one vote', without any ascriptive discrimination, let alone exclusion of nonbelievers or specific religions.[24]

In addition, the institutional setting of associative delivery of public services (e.g. education, care and media) enables a wide variety of divergent service providers (including religious ones) to participate in public, democratic debates and partly also decisions on standards of service delivery, their implementation and critical scrutiny and control.[25] The respective professions (teachers, medical practitioners, the wide variety of caring professions and social workers etc.), clients (students (and parents), patients, care receivers of all sorts), and boards of service providers (and their umbrella organisations) as stakeholders guarantee that the relevant interests are voiced. They also guarantee that expertise and practical experience are an intrinsic part of the process (compared with standard setting performed solely by politicians in parliaments, who inevitably lack such expertise and insider knowledge).[26] The participation of religious providers may help challenge the strong ideological bias hiding behind 'professionalism' and 'secularism' (sect. 5.3). The process should be made transparent to issue- and arena-specific publics[27] and it can and should be supervised by the general public, media, political parties, parliaments and the respective state departments. Co-operation in these public-private forms of governance may contribute not only to better informed, more effective and legitimate decisions on standards, their implementation and control, but also to trust and to a two-way redefinition of cognitive and normative frames. This will allow criticism of both aggressive secularism, masked as 'neutral' and 'public', and the imposition of illiberal and anti-democratic religious particularism.

7.4.2 Why associative democracy is conducive to the flourishing of representative political democracy

AD shares a concept of democracy with classical social democracy and recent varieties of strong or empowered democracy that is not reduced to representative democracy and not confined to traditionally understood 'politics'. Peoples themselves, and not only their representatives, should have opportunities to participate wherever their interests are relevantly affected by collective decisions in all societal fields and on all levels of decision-making. This increases the opportunities for meaningful participation and also increases its complexity and the need for selectivity. In addition to the well-known general constraints on participation (time, information, qualification, loyalty or commitment), people have to decide whether or not to participate and, if so, in which arenas and on which levels. Contrary to assumptions that the multiplication of arenas, issues and levels would confuse people or would weaken participation in representative political party democracy by siphoning away energy from 'politics', we have good theoretical reasons to assume that a positive interaction exists between broad participation and narrowly conceived political participation. Learning democracy by doing democracy and practising it in all relevant fields of life contributes to create participating 'political citizens'. This positive correlation is also empirically corroborated (Verba et al. 1995; Fung 2003). Hence, the weakness charge is not plausible in this regard.

Yet, compared with associationalist theories of civil society and of strong or empowered democracy, AD is more modest and sober. It strikes a different balance between participation (voice) and exit, and it is more 'libertarian' or minimalist in criticising the 'seedbed-of-virtues' assumptions and the demands of democratic congruence. If plausible, the proposals of these alternative theoretical strands would be clearly more conducive to the flourishing of representative political democracy than AD. AD strikes a different balance between 'liberalism and democracy'.

7.4.2.1 Exit, voice and loyalty

Theories of participatory democracy demand high levels of political and societal participation of people. Theoretical reflection shows that participation depends not only on institutional opportunities but also on resources. These include available time, relevant information, education and expertise, participation skills and also loyalty, and are unequally distributed among classes and groups. Empirical studies have repeatedly shown that actual participation has a strongly elitist bias; the farther away from peoples' everyday activities and on the higher levels, the stronger the bias works. This explains the preference for the devolution of decisions to local political levels and for social democracy. Compared with strong and empowered democracy, however, the structural dilemma for all participatory democrats to achieve higher degrees of participation in complex political decisions on higher federal and on supra-national levels is moderated by AD's explicit institutional design to make the state on all levels as 'thin' as possible, by an active displacement of traditional parliamentary politics (a consequence of its criticism of parliamentary sovereignty) to lower levels (democratic subsidiarity) and, most importantly, to relatively autonomous societal fields. To the degree that this can be achieved, the inevitable elitism of traditional political participation and representative decision-making loses some of its sting.

The possibilities of meaningful societal participation are obviously enhanced by associationalist designs of service delivery. However, even in this regard, AD is more moderate than empowered democracy, which expects (too) much from participation or voice. This may be shown by shortly explaining the complex trade-offs between voice, exit and loyalty (Hirschman 1970; Warren 2001: 103-109; Korver 2002). Paul Hirst has increasingly privileged exit over voice in his later explications of associative democratic service delivery for good reasons.

First, even in social democracy, voice is much more demanding and tends to be elitist. In principle, exit is less demanding because voting by ones feet is open to all, if actual exit options are available (guaranteed by a publicly financed voucher system). It is also less controversial because changing schools, for example, is mostly an accepted side effect of mobility. Second, the assertion that easy exit increases the voluntarism of staying, thereby breeding loyalty, seems prima facie theoretically and empirically sound. Third, but more dubious, the hope is widely shared that free exit will contribute to voice.

The arguments that exit is less elitist, easier and open to all depend crucially on available exit options: voice becomes more important the less exit becomes possible. It is the most important in 'closed institutions' that are based on forced membership, like prisons or psychiatric institutions (where it is usually absent) and states (if they forbid or restrict exit but also if the right to exit is not matched by real entry options due to restrictive immigration policies).[28] Yet, the argument that free and easy exit contributes to voice and loyalty (if considered in more detail), seems implausible for two reasons. First, high degrees of exit and of voice may not be equally possible. Free exit does not stimulate the need to participate because instead of raising your voice, you can leave. Free exit may also only weakly contribute to the motivation to participate because freely staying increases loyalty to the association or organisation, but pre-existing high degrees of loyalty seem to be much stronger sources of motivation to participate. High degrees of loyalty, however, result from long-term membership, from being treated with respect and concern, and from opportunities to exercise voice.[29] Second, as a means of communication in strategies to increase the chances for voice inside organisations, the threat to exit requires much loyalty and a credible, organised and massive threat (making leaders vulnerable or threatening the existence of the organisation). It also requires resources and a high degree of strategic arts.

7.4.2.2 Limits of democratic congruence: AD and minorities within minorities

If plausible, these arguments show a structural dilemma for all approaches that try to ameliorate the position of vulnerable minorities inside minorities by giving them more voice. This is the preferred option of republicans, (empowering) deliberative democrats (Fung & Wright 2001) and feminists (Okin 2005: 72ff; Deveaux 2005: 343, 348f; Moore 2005: 283; Phillips 2005). In my view, AD is more sceptical for two reasons. First, state-imposed policies of democratic congruence are incompatible with meaningful notions of associational autonomy. AD resists this democratic temptation. Deveaux acknowledges an 'important conundrum. In requiring groups to democratise their own internal political processes, and to allow dissenting members to have a role in decision-making, do we not fail to respect their collective, cultural autonomy? And do we not violate a group's own conceptions of legitimacy – which ... are often explicitly anti-democratic?' (2002: 25, slightly changed in 2005: 361f). However, she tends to play down the costs. Second, voice (internal democracy) is the most important and urgent in cases where exit is impossible or extremely costly. Examples include cases of illiberal and anti-democratic groups and organisations that silence the voices of vulnerable minorities (e.g. of feminist Catholics) who seek liberalisation and democratisation of their respective cultures, religions or organisations, as well as cases in which oppositional leaders are threatened with excommunication or are actually excommunicated. It would be foolish to claim that AD has a ready-made answer to this dilemma. This particularly severe irony makes it all the more understandable why AD focuses on exit.

In all other cases, however, in which less isolationist minorities accept public money and other privileges, or want to be represented in the political process, AD provides more opportunities for institutionalised voice compared to rival democratic theories. AD may eventually contribute to enhance voluntary endorsement of internal democracy without imposing it on minorities that do not want to make use of its institutional opportunities. And, finally, it also explicitly requires that the relevant stakeholders (including minorities within minorities) be included in negotiations and deliberations. Compared with traditional religious or linguistic pillarisation (e.g. in the Netherlands and Belgium respectively), and with neo-corporatist settings, the relevant stakeholders cannot solely be the entrenched, conservative organisations and leaders of minorities. In all of these cases, AD and modest versions of deliberative democracy join hands.[30] In my view, democratic government should impose minimal requirements of even-handed representation to prevent illegitimate exclusions. To the degree that this can actually be achieved, the standard realistic objections against democratic institutional pluralism and AD (chap. 9), (namely that they favour only the most purist conservative organisations and privilege the 'worst' radical leaders) are pointless.

Before discussing how the institutional design of AD addresses these and other normative dilemmas of institutionalisation (chap. 8), I conclude by summarising how it may help to resolve the problems of accommodation of non-liberal and non-democratic practices of religious minorities and the plight of minorities within these minorities. As we have seen, various theoretical traditions share a more or less pronounced institutionally pluralist approach to accommodate legitimate needs and claims of different minorities: liberal nationals (Kymlicka,

Milller) and multiculturalists (Margalit, Raz), liberal communitarians (Selznick), communitarian liberals (Etzioni), structural accommodationists (Glendon & Yanes 1991, McConnell), liberal pluralists (Galston 2002), and 'joint governance approaches' (Shachar 2001; Swaine 2001, 2003a, 2005; Holder 2005; Moore 2005). My AD proposal explicitly favours power sharing in systems of multilevel governance. It starts from differentiated moral and legal standards and explicitly takes into account many levels of governance and of government, many actors (individuals; families; minorities and their associations and organisations; minorities within minorities; local, provincial and federal government; international polities like the EU and the UN; NGOs and SMOs) and a broad policy repertoire. Instead of betting on one strategy exclusively, e.g. external control and intervention (as classical liberals and republicans); or internal voice (as deliberative democrats); or voluntarism and leave them alone/self-government (as libertarians), AD prefers a minority-, context- and issue-specific mixture of policies. This includes leaving minorities alone as much as possible (maximum accommodation) and making use of external legal intervention only to protect the basic needs and rights of individuals and vulnerable minorities inside minorities. Policy repertoires also include applying stricter standards of public scrutiny and external control in cases when minorities ask for legal support, subsidies or other privileges from the state. In addition to legal sanctions backed by the (threat of) use of violence, governments (and obviously all other actors like NGOs, parties, media lacking this specific means of state policies) should make use of non-violent sanctions, positive inducements and persuasion, wherever prudent. The choice of appropriate policies depends upon the type of minority, the issue-specific conflicts of predominant practices with minimal or with minimal liberal morality and law, the specific goals of associations, and the degree of voluntariness and vulnerability of minorities.

Space prevents the comparison of the specific details of this approach with other approaches that share most of its basic tenets.[31] However, I think that liberal-democratic institutional pluralism, 'joint governance' and AD in particular provide the best opportunities to deal with problems of the protection of minorities and minorities within minorities. Yet it seems only fair to say that none of the available approaches can adequately solve the dilemmas of protecting vulnerable minorities within illiberal, anti-democratic and isolationist minorities. Here, it is most difficult to find morally defensible balances between individual and associational autonomy and external interference.[32] What we can and should do is guarantee basic needs and rights,[33] increase real exit options and try to strengthen the voice of insider minorities by means that do not override associational autonomy. For the rest, we can only hope that the fact that minorities (are forced to) live in and have to cope with modern societies will do some work in the long run. Requiring less (e.g. by granting full sovereignty) would sacrifice vulnerable minorities. Requiring more would impose specific liberal ways of life and sacrifice meaningful free exercise and associational autonomy.

It is also fair to say that all theories of democratic institutional pluralism or liberal-democratic joint governance (including AD) present fairly general, institutionally under-determined models. Clearly, the main research task ahead is to demonstrate what AD requires in specific countries, fields, and with regard to specific minorities, and this is what contextualised morality or 'grounded normativity' is all about (see chap. 10 for education).

8 Dilemmas of institutionalisation: associative democracy, church autonomy and equal treatment of religions

Here, institutionalisation is understood to contain the following conse-cutive steps: the development of mutual expectations by which new (immigrant) religions are 'here to stay' and also seen to be so; of their own organisations; of the different varieties of their public recognition; and of organised structures of selective cooperation at different levels of government (sect. 8.1). Institutionalisation is always a conflictive, two-way process. It involves many actors and is influenced by differen-tial opportunity structures (sect. 8.2). Institutionalisation includes pro-mises but also poses risks for religions, religious minorities in particu-lar (sect. 8.3) as well as for governments (sect. 8.4). As examples, I dis-cuss the empirical patterns of Muslim representative organisations in European States and the US (sect. 8.5) before drawing normative con-sequences from the fact that none of these patterns seems to provide appropriate solutions to the many dilemmas of institutionalisation (sect. 8.6).

8.1 Claims making, organisation, negotiations and selective cooperation

The long-term presence of new religions initiates processes of institu-tionalisation in every nation regardless of their regimes of governance. Newcomers raise claims to the permitting of their divergent religious practices in private and in public organisations (sects. 5.1 and 5.3). They have to *organise* (e.g. in local mosque associations) and to come up with representatives or spokespersons in order to be able to raise these claims effectively and to negotiate with management in the respective organisations and with public administration in neighbourhoods and municipalities. The capability to negotiate requires answers to ques-tions such as: who is negotiating? Whom is he/she representing? How representative are the spokespersons, interlocutors and organisations? How binding are concessions, compromises and agreements? (Bader 1991: 241f) These external pressures on organisation, leadership and mobilisation increase if, as usual, their claims are not smoothly accom-modated but more or less strongly resisted because they ask for the adaptation and change of implicit or rule-guided organisational and administrative customs and practices. In addition, the organisation and leadership of newcomers tends to become more stable and structural, as with all conflicts of longer duration.

Some claims (e.g. building mosques, funeral ceremonies or using cemeteries) require exemptions from rules and regulations of local public administration (zoning, building, parking and cemetery requirements) and induce a shift from private corporate governance to public government as addressee. They also require exemptions from state and federal laws, which is more obvious for claims to exemptions from tax law, labour law, military conscription, general admission rules (for ministers of religion), and for required changes in anti-discrimination law and/or blasphemy law (sect. 5.3). This stimulates a tendency to develop more centralised or umbrella organisations and leadership – from neighbourhoods to the municipal, state and federal levels of government as addressee. It also contributes to the politicisation of claims making, organisation, leadership and mobilisation,[1] particularly if these claims are resisted, as is initially and normally the case with exemption claims. This is much more so with claims to real respect and symbolic signification of the presence of religious newcomers (sect. 5.4) and even more so with claims to participating in the political centre in debates and decisions on rules (sect. 5.3). Centralisation and politisation are reinforced by counter-mobilisation of old religions, nativists and aggressive secularists. Increasingly, religious newcomers are drawn into lobbying and coalition building, and into traditional pluralist politics, whether they like it or not. Conflictive processes of 'negotiations *cum* deliberations' are an unavoidable side effect of claims making arising quasi-spontaneously. Eventually, as conflicts and negotiations become more routine, mutual expectations regarding ways and means of interaction, representative organisations and leadership of minorities, and some minimal trust between the parties emerge in all states, fairly independently of their regimes of government (Bader 1991, chap. X.4).

Yet, none of these processes are purely spontaneous processes from below, isolated from external impacts. They are strongly influenced by two clusters of variables.

First, new religious minorities do not act from scratch. Their claims, and also their ways of organising and mobilising, their strategies and actions 'in politics', are influenced by their respective doctrinal and organisational traditions. The internal organisational structure of religions shows huge variations in terms of formalisation, centralisation, hierarchy, democracy/autocracy and leadership. Christian church(es) differ from the Buddhist *sangha,* the Islamic *umma* and mosques, Hindu temples, Jewish councils and synagogues and from formally unorganised religious leadership in 'tribal' religions (chap. 1, note 16).

Furthermore, within Christendom, the spectrum reaches from the pole of the highly formalised, centralised, hierarchical, autocratic and international Roman Catholic Church via Orthodox and Lutheran or Anglican (Episcopal) national churches to fairly decentralised, radical Protestant congregations and informal sects. These organisational differences are related to differences in terms of strategy and action repertoire: from militant proselytising by military force to strict non-violence, civil disobedience and *satyagraha*. Less formalised, centralised and hierarchical structures seem to be less capable of representative and effective central negotiations, deliberations and compromises, and the respective religious communities (e.g. Muslim communities) are seduced and pressured into developing central or umbrella associations and leadership, particularly in institutionally pluralist regimes of religious government. In addition, these processes inside states are not neatly separated from the 'rest of the world'. They are increasingly international, particularly under conditions of *'glocalisation'*, evidently for those universalist religions that are internationally organised (the Roman Catholic Church) or have global pretensions (such as the 'unorganised' and officially 'leaderless' Islamic *umma*; backed by some 'Muslim states' like Saudi Arabia). However, this also applies to traditionally fairly parochial and formally unorganised 'tribal' religions (Tully 2003) and 'new age religions' inspired by Hindu and Buddhist traditions. Internationally organised or oriented religions and some foreign states have interests and also the means to influence processes inside states. Together, these differences in internal structure and international organisation and orientation help explain why new religious minorities show divergent patterns of organisation, mobilisation and institutionalisation within the same state.

Second, patterns of claims making, organisation, negotiation and selective cooperation are strongly influenced by divergent regimes of governing religious diversity and by differences in the general political opportunity structure. This helps explain why the same religious minority organises, mobilises and acts differently in different states (for Muslims in different European countries and the US, see section 8.5). Incorporation of religious minorities in all its dimensions inevitably includes many actors, but most prominently states on various levels.[2] All states have an interest in guaranteeing smooth public administration, public order, security and toleration, and in preventing violence and conflict escalation (policing religions). In addition to these general 'reasons of state', states with liberal-democratic constitutions should have (and to different degrees also actually have) an interest in guaranteeing the basic rights of all residents and minimally 'civilising and democratising' their citizens by appropriate policies. These state interests also

work in favour of a certain minimum of regular negotiation and national institutionalisation.

8.2 Differential opportunity structures; selective recognition and cooperation

Irrespective of divergent regimes of religious government, no liberal
state can avoid 'recognising' religions administratively and/or in legal
or jurisprudential practice to a certain degree (paras. 1.3.3.3 to 1.3.3.5).
In deciding whether individual claims to exemptions should be
granted, they all have to deal with the nasty questions of 'defining' religions either by legislation or jurisdiction. In deciding whether religions
or related organisations should be granted tax exemptions, states use
thresholds in terms of minimal numbers of adherents and minimal
duration and stability, and they do so regardless of whether these administrative practices are governed by legal rules and judicial control,
as they should be in liberal states, or not. If states grant FBOs public
money in care (as all liberal states do) or in education (as most states
do), these contested thresholds in terms of numbers, territorial concentration of clients/students, organisation, credibility and duration of service providers are usually and inevitably much higher.

Irrespective of countervailing ideologies and normative 'models', the
emerging pattern of selective (administrative, legal and judicial) recognition of religions and of selective institutionalised cooperation in all
liberal states involves two normative problems, which should be openly
acknowledged by all, instead of myopically used as weapons against defenders of NOCOP or AD. First, legal and other privileges, fiscal and
monetary 'gains' for religions go hand in hand with 'losses' in formal
autonomy of religions or with increases in corresponding standards of
state regulation and control (from minimal fiscal accountability to the
application of more demanding liberal-democratic standards of nondiscrimination laws). Second, the increase in privileges for religions is inevitably tied to increasing minimal thresholds, which work to the disadvantage of very small, new religious minorities, even if this is not intended and states try to counteract this unintended effect by explicit
minority policies.[3]

These problems are sharpened by institutionally pluralist regimes of
government (including AD), which provide opportunities for religions
in setting standards, implementation, control of services, selective cooperation with governments, and also some formal representation of
organised religions in the political process on all levels, particularly at
national and supra-state levels. They are characterised by much more
demanding systems of public recognition of religions, e.g. as 'Kör-

perschaften öffentlichen Rechts' in Germany as an extreme case, and by higher thresholds of systems of institutional interest intermediation. Moreover, they considerably increase the demand or need for religions to develop more centralised, representative organisational and leadership structures than those needed for lobbying in civil society and politics in NEPP.

8.3 Dilemmas and strategic problems for religions

All regimes, but especially institutionally pluralist ones, pose serious strategic problems for religions in general and for religious minorities in particular. The first is how to deal with the trade-off between autonomy and privileges, on the one hand, and political influence, on the other (the autonomy dilemma). The second refers to how one deals with problems inherent in institutionalisation (the organisation and mobilisation dilemma).

Ultra-orthodox Christians and Jews want to be left alone completely, hoping to achieve maximum autonomy by not asking for any privileges except those involved in being left alone. They only end up going to court, organising and mobilising when states do not guarantee the required exemptions. The strictest possible 'separation of state and religions' has also been propagated by Protestant Free Churches and by sects in a historical context of established churches and massive state interference into core issues of doctrine and internal organisation. Today, all states with liberal-democratic constitutions claim to respect church autonomy, and actually do so in different ways, which has softened the autonomy dilemma considerably (para. 1.3.3.4). It is also common practice that religions are free (as they should be) in their choice of whether to ask for registration, legal and judicial recognition or the more demanding public recognition needed for exemptions or additional privileges. Still, the choice is difficult because increasing privileges and opportunities of cooperation go hand in hand with more demanding criteria of recognition and more opportunities for governments to legitimately interfere with practices (Ferrari 2005: 7f), but also with clearly more illegitimate ways if governments try to impose their own 'liberal' and 'democratic' definitions of the respective religions. Honesty demands us to state at the outset that institutionally pluralist regimes pose some serious dangers such as increasing external pressure to adaptation, calculability, moderation, heightened internal control and disciplining of members and constituency, and even of intervention in contested core issues of religions. This all makes the choice more troublesome. Moreover, the choice is even more exacting for new and for small religions because the chance is much greater

that governments and administrations (having accommodated the practices of old religious majorities or even seen them as 'neutral') will define their 'strange' religious practices as illegitimate or illegal, and because small religions may be more in need of exemptions and positive
privileges but have less power to resist illegitimate state interference
(Robbins 1987: 145).

All religions have to face the dilemmas of organisation and leadership, of centralisation and institutionalised cooperation known from social movement studies (Bader 1991, chaps. VII and VIII.3). If religions
want to reap the benefits of registration, legal and judicial recognition
and material and political privileges and if they want to be politically effective in public and in negotiations on all levels of government, there
is a growing need to develop effective and representative organisations
and leadership. This is especially true for new religious minorities because they have to challenge established power balances and routines.
Yet, organisation, leadership and centralisation come at a price. Formal
organisation implies tendencies of bureaucratisation (organisation
costs, material interests of functionaries, tendency of conservatism, ritualism and rigidity) and oligarchisation (difficulties of controlling the
illegitimate power and domination of leaders).[4] This explains why
more communal, congregational and democratic religions (e.g. radical
Protestantism) are more critical and reluctant compared with Episcopal, hierarchical and autocratic churches, but they also have to address
the trade-off with political clout. Lobbying central government or supra-national polities increases the demand for religions to develop federal and even supra-national representational structures and – to repeat
– this demand is much stronger in institutionally pluralist systems.[5]
One way in which religions can respond is by organisational centralisation, which promises to overcome the negative effects of competition
between denominational organisations and leaders within one religion,
i.e. internal conflict instead of cooperation; the lack of (or lower degrees of) information, communication, and co-ordination; the lack of
minimally required unity in terms of issues, opinions, decisions and
action; ritualised battles amongst organisations and leaders; dogmatic
struggles over the 'purity' of the doctrine and the respective 'purification' and essentialisation of religion.[6] These effects, which are well
known from the radical Protestant denominational model, are highlighted by traditional theories and are used in external strategies of 'divide and rule' by opponents. The optimal response would then be the
organisational model of the *una sancta Catholica et apostolica eglesia'*,
the Roman Catholic Church representing all Catholics in all issues on
all levels in all countries.

However, organisational centralisation also has its serious downside
(ignored by Pfaff & Gill 2006), and competition between organisations

and leaders has often neglected positive effects. Inside one organisation, it tends to stimulate higher participation of members and more
democratic opinion and decision-making, as well as the capacity to
adapt, learn and innovate. Between organisations and leaders of the
same religion, it prevents the control and monopolisation of the religion by one organisation; it allows higher degrees of organised heterogeneity of the religion and at the same time more specialisation and internal unity of the competing religious organisations. It also tends to
broaden and deepen the involvement, motivation of believers and the
base of mobilisation, and it increases the capacity for innovation and
adaptation. In this regard, a model of a more or less loose federal association of independent organisations, like the Board of Jewish Deputies
in the UK, seems to be more appropriate, although it may be difficult
to transplant to the international level. The higher up and the more diverse the constituency and its organisations in terms of doctrinal differences or even cleavages, and in terms of ethnic and national composition, the more difficult is co-ordination and effective and legitimate representation.

In addition, institutionalised cooperation confronts religions with a
structural mobilisation dilemma: how to save the benefits of institutional pluralism (secure rights, legal and public recognition, public
money, cooperation and some representation in the political process)
without the usual losses of initiative, motivation, spontaneity, activism
of religious constituency and members on which the mobilisation potential and the relative power position of the organisations are based.
The difficulty in finding workable solutions for this dilemma (the practical version of 'Veralltäglichung des Charisma') is vividly demonstrated
by the different historical waves of evangelisation in opposition to established, bureaucratised Protestant churches or by the mobilisational
power of recent Pentecostalism compared with stuffy, saturated Anglican churches.

8.4 Dilemmas and strategic problems for liberal states

These problems of religions are mirrored by serious dilemmas and
strategic problems for liberal states and, again, no one best solution is
available. Liberal states (as all states that want to guarantee security,
public peace and order) have to choose a context-dependent mixture of
policies of persuasion, positive or negative sanctions, or repression,
which may have counterproductive effects. In addition, liberal states
are restrained in their means by the rule of law, due process and constitutionally guaranteed civil and political rights and freedoms of communication. The inherent tension between security and public order

and these constraints increases dramatically under conditions of (defined or real) emergency, as the recent internal and external 'war on terrorism' painfully reminds us.

In guaranteeing smooth administration, the choice is between a government that is separated as far as possible from all 'interest groups' (including religions) and governance, selective and gradual cooperation with relevant stakeholders, including religions. State definition of rules and standards, implementation and control may at first sight promise better rule compliance, accountability and control. However, it is confronted with serious problems of efficiency and effectiveness, which increase dramatically in complex matters where governance promises much better results. In addition, governance has problems in living up to a traditional understanding of the rules of law and democracy.[7]

The task of the liberal state in guaranteeing the basic rights of all citizens and residents, particularly those of vulnerable minorities, requires external intervention in cases of serious violations (sects. 4.4 and 4.5). Systems of selective registration and legal recognition of religions seem to provide better chances here compared with strict 'separation' and absolute autonomy or libertarian 'leave them alone', although these systems also cannot resolve the difficulties in cases of small, formally unorganised sects.

Systems and policies of selective financing and cooperation that apply more demanding liberal and democratic standards may increase chances of illegitimate state intervention in the core of religions (sect. 4.3) and they are vulnerable to charges of unequal treatment. On the one hand, policies to finance and cooperate with the more civilised, liberal and moderate religious organisations may contribute to stem radicalisation and religious fundamentalism. However, they may also backfire because the external influence in the development of religious minorities may be seen as illegitimate, the 'moderate' organisations and leaders may be accused of being traitors, and the excluded organisations may radicalise. On the other hand, systems and policies of 'absolute separation' – no public money or privileges in education and care, for houses of worship, religious instruction in schools or (the education of) Imams – may also contribute to radicalisation and fundamentalism. This is particularly so if they are (or are seen to be) unfairly excluding only certain new, 'strange' religions like Islam(s), if their individual and associational religious freedoms are partly infringed, and if accommodation of their legitimate religious practices is absent, reluctant or delayed. If governments do not provide money and assistance, foreign states and international terrorist networks are eager to do so and actually finance mosques, madrassas and Imams. If public money and assistance is not provided as a regular part of policies of incorporation of minorities but only as a delayed reaction to perceived or actual processes of segregation and radicalisation and with the explicit intent of 'liberalising and democratising' the 'Muslim community' (as, most prominently, in France), the chances of de-legitimisation of 'collaborating' religious associations and of radicalisation of the excluded ones are much higher.

Systems of selective cooperation depend on and stimulate the emergence of representative organisation(s) and leader(s) on national and supra-state levels, and even otherwise fairly separationist countries initiate such processes for reasons of counterinsurgency or state-imposed 'integration'. Here, the policy choice is either to wait until these structures develop more or less spontaneously from below or try to organise the process from above through direct state policies intended to externally initiate, stimulate, influence and steer these processes. The disadvantage of the first option is that self-organisation may be completely blocked by internal doctrinal, ethnic and linguistic differences, cleavages, organisational rivalry and leadership competition. Moreover, it may take a very long time, with no representative organisations and leaders' administrations to cooperate with in the meantime. The disadvantages of the second option is that the whole process may be seen as illegitimate external imposition, that it provides states with chances to intervene in the core matters of religious belief and practice incompatible with religious freedoms and autonomy, that it massively contributes to internal splits and cleavages and that it de-legitimises 'collaborating' 'moderate or liberal' organisations and leaders. In addition, neither option guarantees that it will win, and not more traditionalist or conservative organisations and leaders.

8.5   Representative Muslim organisations in Europe and the US

The diverse patterns of the emergence of representative Muslim organisations at the national and supra-state level in Europe and the US, very roughly summarised here, vividly demonstrate these dilemmas.

8.5.1 Institutionalisation of Islam in Europe

The common element of all regimes of selective cooperation is 'the need to promote the constitution of an organization or a coordinating body that represents the largest possible number of the Muslim communities present in a country, independent from the religious and national currents into which they are divided.' (Ferrari 2005a: 10) In those *European* countries in which legislation and jurisdiction on religious matters is focused at the national level, 'Muslim communities are condemned to remain at the edges of the system of relations between the state and the religious groups' without an institution of this type.

In some countries, the Muslim community was recognised by law fairly early on: In the Austrian Hungarian Empire in 1912, in Poland in 1936 and in Austria in 1979. In other countries, legal recognition and actual representative organisations came much later: In Belgium, Islam was recognised in 1974 but the first elections only took place in 1998; in Spain in 1992, in France in 2003. In the UK, Italy, and Germany, until now no representative organisation of the Islamic communities exists or is legally recognised.

This divergence can only be partly explained by the time and size of the respective Muslim settlements and by internal differences in the respective Muslim communities.[8] It is also the result of imperial and colonial traditions (in Austria, the UK, France and the Netherlands) and of legal regimes: whether a unitary organisation is required (as in Germany and Italy), whether a federation of independent organisations or even several independent organisations is/are accepted (as in Sweden and Norway). In addition, differences in state policies have a considerable impact: (i) whether governments facilitate fairly autonomous Muslim representation (as in Austria) are more neutral and/or reluctant (as in the UK and Germany (Pfaff & Gill 2006: 814f, 820-822)) or try to impose their preferred unitary pattern of representation and their preferred organization and leaders, as in Belgium and France; (ii) whether they follow pro-active policies of selective cooperation, which are part and parcel of their normal religion and/or multiculturalism policies, or reactive policies of 'fighting terrorism' in isolation from (as in France) or combined with radical changes in the traditional regimes of religious government and minority incorporation (as recently in the Netherlands).

The French attempts to create a single, national representative Muslim body with which to negotiate and deliberate, and also draw legitimacy for the state's decisions, may illustrate problems of such a reactive, late, top-down approach. Since the 1980s, different Left and Right governments (from the helm of the Ministry of the Interior) tried to create such an *instance représentative* as an 'identified interlocutor' in three major efforts (see extensively Bowen 2006: 42-62). First, in 1989, as a direct response to the 'Islamic threat' symbolised by the first foulard affair and the fatwa against Salman Rushdie, Pierre Joxe set up the *Conseil de Réflexion de l'Islam de France* (CORIF) as an advisory body presided over by the rector of the Paris Mosque. It collapsed in the following year. The second effort was made by Charles Pasqua, who formed a new Representative Council of French Muslims in 1995 around the *Charte du culte musulman en France*, leaving out major players like the

UOIF and the FNMF. The council never had any authority or influence. The third attempt began with Jean-Pierre Chevènement's creation of the Consultation of French Muslims in 1999 and, after laborious state crafting, eventually produced the *Conseil français du culte musulman* (CFCM) in 2003. I briefly point to some of the inherent problems.

First, these attempts show that France 'is caught in a dilemma faced by most efforts to construct legitimate representation from the top down: those willing to be "co-opted" are also those with the least legitimacy' (Bowen 2006: 55). Seven Muslim organisations have been entangled in power struggles for representation and leading roles in this process. Attempts by Joxe and Pasqua to privilege the Paris Mosque, and by Sarkozy to guarantee that Dalil Boubakeur, the State's 'favourite moderate Muslim', would be the first President of the CFCM have been vigorously opposed and failed. Some attempts have clearly been untimely and strategically unwise.

Second, possibly motivated by the consideration that 'Islam is today the only religion without a national unified organization' (*Libération* 21 February), Sarkozy aimed to end this seemingly endless struggle for power by 'devising rules for selecting members to the Council that would be at least minimally acceptable to all' and by ensuring that 'the two associations with the strongest control over participating mosques (the UOIF and the FNMF) did not end up controlling the Council' (Bowen 2006: 56). Eventually, under strong time pressure and state interference, an agreement was reached about the composition of the CFCM and about electoral procedures, and the elections were held in April 2003. State administration not only initiated this process, it also financed the elections and massively influenced procedures and composition of the Council. Still, some think that it has '*pleinement joué son rôle de médiateur et de facilitateur en veillant à ne pas exercer de tutelle*' (Sevaistre 2004: 41) and some scholars like Ferrari (2005b: 10) seem to agree.[9] I agree with John Bowen that this judgement seriously underestimates the second aim of the French administration and its impact on the negotiations about the composition of the Council and the electoral procedures. The roles of facilitator and mediator and the role of the interested party have not been clearly separated, and cannot be in principle. French administration indeed interpreted and used its self-proclaimed competencies in a 'Bonapartist' fashion (Terrel 2004: 71-74; Bowen 2006: 60).[10]

Third, the second main aim of the French administration has explicitly and consistently been to control and domesticate Islam, to assimilate Islam into the republic, to create a moderate, liberal and privatised 'French' Islam and to fight 'the idea of a 'community' that runs counter to French Republican principles' (Jean-Pierre Raffarin, *Le Figaro* 5 May

2003), instead of allowing the free association and organisation of the
different 'Islam(s) in France' on their own terms. It has been unambiguously expressed and made clear 'that the State intended the CFCM
to be its instrument in promoting its sort of Islam and ridding France
of all other sorts'. Prime Minister Raffarin ordered the CFCM to serve
as 'the enlightened word of French Islam to fight against deviant tendencies which could threaten social cohesion' (Bowen 2006: 62).

The French case vividly demonstrates two points. First, state interventions into the organisational structure and even more so into core
matters of faith are clearly beyond the threshold of morally legitimate
interference and also seem to be incompatible with the respective constitutional and legal regulations in France and with ECHR (European
Convention on Human Rights), Art. 9. Second, they also conflict seriously with proclaimed state neutrality (both in the older and in the
more refined recent versions of *laïcité*) and with constitutional and legal regulations on equal treatment of religious groups.

Two more general, empirical conclusions for European countries
seem in order. First, the importance of the existence or absence of a national representation of Muslims (whether legally recognised or not)
depends very much on the regime of religious government. The absence of a representative Muslim presence at the central level in the
UK, where no form of legal registration and recognition of religious
communities exists and negotiations are mainly local, is much less serious than in Italy or Germany. Here many legal and monetary privileges are exclusively granted to centrally and publicly recognised religions and the absence of central recognition cannot be compensated
for by cooperation at local or provincial (*Länder*) levels (Ferrari 2005b:
7-9).

Second, we see the emergence of three different patterns of central
Muslim representation: a more 'church'-like central, unitary organisation (mainly as a result of state imposition) as in France or Belgium, a
confederal association that represents the common interests of independent Muslim organisations in a co-ordinated and legally recognised
way (as the Spanish *Comisión Islamica de España*),[11] and the representation of Muslim communities by several independent, loosely co-ordinated, publicly recognised organisations (as in Sweden (Otterbeck
2004) or Norway). At present, it seems unlikely that one and the same
representational pattern will emerge in all member states of the European Union.[12]

8.5.2 Institutionalisation of Islam in the US

The situation in the US differs from the European one in three main
aspects: (i) the impact of denominationalism on all religions, (ii) the

fairly limited system of selective cooperation, and (iii) the absence of state-induced or imposed patterns of organisation and representation.

The religious landscape in the US emerged and developed in opposition to European church-like structures (both Catholic and Protestant) under the predominance of radical Protestantism and its typical denominational structure. At the basic level of local religious communities, congregationalism is characterised by an associational pattern that shows fairly high degrees of voluntarism, by a non-profit organisational form led by laity, and by the fact that congregations are 'more than houses of worship or prayer but become authentic community centres with different kinds of educational and social services, fellowship and recreational activities, and task-specific associational networks' (Casanova 2005: 25).[13] This originally radically Protestant congregational pattern has been historically adopted by other immigrant religions, first by Catholicism, next by Judaism and now also by Islam, Hinduism and Buddhism, fairly 'irrespective of their traditional institutional form in their home settings', whether they are characterised by a quasi-congregational structure like Islam or not (like Buddhism and Hinduism) (Casanova 2005: 23). Christian churches, synagogues, mosques, masjids and temples are transformed into congregations. At the level of denominations properly speaking, American Protestantism 'emerged as doctrinally or ethno-racially differentiated plural denominations', whereas 'the hierarchically organised Roman Catholic Church was able to incorporate all Catholic immigrants (with the exception of the Polish National Church) into a single American Catholic Church through the ethnic parish system. American Judaism also became differentiated into three main denominations (Orthodox, Reform and Conservative). It is still unclear whether various branches or traditions of the other world religions will become institutionalised as separate denominations in America or whether other denominational divisions will emerge' (Casanova 2005: 26). At the national level of 'imagined community' at which immigrant religions 'gain symbolic recognition and are thus incorporated into the nation as 'American', Casanova thinks that this incorporation takes place 'irrespective of whether they also develop national organizations'.

Second, contrary to 'separationist' ideology, the US also has practices of selective legal recognition and support of religions. Yet, an elaborate system of selective cooperation as in Italy, Austria or Germany is absent, particularly at the federal level. Not many privileges can be gained, there is no central 'negotiation table' that would require some form of public recognition of religions and of structured selective cooperation. Religions are not induced by positive incentives to develop national organisations and federal administration is not in need of interlocutors representing religions (supply and demand sides do not stimulate their emergence).

Third, unlike France or Belgium, the state does not attempt to impose a uniform organisational and representational pattern. On the one hand, the result is that religions (new minority religions included) are inspired to develop national organisations or associational structures only or mainly in order to more effectively propagate and proselytise, to influence civil society and – like all other interest organisations – to lobby. Lobbying means trying to influence legislation, administration and judiciary, informally and indirectly. It also means trying to gain national symbolic recognition to extend the denominational forms of American civil religion from Protestant-Catholic-Jewish to 'Abrahamic' or eventually to incorporate all world religions and become 'the first new global society', because this process is not so independent of national organisations, their power resources, mobilisation and strategies as Casanova (2005: 26-28) assumes. On the other hand, the state's interest in national representatives of religions (including new minority religions) is limited to symbolic demonstrations of its neutrality and, because of American religious pluralism, at ceremonies in response to terrorist attacks.[14]

Islam has now taken root in the US as one of the major American religions. As in European countries, the internal challenge confronting Islam is how to supersede linguistic, ethnic, national and doctrinal diversity, 'how to transform diverse immigrants from South Asia, which today constitute the largest and fastest growing group of Muslim immigrants, from Arab countries and West Africa into a single American Muslim umma' (Casanova 2005: 29). Two cultural options seem to compete: the segregated, defensive sub-cultural 'Nation of Islam model' versus a public, self-assertive, powerful and cultural option within American competitive religious and cultural pluralism, 'which many Muslims view as an actualization of Islam's universalism' (Islamisation of America to counterbalance the Americanisation of Islam). Like earlier Catholic and Jewish minorities, Islam is also confronted with the related pressure to choose an appropriate organisational and representational structure.

> (i)t is still an open question which kind of internal denominational structure Islam in America is going to assume: whether it will succumb to what Niebuhr called 'the evil of denominationalism', which he saw grounded in socio-economic and ethno-racial divisions or it will organize itself into a national church-like umma, able to bridge its internal ethno-linguistic and juridical-doctrinal divisions. American Protestantism, Catholicism and Judaism (three main denominations and the Board of Jewish De-

puties representing common interests – V.B.) represent in this respect alternative denominational models. American Islam is likely to develop its own distinct denominational pattern, while sharing some elements with all three (Casanova 2005: 30).

In contrast with Europe, this choice is not massively crafted by state administrations, and this fact considerably alleviates the related problems of church autonomy, equal treatment of religions and relational state neutrality. Islam(s) in America is/are less forced into an imposed 'American Islam'. The 'Americanisation of Islam' from below is more the unintended but welcome by-product of the American system of religious governance than the result of intentional state policies to 'Americanise Islam', compared to attempts to create a 'French' Islam from above.

8.6 Associative democracy, church autonomy, legal and substantive equal treatment

All existing regimes of religious governance and all alternative institutional designs have to deal with tensions among normative principles. No ideal model – neither an idealised NEPP nor AD – can maximise or optimise them all. Here, I focus on two trade-offs involved in my analysis of institutionalisation: on the autonomy dilemma and on legal or substantive equal treatment.

The American denominational regime and European regimes of selective cooperation both guarantee individual religious rights, which is an important similarity. The latter provide more legal and substantive privileges and more representation in the political process for recognised religions but also permit more involvement by public powers (interventionism) in religious matters that potentially or actually infringe on church autonomy. Recognition of and cooperation with religions by the state is inevitably selective and this selectivity is reflected in the pyramid of plural legal statuses established by states for various religions. Systems of public recognition and cooperation are also more rigid and less open and pluralist. On the face of it, the American regime clearly seems preferable because it respects church autonomy more fully, it guarantees a more, though also not a totally, equal legal treatment of all religions, particularly of minority religions, and it is more flexible and pluralist. Can AD overcome some of these serious shortcomings of existing regimes of public recognition in Europe and also avoid some of the deficiencies of existing American denominationalism?[15]

8.6.1 Church autonomy or selective recognition and cooperation?

In all liberal-democratic regimes, the autonomy of religions is restricted by moral and legal requirements to guarantee essential basic rights of members and non-members. Within these constraints, autonomy rights with regard to the doctrinal and legal core and the internal organisational structure of religions are necessary to guarantee a wide and well-defended space of freedom for all religions, including the smallest, newest and 'strangest' ones. The legal instruments to guarantee individual and collective religious freedom should be equally and indiscriminately available to all religions, but this requirement has often not been applied in European countries in the face of Islam and new, spiritual religious movements (Ferrari 2005a: 9). Autonomy rights for religious core organisations, however, do not equally cover FBOs in education and care. All regimes rightly and legitimately impose requirements of fiscal accountability and differentiated applications of anti-discrimination law, labour law and co-determination law on these organisations if they are partly or fully publicly financed. The meaning, extent and limits of religious autonomy and the depth and width of legitimate exemptions are contested and continually negotiated both in Europe and in the US (paras. 1.3.3.5 to 1.3.3.8). I agree with Ferrari that 'public administration can graduate its support within certain limits and maintaining certain proportions' (2005b: 16). However, I suspect that the broad reference to 'the democratic and secular rules of the state' and the perceived 'impact of religions on civil co-existence' may do more harm than good in this regard (see para. 4.3.5 for the slippery slope in public trust theory). I have advocated a more offensive 'libertarian' position to safeguard the associational autonomy of religions, which also extends to the question of national representation of organised religions in the political process. AD, similar to European cooperation regimes, provides opportunities for cooperation that is inevitably selective. However, it clearly insists that central organisational and representational structures by the respective religions emerge as far as possible from below, to avoid the second great threat to religious autonomy through external state-crafting from above.[16] Here too, autonomy rights should be defended and as clearly as possible distinguished from 'rights to cooperation' (Ferrari 2005b: 16).

8.6.2 Equality, selectivity, legitimate and illegitimate exclusions

Registration, administrative, judicial and legal recognition of religions are inevitably selective in terms of time and durability of settlement, minimal numbers of adherents and stability of association/organisation. Minimal thresholds and inevitable selectivity, however, increase in steps when it comes to material and other privileges, particularly (i) when systems of official cooperation between administrations and publicly recognised religions emerge, (ii) when FBOs participate in standard setting, implementation and control, and (iii) when some religious organisations gain rights and opportunities of representation in the political process. 'Reasons of history, number of adherents, social roots, and so on' (Ferrari 2005a: 8) clearly matter in existing regimes and, according to a contextualised theory of morality, legitimately so. Yet, selectivity means inclusion and exclusion, and the normative problem is how to prevent illegitimate exclusionary effects, inflexibility and rigidity, which are particularly serious for religious minorities.

The establishment of private, faith-based schools and care institutions requires a certain minimum number of students and clients and also the size of territorial concentration, even independent of public financing and recognition. Very small or dispersed religious minorities are quasi-'naturally' excluded. Public financing requires the definition and application of contested minima in terms of numbers. Equality before and under the law requires that these thresholds (which may be different for primary, secondary and high schools, etc.) have to be applied equally and indiscriminately to all applicants, irrespective of faiths. Also, fairness requires that they are as low as possible to prevent exclusion of minorities not based on justifiable grounds of feasibility or workability. All service delivery, whether publicly financed or not, has to live up to contested minimal standards of provision but public financing and recognition may add more demanding standards. Again, these standards should be applied equally and indiscriminately to all applicants, and fairness as even-handedness requires that public authorities do not impose 'biased' contents and procedures on religions, on religious minorities in particular (sects. 5.2 and 5.3).

Because numbers and standards of service delivery are hotly contested, it is crucial that organised religions are involved in negotiations and deliberations at the municipal, provincial/state and national levels where decisions are made. Regimes of governance of education, care or media differ widely among countries, and the higher the levels of decision-making competencies the stronger the incentive for and the pressure on the respective religions to develop representative national or federal peak organisations. Furthermore, systems of associative governance of sectors (e.g. education and healthcare) increase the thresholds considerably because the respective councils (analogous to the tripartite neo-corporatist socio-economic councils) impose stricter limits on the number of participating parties (i.e. public authorities; representative organisations of service providers as employers, of professions and of clients). Unlike parliaments, they have to be working bodies if they (i) promise to deliver the gains of organised interest intermediation: increase the deliberative character of negotiations; (ii) foster less particularist, more other- and future-regarding definitions of interests and preferences; (iii) find more innovative, less biased definitions of situations and issues, and new, unexpected, more 'fact and future regarding' ways to solve problems;[17] (iv) increase trust among participating parties with divergent and partly conflicting interests; (v) deliver better informed and more efficient and effective standard setting, implementation and control. The requisite exclusion for functional reasons, which may vary in different sectors, is still an 'unsettled empirical issue' (Cohen & Rogers 1992: 445) and a matter of institutional tinkering. Yet, two points seem plain to me. First, the existing systems at sector, national and EU levels are needlessly and unfairly exclusive. Second, even less exclusive or closed systems are confronted with the problem 'to find a reasonable trade-off between (morally recommendable) inclusion and (functionally required) workability' (Bader 2001: 39).

Developed sectoral systems of representation of religious organisations are scarce (e.g. for public media in Austria) and standard setting and control in education and care seems to be reserved for public authorities only (parliaments, departments of education or healthcare and state inspections). Often, national public recognition of one religious organisation is only required for religious schools even if the educational system is federal as in Germany, where the requirement of legal recognition as 'Körperschaft öffentlichen Rechts' has impeded Muslim religious instruction at the Länder level. (And this is neither functionally required nor fair because the requirement of one national organisation for all Christian denominations would be clearly outrageous.) At the national level, existing systems of public recognition in European countries are often needlessly and unfairly exclusive. Criteria for recognition are vague and not applied indiscriminately; there is too much discretionary power by public administrations and too little judiciary control,[18] which is a disadvantage that would be even more serious if the actual recognition that is needed for any negotiations were left to administrations alone.

In addition, this unfair selectivity of existing national regimes[19] is stabilised by two aspects characteristic for all systems of organised interest representation: their rigidity (how vested their constituent organisations are), and the respective lock-in effects (Bader 2001: 43f). Once established, systems of public recognition of religions tend to become quasi-permanent because they endow religious organisations with public status, subsidies and power, which they may use to freeze their position and to exclude newcomers, and also because it takes quite some time before demanding legal recognition of newcomers is successfully completed.[20]

This selectivity is reproduced at the level of the European Union in the informal initiatives of the *European Commission* (Massignon 2003: 4ff). In 1994, the initiative 'A Soul for Europe' was established for funding inter-religious seminars and projects. This initiative includes two representatives each from Catholicism, Protestantism, Judaism, Islam, and agnostic or atheistic Humanism, independent of the relative size of their respective traditions.

In addition, there are '(t)he twice-yearly briefing sessions following European summits organised by Forward Studies Unit, a think tank attached to the Commission Presidency. By 2003, there were 50 invited partners, religious representatives, religious NGOs and European offices of religious orders. Unlike the "Soul for Europe" initiative, Buddhists, Hindus, Christian Scientists and Scientologists also take part. Protestant Churches are more widely represented by Evangelicals, Pentecostalists and Quakers. A diversity of Muslims and Jewish organisations are invited. The Russian Orthodox Church opened an office in Brussels by the end of 2002. So did the Catholic Church of Ukraine in 2003'.

This informal representation is clearly more pluralist and open than existing representations at the level of member states but has 'structural limits. In the absence of official relations between the religions and the European institutions, developing strategies to influence the European decision-making process and even simply obtaining information on developments in European integration requires considerable resources. The Catholic, Protestant and humanist networks – the most structured organisations at the EU level – are not on an equal footing'.[21] Massignon proposes the establishment of a consultative NGO status by European institutions, comparable to the European Council, to complete the fulfilment of this informal pluralism, which she sees threatened by attempts of the Churches seeking an official recognised status. 'This development would automatically define who was included and who was excluded. Lacking expertise, the European Commission is already inviting the more structured groups, KEK and COMECE, to seminars of dialogue on specific topics concerning EU policy. In the same way, there are unofficial tripartite KEK, COMECE and European Council meetings before each new EU Presidency' (chap. 5).

Can AD avoid or soften this unfair selectivity, fixity and closure of existing systems of selective cooperation at national and at the emerging European level and, if so, how, by which proposals?

First, AD tries to keep the thresholds for representation and cooperation as low as compatible with workability requirements, and also to include the relevant stakeholders. For (national and European) *advisory councils* (religious councils, 'ethics councils') that are not involved in decision-making and implementation, the thresholds can be much lower than those of sectoral councils. Also, AD vigorously insists that the voice of relevant vulnerable internal minorities should be represented in the former, if they so wish and are sufficiently organised. In *sectoral governance bodies*, the thresholds are higher but minorities can and should be represented. As with all organised interest representation, however, the wish to be represented, the capacity to make claims, and a stepwise, increased, minimal organisational capacity are required.[22] For three reasons, AD is more open and flexible than existing neo-corporatist types because it does not overemphasise the demands of encompassment, integrative capacity and scope of responsibility of the represented organisations; it keeps the type of representative organisation open (one centralised vs. federations or some independent organisations); and it does not insist that Muslims are represented by one organisation while Christians are represented by several denominations. In addition, representation is not equally important in all sectors to all religions. It need not be the same religious organisations that provide services in the different sectors, and a central, nation-wide, 'public' or legal recognition is not required for representation and cooperation on provincial or local levels.[23] In all of these regards, associative interest representation is less exclusive than existing ones, but it also has to accept the abovementioned challenge to find a reasonable trade-off between inclusion and workability.

Second, highlighting the inevitable selectivity of formalised systems of representation and cooperation should not make us forget that systems (such as US denominationalism) that restrict interest representation to informal ways of influencing governments through network building, lobbying etc. are even more vulnerable to inequality charges because old, big 'established' religions have huge and unchecked advantages in terms of power resources and strategies.[24] AD's less exclusive, more open formalised system is thus an interesting alternative, also at the European level, which Massignon neglects in her conclusion that formalisation of an official recognised status would 'automatically' privilege the big, old religions.

Third, AD promises a more sensible tension balance between equality before the law and more substantive equality. Yet this promise partly depends upon the effectiveness of the proposed measures to counteract vestedness and lock-in effects. AD demands and tries to institutionalise procedures of external review and evaluation at regular intervals for the renewal of grants and of the legal status of privileged organisations after accreditation (Cohen & Rogers 1992: 444, 450). The threats of withdrawal or amendment must be serious and credible and the gains of accepting such scrutiny must be considerable for religions and FBOs (chap. 10). These are important measures but one should not underestimate the difficulties of external scrutiny and control in terms of time, information and access to insider knowledge. These difficulties are alleviated by democratic and transparent internal organisational structures that increase the possibilities of external control and accountability considerably (Mansbridge 1992). However, honesty requires me to clearly state that the version of AD I am defending resists the temptation to impose democratic internal structures (its own favourite democratic stakeholder model of 'corporate governance') on FBOs,[25] although it places the burden of proof for exemptions clearly on them and it requires adequate standards of financial accountability. In any case, the most important effect of putting systems of public scrutiny and control in place is an indirect one. Working in the shadow of hierarchy stimulates meaningful internal, pro-active self-control considerably. In addition to (the threat of) withdrawal, the fixity and rigidity of formalised systems of cooperation can be counteracted by choosing 'softer law' instead of hard or even constitutional law. More precisely, if systems of selective recognition, representation and cooperation are part of the constitutional law of countries, constitutions should, to repeat, only contain procedures, criteria and standards but not name specific religious organisations.

Proposals like these promise better balances between competing principles for national systems of cooperation and for possible supranational regimes of religious governance in the EU 'halfway between the pluralist interdenominational American model and the classic European model of a hierarchy of recognized religions' (Massignon 2003: 6). To indicate these possibilities, I apply some of the general proposals to counteract unfair exclusive effects and structural inequalities of emerging European governance arrangements in the spirit of associationalism to religious governance.[26] Phil Schmitter's proposal (2000: 56ff) to establish functional sub-parliaments or standing committees to formalise functionally diverse, pluralist representation and expertise in the legislative process of the EU may be extended to give religions a more formalised advisory role in European rule making. The proposals by Joerges (1999: 311ff; 2001: 140) to increase the deliberative character of the negotiations in existing European 'comitology' and, at the same time, the pluralism and openness of European regulatory policy are also relevant because they are explicitly meant to heighten sensitivity regarding cultural issues, including religious differences in administration and implementation. Again, the problem with existing practices is that they are less open, fair, transparent and accountable than they could be. The most elaborate proposals for tackling unequal access, expertocracy and problematic informality of emerging European Governance Arrangements (EGAs) are Schmitter's principles for the chartering, composition and decision rules of EGAs in an associational spirit, to increase the democratic legitimacy of the delegation of powers to these political institutions (2001). If applied and worked out in practice, they allow the formalisation of the representation of functional, cultural and religious interests in a more open, flexible, pluralist way without a dramatic decrease in efficiency and effectiveness.

Whether such a realistic utopia can be realised is one of the most intriguing open issues of our times. It would combine the best of the existing US denominationalist and the European selective cooperation regimes of religious governance. AD, as we have seen, shares with NEPP the open, pluralist, largely voluntarist character, and also the trust in the beneficial working of an adequate liberal-democratic institutional environment on new religious minorities instead of direct state 'integration' policies to impose liberal and democratic institutions and virtues. However, it hopes to avoid its downsides by offering religions a fairer, open and flexible system of institutional pluralism, of selective recognition, representation and cooperation with old and new religions, which it shares in principle with European NOCOPs.[27] Basically, I am convinced that it is possible to combine the best aspects of these competing models, and I have tried to indicate how this could be done. However, I have also made it clear that it is hard to find sensible balances among conflicting moral principles, and that trade-offs with other normative principles like efficiency, effectiveness and workability are involved. Even if it seems possible to find better, more sensitive solutions to some of these trade-offs, one still has to deal with realistic challenges of feasibility and inevitable counterproductive effects. After all, the way to hell is paved with good moral intentions.

9 A realistic defence of associative democracy

Associative religious governance, like consociationalism and multiculturalism, may be vulnerable to the following realistic objections. Notwithstanding its morally good intentions, it is said to lead to disruptive conflicts between secular or religious majorities and religious minorities, it threatens the stability of the polity and undermines minimally required social cohesion and political unity. It does so because it empowers minority organisations and leaders who, for structural reasons, tend to engage in separationist strategies, because it does not create but eventually undermines minimally required conciliatory attitudes, because it does not create but inevitably undermines minimal civic and democratic virtues and also loyalty and commitment to the polity. It is also said to severely restrict or exclude opportunities for non-communal everyday interactions in public institutions and encounters. Some of these general objections may be less to the point regarding religious minorities, e.g. the nasty consequences of categorisation and stigmatisation because religious belonging may be more voluntary and because even all existing forms of institutionalisation of religions are clearly based on self-definition (Bader 2003c: 146ff). Others, such as rigidity, seem less serious because AD is more flexible, open and choice-based than existing varieties of religious institutional pluralism.

I will first refute the objections that involve vicious context-independent effects or 'institutional structures' and 'measures' (Horowitz 1991a: 452) because they are more accessible for 'deliberative action' (458) than contexts and conditions, which may be very hard to influence via politics, at least in the short and medium term. However, institutional and policy proposals in the spirit of AD may not be equally feasible in all contexts (sect. 9.8).

Realistic evaluations are complex and contested (Bader & Engelen 2003: 384). Hence, my attempt to refute charges against religious associative governance cannot mobilise consensus amongst social scientists. It is also not intended to play down the difficulties of institutional design but to undermine the *prima facie* evidence of the challenges shared by most libertarians, liberals, republicans, deliberative democrats and postmodernists and, increasingly so, in actual political talk against 'Multiculturalism', 'Communalism', 'religious pillarisation', and 'parallel societies'.

9.1   Context-independent vicious effects: undermining stability?

Institutional pluralism is said to undermine the *stability* of society and polity, to disunite and 'balkanise' the country regardless of groups and contexts (Lind 1995; Hollinger 1996; Offe 1998a; Barry 2001). This ostensibly general effect of all forms of institutional pluralism is hotly contested, as the theoretically guided and empirically informed old discussions between representatives of consociational approaches (Lijphart 1968; Van Dijk 1995), integrative approaches (Horowitz 1985) and control approaches (Lustick 1979) have clearly shown. Obviously, stability may mean many things (Bader 2001e): it may mean stable patterns of gross inequality, a stable repressive state, stable patterns of oppressive cultures. It may also mean a relatively stable rule of law, stable minimal government, and minimal security and safety as in Lijphart's 'civil peace and a democratic system of government' (1985: 87) as well as gradual non-disruptive rates of cultural change (Bader 1997a: 48). Only the latter kinds of stability are worth defending from a liberal-democratic point of view. If religious institutional pluralism were to threaten the minimally required stability of government and rule of law, for instance, even coercive integration of religious minorities by a strong repressive majoritarian state may be preferable. This is because stability in this sense is an important prudential aim intimately connected to the basic right to life and security (sect. 2.2; Lustick 1979: 332ff).

The supposed integrative or disintegrative effects of institutional separation and cultural pluralism depend on two clusters of variables (para. 6.4.2). First, on whether they are relatively freely accepted by both minorities and majorities, and whether the resulting centrifugal or centripetal strategies point towards the same solution. Second, on contextual variables addressed below. If one focuses on institutions and policies, bracketing contexts, the presumed disintegrative effects refer to issues of minimal social cohesion and political unity (sect. 9.2), of civic and democratic virtues (sect. 9.3), whether the opportunity for separate institutions creates 'parallel societies' undermining everyday inter-religious encounters and their presumed beneficial effects generally (sect. 9.4), in schools, parties and workplaces (sect. 9.5), and in public spaces (sect. 9.6) in particular, and whether it breeds or creates religious fundamentalism or even terrorism (sect. 9.7).

9.2 Undermining social cohesion and political unity?

The fear of disintegrative effects is very often based on uncritical assumptions regarding social cohesion, which are incompatible with
functionally and culturally differentiated societies. Modern societies require much less social cohesion, and minimally required social cohesion rests less on moral principles, shared cultures, virtues and 'reasonable public deliberation' than moral and political philosophers still
largely assume (Bader 2001e). Moreover, the thick versions of 'shared
values, cultures, habits and virtues' are often incompatible with the presumed 'neutrality' of the liberal-democratic state in all matters of the
Good Life.

   Yet, all versions of institutional pluralism are also said to undermine
minimally required political unity. Again, this objection has an institutional and a cultural side. Power sharing arrangements are obviously
incompatible with unitary or monist polities. Processes of erosion of
traditional state monopolies and historical cases of institutional design
of multilevel polities show that institutional differentiation and systems
of complex divisions of powers do not in themselves threaten minimally required state unity. The institutional core of federal states can
be very thin (e.g. some common framework legislation, common
armed forces). The 'institutional compartmentalisation' (e.g. in full-
fledged religious pillarisation) of society together with institutionally
plural multilevel polities evidently makes the institutional core of the
overarching polity very thin indeed, without threatening the unity of
states like the formerly 'pillarised' Netherlands or Switzerland.[1]

   An institutionally minimalist centre can also be culturally more neutral than a state trying to legislate or regulate almost everything and
trying to institutionalise a state monopoly in the provision of services
of all kinds. A thin and culturally fairly neutral state is praised by committed libertarians (Kukathas 1998: 690; 2002) and associative democrats (Hirst 1994: 67-70) and it should also be advocated by committed
political liberals. Yet, at the same time, it can also be seen as undermining minimally required political unity. It is claimed, then, that the
disentanglement of liberal-democratic political culture and virtues from
ethno-religious or national culture dramatically weakens civic and democratic culture and virtues as well as commitment for the common
cause.

9.3 Undermining civic and democratic virtues?

That pre-existing traditions and habits of conciliation and toleration
make the establishment and functioning of institutional pluralism in

general more feasible is uncontested. Whether Democratic Institutional Pluralism (DIP) itself stimulates conciliation (as Lijphart has argued) or undermines it (as Horowitz has claimed) is one of the core issues in debates on consociational democracy. If, in a first step, one accepts the restriction of this discussion to the conciliatory attitudes of
elites or political leaders, 'making moderation pay' (Horowitz 1991) is
important, and DIP would be weak if it only drew upon already existing motives for conflict resolution among the leaders of groups (Horowitz 1991a: 116) or if its institutional proposals did not alter the structure of political incentives (121). DIP can, however, offer meaningful incentives to minority organisations and leaders if representation in the
political process is not merely symbolic (vs. tokenism), if it has some
bite (vs. fake democracy), and if it has real and meaningful distributive
effects. This is precisely what DIP, AD in particular, is all about (Lijphart 1985: 104).

The general claim that all forms of DIP would undermine civic and
democratic virtues, political loyalty and commitment of all citizens and
residents is not plausible. The core of the objection seems to be the following: DIP strengthens particularist communal cultures and virtues
(intra-group 'bonding') and consequently weakens common civic and
democratic culture and virtues (inter-group 'bridging'). If liberals and
deliberative democrats raise this objection, they defend the ideal of a
purely public or 'political' culture, completely 'neutral' and disentangled from all religious and national cultures, and claim that purely
civil and democratic virtues are strong. Yet the objection to this presumed effect of DIP is not plausible, as DIP may actually contribute to
the forging of a common political culture that is more relationally neutral than the presumed neutrality of monist states and national public
cultures without being weak.[2]

The objection is more suited to stronger versions of liberal nationalism and, particularly, of national republicanism, criticising the weakness or even impossibility of a completely disentangled public morality,
culture and virtues that are not based in national culture and one or
other version of a 'civic religion'. In my view, DIP, particularly associative democracy, allows for a more reasonable balance to be struck between the fiction of complete disentanglement and the overly strong,
exclusivist and assimilatory concepts and practices of republican, reli-
gion-based national culture and virtues (Bader 1997b: 785-789, and
1999: 391ff). Relationally neutral political culture and democratic virtues cannot and need not be completely disentangled from existing majority and minority cultures and religions. Consequently, common virtues promoted and stimulated by AD would not be as weak as these
critics claim.

More importantly, AD proposes not only multi-level polities but also promotes multi-layered schemes of overlapping, partly competing and partly reinforcing obligations, loyalties and commitments (Bader 2001d, 2005c, 2006). By accepting a certain trade-off between inclusiveness and motivation,[3] AD allows for a better balance to be struck. Local, regional, central, supra-state, plus global virtues, obligations and loyalties (e.g. the global obligations of universal religions) partly conflict, but may also partly enhance each other. In addition, these political obligations and loyalties have never been as exclusively focused on the 'nation-state' as centralist monists assume. They have been intimately linked with ethno-religious and national obligations and parochial or 'communal' loyalties. Particular obligations and loyalties often compete with more universal ones, but AD again offers a setting that more often allows for their mutual re-enforcement. To the degree that 'communal groups' have meaningful autonomy and group representation, and further experience this as satisfying (or minimally as the least of worst-case settings), they can and usually do accept obligations towards the overarching polity (Swaine 2001, Kymlicka 2005: 69f), allowing strong commitments to develop. Whether this actually happens depends on numerous contextual factors, though I do claim that the structural design of AD itself does not preclude, but rather facilitates the development of such strong commitments. In turn, it should not be forgotten that attempts to impose demanding, thick versions of liberal, democratic or even inter-cultural virtues on resenting ethno-religious minorities are morally questionable and risk serious counterproductive effects.

9.4 Separate institutions and 'parallel societies'? Undermining beneficial inter-religious everyday interactions?

Critics often focus on the more radical, 'pillarised' versions of DIP. In particular, they claim that DIP cannot provide minimally required common, public institutions (mainly schools and political parties) in which these virtues, loyalties and commitments can actually develop (the seedbed of virtues thesis) and in which minorities and majorities actually interact in common causes (the everyday interaction thesis (para. 6.1.2). A detailed analysis of this complex, hotly contested issue is far beyond the space limits of this section. What I intend to show instead is that the effects of interactions in organisations and in public spaces clearly depend on the degree of voluntariness of inclusion into common public organisations, on the degree of voluntariness of separate institutions or territorial segregation, and on other contextual factors. I start with more or less fully compartmentalised societies (sect. 9.4), then I focus on the vices or benefits of communal vs. common schools, religious vs. non-communal parties, and ethno-religious vs. common employment and entrepreneurship as relevant organisational issues (sect. 9.5) before turning to interactions in public spaces (sect. 9.6). I conclude with a strong defence of associative religious governance: high degrees of voluntarism and real choices between communal and public institutions, better exit options, more equal chances and overlapping membership in divergent associations all tend to have a beneficial impact on the kind of inter-religious interactions, which tends to foster minimal as well as more demanding civic and democratic virtues.

My criticism of the philosopher's model of the millet system (para. 6.5.1) has shown that complete separation without any inter-religious interaction exists only in textbooks, not in reality. Yet, DIP allows for different degrees of separation from the cradle to the grave in work and employment, in healthcare and recreation, mating, friendship and marriage, social services, arts, sciences, education, media, political movements and parties as well as territorial segregation in neighbourhoods or areas (Bader 1998a: 204, Figure 1). Historically, high degrees of institutional completeness of minorities emerge under conditions of exclusion from common institutions or as a powerful reaction (by national or religious minorities) to enforced inclusion in institutions of the dominant (secular and/or religious) majorities. Only tiny ultraorthodox religious minorities have more voluntarily chosen maximum isolation and institutional separation across the board. People who raise the spectre of 'parallel societies' of Muslims today in politics and in theory usually forget to mention the important structural reasons for separation and segregation. In addition, the overwhelming majority of Muslim immigrants does not choose freely for, nor claims full separation, and their demand for separate institutions (e.g. in education) can also be understood as a reaction to resistance of their legitimate demands for accommodation (or the extremely slow pace and degree of accommodation (sects. 5.2 and 5.3). Residential segregation is also mainly caused by structural characteristics of housing markets in large cities and only partly the result of voluntary self-segregation. In my view, failures to accommodate their legitimate demands, together with imposed inclusion in 'neutral institutions of majorities' largely explain the reactive and defensive self-separation and self-segregation of religious minorities and also partly the feeding ground for political radicalism.

Critics tend to overlook the potential of DIP to prevent reactive attempts to more full-scale separation. They also claim that opportunities for voluntary and partial institutional separation in themselves would lead quasi-naturally to ever more radical claims for institutional completeness or full-scale separation, independently of contextual variables, and hence block the presumed beneficial effects of everyday interaction. Before addressing this issue, it is important to repeat that even high degrees of separation and low levels of everyday inter-group contacts can go hand in hand with actual (gritting teeth) toleration, live-and-let-live, and even with acceptance of basic principles of multicultural states (Kymlicka 2005), as we have seen in the case of the millet system and as traditional Dutch pillarisation has also shown. Low density and intensity of interaction in contexts of potential or actual hostility between groups, or of harsh patterns of discrimination is by far preferable to (imposed!) high density and intensity. Whether the effects of interactions are beneficial depends on the degree of voluntariness, the absence of serious threats, of serious patterns of discrimination, severe socio-economic inequalities and of negative sum games (para. 6.1.2). The generalised objection to DIP is clearly contradicted by all of the evidence found in organisations and public spaces.

9.5 Public schools, political parties, workplace interactions

Let's first have a short look at the character of interactions in public and private organisations and their capacities to create civil and democratic virtues.

The claims that governmental schools favoured by nationalists and also by civic republicans and deliberative democrats (e.g. Gutmann 2002; Bauböck 2002; Valadez 1999; Williams 2001) have beneficial effects because they already practice multicultural and inter-religious citizenship in everyday interactions between a huge diversity of students (and teachers from all backgrounds), and that 'communal' schools have vicious effects are extensively discussed in chapter 10. For now, it is enough to announce some serious doubts and also to require that comparisons should be fair – not comparing ideal models with muddle (McConnell 2002: 129-133) – and contextualised.

Authors who share doubts regarding government schools and also do not believe that armies or prisons will adequately compensate for serious defects of schooling are looking for other common institutions, mainly non-communal political parties. The cleavage of party systems along communal lines often has strong centrifugal effects, particularly in the case of ethnic parties (Horowitz 1985: chap. 7). Strong non-communal parties are hence favoured by most political theorists, maybe with good reasons. Communal parties are said to be 'particularist parties' that behave like interest groups, whereas non-communal parties are said to pursue the 'public interest', i.e. the 'common good'. This involvement in a common cause is said to create civic and democratic virtues (parties as schools of democracy), along with a strong common

loyalty and identity, which transcends more parochial groups (Rosenblum 2003). Again, the ideal is praiseworthy but some sobering remarks are in order.

First, depending on the setting, interest groups (particularly social
movements and SMOs) do not only aggregate interests but also serve
to 'intermediate' interests, while non-communal parties do not always
foster the emphatically understood 'public interest'.

Second, the analytical distinction between communal and non-communal parties can be highly misleading if applied to existing parties. It
is only in predominantly ethnically homogenous polities that 'non-eth-
nic parties' (Horowitz 1985: 334ff) may seem ethnically neutral, and it
is only in culturally fairly secularised societies that secular parties seem
religiously neutral. In all other cases, their presumed neutrality (together with that of the polity) is one of the main reasons why communal (ethnic and/or religious) parties develop and why non-communal
parties may end up as de facto ethno-religiously or secularly biased parties.

Third, historically, religious communal parties in democratic political
systems have contributed to the integration of religious minorities into
democratic polities, as well as the liberalisation and democratisation of
the respective Churches (sect. 3.6) and this may happen with Islamic
political parties in liberal-democratic polities (e.g. in Turkey or if they
were to emerge in Europe).

Fourth, AD can have many beneficial effects: By guaranteeing meaningful autonomy, selective cooperation, and political representation for
ethno-religious minorities, it reduces the demand for separate religious
political parties and it helps prevent communal cleavages from completely conquering and segregating party systems. Proportional representation rules tend to generate more parties, thereby also increasing the
chances for fairly small ethno-religious minorities to create their own
communal parties if they so wish. It also guarantees the possibility of
crossovers (membership, candidacy in non-communal parties) and
makes voting for non-communal parties strategically easier. Depending
on the issues and on the perceived seriousness of ascripitive clefts, this
may open up a centripetal dynamic (absent in Horowitz's analysis) in
which communal parties lose and/or more moderate communal parties and leaders may win from radical (fundamentalist, separationist)
ones. Rather than inevitably leading to ever more radical fundamentalism, competition among ethno-religious or national parties and leaders
may also generate rivalry between strong, moderate and integrationist
organisations, on the one hand, and small radical, fundamentalist and
separationist ones, on the other (Bader 1991: 246ff).

The formation of communal parties is, to repeat, guaranteed by freedoms of political communication and association. Whether they actu-

ally emerge depends mainly on the actual degree of communal segregation and of structural inequalities along ethno-religious cleavages, on
the one hand, and on the actual degree of openness and inclusiveness
of non-communal parties for minority membership, candidates, MPs
etc., on the other. It is only if non-communal parties are really inclusive and succeed in developing even-handed inter-ethnic and inter-religious cultures, that the high expectations of parties as schools of civic
and democratic virtues may come true.[4]

To the degree that government or associational education and non-
communal political parties do not create civic-democratic virtues and
do not provide the basis for actual practices of inter-cultural moderation and toleration, the main hope left would be that everyday interactions in work organisations and in unorganised public spaces might
teach these virtues in the normal course of practical life. This hope is
strongly articulated by Rosenblum (2000: 189), Spinner-Halev (2000:
88ff, 178ff) and Estlund (2003). To make a long and complex story
short, not unlike in schools, the character of everyday interactions in
workplaces depends on (i) the numerical and power relations between
majority/majorities and minorities and the respective demographic
composition of the employed (degree of actual 'mixing'; Estlund chap.
4 and 5); (ii) the degree of inclusiveness of selection and of actual and
effective anti-discrimination in the structure and culture of organisations (Estlund chap. 8; Engelen 2003: 522ff); and (iii) the degree to
which respective minorities are included in co-decision systems of democratic corporate governance.[5] Here again, it is important to recognise two dangers of idealisation.

First, actual workplaces diverge from the ideal of actually fairly free
entry (voluntarism), wide heterogeneity of demographic composition
(inclusiveness), anti-discriminatory practices and culture, and workplace democracy. Only if they are not demographically homogeneous is
there a chance that they can foster connectedness in a diverse society
('bridging ties' and the related minimalist civic virtues). Only if they
are democratic at least to a certain degree can they work as schools of
democracy.

Second, it is crucial, however, to recognise that (i) voluntarism of entry permits self-segregation and limits the ability of associations in civil
society 'to draw together individuals across lines of social division that
they prefer not to cross' (Estlund 2003: 129) whereas economic compulsion contributes to demographic heterogeneity of the employed;[6]
(ii) being bound to 'work together' fosters connectedness across ascriptive cleavages, increases the chances for 'bridging ties' not only at workplaces, and it breeds minimalist civic (Estlund 2003: 138), though not
necessarily democratic virtues; (iii) the often plainly neglected fact that
'even hierarchically organised, non-union workplaces can foster social

ties and civic skills that are essential in a diverse democratic society' (137). However, the 'ambiguity of compulsion and hierarchy' (130ff) does not imply that we would have to sacrifice the ideal of workplace democracy because less hierarchical, more cooperative models of organising work are possible and developing (Estlund chap. 3; Engelen 2000 chap. 2), and they are obviously more conducive to foster bridging ties and civic virtues. In addition, firms, sectors, regions and national regimes of economic governance differ widely regarding degrees of 'workplace democracy' (Rogers & Streeck 1995), and higher degrees can and should be stimulated in different ways with the intended side effect of breeding democratic virtues.

Hence, a sober analysis of actual workplace regimes and interactions is not discouraging. However it should also be emphasised that actual interactions foster minimally beneficial effects only if the structure (of hiring and firing, of pay and promotion) and culture of organisations of work is not too exclusive, internally segmented and discriminatory. As in other cases, the segregation of ethno-religious minorities into 'niches' of labour markets and immigrant entrepreneurship is mainly caused by structural closure and discrimination and certainly not by voluntary self-segregation.[7]

9.6 Everyday interactions in public spaces

In themselves, everyday inter-communal interactions in public spaces such as cities and neighbourhoods are mostly fleeting and superficial compared with more regular and repeated interactions at workplaces. They are clearly more limited in cases of high degrees of territorial segregation. Ethno-religious areas or neighbourhoods in 'metropolis', characterising the experience of most immigration societies again result from a mixture of involuntary choices caused by capitalist housing markets, strong 'nativist' discrimination; from chain migration and migration networks; and from more voluntary but still reactive decisions. They may provide shelter in fairly hostile environments, create opportunities of employment and ethno-religious niche markets for entrepreneurs, and guarantee minimal social security (particularly for 'irregular' immigrants and in the absence of developed welfare states for residents). Minimal territorial concentration is also required to practice communal religions, for houses of worship, communal schools, hospitals and newspapers. Also, it makes communal friendships, recreation, mating and marriage easier. In addition, it creates better opportunities to retain and transform cultural (including artistic) and religious minority practices more on their own terms and to better resist assimilatory pressure by religious or secularist majorities and 'their' state.[8]

Everyday interactions in mixed neighbourhoods may not foster bridging-ties and civic virtues as idealists commonly assume[9]. However, under conditions of mutual suspicion, mounting ethno-religious stereotyping, 'racism and counter-racism', they can also be the breeding ground of violent confrontations, whereas communally fairly homogeneous neighbourhoods may teach minimal toleration (para. 6.1.2). In addition, they may provide fairly safe spaces and social environments – 'cultural comfort zones' (Estlund 2003: 67f) – for the development of self-respect needed to play the 'game of marbles', the 'struggle for everyday recognition' on the streets and in mixed city areas,[10] because ethno-religious segregation is never complete and many inter-communal encounters are inevitable.

Policies of forced spreading, to prevent self-segregation and to increase inter-communal encounters, often motivated by emancipatory concerns, tend to produce counterproductive results, apart from the facts that they are morally and legally more than dubious (freedom of settlement) and extremely hard to realise. Morally and realistically, the problems are not ethno-religious neighbourhoods per se but ghettos. The appropriate policies are not imposed cultural assimilation and spreading but socio-economic empowerment and providing opportunities for those who want to move out of ethno-religious neighbourhoods.[11]

Experience also shows that it is extremely difficult for immigrant minorities to resist long-term acculturation processes, which emerge not only from intentional assimilation policies but from living in a different society that provides new chances and opportunities, not only risks and threats. As a rule, second- and third-generation migrants tend to move out of ethno-religious neighbourhoods (if not prevented), to shed traditional cultural practices, and to give up self-segregation strategies. Only orthodox religions tend to retain and purify dogma and practices following isolationist strategies (Isaijw 1990). Policies of imposed assimilation and integration and enforced spreading are signals of 'democratic impatience' (Vermeulen & Penninx 1995). They claim the moral high ground but clearly lack the trust in the seductive capacity of the praised 'open' character of 'postmodern' societies and liberal-democratic polities. They also lack determined efforts to make them actually more open and diverse and to really convert the rhetoric of equal opportunities so that it works everyone.

In summary, the core of Nancy Rosenblum's forceful criticism of institutional pluralism (1998) is correct in that a compartmentalised society minimises the opportunities for everyday encounters and also virtually excludes crosscutting memberships in divergent associations and their expected beneficial effects on overlapping, not strictly segmented obligations, loyalties and identities. It is particularly telling because she

too is rightly sceptical of the high democratic expectancies of deliberative and associative democrats that membership and participation in
associations would actually function as a seedbed of democratic virtues
(para. 6.1.2). She also explicitly criticises policies of liberal congruence,
defended by many liberals and republicans. Yet, this criticism has to be
qualified in two regards. First, minimal toleration can emerge even in
fully 'pillarised' societies, and high density and intensity of everyday
encounters are not beneficial in all contexts. Second, habits and virtues
of conciliation and the toleration of elites emerging from institutionalised interactions, negotiations and deliberations among communal
and non-communal groups in pillarised systems are no small achievement. Policies of imposed spreading to increase intermingling tend to
threaten the minimal virtues of both elites and rank and file (violating
the non-infringement proviso). AD focuses on policies of socio-economic empowerment of minorities. It does not confine people to their
communities but creates meaningful options for voluntary exit and
considerable increases in voluntary everyday encounters of 'ordinary
people' in all kinds of organisations and public spaces. If this can actually be achieved, the chances increase that more demanding virtues will
actually be learned by both 'elites and the masses'.

9.7   Creating religious fundamentalism or terrorism?

DIP is said to create political fundamentalism because it stimulates the
radicalisation of communal parties and of other communal organisations and leaders, it provides the feeding ground for essentialising and
purifying cultures/religions, and even for ethno-religiously legitimised
terrorism.

I have already refuted claims that communal parties would inevitably
radicalise and select the wrong leaders and that institutional pluralism
would foster conflicts.[12] In turn, one has to ask whether integrationist
conflict-regulating proposals like 'a single inclusive unitary state' and
the adoption of 'majoritarian but integrated executive, legislative and
administrative decision-making,' of 'a semi-majoritarian or semi-pro-
portional electoral system' (vote pooling, president elected by 'superma-
jority'), or of 'ethnicity-blind public policies' would have the intended
effects (Sisk's summary 1996: 71). We indeed lack 'whole-country empirical examples of working systems', and we also have good theoretical
arguments about why this may not be effective. Minorities may have
good reasons to question the presumed neutrality and inclusiveness of
the single unitary state and its ostensibly difference-blind public policies. If they do so strongly, integrationist proposals generate and foster
radicalism. In such cases, only the strong, repressive state advocated by

defenders of a 'control' approach may succeed in coercively assimilating or completely disempowering minorities, if it is not too late for such strategies to be successfully applied (Bader 1991: 313ff). In such cases, Lijphart's claim (1985: 101ff) that consociationalism is the only more or less available democratic setting for conflict resolution in deeply divided societies gains in plausibility. Political empowerment of minorities may help to make states and policies more relationally neutral.

Empowering religions not only politically (as in consociational democracy) but also socially (as in AD) is again said to contribute to the radicalisation of organisations and leaders and to fundamentalist political conflicts because the provided resources and opportunities can be used for 'integrative' and also for antagonistic and separationist ends, depending on definitions of ends and strategies. This is the currently most often heard and fashionable argument of republican critics. We have already seen (sects. 8.3 and 8.4) that the general argument regarding radicalisation is implausible, particularly if religions are granted meaningful autonomy and opportunities to run their own institutions. If they vie for legal recognition and public money to get important things done, there is a strong incentive towards 'moderate' strategies and also to prevent 'the worst from getting on top'. Public administrations then have a legitimate right of oversight that may also help to prevent radicalisation if prudently and pro-actively used. All this cannot prevent small, radical organisations and leaders from emerging. However, it helps to prevent the radicalisation of whole minorities, which may result from not accommodating the legitimate wishes of religious minorities characterising assimilationist policies, from ineffective policies of socio-economic empowerment, and from reactive and badly timed selection of 'moderate' organisations/leaders from above (sect. 8.5).

DIP is explicitly meant to shield ethno-religious minorities from morally illegitimate assimilatory pressure but critics claim that its institutions and policies would inevitably result in state- and policy-imposed categorisation of minorities ('ethnicise' and/or 'religionise' immigrants) and in essentialising cultures. This may be an unintended, counterproductive side-effect of inflexible and rigid multiculturalism policies. However, even in this case, it has to be compared with counterproductive categorisation (as 'others', 'strangers') and with reactive 'essentialism' as a consequence of societal marginalisation and of state-imposed assimilation policies.[13] AD is the least vulnerable to these charges because it creates meaningful options for exit, desegregation and voluntary interactions on all levels, which may stimulate the development of cultural and religious blending or hybridisation on their own terms. In addition, self-chosen cultural and religious conservatism is clearly not the feeding ground for political fundamentalism but may actually be very important in stemming religious and political fundamentalism.

DIP was recently also made responsible for the emergence and mushrooming of religiously legitimised terrorism[14]. Yet, it is ironic that the same political leaders and theorists mounting these charges increasingly appeal to orthodox Muslim communities, organisations and leaders to help prevent terrorism. To make a complex story short, it seems increasingly evident that Islamicist, Al-Quaida-like terrorism worldwide (but particularly in the West) is not produced by accommodationist policies and institutions, by voluntary self-segregation or by conservative religious and political Muslim organisations and leaders. It is executed by uprooted, completely 'footloose' young (fairly well-educated, second-generation, male) individuals, loosely integrated into global, informal networks who learn about Islam not from their parents or learned religious leaders, certainly not from 'traditional' or 'conservative' ones, but from unlearned, self-declared imams or internet sheiks inventing their purified version of a global Islam and a footloose virtual *umma* (Roy 2002). Quite contrary to the critics' claims, DIP and AD may actually help to fight terrorism by accommodating legitimate religious needs and collective, publicly visible practices of Muslims, by stimulating but not imposing responsible organisations and leaders, and by integrating youngsters into the diversity of networks and organisations of a broad and vibrant Muslim community (Frey 2004 chap. 5).

I hope that I have undermined the plausibility of the main charges by critics that AD would intrinsically have all these vicious effects. However, by highlighting the potentially beneficial effects of AD's institutional and policy proposals, I do not claim that they would be beneficial under all circumstances and in all situations. My claims that AD does not undermine or is parasitic on pre-existing virtues and attitudes of conciliation does not include that they would be stable enough to survive heated communalist mobilisation. That AD does provide better opportunities to prevent radicalisation does not mean that it also would provide the best institutional and policy capabilities in emergency contexts when situations tend to get completely out of control for reasons not related to the institutional structure but, quite often, for contingent external events like wars or 9/11. AD may be good in preventing, but bad in fighting political fundamentalism and terrorism. In addition, AD may be suited for a fairly egalitarian society but may be bad for bringing such a society about.

9.8 Is assiociative democracy feasible in all contexts?

The second step of my refutation of objections addresses contexts. Contexts matter, but they do not completely determine institutions and policies, although the degree of choice and the range of feasible institutional design may be higher or lower. Conversely, institutions and policies may change structures, although not always with the intended effect and within the desired time span. At this juncture, I have selected some of the most important contextual factors, indicating their anticipated impact on conflict dynamics and institutional options under *ceteris paribus* assumptions.[15]

Two types of external conditions are often highlighted: economic and political opportunity structures. Fairly steady economic growth allows for long-term positive sum games, and tends to moderate conflicts between groups, including ethno-religious minorities. However, as with all other contextual factors, some *ceteris paribus* conditions, in this case unequal distribution and rising expectations counteract this effect. Zero-sum and negative-sum games tend to foster distributive competition and stimulate potential conflict situations actually being defined as conflicts (Bader 1991: 344).

Broadly understood, the political opportunity structure includes: the character of the state ('owned by the majority' versus degree of ethno-religious neutrality; the degree of legislative, executive and judicial power sharing), and the predominant state policies regarding minorities (repression or facilitation). Conditions for DIP and AD are clearly more difficult if majority states such as France try to repress any form of minority autonomy, political representation and also the retention of minority cultures. Furthermore, the conditions for DIP and AD are obviously much better under stable, established and broadly accepted liberal-democratic constitutions and politics. For example, the role of religious parties will be evaluated differently if liberal-democratic polities are seriously threatened by illiberal and anti-democratic religious majorities and 'their' parties (e.g. if the BJP were to threaten to overthrow the Indian constitution or the divergent Muslim parties in Turkey were to threaten the liberal-democratic character of the Turkish state). This also applies if ethno-religious parties emerge and mobilise in deeply divided societies after the breakdown of imperial, authoritarian, dictatorial or totalitarian governments, as in the former Soviet Union or former Yugoslavia.

In general terms, it is more difficult, though not completely impossible, that AD will emerge and develop under the conditions of post-conflict development and under the conditions of threatened transitions to liberal democracies than under conditions of well-established liberal-democratic polities.[16] The chances for the development of flexible and open forms of DIP are better under (different varieties of) proportional representation systems than under majoritarian systems. Also, the existence of fairly stable and broadly accepted traditions of civil and democratic culture, habits and practices is clearly more favourable to DIP. Yet the absence of traditions of toleration and accommodation does not absolutely prevent its development. Even if accommodation and attitudes of conciliation are limited to elites, this allows for policy styles and traditions of political negotiation, bargaining and diplomacy (seeking compromise), and also for limited but important forms of persuasion or deliberation (seeking consensus) that are conducive to the more flexible and open forms of DIP, which are absent in adversarial, majoritarian systems. Finally, a high degree of overlap between party clefts and overall societal cleavages has an important impact on forms and types of DIP, but I have tried to show that AD provides better opportunities to prevent this.

Even well-established and fairly stable forms of DIP may turn out not to be sufficiently robust and stable under emergency conditions, external threats of war and terrorism and internal nationalist mobilisation threats. Late Ottomanism did not survive the onslaughts of nationalist mobilisation in the Balkans (Mazower 2005 for Salonica) and in Turkey (Birtek 2006), Lebanon (Lijphart's favourite consociationalist country) had to endure endless civil war and external interventions, and the politically pluralist and innovative structure of the EU may not be robust enough regarding new international relations even if reforms to strengthen common foreign policies and security were to be successful (Kalyvas 2003). External and internal 'wars' of all kinds are not conducive to 'diversity', to say the least. And the unifying and homogenising tendencies of institutionally monist polities (whether liberal-democratic or not) may provide comparative advantages in terms of institutional and policy capability for deterrence strategies under conditions of emergency. Deterrence may be quicker, more resolute and coherent and commitment and mobilisation may be higher but this in itself does not make deterrence strategies the better option. DIP and AD seem much better in preventing emergencies, particularly inside polities and also in post-conflict development when one has to clean up the mess produced by deterrence and war. However, they may be less effective under these conditions.[17]

It should be clear by now that no institutional or policy model fits all minorities in all polities, fields, contexts and situations. From a practical perspective, the different options offered by AD can be seen as the pieces of a bigger puzzle, to borrow an image from Sisk. The task of 'constitutional engineering' (Lijphart) or better of institutional design is to strive for a good fit, balancing principles and institutional trade-offs with regard to all of these context-specific factors. At this point, it should also be clear why I have argued that the trajectory from inclusion in monist institutions of the majority (figure 7.1, cell 1) to inclusion in monist 'neutral' institutions encounters so many practical and institutional difficulties. Liberal, republican and deliberative democratic defenders of such a trajectory should seriously rethink their institutional preferences and become more receptive to associative democracy. Once scrutinised in more detail, their ritualised objections that all varieties of institutional pluralism suffer from elitism, from the 'Russian doll phenomenon', and from inherent instability have lost much of their persuasive force. In this regard, it is particularly disappointing that, in their quest for institutional alternatives, sophisticated feminists such as Phillips (1991: 153) and Williams (1998: 213ff) should employ fairly unsophisticated and misconstrued models in their refutation of consociational democracy, neglecting AD completely.

10   Associative democracy and education

Educational systems differ widely among and within states in terms of financing, organisation, school types, regulation and control, centralism, homogeneity, choice and so on (Glenn & Groof 2002, 2002a; Fase 1994: 207ff; Leenknegt 1997; Leiprecht & Lutz 1996). These systems are embedded in predominant cultures and institutional legacies and characterised by remarkable, stunning complexity, which is why they cannot be simply exported or imported. Schools are confronted with divergent, conflicting demands and claims by parents, students, teachers, ethnic, religious and national communities, politicians and educational authorities. Educational regimes have to find sensible balances between conflicting moral principles, and they have to respond to legitimate realistic concerns (whether they are effective in achieving their aims) and to prudential standards (efficiency, comparative costs), which may conflict with moral principles and with pedagogical aims: large schools may provide 'economies of scale' advantages but comparatively poor educational environments. These tensions and trade-offs cannot be resolved once and for all and there seems to be general agreement in the debates on educational 'design' that none of the existing educational regimes provides optimal solutions for all these problems in all contexts, which is yet another reason why entire regimes cannot simply be exported or imported.

Yet we can learn because educational systems, given the variety, have to resolve the same problems. We can compare their respective balances of normative principles and their practical solutions, and my general claim has been that AD provides excellent opportunities to overcome ritualised theoretical oppositions and institutional bottlenecks. For reasons of space, I have to reduce the complexity of debates on educational systems drastically. I focus on primary and secondary schools but do not discuss the structure of schooling, even if the issue of comprehensive vs. divided school systems is much more important in improving education than the old issue of governmental vs. non-governmental schools. I focus on recent educational regimes and neglect debates on their history and on developmental stages.[1] I bracket both home schooling, where tensions between the freedoms of parents and the proto-freedoms of children, civic virtues and equal opportunity may be most serious, and also private non-religious schools (the 'merits of choice', generally). Instead, I focus on heated battles between national-ist, (neo-)Jacobin or more moderate civic republican defenders of gov-ernmental schools and pluralist defenders of publicly financed non-governmental religious schools. These battles characterised much of European school wars in the 19th century as well as recent conflicts both in the US and Europe.[2] Yet, my focus should not be misunder-stood as a general plea against home schooling (or to confuse manda-tory education with education in governmental schools), or as a Chris-tian-Democratic plea for religious non-governmental schools as the only or main alternative to governmental schools. Quite to the contrary, my main intent is to advocate associational school choice in a broad sense, i.e. the possibility of a wide variety of self-organisation in school-ing on a religious and a non-religious (e.g. humanist, philosophical, pedagogical) basis (Dijkstra et al. 2004: 84).

To simplify things, 'governmental schools' here are understood to be owned, run and financed by (a flexible combination of) governmental (federal, state, municipal) authorities. 'Non-governmental religious schools' (even if their legal status may be 'public' or semi-public as in England) are owned and run by (central or local) religious organisa-tions or associations whether (partly or fully) publicly financed or not (Glenn & Groof 2002a: 70f).

I will concentrate on recent discussions in the US in a comparative perspective for four reasons. First, the US has been exceptional in out-lawing any direct and indirect public financing of FBOs in education for quite a long time whereas 'nearly all advanced democracies' (Wolf & Macedo 2004: IX) allow this. Second, indirect public funding by vou-chers has been deemed constitutional 2002 (in the *Zelman* ruling) but certainly not obligatory and direct funding still meets massive opposi-tion. Third, private education is clearly 'under-regulated' (Witte 2004: 358, 361) or not regulated and controlled at all. Fourth, and most im-portantly, theoretical discussions and practical policies are still guided by strong dichotomies between private/public and market/state. They are legally less open for divergent public-private and semi-public con-structions and this also hinders the perception and recognition of insti-tutional experiments with other modes of governance (democratic school governance, networks among private and between private and public providers and associations, communities) beyond the increas-ingly misleading confrontation of either 'market/private hierarchy' or 'state'. My claim here is that these dichotomies not only govern the leading (moral, legal, political) ideologies and philosophies and the ideal normative model (idealised American Denominationalism, NEPP, sect. 8.6) but form considerable obstacles for practical experimentalism and actual 'muddling through', although important experiments with new models of school governance actually take place, e.g. in Texas and Kentucky (Liebman & Sabel 2003). Hence, recent debates in the US provide an excellent opportunity to substantiate my claims that AD allows these imposed 'choices' to be overcome.

The charges that institutional pluralism produces vicious effects (chap. 9) are particularly fierce when it comes to education, especially regarding religious schools and public financing. Religious schools are said to produce extremism, social fragmentation, greater inequality and erosion of civic values.[3] As in other campaigns under the spell of panics and security threats, these accusations are generalised, completely independent of contexts, immune to empirical refutation, and they are repeated – in more moderate versions – by all civic republican and deliberative democratic opponents of (publicly financed) religious schools. Instead of countering these accusations with a rosy picture of unconditionally beneficial effects of religious schools, we should gain some distance and soberly discuss the respective moral, realistic and prudential claims and the available evidence to avoid both the 'myth of the common school as the sole legitimate and effective *maker of citizens'* (Glenn 2004: 351) that 'will not stand up under scrutiny' (vs. model-muddle shifts) and the myth of choice utopias or voucher utopias. In doing so, I focus on civic and democratic virtues because these clearly form the most vigorously contested issue and because the available empirical evidence regarding cognitive performances seems to prove the superiority of religious schools both in Europe and in the US, whereas the dearth of evidence regarding civic competencies and virtues is more open to debate.

Here are the more specified claims I want to defend:

1. An unconditional priority for democracy, let alone for democratic majoritarianism, does not live up to our considered moral convictions and to constitutional constraints. It is more reasonable to accept that, in education, we also have to deal with tensions and conflicts between moral principles (moral pluralism) (sect. 10.1).

2. A sensitive division of and cooperation between educational authorities (parents, students, teachers, communities and public authorities) is more reasonable and productive than the ritualised opposition between (parental) 'free choice' and (state) authority (sect. 10.2).

3. Teaching civic and democratic virtues is as important as it is hard to achieve. Civic minimalism is more agreeable, robust, productive and much easier to 'control' than democratic maximalism (sect. 10.3).

4. Learning civic and democratic virtues by doing and by everyday interactions in classes, schools and school environments is at least as effective as by teaching. However, religious schools can be as inclu-

sive and effective as governmental schools and the trade-off between bonding and bridging ties may be less harsh than assumed
(sect. 10.4).

5. Educational regimes, which provide either direct and/or indirect
   public financing for religious schools, are more just and more effective regarding equal opportunities for all students (sect. 10.5).

6. All schools have to be minimally regulated and controlled with regard to minimal standards of cognitive competencies and civic virtues, although publicly financed schools may and should be controlled in a more demanding but still minimally invasive or obtrusive way by government authorities. More demanding controls
   should be internal controls by schools and associational providers
   that should be involved in standard setting and inspection (sect.
   10.6).

7. Mixed educational regimes are preferable not only for reasons of diversity and choice but also of effectiveness, adaptation and innovation compared to governmental schools, only even if the latter allow
   for federal diversity and experiments with new, choice-based types
   of schools (sect. 10.7).

8. AD provides a general institutional framework that is open and conducive to a contextually sensitive design of educational regimes. It
   proceeds bottom-up via democratic experimentalism instead of
   functioning in a top-down imposition of educational dystopias
   through state crafting, or simply by accepting entrenched status-
   quo educational arrangements (sect. 10.8).

10.1 Democratic versus pluralist education?

The constitutions of liberal democracies are originally historical compromises of competing liberal and democratic traditions, where the
principles of freedom and equality often conflict in general as well as
in education. Upon closer scrutiny, we have to distinguish four different tensions and the respective trade-offs.

First, the internal tension within individual liberty between the freedoms of parents and the proto-freedoms (growing autonomy) of children. Guaranteeing associational freedoms for adults that result in the
creation of diverse schools has to be balanced against the proto-freedoms of the children who will attend these schools. Parental associational freedoms are not co-extensive when it comes to respecting the
increasing liberty of children as they mature (sect. 10.2). This *liberty-
liberty* tension has partly been dealt with already (sect. 4.4), where I defended the position that the basic needs and interests of children have
to also be externally guaranteed against parents and 'communities' if

violated, whereas their best interests should primarily be catered to by their parents as trustees before students are able to care for themselves. Here, I assume that parents actually act in the basic and best interests of their children as long as these maturing students are unable to speak for themselves. To avoid misunderstanding my claim in this regard, I have to highlight that AD, although it accords great value to parental and associational freedoms, does not neglect or simply overrule the independent interests of children, either in developing their capacity for exercising their own agency and autonomy or in adequate/ equal educational opportunities. My concept of differentiated morality allows me to combine minimal standards with more demanding ones, if the non-infringement proviso is not violated.

Second, the tension between educational freedoms and 'liberal' non-discrimination (equal respect and concern). This *liberty/nondiscrimination* tension is partly dealt with in chapter 5 and is more fully addressed in sections 10.3 and 10.4, where I argue that all schooling has to guarantee nondiscrimination as part and parcel of civic minimalism.

Third, the tension between educational freedoms and more demanding or substantive educational opportunities that are adequte if not equal. This educational variety of the famous *liberty-equality* tension is addressed in section 10.5.

Fourth, the tension between educational freedoms and the more demanding requirements of democratic citizenship and democratic virtues. This *liberty-democracy* tension is addressed in sections 10.3, 10.4 and 10.6.

We can expect that the solutions to the respective trade-offs may run counter to instead of reinforcing each other. This is why one should clearly distinguish them instead of lumping them together in the famous opposition between civic republican or pluralist, or democratic versus pluralist education.

Freedoms of religion and education are constitutionally guaranteed by international and regional human rights laws, by constitutions, laws and jurisdictions both in the US (McConnell 2004) and in Europe (Vermeulen 2004: 36-38; Harris 2004; Glenn & Groof 2002: 581; 4.1). All reasonable civic republicans accept that democratic decision-making, particularly majoritarianism, and state authority in education has to be constrained. In turn, all reasonable defenders of educational pluralism accept that democratic polities have a legitimate interest to guarantee minimal standards of nondiscrimination, adequate or equal educational opportunities, and education to citizenship in all schools. Important as it is, this general agreement cannot prevent serious disagreements regarding the amount and limits of legitimate discretion for democratic legislation and educational administration,[4] the forms and degrees of judicial control and, particularly, how to balance the competing 'values', how to interpret them, how to operationalise them, how to regulate and control them, whether and if so under which conditions to allow exemptions, and so on.

As we know from experience in all liberal-democratic countries, educators, politicians, judges and philosophers as well as ordinary people continue to reasonably and seriously disagree on the various issues. I am convinced that it does not help to try to resolve the tensions by engaging in the age-old battles about which of the principles or 'foundational values' – in Rosenblum's wording 'pluralist education' versus 'democratic education' – is more 'fundamental' or has 'priority' (2004: 148, 158) in general, independent of the issues and various contexts.[5] In general, indeed, 'we simply can't tell' (Rosenblum 2004: 159). What we *can* tell is that the tendency of some radical libertarians and liberals, as well as pluralists or free choice apologists, to reject any public regulation and control of 'private' schools is beyond the limits of reasonable balancing. However, this is not what reasonable defenders argue for.[6] Yet, their defence of civic minimalism, their plea for the least invasive or least obtrusive forms of regulation and control, and their warning against imposing (maximum) democratic congruence should be taken seriously, particularly by civic libertarians such as Rosenblum. In turn, the tendency of some radical democrats and egalitarians to solely allow governmental schools and to enforce their versions of democratic homogeneity are beyond the limits of reasonable balancing. Their attempts to impose 'democratic maximalism' in civic education and maximum regulation and control on all schools should be seen with moral suspicion (it easily violates the *non-infringement proviso*) and sober realistic scepticism. What we also know is that these tensions may be less tragic and may allow smaller trade-offs if we appropriately design institutions and policies (Glenn & Groof 2002: 581; Eisgruber 2002: 83).

10.2 Parents or the state? Division of educational authority

Children are neither 'owned' by their parents nor by any other collective body, and a proper division and allocation of authority has to recognise and balance the legitimate needs, interests and perspectives of different stakeholders (sect. 7.3). Contrary to radical pro-choice advocates who stress parental interests exclusively,[7] and contrary to some radical Jacobin advocates of public education in France who stress only the overriding interests of 'the republic' (Meuret 2004) (in both cases, the legitimate interests of maturing students are neglected or overruled without consideration),[8] we have to take into account not only parents, citizens and (cooperating but also competing) governmental authorities but also students (and their associations), teachers (and their professional associations and unions), schools and the respective associations of public and communal providers of education whose perspectives often conflict with each other.

To find a proper and workable allocation of educational authorities is certainly no easy task. First, parental authority can be legitimately overruled in general as well as in education when the basic interests of children are at stake, but parents are normally better guardians of their best interests before they reach maturity.[9] Second, giving proper voice and representation to pupils depends on contested thresholds of maturation. However, at least in secondary and higher education (and obviously universities) they should be treated as (proto-) citizens with relevant interests, perspectives and opinions. Third, the different stakeholders do not all have the same intense interests or competence in all issues. A proper allocation of authority therefore certainly does not imply giving them all equal say in all matters. Fourth, combining divergent, partly overlapping but also conflicting interests and educational perspectives in institutionalised deliberation, representation and decision-making (at the school level and when it comes to setting standards, regulations and controls) certainly raises disagreement and prevents statism and/or professionalism under the guise of neutrality and the best interests of children from ruling supreme. It is more heterogeneous and maybe disorderly but it need not and does not lead to chaos because it is guided by a strong common concern. Moreover, representation has to be constrained by workability requirements (sect. 10.6).

10.3 Teaching virtues: civic minimalism or democratic maximalism?

As we have seen, teaching civic and democratic virtues is difficult because virtues combine competencies and attitudes, because the content of civic and democratic virtues is contested (the longer and thicker the list of virtues the more so), and because learning virtues by direct interactions may be more important than teaching virtues. In line with my general plea for moral minimalism, I also defend minimalism in education because it allows for the 'economisation' of moral and political disagreement on virtues that is paramount in educational debates, because minimalism is relationally more, though not completely neutral (Gutmann 2002: 37), because it can mobilise broader agreement and is hence more robust, more legitimately imposed and better to control in all schools. However, minimalism is also contested and means different things: minimal virtues related to minimal morality, minimal liberal virtues, and minimal democratic virtues (para. 6.1.1).

To reiterate, the short list of minimal virtues to be taught and learned in all schools contains civility, moderation, self-discipline, trustworthiness, 'gritting teeth' toleration, law abidingness and a minimal sense of justice. Obviously, this minimum in itself is very demanding. In addition, although more demanding, minimal liberal-democratic virtues such as agonistic respect of all as legally and politically free and equal (related to principles and rights of nondiscrimination and non-repression) and minimal mutuality and reciprocity should also be taught in all schools, not only in governmental or publicly financed non-governmental schools. To prevent 'malfare' or 'evil' (Glenn & Groof 2002: 150), schools 'must not promote or foster doctrines of racial or other ethnic superiority or persecution, religious intolerance or persecution, social change through violent action or disobedience of laws'.[10] The wording of this core in (constitutional) laws and regulations in different states varies, is very general and lacks detailed prescriptions. It commonly focuses on 'values' instead of virtues, and also often adds more demanding democratic and pluralist virtues without due consideration.[11]

All reasonable pluralists defend the minimalist core that a pluralistic society should be 'committed, above else, to peaceful coexistence' (McConnell 2002: 88), to 'live and let live' (97) and also in teaching values and virtues. However, McConnell quite unfortunately fails to specify the respective virtues and also what 'within the limits' (100) or 'bounds of reasonableness' (101) means. That 'there is no set of agreed-upon values for democratic citizens' is certainly a bad excuse for not spelling out the substantive content of the core of civic minimalism for education, and this is rightly criticised by Gutmann (2002: 38) and Rosenblum (2002: 165, 171). The core clearly includes virtues related to 'nondiscrimination', which is a liberal as well as a 'democratic' value. McConnell's silence may be motivated by hesitations to impose nondiscrimination legislation without exemptions on all schools (sect. 4.3). Nevertheless, allowing religious, but not 'racist' or 'sexist' criteria in the selection of teachers and maybe the students as well (sect. 10.4) certainly does not permit teaching religious intolerance and discrimination, and allowing the teaching of religious views that oppose sex and gender equality or even 'racial' and ethnic equality does not exempt religious schools (even ultra-orthodox ones) from the requirement of teaching values of anti-discrimination.[12] Similarly, opposition of authoritarian religions to minimal democratic virtues of participation does not exempt religious schools from teaching democratic minimalism.

The trouble then is that teaching values is not the same as learning virtues, and this points towards a more general problem. In principle, teaching and learning values is no more difficult than learning mathematics or history, but teaching virtues not only requires providing information and acquiring cognitive skills or competencies but also the respective attitudes. We have already seen (para. 6.1.2) that, contrary to Gutmann's claim (2002: 42), compared to primary socialisation and non-school everyday interactions (Rosenblum 2002: 148f; Garnett 2004: 332; Estlund 2003) schools may not be the 'best place' for learning civic and democratic virtues. However, more than just appropriate curricula, textbooks and teacher guides, schools require virtuous teachers who exemplify civic and democratic practices (Eisgruber 2002: 75; Gorard 2004: 133), as well as adequate teaching practices. This enables a learning-by-doing of civic and democratic practices by fostering a predominant civic-democratic culture or 'climate' not only in civics classes, but in all courses, classrooms, schools and the greater school environment. Ultra-orthodox religious schools are certainly not among the places that foster the learning of civic-democratic virtues. However, the same is also obviously true for many governmental schools.

The available empirical evidence on cognitive performances points to a superiority of religious schools both in Europe and in the US,[13] whereas the 'dearth of evidence' regarding civic competencies and virtues allows more debate, although 'all we know' is certainly not negative and the available results 'seem to put the onus on those who question the civic competence of students educated outside of the traditional public school' (Campbell 2004: 208). The claims by civic republicans that governmental schools would do better in principle and practice compared to religious schools may or may not be true in ideal worlds; they are certainly not corroborated by any evidence in the real world. The political sensitivity of the issue partly explains why so few studies have been undertaken, but this is also due to the complexity of this kind of research. Evidence regarding cognitive civic competencies can be attained by comparing the results of examinations, tests or essays, and all available evidence points in the same direction as other cognitive competence research: religious schools do slightly or significantly better.[14] Researching the non-cognitive or 'attitudinal, affective, behavioural' aspects of civic and democratic virtues is methodologically and empirically much more difficult, but available studies also favour religious schools, although the evidence is shaky.[15] The modest attempts to explain these differences include stronger informal relations between boards and parents in religious schools, a higher commitment and participation of parents, more and more direct interaction between parents and teachers, the importance of a conservative, discipline- and value-oriented education (Dronkers 2004: 300), and a more shielded school culture in religious schools (the same reasons that help to explain the generally higher cognitive outcomes). These results may irritate liberals and democrats, they may also point towards yet another dilemma that a more liberal and democratic educational practice may not be better but worse in producing educational achievement and maybe also civic virtues. However, they should certainly contribute to a moderation of exaggerated hopes regarding 'public schools of democracy' and of myopic criticism of all religious schools. Above all, they should lead to concerted efforts to improve the teaching and learning of civic and democratic virtues in both.

The results, however, may be influenced by higher social segregation and a more homogenous religious and also ethno-racial composition of religious schools and its supposedly beneficial impact on direct interactions, as defenders of civic republicanism often claim.

10.4 Learning virtues: education, segregation (bonding) or inclusion (bridging)?

I distinguish analytically between segregation on the basis of class and educational background of parents (class segregation), 'racial' and 'ethnic' segregation, and religious segregation.

Almost all scholars agree that class segregation in governmental schools characterises all regimes of residential assignment. Residential class segregation (neighbourhoods, inner city areas vs. suburbs, cities vs. rural areas) is systematically reproduced by 'catchment areas', 'zones' or 'districts'.[16] Attempts to fight social segregation and class flight (normally combined with ethno-racial segregation and 'white flight') by legally enforced desegregation ('bussing') have been massively resisted. Their constitutional and legal status remains at least dubious (Vermeulen 2004: 56ff), and they eventually turned out to be ineffective.[17] Attempts to fight residential class segregation directly by imposing mixed class neighbourhoods ('spreading') are incompatible with moral and constitutional and legal rights of free movement and settlement and obviously unachievable under conditions of capitalist housing and renting markets.

Attempts to make residential assignment more fluid and flexible, to allow more choice for parents and students to escape from the 'poor neighbourhood-poor public education' trap – as in New Zealand (Glenn 2004: 344f; Glenn & Groof 2002: 377ff) – or to introduce charter schools, magnet schools and the like are also vulnerable to the class segregation charge. Furthermore, without proper public financing, they may even magnify educational inequalities, as has been the case with all private schools that have traditionally been elite schools.

In summary, contrary to the ideal picture of civic republicans, mandatory residential assignment in governmental schools reproduces class inequalities in all existing educational systems, and the use of state enforcement is morally and legally forbidden or dubious and ineffective. Voluntarism permits self-segregation and 'it is quite impossible to prevent those who have adequate resources from escaping schools that they deem to be bad, which reinforces the existing social hierarchy' (Meuret 2002: 262). Hence, apart from the clearly preferable strategy of fighting class inequalities directly, the only alternative for committed egalitarians to allowing school choice and publicly funded 'private' schools would be the exclusive enforcement of governmental schools by proscribing all of the other alternatives. This is an option that is incompatible with moral and legal requirements of freedom of religion and education.[18] If not properly regulated, voluntarism may magnify the self-segregation of the rich and powerful. However, at least in education, force or imposition is not a viable alternative. We have to trust voluntarism and look for adequate ways of public financing and regulation and control.

Civic republicans also accuse religious schools of increasing class segregation or of delivering 'poor' education. However, they should at least be aware of the fact that most educational regimes that recognise and subsidise religious and other 'private' schools impose rules that do not allow discrimination on the basis of 'family income' (Glenn & Groof 2002: 585), and that, depending on the type and degree of funding, they show less class segregation than comparable governmental schools.[19]

Religious schools are also generally independent of contexts and regulations, accused of increasing 'racial' and/or ethnic segregation compared with governmental schools (assumed to be desegregated or mixed). The following four arguments help to refute this charge:

First, all existing rules and regulations of publicly funded religious schools clearly proscribe racial or ethnic discrimination in student admission[20] and all reasonable defenders of free choice explicitly defend these nondiscrimination rules.

Second, ethnic and religious discrimination and segregation overlap in reality (para. 6.4.1) but their analytical distinction is morally, legally and also descriptively important though often ignored in phrases such as 'along ethnic or religious lines' (Harris 2004: 120). Many rules and regulations of (publicly funded) religious schools allow a more or less neatly qualified religious selection of students, while explicitly banning ethno-racial selection.[21]

Third, comparatively speaking, the record of religious schools regarding degrees of racial and ethnic segregation is mixed, depending on the actual overlap of ethno/racial and religious cleavages. Muslim schools in Western countries tend to attract mainly second-generation immigrants, who may be categorised as ethnically homogeneous, 'nonwhite' (e.g. 'Asian' or 'Arab'), even if they are composed of quite heterogeneous ethno-linguistic minorities, whereas Catholic schools attract mainly pupils from longstanding religious majorities or minorities (former immigrants). Empirically, they are ethno-racially more hetero-geneous in many countries than comparable governmental schools.[22]

Fourth, ethno-racial and class segregation often strongly overlap, par-ticularly in cases of developing immigrant underclasses and residential segregation. If not properly funded, religious schools (e.g. Muslim schools) tend to be schools of the poor (contrary to the charge that school choice would favour the rich only)[23] and contribute to reprodu-cing ethno-religious and class inequalities. Combined with the strong class segregation effects of residential assignment in public education ('black' governmental schools) and of inadequately funded and regu-lated school choice, this will result in a continuation or even strength-ening of overall class segregation in education and its detrimental ef-fects for cognitive results.

Even in this specific case, however, the civic-republican policy re-sponse is to fight ethno-racial and class segregation by forbidding or not publicly funding religious schools in order to achieve more equal educational opportunities and really 'mixed' schools, which runs into the troubles already discussed. Imposing school desegregation is mo-rally and legally dubious and ineffective without housing desegregation ('white flight' is 'class flight') or allowing non-residential assignment and school choice that is properly financed and regulated.

Furthermore, criticism of an unqualified contact hypothesis (para. 6.1.2) creates the expectation that the anticipated benefits of direct in-teraction in 'mixed' schools very much depend (i) on the majority/min-ority ratio and the related power relations in schools and classes; (ii) on the specific ethnic and religious composition of the student population; (iii) on the presence or absence and the seriousness of everyday racism, classism, sexism and religious discrimination. In adverse contexts, di-rect interactions amongst students tend to breed hostility instead of tol-eration, and more segregated schools provide better teaching and learn-ing opportunities and may at least prevent 'teaching' the wrong prac-tices (serving as a breeding ground for 'vices'). The crucial question, then, is how to break through vicious self-reinforcing circles and create beneficial ones, both in governmental and non-governmental schools. This is the strategic problem to be solved, and in my view, voluntarism of student enrolment is crucial (Macedo 2002: 18, McConnell 2002). Self-segregation of the 'rich white' is also remarkably different, both morally and empirically, from possible/actual self-segregation of poor ethno-religious minorities for two reasons. First, the range of choices and options is much broader for the former whereas it may be practi-cally zero for the latter. Second, only the latter are confronted with a big trade-off between adequate/equal educational opportunities and a school environment, which is shielded from unfriendliness, hostility or outright racist, ethnocentrist or religious discrimination, and which provides opportunities 'to raise children in a sort of cultural comfort zone in which skin colour and identity are a source of shared pride and not a daily source of tension' (Estlund 2003: 67). If increased ethno/racial-religious heterogeneity in governmental schools goes hand in hand with dormant or open tensions and discrimination of all kinds, more homogenous schools clearly provide better pedagogical environments fostering increased parent-teacher interactions, higher participation of parents and a conducive learning culture and help to decrease dropout rates and increase cognitive results.

If schools are properly funded, higher degrees of segregation in 'separate' schools (as in neighbourhoods) tend to create stronger bonding ties, communal cultures and identities, which may foster school effectiveness. However, they also tend to weaken bridging ties and thick 'national' culture, identity and loyalty (Estlund 2003: 179-181; see Gorard 2004: 133). Even this trade-off between 'bonds of commonness' and 'bonds of diversity' has to be qualified. First, weak bridging ties and thin national identities and loyalties may be strong enough and morally preferable to thick ones. Second, fair freedom of choice in combination with adequate public funding helps considerably to increase minimally required toleration and thin overarching identities and loyalties. Third, imposing desegregation has counterproductive effects. In addition, the trade-off is not only big for some religious schools where class, ethnoracial and religious cleavages massively overlap, it also holds for many governmental schools, and we should stop reproducing red herrings and the 'hypocrisy' (McConnell 2002: 132) inherent in these model-to-muddle shifts.[24]

As with neighbourhood segregation, in education, we may also have to face a trade-off between high overall diversity and high school diversity. Religious schools may be internally more homogenous regarding teaching, pedagogy and the religious composition of students, even if they are also committed to teaching ethno-cultural pluralism and to informing students about religious diversity, as they should, from a distinct, recognisable religious perspective. Yet, governmental schools may not inform students about religious diversity at all and may not be committed to, or do not effectively teach any, even not a committed pluralist perspective (the 'mush' argument).[25] The price for a high degree of ethno-cultural and religious diversity in education, which seems to be fostered by pluralist educational systems allowing school choice, seems to be a lower degree of diversity inside schools or classrooms.

Still, the different trade-offs mentioned may not be as big, the balance may not be as difficult, and the choices may not be as tragic as is often assumed, and exclusive governmental schooling is certainly not the best or only way to find sensible solutions. The tension between class and ethno-racial segregation and 'social justice', equity or equal educational opportunity (Glenn & Groof 2002: 577) may be moderated by appropriate systems of public financing of religious schools and more choice in public education. To the degree that it really exists, the tension between freedom of choice-autonomy (allowing strong bonds of sameness, communal cultures/identities and loyalties) and civic-democratic virtues, bridging ties ('social cohesion') and national culture, identity and loyalty (Harris 2004: 99f, 120) may be alleviated by appropriate public regulation and the control over the teaching of civics. The tension between teaching and practising cultural diversity in schools and in the overall educational system may be alleviated by appropriate but minimal content regulation. In brief, it all depends on institutions and policies, and existing regimes often already show good practices neglected by political philosophers' deep incompatibilities and tragic choices.

10.5 Social justice and equality and religious schools: no aid or fairly equal public funding?

International human rights law and European covenants and jurisdiction oblige states to permit freedoms of education in all their consequences for religious schools. However, it is an open, debated issue whether they also obligate states to fairly equal public funding or not,[26] as the constitutions and laws of some states such as the Netherlands and Belgium clearly do. As we have seen (para. 1.3.3.6), only Greece, Bulgaria, and most Swiss cantons and, until fairly recently, Italy and the US reject any and all public financing, although the latter two have now allowed some indirect financing (Glenn & Groof 2002: 4, 578; Wolf & Macedo 2004: 67; Campbell 2004: 190f). For reasons of space, I cannot deal with the stunning complexity of existing systems of direct and indirect public financing.[27] This complexity and lack of transparency explains why it is difficult to accurately calculate the comparative overall amount of public money for non-governmental religious schools in relation to governmental schools. However, roughly the following picture for various groups of countries emerges. Some states (Austria, Belgium, the Netherlands, England and Wales) cover virtually all costs (*full funding*); the Scandinavian model (Denmark, Finland, Sweden) is characterised by large subsidisation, and *partial funding* is known in many other countries as well (e.g. Australia, Germany, Hungary and countries where public funding depends on contracts, as in France or Spain). Finally, only a tiny minority totally rejects any public funding.

Three important lessons seem to emerge from more detailed studies of existing systems of financing.

First, notwithstanding the lack of transparency and mixed records of public funding, one straightforward lesson 'from this varied experience is that equity in access to educational opportunities is best served by funding approved non-public schools on the basis of parity with government-operated schools. Otherwise, it is inevitable that family income will play the major role in determining whether parents can exercise their right of educational freedom on behalf of their children' (Glenn & Groof 2002: 587; Dronkers 2004: 288, 305; Gorard 2004: 151). The reasons and motives for choosing non-governmental schools are various and mixed: historical strength of the non-government sector, proximity, disappointment with the quality of government schools in addition to religious, philosophical or pedagogical convictions. However, the evidence is plain that 'those nations which guarantee equal financial treatment of public and private schools, and thus provide a 'level playing field' on which parental choice of schools is not influenced by financial considerations, have the highest proportion of pupils enrolled in private (usually religious) schools' (Glenn & Groof 2002a: 253).[28]

Second, fairly equal public funding not only helps to fight class segregation, but also ethno-racial segregation, as we have seen in section 10.4. In addition, most states provide supplemental funding (either directly to schools in the form of higher coefficients per student or in the form of income-related tax credits) to serve pupils from poor and/or ethnic minority families[29] and children (e.g. handicapped) needing special education.

Third, most systems combine direct subsidies for the construction and maintenance of schools, teachers and staff etc. and for the number of enrolled students with indirect subsidies for students and parents (like vouchers or tax credits). Apart from apparent moral advantages, this mixed approach[30] also has prudential and realistic advantages compared with voucher funding only, for example. It allows more stability and predictability to run schools without making them insensitive to considerable changes in student enrolment, and it allows better public control of what schools actually do with supplementary funding for 'poor, minority, and immigrant' students, for instance. Systems that are exclusively voucher-based are plagued with huge information problems, and exit alone has too little impact on actual change and performance if not combined with voice (sect. 10.6).[31]

Against this background, I will now try to develop a complex argument in six consecutive steps of why we all (but particularly egalitarian civic republicans, especially in the US) should defend the moral obligation to fairly equal public financing of religious schools, maybe not in an ideal world but certainly under conditions of structural inequalities.

First, freedoms of education include the free establishment and running of religious schools and forbid enforcing a monopoly for governmental schools. This is why all of us (and not only libertarians and pluralists) should favour mixed or pluralist educational systems: neither a monopoly for governmental schools nor a situation where there are no governmental schools and no public financing, as some libertarians (Lieberman, 1989) propose.

Second, if governments fund some non-governmental schools, including some religious schools, they have to treat all of those that live up to minimumal standards equally. This is why all libertarians and liberals for reasons of equal treatment and nondiscrimination are morally and legally obliged to defend fairly equal funding (para. 4.1.4 and sect. 5.2).[32]

Third, private schools, including religious schools under ideal conditions of equal distribution of socio-economic resources and opportunities, may not require public funding (para. 4.1.4). However, structural economic, educational and residential inequalities require changes in the residential assignment regimes of students in governmental schools and fairly equal funding of non-governmental schools, to achieve fairer and equal educational chances for all pupils (independent of socio-economic status, parental education or all ascriptive categorisations) instead of reproducing societal inequalities in the educational system. Only defenders of 'libertarian archipelagos' in education may be more or less immune to such arguments. This is the major reason why civic republicans (if they are really committed to more substantive notions of equality) should favour fairly equal funding in the real world. Furthermore, a more substantive notion of equality morally requires more than equal funding and preferential treatment to all schools that serve pupils from poor and/or ethnic minority families either directly (e.g. additional funds, teacher training), to enrolled students by way of a weighed voucher system,[33] or through income-dependent tax grants for parents.

Fourth, free choice for parents is a formal, empty or illusory right (Glenn & Groof 2002a: 247), it is a 'dead' term without adequate public subsidies. If tuition fees are allowed and have to be paid, then there should be either income corrections or grants.

Fifth, if (and to the degree to which) governmental schools cannot and do not live up to the principle of 'neutrality', at least in the considered opinion of parents/students who fear that these schools unduly promote a specific secularist way of life in the content and practice of their teaching, even defenders of 'strict neutrality' in the real world (and obviously all proponents of relational neutrality and fairness as even-handedness) should favour fairly equal funding (Monsma & So-per 1997; Glenn & Groof 2002a: 245f; 2002: 4). If governmental schools cannot or do not live up to the requirements of legitimate or reasonable pluralism or cultural diversity of all sorts in content and practice of teaching, defenders of a more demanding 'ethos of plural-ism' should also favour pluralist school regimes and fairly equal fund-ing to realise more overall pluralism in education.[34]

Sixth, if states depend considerably on religious schools to live up to their obligations to provide education for all (for whatever historical or recent reasons), i.e. if religious schools meaningfully help in the rea-lisation of mandatory public services, fairness requires that they should be equally publicly funded.

Public funding is and obviously should be conditional (minimal standards). This is why all reasonable defenders of non-governmental schools should favour public regulation and control of all schools.

10.6 Public regulation and control

As with financing, the forms and ways of regulation and control of gov-ernmental and non-governmental schools are complex and differ with-in and among states. They usually concern conditions of accreditation and withdrawal, input (general curriculum frameworks, specified curri-culum plans, textbooks and teacher guides), output (examinations, tests, essays and performance indicators) and also throughput control. The standards of regulation and control are various. In addition to questions of what is regulated and controlled, as well as when and how it might be, there are numerous actors as far as who is in control: cen-tral, provincial and local governmental educational authorities; self-con-trol by schools and school boards, plus control by associations of provi-ders and 'market' control by clients (parents and students). I have to re-frain from a detailed comparative description and evaluation of the various regimes of regulation and control and also do not sketch aggre-gate country templates that often reproduce myths like 'the unregu-lated American' systems versus the 'excessively' over-regulated Eur-opean regime. In addition, meaningful (parental, teacher and school) autonomy versus legitimate public control implies tensions and trade-offs not only for religious schools, as is often assumed, but also for governmental schools. I start by briefly stating the general tension be-tween autonomy and control and the dangers of extensive interpreta-tions of the 'public trust theory' (para. 4.3.5) in order to avoid the unat-tractive poles of full control versus no control. For moral and pedagogi-cal reasons, we have to look for effective but also the least obtrusive or invasive forms of input, output and throughput control. To avoid state-imposed standards, which are often rightly perceived as secularist and professionalist, I advocate the involvement of different kinds of providers in the debates and settings of minimal moral and minimal liberal-democratic standards all schools have to live up to. More demanding standards should not be enforced but agreed upon, which considerably raises the chances of effective implementation and self-control.

The tension between autonomy and control is widely and rightly recognised for both religious and governmental schools. The 'heightened demand for measurable educational results' (Glenn & Groof 2002: 579f), stimulated by civic-republican fervour and by 'free choice' as well, conflicts with the minimally required pedagogic autonomy for teachers. Making teaching contents, methods, lessons and also students' results ever more visible, transparent and comparable leads to 'teaching to the test'. In many countries, there is evidence of attempts to minimise central regulation and reduce external control of governmental schools (Liebman & Sabel 2003 for the US). Yet, over-regulation and invasive control are particularly dangerous for religious schools because they tend to override not only pedagogic autonomy but also constitutionally and legally guaranteed freedoms of religious education.[35] This tendency is particularly used in the US by some strong ('unreasonable') defenders of freedom of religion, free establishment and 'choice' as the core argument against any form of public regulation and control, however minimal and 'unobtrusive' (Campbell 2002: 207; Wolf & Macedo 2004: 3). Reasonable pluralists such as McConnell (2002); Witte (2004: 357f); Glenn (2004: 348); Groof (2004) and Esbeck (2004) accept that all schools have to be minimally regulated and controlled but rightly point out that 'it is very tempting to use subsidies as a way to make non-public schools into instruments of public policy' (Groof 2004: 175). 'With public dollars come a wide variety of government regulations' (Wolf & Macedo 2004: 3). State authorities often cannot resist the temptation to use the 'backdoor strategy' (Galston 2002: 321, Witte 2004: 366) to impose specific perspectives and ways of life, pedagogies and ways of organising on religious schools.[36]

I have already explained, on the one hand, why moral minimalism requires minimal external controls of all religious organisations including churches, why controls may legitimately be more demanding for FBOs compared with churches and for FBOs in education compared with care (para. 4.3.5). On the other hand, respecting the educational consequences of religious freedoms clearly means that the standards should not be maximalist but minimalist although liberal-democratic. The freedoms of *richting* (i.e. the right to shape a school according to a religious or philosophical worldview or pedagogy) and of *inrichting* (i.e. of internal organisational structure or 'organising authority' (Groof 2004: 166) should be respected and also defended by all reasonable civic republicans. They require that the controls are as unobtrusive as possible. It is obviously difficult to find the 'right' balance (Glenn & Groof 2002) or 'appropriate' balance (Harris 2004: 104) and to avoid the dangers of over-regulation and under-regulation (Witte 2004: 358). Here, as in all other cases, the fact that standards and controls should be 'reasonable' (*Pierce*, quoted in Glenn 2004: 342) does not solve the tension but only indicates the difficulties involved.

If all schools, including 'private' or independent religious schools, which do not ask for or accept public money, have to be minimally controlled, does public financing make a difference at all empirically?[37] Should it make a difference morally speaking? (Wolf & Macedo 2004: 8) In other words, what is the normative worth of the public trust theory in education? In my view, its main impact lies in legitimate rules requiring schools to be non-profit organisations (actually required in all liberal-democratic countries and in legitimate control of financial affairs: private schools may waste their own money if they so wish but publicly financed schools are accountable to standards of efficiency and effectiveness).[38] Its impact is much weaker and more dubious with regard to the selection of teachers and students: private religious schools not publicly funded are still subject to nondiscrimination in employment and student selection. It is even weaker regarding matters of content and pedagogy: they have to teach 'nondiscrimination and non-oppression' and obviously if they want their examinations to be publicly accredited, schools must teach the minimal cognitive content of the curriculum. In the end, the moral intuition, spelled out by the public trust theory, that public funding of schools also makes a big difference in terms of content control, seems correct only *prima facie* (see Martinez-Lopez quoted in Glenn & Groof 504). The moral trade-off between autonomy and control seems smaller than the empirical trade-off, which may also be exaggerated in phrases like 'the more choice, the more regulation/control' (Wolf & Macedo 2004: X).

Finding reasonable balances then crucially depends on finding the least invasive or obtrusive but still effective means of public regulation and control. Regulation and control of accreditation ranges from detailed specification in advance of maximum conditions regarding the numbers of expected and actually enrolled students, facilities, geographical spread, qualification of teaching staff, trustworthiness of provider, mission and curriculum guide, etc. to more lenient rules and practices and shorter periods between recognition and public financing. (This detailed specification has been approached by Russia (Glenn & Groof 2002: 589) and, to a lesser degree, by France and Germany.) In some countries, accredited schools are controlled regularly (e.g. in England and Wales every six years), in others only after a 'notice of complaint', and withdrawal of financing or accreditation is open to judicial

appeal. In my view, fairness requires low thresholds in terms of numbers of students and short waiting periods before financing is granted
because high numbers and long periods (e.g. in France it is five years
and in Germany up to six years) tend to exclude or discriminate against
smaller and new religious minorities or alternative candidates and directly or indirectly privileges established providers.

Input regulation can be detailed and specified in all possible regards.
In addition to general curriculum guides or frameworks, which are accepted in most countries,[39] some countries require that curriculum
plans specify in detail not only subjects[40] but also courses, minimum
number of lessons or hours, schedules or even prescribe textbooks and
teacher guides. The more detailed these regulations and controls, the
lower the autonomy of the teachers and schools in general and for religious schools in particular. Opposition to this tendency is mounting,
even within governmental schools.

Morally more apt alternatives are 'outcome driven approaches' (Groof
2004: 180) or output control, often praised as 'smart regulation'
(Glenn). They require final attainment targets following from general
curriculum guides or frameworks. However, they leave schools and teachers 'free to express its distinctive character and its method of teaching and to a considerable extent in the content of teaching, as well as
in other aspects of school life' (Groof 2004: 172). To make outcomes
comparable and to test whether cognitive and non-cognitive achievements live up to the minimum standards, they also require common,
state or nation-wide examinations at least at the end of primary, secondary and high school education that are hotly contested in federal
education regimes such as Germany or the US. The kinds of examinations differ widely (oral, written, from multiple choice to open essays,
course work) and legitimately so. Yet, common examinations can also
be used as a backdoor strategy to impose statism and professionalist secularism on all schools. This danger can only be effectively prevented
by integrating the different educational providers in setting standards
and preparing common examinations (see below). One should also be
aware of the danger of introducing testing in all schools and classes all
the time, starting in pre-schools (teaching to the test from the cradle to
the grave).[41]

When it comes to examinations in civic education, for example, essays (e.g. in the CBEES 'curriculum-based external exit examination
system' in Alberta) are preferable because they avoid the 'negative outcome of standardized testing' (Campbell 2004: 209). However, they
can only test cognitive outcomes. The pedagogical climate of a school,
its 'atmosphere, ethos or culture', the character of interactions in
classes, school and school environment as well as the actual learning
of civic and democratic virtues can only be controlled, if at all, by

throughput control or external inspection in classes or schools (Eisgru-ber 2002: 70, 82). Some countries like France (Meuret 2004: 247f), go very far in this regard at least in theory, others are much more reluc-tant[42] and most exempt religious instruction classes from inspection. Throughput control, particularly unannounced state inspection, is clearly the most effective control if 'we' really want to know what is ac-tually going on in classrooms and schools but it is also the most inva-sive one. Our desire to know and to control (the ceaseless 'quest for control') generally stimulates the tendency towards massive over-regula-tion but particularly if it is driven by dramatised 'fringe' cases and by the logic of moral and political panic instead of focusing on 'typical si-tuations' (Witte 2004: 335ff, Wolf & Macedo 2004: 24f) and the 'really important, long-term concerns'.

To summarise, in a comparative perspective, we have many com-bined moral and pedagogic reasons to prefer regimes that are mainly output-oriented and 'humble' but maybe not so 'devolved' (Witte 2004: 362).

All standards and procedures of regulation and control, even if mini-mal, crucially have to be 'objective' (Glenn & Groof) or in my language, as relationally neutral and even-handed as possible. Instead of counter-factually assuming that government authorities and teaching profes-sions are 'neutral' by definition, institutions and processes of defining general curriculum frameworks, final achievement targets and also ex-aminations should try to guarantee that the divergent perspectives be included. This is particularly relevant if one realises that worldviews or perspectives are not only important when it comes to religious instruc-tion (sect. 5.2).[43] It is remarkable that only a few countries have tried to set up fair and even-handed institutions and procedures for setting standards and control. Most seem to trust that fairly non-transparent institutions and committees composed of state officials and co-opted teachers and scientists (as the *Onderwijsinspectie* and *Onderwijsraad* in the Netherlands) are the best in realising 'neutrality and objectivity'. Belgium is the exception; it has a 'longstanding tradition of consulta-tion with educational networks and stakeholders' (Groof 2004: 171).[44]

10.7 Associative democracy, standard setting and control

This is an example of associational standard setting and control as pro-posed by AD. It combines governmental and non-governmental institu-tions, general and specific publics instead of trusting the wisdom of either professionals in the field, state authorities or (religious, philoso-phical, pedagogic) educational providers.[45]

Like all forms of selective cooperation (sects. 8.3 and 8.4), it requires thresholds in order to be workable. To establish and successfully run a publicly financed religious primary school for example, a certain minimum number of students is required, which depends on years of mandatory education, prescribed minimum/maximum students per class, geographical location and the wealth of a country, etc.[46] It only makes sense that umbrella associations ('networks' in Belgium, 'systems' in Australia) be present at the table to deliberate and negotiate with other umbrella organisations, government educational authorities and other relevant stakeholders after a certain minimum of such schools have for some time been in successful operation. The providers must also express the desire, not to mention the organisational capacity, to be represented in educational councils that advise or co-decide standards and control. In addition to the external public control according to negotiated and agreed minimum standards, AD places its trust on different forms of self-control by educational networks or umbrella associations of providers,[47] by schools themselves, which may develop and implement more demanding standards, and also by parents and students who act as 'private quality controllers' (control by more or less well-informed clients or 'consumers'). Self-control can be more routine, less invasive, more enhancing (promoting quality instead of only supervising and reporting). However, as opposed to what some school choice evangelists propose, to work properly, it should be backed by external public control (it has to work in the shadow of hierarchy).

External control is mainly punctual, *ex ante* and/or *ex post* and it depends on the quality and selectivity of provided information, which is why its effectiveness should not be overestimated. Hence, internal routine self-control *in actu* and continuous adaptation and change of practices are paramount, although the possibilities very much depend on the forms of governance of the schools. Many countries have laws that regulate democratic participation and co-decision (democratic governance) by the relevant stakeholders (teachers, other staff members, students and parents)[48] and these or similar systems are also proposed by deliberative democrats, empowered (deliberative) democrats (Fung & Wright 2001: 9f) and AD.

However, associative democracy, like civic libertarianism, takes associational religious freedoms more seriously and is more hesitant to impose democratic congruence on all FBOs in education without due consideration. It does not want to overrule the 'organisational authority' of providers[49] and may even allow exemptions from participation and co-decision laws where religious providers can reasonably and plausibly demonstrate (and the burden of proof is clearly theirs) that even moderate forms of democratic school governance would be incompatible with the core of the religion as they define it. Yet this may then be a legitimate reason to withhold public subsidies. If this is done, it weakens internal control considerably and also makes external control more difficult. This indicates the first serious problem for AD.[50] However, we have seen that the overwhelming majority of religious schools do not ask for such exemptions and, more importantly, seem to provide a school structure and culture that seems to be more conducive to effective cooperation between parents, students and teachers than comparable governmental schools.[51] Furthermore, in this regard, the trade-off between public control and diversity is not as big as is often assumed in general statements that governmental schools increase the chances of effective civic and democratic education, regulation and control at the risk of 'treating all the same' instead of 'all equal', whereas nongovernmental schools would be good for diversity but bad for democracy and public regulation and control.

Compared with either external governmental control or 'market control' by clients only, mixed regimes of regulation and control are also preferable for other reasons because the latter are external, they perform poorly in situations of routine control and slight, continuous improvement of practices, and both have to tackle serious information problems. Information problems may be better resolved by governmental authorities, although there is no reason to take this issue lightly. One cannot just assume that parents and students as choosers and private quality controllers are well informed. They are confronted with serious difficulties to get adequate, relevant (i.e. selected), reliable and comparable information (Minow 2000). These are difficulties that can be resolved only on the basis of publicly regulated information provisions because voluntary agreements have proven to be ineffective (Engelen 2005). 'Markets' in services do not solve information problems automatically, but may help to resolve them only if properly regulated. Otherwise, more school choice increases formal autonomy only, instead of meaningful substantive autonomy, and clients tend to escape from the bewildering 'freedom of choice' by either traditionally staying where they are or by fairly volatile entries and exits. Associative democracy's choice of exit over voice should hence be more circumscribed in order to respond to the two downsides of exclusive exit strategies (a second serious problem for AD): the information problem and the problem that only voice guarantees some continuing impact on increasing the quality of teaching practices. In summary, mixed systems of control seem the most able to guarantee what is paramount: improving the quality of all education in all schools for all pupils (Gutmann 2002: 43; Rosenblum 2002: 153) instead of only guaranteeing the bare minimum.

10.8 Monopoly for governmental schools or libertarian market archipelagos? Regime pluralism: the case for associative democracy

Organisational or institutional pluralism is not only conducive to a more culturally diverse education in terms of content and pedagogy, it is also better for the overall effectiveness, efficiency and for higher degrees of adaptation and innovation compared with an ideal model of organisational monism.

A state-enforced legal monopoly for governmental schools no longer exists in liberal democracies (as it did in some Swiss cantons until 1969) but some states (in Scandinavia, Italy and Switzerland) approach a factual monopoly. Yet even if it did exist, it would not *eo ipso* mean that governmental schools would be completely homogenous or monolithic,[52] for two main reasons.

First, even in highly centralised systems of government and education – as France (Meuret 2004: 245; Glenn & Groof 2002: 247), Portugal (Glenn & Groof 2002: 415), Italy (Ribolzi 2004: 269f) and also the Netherlands – there is always some delegation of educational authority to lower levels, whether legally or in actual practice. In all federal systems, educational authority is explicitly divided and more or less radically devolved, so that actual regimes of educational governance (in terms of funding, of regulation/control of content, pedagogy and organisation) can differ markedly within a country/polity. This can be within provinces (Canada),[53] 'states' (US) or *'Länder'* (Germany), Swiss *cantons,* or provinces or regions (Belgium and Spain) as well as within the same unit among school districts, municipalities, schools and classrooms: the more this is the case, the more decentralised and devolved actual competencies are.[54]

Second, and increasingly so since the 1990s, more countries have begun to permit and subsidise alternative, non-governmental ('independent') and non-religious schools like magnet schools, charter schools, city colleges or city academies.[55]

Hence, governmental schools may allow more diversity in content and pedagogy of education than critics suggest. However, in such a system, it is more difficult to resist the temptation to impose specific statist and professionalist and secularist philosophies and the newest 'educational reform' fads on all schools. This is because governmental schools lack the constitutional, legal and institutional means to resist such modelling, particularly if they are guided by strong nationalist assimilation[56] and aggressive *laïcist* agendas. Institutionally and organisationally pluralist regimes provide more guarantees and chances for legitimate diversity in education if shielded against the fervour of statist over-regulation.

In turn, there is reasonable doubt that exclusive 'school choice', the libertarian utopia of independent, loosely connected school archipelagos would provide a 'panacea' (Gutmann 2002: 41f, 45, 174 vs. Chubb & Moe) or a 'magic solution' (Glenn 2004: 354), particularly if they are not properly regulated and controlled and adequately funded.

All reasonable pluralists quite outspokenly favour regime pluralism in education, and AD proposes a much broader set of associational self-organisation in education compared with Christian-Democratic defenders of pluralism, who focus on religious schools as the only or main alternative to governmental schools. The position of civic republicans is much less clear, however. On the one hand, they seem to accept, rather reluctantly and with hesitation – as a regrettable 'fact of life' – that non-governmental, particularly religious schools are constitutionally guaranteed.[57] On the other hand, they still seem to be unprepared to accept public financing, let alone opt for adequate levels of public financing for reasons of fairness and to realise equal educational opportunities for everyone in the real world. They also seem to advocate comprehensive and fairly obtrusive regimes of public regulation and control.

Defenders of school choice and of AD (Hirst 1994: 201ff, Bader 1998a: 195ff) share a strong emphasis on voluntarism (choice for parents and students), on legitimate autonomy of teachers, schools and associational providers, and on legitimate ethno-cultural and religious diversity of the overall educational system. In addition to these moral reasons, they also share more contested prudential arguments[58] that regime pluralism increases competition and, directly or indirectly, the overall effectiveness and efficiency of educational systems. In contrast to most pluralists and school choice theorists, however, associative democrats are in possession of more sophisticated conceptual and theoretical resources in many regards. They oppose the wrong, exclusive choice between either state (civic republicans) or market (school choice). They can also use the full set of modes of governance in education: private (profit/non-profit) schools/hierarchies; schools owned and run by (religious, 'philosophical' or pedagogic) associations and communities and/or their roof organisations; governmental schools (public hierarchies); networks or 'partnerships'[59] among private, semi-private and public schools and within and among roof organisations; all cooperating and competing on a more or less strongly regulated market (see also Glenn & Groof 2006a: 66ff).

The inherited legal private vs. public dichotomy is also inadequate to describe the various forms of private, semi-private or semi-public and public organisation in education. AD advocates a fairly large percentage of associational educational providers, which are public but non-state or non-governmental. Moreover, this dichotomy increasingly impedes the asking of questions that are normatively really relevant: whether schools perform better or worse regarding cognitive and non-cognitive outcomes, and whether effectiveness and efficiency depends more on adequate financing, regulation and control of educational service delivery than on dubious legal constructions.

As in all human services, 'private non-profit organisations', particularly associational ones, also seem to be superior in education compared to governmental bureaucracies and private profit organisations (in unregulated or poorly regulated markets) in providing 'quasi-collective services' on 'quasi-markets' (Harris 2004: 119). 'In particular, the importance of maintaining face-to-face communication between parents and teachers while producing these quasi-collective services requires a less bureaucratic form of governance and administration. Private non-profit organisations seem to be able to deal better with the two-sided, face-to-face demands of supplying quasi-collective services than private, profit-seeking organizations or public organizations.' (Dijkstra et al. 2004: 86f).

Because AD is situated most self-reflexively in the broad tradition of institutional pluralism, it is able to more fully use its concepts (e.g. division, delegation and limitation of powers, sovereignty and authority),[60] theories and strategies (e.g. cooperative competition), plus the many experiences with resolutions of problems of political IP (e.g. federalism), of social pluralism and of minority pluralism, and practical experiments in other fields, including educational governance.

Finally, institutionally pluralist arrangements, 'mixed' or 'poly-centric' systems or regimes show considerable advantages when it comes to fairly quick and smooth adaptations in response to internal or external challenges or crises. This is true not only in the economy, but also in welfare systems, systems of care and healthcare, pensions, as well as in education, because they allow piecemeal, incremental changes instead of full-scale system change.[61] In addition, they quasi-naturally form laboratories, a much richer variety pool for experimenting with new alternatives, finding better practices, selecting them and stabilising them. In brief, they have a superior capacity for innovation.

10.9 Educational design and practical democratic experimentalism

As I have stated in the introduction to this chapter, the complexity and contingency of educational regimes of governance, their cultural-political embeddedness (Galston 2004: 321), path dependency and also their 'institutional inertia' (Wolf & Macedo 2004: 70ff, 198) prohibit the 'wholesale export' (Campbell 2004: 209) or 'import' (Wolf & Macedo

2004: 4f) of systems (generally: Zeitlin 2003). There are no 'simple lessons' (Wolf & Macedo 2004: 2). Moreover, there is no one institutional design that can resolve all the trade-offs and fit all of the circumstances. One optimal or utopian educational system is impossible. However, since all of the various systems are confronted with 'many stubborn problems' (Glenn 2004: 339), we can compare how they try to resolve them, find better practices by using divergent, contested but still reasonable normative (moral, prudential, realistic) standards.

Mixed or pluralist regimes provide better chances for this type of learning because they allow for 'incremental' (Wolf & Macedo 2004: 5f), routine changes and do not require mega-planning and the almost inevitable risks of 'mega-failures' (Scott 1998) that normally go hand in hand with such endeavours driven by political and technocratic elites in general, but also in education (as in the Netherlands). Incremental change and democratic practical experiments also require a lot of prudence ('design with care', Glenn 2004: 340f). Good design is of 'central importance' (Glenn 2004: 353) and 'details matter a great deal' (Wolf & Macedo 2004: 9), indeed. Together with other proponents of democratic experimentalism, AD is clearly opposed to top-down, expert- or elite-driven 'Grand Design' and stresses the involvement of educational stakeholders and their practical knowledge. However, it also insists on a modest but important role for political theorists (Bader & Engelen 2003). As this chapter has hopefully shown, it provides some useful general guidelines and rules of thumb for experimental change of funding, regulation and control of education that should be further explored and applied in specific countries because the proof of the pudding is eventually in the eating (Bader 2001a: 61).

Conclusions

In my Introduction, I claim that the threats and promises of new religious diversity urge us to rethink our moral principles, our cherished institutional models of the relations between religions, states and politics, and our traditional policies of incorporation. On all these levels, I hope that I have shown that we should stop reproducing outworn oppositions that stand in the way of finding promising alternatives or third ways. The ritualised opposition between universalist principles of neutrality and justice and particularist partiality and perfectionism can be overcome by moderate universalism, relational neutrality and fairness as even-handedness in matters of cultural practices. On the one hand, the set of institutional choices is not limited to the 'ideal model' of a strict or complete constitutional, legal, administrative, political and cultural separation of state and organised religions that is shared by the overwhelming majority of libertarians, liberals, democrats, republicans, socialists and feminists. On the other hand, the set of institutional choices is not limited to the existing patterns of 'establishment' of dominant religions and corporatist types of religious governance shared by many communitarians and traditionalists. Associational governance of religious diversity is a form of institutional pluralism that shares the advantages of institutionalising religious pluralism with the openness and flexibility of American denominationalism and non-establishment. The set of relevant policy choices is limited neither to old or new liberal or republican policies of assimilationism masked as neutral, secular and purely civic-democratic, nor to policies of accommodation of all ethno-religious cultural practices even if they violate basic rights.

My contextualised political theory requests that we take moral pluralism (i.e. the tension among moral principles, the complexity of practical judgement and the limits of theoretical knowledge) really seriously without having to accept the paralysing consequences of 'everything goes', 'all is relative' or 'it all depends'. Minimal morality defines the minimalist but tough standards of basic rights, the moral constraints of toleration and accommodation, which have to be guaranteed by all polities independent of contexts and groups. Differentiated morality explicitly invites us to develop more demanding liberal, democratic, egali-

tarian and pluralist standards and policies, provided that their design
and implementation do not infringe on basic rights, as has been and
still so often is the case with imposing liberty, autonomy and equality,
without due consideration, on all people in all spheres of life and all
contexts.

In this conclusion, I summarise the new perspectives for the design
of institutions and policies that follow from my theoretical position,
which combines a contextualised moral theory with an institutional
turn in political theory. As could be expected from an explicitly contextual moral theory, my preferred institutional alternative AD (and my
preferred policies of maximum accommodation within the constraints
of moral minimalism combined with facilitation of freedom of exit, entry and good practical examples of fair and pluralist incorporation) also
have to address serious tensions amongst moral principles and rights
and also between moral, prudential and realistic arguments. For this
reason alone, I cannot offer alternatives that pretend to present one optimal institutional setting or policy for all countries, fields and contexts,
even if the inevitable trade-offs can often be softened by intelligent institutional design and end up being not as big and 'tragic' as often assumed. I focus on the most serious trade-offs and try to demonstrate
my 'art of balancing' before indicating expectable objections by those
who neglect the trade-offs or offer context-independent hierarchies and
simple solutions. I conclude by indicating some of associationalism's
serious problems that need to be further explored.

Let me start with the tension between individual and associational
autonomy that is inherent in any comprehensive understanding of the
liberal principle of freedom. In chapter 2, I opt for a differentiated approach to autonomy and defend a minimalist morality of basic rights
to security and subsistence connected to a thin notion of agency and legal autonomy. In my discussion of 'hard cases' (chap. 4), I apply this
concept of moral minimalism in my plea for maximum accommodation within these moral constraints ('leave them alone'), to show how
the basic rights of vulnerable minorities within minorities (particularly
minors and women) can be safeguarded; I also try to show that one
cannot hope that law and external intervention by the state alone could
solve these problems. A broader policy repertoire also includes other
external agents, other forms of sanctions and, most importantly, also
inducements. In chapter 7, I show what AD can do (i) to provide real
exit options in addition to guaranteeing exit rights, (ii) to strengthen
the voice of minorities within minorities, (iii) to convince non-liberal
minorities not only via persuasion but via good examples of fair and
pluralist incorporation and (iv) to trust in the seductive power of really
pluralised societies. In my view, this is all we can reasonably do without violating the 'reasonable, deep pluralism of the Good' and without

overriding associational autonomy. It may not convince determined comprehensive liberals and republicans who require the application of more demanding lists of rights and, particularly, of the full set of modern nondiscrimination rights, on all groups and organisations, and in all fields. However, these attempts to maximise individual autonomy have to pay the moral price of neglecting associational autonomy. In addition, they encounter realistic objections. Policies to enforce assimilation on dominant ethno-religious cultures (masked as 'secular', 'neutral' or 'purely civic') by legal and other sanctions are most likely to provoke reactive ethnicisation, religious fundamentalism and radical communal organisation, mobilisation and conflict if minorities command sufficient resources to resist. If these policies succeed in individualising and isolating people belonging to minorities (the 'socio'-logic of power asymmetries) and if they (have no other choice than to) use individual assimilation strategies trying to suppress or forget 'their old culture', they are most likely to eventually be less 'integrated', compared with those who try to find productive combinations of both cultures (Berry et al. 2006).

My liberal or libertarian plea for AD against attempts to maximise democracy completely resists the temptation of democratic congruence. The specific modern version of this old tension between liberalism and democracy is particularly pressing for associative democracy regarding those organisations that are not shielded by intimacy. This is because AD, together with other theories of democracy, shares a strong moral emphasis on democratising the internal structure of 'non-political' or private associations and organisations. It favours co-determination laws not only for private profit organisations of all kinds but also for non-profit organisations above a certain size. Exemptions from such laws for churches seem less problematic and more broadly shared than (in consecutive order) exemptions for political parties, for FBOs in care (sect. 4.3), and FBOs in education (sect. 10.6). More emphatic democrats either find all these exemptions unacceptable, or at least the latter ones. Yet the question is then whether this is still a 'tolerable democracy'. However, my argument that we might consider exemptions from participation laws and co-decision laws for FBOs, that we should not overrule the organisational authority without due consideration where religious providers can reasonably and plausibly demonstrate that even moderate forms of democratic governance would be incompatible with the core of their religions as they define it (and the burden of proof is theirs), is clearly more debatable because such exemptions may be seen to undermine the effectiveness of nondiscrimination and co-decision laws.

All institutional settings and policies have to address the old tension between the principles of equality and liberty or diversity, given that it is impossible to maximise or optimise substantive equality ('all equal') and diversity ('all different') at the same time, although appropriate institutional design may soften this trade-off. Where determined egalitarians try to realise a more or less complete equality of resources, opportunities, rewards or capabilities, I strike a different balance. Associative democracy is more moderately egalitarian in defending tough but minimal and contextualised standards to guarantee basic needs and social security for all, which are already extremely difficult to realise. However, it allows more unequal distributions (and more freedoms) if this threshold is satisfied. In addition, I have defended affirmative action policies (e.g. in education) to guarantee adequate though not necessarily fully equal educational opportunities for poor and minority students by a combination of a weighted voucher system and additional direct public funding of schools. Proposals like these are clearly more egalitarian and strike a different balance than classical liberals, neo-liberals and libertarians, who have criticised *all* affirmative action as a morally intolerable violation of liberty and equality before the law.

All regimes of religious governance lead to a certain institutionalisation and also require some forms of public (administrative, political, legal or constitutional) recognition of religions (chap. 8). Public registration (e.g. for granting tax and other exemptions) requires criteria and thresholds in terms of numbers, time and durability of settlement, minimal stability and credibility, etc. Because it is inevitably selective, the rule of law minimally demands some forms of judicial control of administrative discretion. All regimes of religious government privilege recognised religions and FBOs in care (and almost all of them also in education) either by indirect or direct public funding. However, distinct from NEPP, institutionally pluralist regimes also provide opportunities for religions in setting standards, implementation and control of services, selective cooperation with governments, and also some formal representation of organised religions in the political process, particularly in problem definition, public deliberation and presentation of decision-making alternatives. This involves more demanding systems of public recognition of religions and higher thresholds of institutional interest intermediation. At the same time, it stimulates the emergence of and increases pressures on representative, more centralised organisations and leaderships that may infringe upon *church autonomy* or the associational autonomy of religions. We have also seen that the political opportunity structure strongly influences the patterns of organisation and representation of religions, whether they develop one centralised monolithic organisation, a confederation or several independent, loosely co-ordinated organisations (sect. 8.5). The situation in the US differs from most European countries because it provides fewer incentives for central organisation and representation (a consequence of the fairly limited system of selective cooperation between governments and religions) and because state-induced or state-imposed patterns of organisation and representation (which characterise both French statism and religious neo-corporatism in European countries) are virtually absent. AD also clearly insists on building associations from below and opposes 'state crafting', an important selective affinity with American denominationalism. This alleviates the autonomy dilemma considerably.

Systems of selective cooperation in care and education, however, are inevitably more selective, rigid, less open and diverse. Here, the normative problem is how to prevent illegitimate exclusionary effects, inflexibility and rigidity, which are particularly serious for religious minorities. This makes the dilemma of legal and substantive equal treatment more pressing for AD as well, because it is not easy, to say the least, to find a reasonable trade-off between morally recommendable inclusion and functionally required workability. Instead of neglecting the fact that there is a problem to be solved, I have proposed ways to keep the thresholds for cooperation and representation as low as compatible with workability requirements and to counteract vested interests and lock-in effects, which may indicate directions to soften the trade-off. American denominationalism and other systems (which restrict interest representation to informal ways of influencing parties and legislations through network building and lobbying) cannot in turn prevent informal ways of cooperation (unregulated 'negotiating administration'). They are even more vulnerable to inequality charges because old majority religions have huge and unchecked advantages in terms of power resources and strategies. Not regulating representation and cooperation has serious counterproductive effects, which are comparable to those of forbidding regulated systems of public financing of political parties. Associative democracy's less exclusive and less rigid system is a promising alternative to American denominationalism and to exclusive, rigid, hierarchical neo-corporatist models in European countries and in the EU. It shares the fairly open, pluralist and largely voluntary character with NEPP and American denominationalism, but hopes to avoid its downsides by offering religions a fairer, more open and flexible system of selective representation and cooperation.

Until fairly recently, the US was one of the very few liberal-democratic states outlawing any direct and indirect public financing of FBOs in education. However, this last bastion of American exceptionalism is now also crumbling, although the development of new forms of institutional pluralism does not seem to have affected philosophical and political defenders of NEPP. In chapter 10, I have tried to show that egalitarian, civic republicans and deliberative democrats should seriously reconsider their unconditional opposition against fairly equal public financing of non-governmental religious schools and that associational governance provides promising institutional and policy alternatives to resolve big trade-offs between educational freedoms and democracy, diversity and equality, and educational achievement. Philosophers and politicians should stop dealing in outworn ideal models that prevent us from seeing what is actually going on, and they should try to learn from the practical solutions in their own countries as well as in other countries. In addition, they should learn from the theories of associational governance.

I hope to have shown that associative democracy strikes more reasonable balances among competing moral principles than rival approaches in political theory. Still, the way to hell may be paved with good moral intentions, a reason why I will now elaborate on two realistic objections that were previously mentioned only in passing.

First, even my minimalist proposals for guaranteeing basic needs and social security for all (and certainly more demanding affirmative action policies) need a 'fairly strong and fairly centralised state in order to correct structural inequalities. Strong centres are required to overcome the entrenched powers of the "rich" and organised, the rich states in a federation or rich regions in a state,' or of dominant classes and ethno-religious majorities. 'Proposals to institutionalise pluralism are very vulnerable because they entrust powers to associations in civil society which, on the one hand, may strengthen already resource-rich and powerful collective actors and, on the other hand, may weaken strong centres' (Bader 2001: 46f). It is an open question whether the proposed thin but strong state of AD is strong enough to enable the proposed moderate egalitarian policies, even if one brackets the paradoxes of transformation, agency and strategy (Bader 2001a: 47, 59f). Historical contextualisation, however, may also help in this regard. Strong states may be needed to realise a basic egalitarian threshold and to guarantee basic social security and a certain minimum of adequate, not even fully equal educational opportunities (chap. 10, note 1). If such minimal thresholds are eventually realised after long and determined struggles, which is certainly not the case in the US, less statist egalitarian policies are conceivable and may gain in plausibility. Free choice of social insurance and pensions, in care provision and education, if and when properly regulated, can help reduce the inequalities that characterised traditional free choice systems.

Second, the tensions within the principle of freedom and among freedom and equality also characterise the design of associative service provision. Associative service provisions seem better able to guarantee legitimate and meaningful cultural and religious diversity whereas universalist state provision (say the 'Swedish model') seems better able to guarantee good, high-quality and accessible public services for all. My proposal of a mixed or pluralist regime combining associational (non-governmental, i.e. private and semi-public) with a variable but substantive public or governmental service provision not only in education but also in healthcare, care for children, elderly, poor, and in health, social security and pension insurance plans, is also motivated by three inherent limitations of purely associational service delivery. (i) It is an open question whether determined efforts to really achieve equal opportunities for all in associational provision can be successfully realised, even if properly regulated. (ii) Focusing on easy exit from and entry into competing service providers may have negative side effects for the quality of service delivery compared with internal voice (too much trust on the healthy working of markets and competition). (iii) It also involves considerable problems of information and choice for clients, which has become plain in recent policies to privatise healthcare and health insurance coverage, for instance. It is an open question what a pluralist regime that would have to be different for the diverse fields of service delivery and for insurances would look like in different countries.

In chapter 9, I address the rock-bottom realistic objections to multiculturalism, all forms of institutional pluralism and AD. Associative religious governance is said to foster 'fundamentalist' organisations and leaders, to undermine stability, social cohesion and political unity and to produce violent ethno-religious conflicts. A sober analysis of these generalised realistic objections as well as the related objections to religious schools (which are accused of undermining civic and democratic virtues and bridging bonds, instead of enhancing them) has shown that they are theoretically implausible and empirically untenable, particularly if raised against AD, which is clearly the least vulnerable to these challenges. If policies of fair ethno-religious accommodation are combined with policies to guarantee fair legal, economic, social and political incorporation, as they should be (Bader 2005; 1998a), they are more likely to create fair and stable forms of cohesion and political unity, to create toleration and the appropriate civic virtues and bonds, and at least help to reduce the chances of violent conflicts and terrorism. Combined with the structural refusal to accommodate legitimate religious needs and the absence of determined policies of fair socio-economic incorporation, the rhetoric of civic-republican assimilation is likely to set 'Paris in flames'. Yet I have acknowledged that institutional pluralism in general, and AD in particular (which is good in preventing fundamentalism and violent conflicts or even terrorism), may be bad in fighting terrorism under emergency conditions (sect. 9.8). This is because more centralised, monist institutional structures can assemble quicker, more resolute and coherent deterrence policies. This objection has to be qualified, however, because polycentricity makes societies and polities less vulnerable to terrorist attacks, because deterrence strategies in themselves more often than not produce counterproductive effects that stimulate and radicalise terrorism, and because institutional pluralism and fair accommodation are urgently needed in post-conflict development to clean up the mess produced by deterrence and 'wars against terrorism' under the guise of 'freedom and democracy'. It remains an open question of whether institutionally pluralist polities are strong, unified and robust enough to endure in situations of emergency and to find ways for determined action without sacrificing diversity.

Nowadays, the most important lessons in this regard, if any, are negative ones. We may disagree reasonably about what we should do, but it seems obvious what we should not do. We should not engage in exporting particularist understandings of 'freedom and democracy' through international wars (modern versions of crusades led by the neo-conservative and deeply Protestant Bush administration). And we should not engage in reckless secularist policies of assimilation, as propagated by increasingly fashionable civic republicans and applied by the French administration under the guise of laïcité plurielle. Priority for democracy is clearly opposed to religious and to secularist crusades threatening peace and toleration. This is where sober realism and moral minimalism meet.

The prospects of a less minimalist and more demanding associative religious governance depend on a clear recognition of the many tensions between moral principles themselves and between moral, prudential and realistic requirements. To neglect inherent trade-offs or to promote 'premature solutions, spells intellectual dishonesty and political disaster. There are no easy answers, and to insist otherwise may have a paralysing effect on those who seek solutions.' (Bader 2001: 61, 2005: 86ff). My refutation of the generalised charges by critics should not lead us to ignore the seriousness of problems and dilemmas. Yet, critics should also not be allowed to ignore moral pluralism or to discount serious prudential and realistic constraints. If they do, they have to pay the double price of sacrificing crucial moral principles and rights and of presenting ideal models that conflict with all existing institutions and practices, are not even connected to them and which, in the real world, may be second best or more often even worse.

Contrary to traditional conceptions of 'utopian' design, and also to defenders of ideal models of NEPP, AD self-consciously takes into account the limitations of theoretical knowledge. It presents no top-down 'blueprints' but tries to learn from practical 'muddling through' and incorporates the practical knowledge of different relevant stakeholders in its preferred strategy of practical experimentalism, whereas the focus on ideal models often blinds us from seeing and finding practical ways of resolving serious problems and tensions (chap. 10). The main task for associationalist political theorists is to design more detailed, historically and empirically informed workable solutions for specific countries and fields and to engage in democratic experimentalism, in close cooperation with social movement organisations, NGOs, organised religions, parties, politicians and administrators that may be inspired by the general ideas of associationalism. Only in this way can the practical superiority of the concrete or realistic utopia of associational religious governance be convincingly demonstrated and, hopefully, realised.

Notes

Notes Chapter 1

1   Increasing religious diversity or pluralisation of the religious landscape globally and within Western states seems to be accompanied by an increasing fragmentation of organised 'high' religions, putting pressure on existing forms of institutionalisation of religions and their 'management' by the state (Bouma 1999, 2004), particularly on the rigid version of religious 'corporatism' in some European countries. This is an additional reason to find new, more flexible forms of governance like AD, see 7.4 and 8.6.

2   With what semantics do they signify the distinction between an immanent and a transcendent world (unfamiliar/familiar, far/near, invisible/visible, otherworldly/this worldly, infinite/finite, heaven/earth, sacred/profane)? How is the transcendent described and how is it evaluated? How are the borders between the transcendent and the immanent marked. What is considered sacred, what is forbidden and how is it sanctioned? How is the transcendent shown and how does it show itself and make itself known in this world? Are any special 'mediators' or specialised roles needed to transgress these borders and, if so, how is the relationship between the different kinds of religious elites and lay people structured? Are they belief-centred or centred on practices and how are beliefs and practices related to each other, evaluated, transmitted and learned? Is religious belief orally transmitted or via written text and, if the latter, are there any attempts by experts to make these holy books and texts consistent and systematic? Is the community of practitioners only bound together by shared practices and beliefs or are they complemented by more or less formalised and hierarchically structured organisations?

3   The Supreme Court's mounting difficulties to find defensible definitions of 'religion' under these conditions are excellently analysed by Galanter (1966: 235ff, 260ff) and in HLR Note (1987: 1622-1631, 1647ff). For similar difficulties in France, see: Basdevant-Gaudemet 1995: 132, 137; in Belgium: Torfs 1995: 21; in Italy: Ferrari 1995: 193f; in Portugal: Canas 1995: 299; in India: Galanter 1998: 255ff; 1998a: 273ff vs. Smith 1998: 196ff; in Australia: Cahill et al. 2005. Some of the practical troubles of applying privatised, subjectivised definitions of religion (following an idealised version of radical Protestantism) are analysed in chapters 5 and 8. UN declarations and international covenants (Koenig 2003: 142ff for ambivalences) also try to avoid a clear legal definition of religion, but show predominant interpretations. In the first phase, these are more in line with classical occidental concepts of religion; while in the second phase, a more 'primordialised' interpretation ('race') or a more 'culturalised' interpretation ('ethnicity', 'tradition'; 'cultural human heritage', 'cultural diversity') is predominant. Recently, protests against such 'ascriptive' definitions are gaining in force.

4   Like politics, economics and law, ethics and aesthetics are specific systems of communication.

5   See Bader 2006c for an extensive discussion.
6   See criticism by Salvatore (2004: 1021-1024). For Judaism in the process of ambiguous 'emancipation and assimilation', ritualism and traditional cultural practices have been seen as a burden, the 'true religion' is an 'affair of sentiment, not of practices' (Salomon Reinach 1900, quoted in Jansen 2006).
7   See Casanova's criticism of the Berger-Luckmann thesis (1994: 35ff). In its 'expressivist' variety ('self-expression, self-realisation, narcissism, individual authenticity' in the 'private sphere', in 'free time'), it is also fully endorsed by Taylor 2002. The eventual absorption of practices and beliefs in identity claims is the distinguishing mark of most 'postmodernist' literatures.
8   See note 2 for the shift in international covenants. Eventually, it is said, all religious believers will be 'born again'. However, it is crucial to distinguish between impositions of such '(post-)modernist' definitions (e.g. Smith's version of Hinduism (1998, see criticism by Galanter 1998: 246f, 259; see also Spinner 2005a) and processes of religious change (e.g. Hindus in New York and the possible impact of these changes on the civilisational homes of religions: see Casanova 2005).
9   This was rightly pointed out by Asad. Even the 'informal' communities of 'new age religiosity' are communities, even non-direct interactions on the world-wide-web form 'internet communities'.
10 Eventually, Luhmann has considerably increased his critical distance to the 'modern semantics' of 'privatisation of religious decisions' (1977: 232, 236ff) and also of 'subjective', 'individual' or 'authentic' (2000: 189-192), clarifying that this structural relevance has to be understood as principled recognition of the contingency of all decisions. This contingency of religious decisions has at least two important consequences. First, it creates new problems of consistency (2000: 294). Second, it seems to favour de-institutionalised, more informal, spontaneous, less hierarchical forms of religions which cannot rely on existing, shared communal forms of life but need new forms of 'community'. If this were to actually happen, religions would lose the will and the organisational capacity to be represented in public and in selective systems of cooperation between governments and organised religions (sect. 2.3, 2.4 and 7.4, 8.2).
11 Luhmann 2000: 295, 315f. See also Marty & Appleby 1991. Gill highlights the theoretical irony: 'The primary explanatory variable proposed to account for decreasing levels of religions in society is the same variable pointer for the increase of religious activism: modernisation' (2001: 125 for a sharp criticism of the conundrums of 'non-falsifiable "grand theorizing"').
12 The generalised presumption by Raymond Williams that immigrants are 'more religious than they were before they left home' neglects (i) minorisation (religious identities as opposition to racialisation, see Casanova 2005: 12-14 and 24ff for the US.) and (ii) the huge impact of different political opportunity structures: Why 'Islam' becomes different in the US 'denominationalist' structure, compared with Europe.
13 Asad 1993, Robertson 1987 and Van der Veer 1997. See Mandaville (2001: 74ff) for 'Pan-Islam' (as an attempt to re-imagine the umma from a minority position) and for 'Living and revising Islam and the umma in diaspora' (114ff) from minority situations.
14 Privatisation, then, has to compete with the 'deprivatisation' of religion, seen as a repoliticisation of private relations and moral spheres, and as a 'renormativisation of the public economic and political spheres' (Casanova 1994: 6; Willaime 2004: 328ff for France). Bouma (1999) distinguishes clearly between the issues of 'going public' or not and of 'low versus high temperature': going public can mean both moderate and fanatic. In Europe, this public role is legally or even constitutionally acknowledged in different forms of 'public recognition' in some countries (sect. 1.4). See Robbers

for Germany (1995: 66); Pötz for Austria (1995: 261f: 'Today, the position as a publicly recognised legal body has less a positive legal substance than that it clarifies
that the state does not see religion as a private affair and aims to prevent the privatisation of the religious'); Ferrari 2002.

15 David Martin's term the 'culturalisation' of religions as a consequence of the loss of
direct political clout is better suited to capturing these changes than 'privatisation'.
Culturalisation is obviously eminently 'social'. It is an important insight that the 'depoliticisation' of religion in this sense does not imply any loss of 'social significance'.
Processes of 'culturalisation of religions' may even result in gains in more indirect
political influence, as is clearly the case for the second (Methodist) and third (Pente-
costalist) wave of Protestantism in the USA and in the Americas, that is so bril-
liantly analysed in 'Tongs of Fire' (Martin 1990: 294 et pass).

16 Applying Robertson's theoretically guided construction of world religions is useful
here. World religions can be distinguished along two crucial axes: (i) their 'distinct'
organisational structures, and (ii) their inner-worldly versus otherworldly orientations. Christianity and Buddhism share diverging organisations (churches, *sangha*),
which keep the 'domains' of polities, state and politics and religion apart, whereas
Islam and Hinduism do not have 'distinct structures' (1987: 156) but rather 'organic
connections with society'. 'In both cases, 'church-state' problems do not truly
emerge until something like the self-consciously secular state has been installed'
(156). After the incipient, early phase, Christianity – ending with the Edict of Milan
in 313 and Justinian's promulgations – and Islam were predominantly inner-worldly
oriented (internally opposed by respective mysticisms) whereas, according to Max
Weber, Buddhism and Hinduism were predominantly otherworldly oriented. After
the conversion of king Asoka to Buddhism in India, 'Buddhism became embroiled
in an Asian equivalent of the Western church-state problems, a circumstance which
continues to the present day in the Theravada Buddhist societies of Sri Lanka, Bur-
ma, and Thailand' (155). But even then, the major contrast with Christianity is that
'ideally the *sangha* (the monastic order) and political authority are separate domains'
standing in a relation of 'hierarchical complementarity' (Dumont), whereas in Christian contexts 'church and state have frequently claimed jurisdiction over the same
domains' (155, see also Smith 1998: 187). Obviously, Japan (Shintoism) and China
(the inner-worldly, immanentist Confucianism, see Hildebrandt 2003: 456f) do not
fit into this pattern (see short summary by Minkenberg 2003: 116f).

17 See Hunter (2005) and Saunders (2005) for the explicit statement of the legal and
political framework of this minimalist threshold by lawyers and state-makers in
Western Europe in the 16th century: sovereignty of an increasingly religious indifferent state to achieve civic peace in internal religious wars. It remains an open question, however, whether the term 'secularist' in this legal-political sense has already
been applied to designate the state or whether, as I tend to think, this is an historical
anachronism.

18 Lawyers and state makers in Western Europe in the 16th century explicitly claimed
the sovereignty of a religiously indifferent state to achieve civic peace in internal religious wars and prepared the legal and political framework of this minimalist threshold (Hunter 2005, Saunders 2005).

19 Teubner 2002. See my detailed criticism of Luhmann's theory: Bader 2001e: 141-145.
See recently also: Mayntz & Scharpf 2005. On the one hand, Luhmann himself has
pointed out that, contrary to the other systems, the political and the religious systems are not yet fully functionally, but still segmentally differentiated: no world state
and no world religion. Here, the remnants of history seem to be lasting and this
seems to allow for much more institutional variety. On the other hand, he makes
more productive use of this insight in his discussion of the relationship between glo-

bal society and global religions (plural; continuing religious diversity and segmental differentiation) than in his analysis of the political system and, most disappointingly and unfortunate for our issue, of the relationship between politics and religion and more specifically between states and organised religions. The huge legal, institutional, political and socio-cultural diversity in the relations between states and 'churches' is blatantly absent from his sociology of religion (1977: 282f; 2000, chap. 6). This indicates that he too falls prey to a maximalist interpretation of 'complete separation' as a functional requirement of 'modern society' and the only adequate institutional option for it. Yet, the design of his theory would allow other options in this regard.

20   The more promising alternative here seems to be elaborated by Matthes, Tenbruck and others, which is different from my treatment of the concept of religion: analysis of the everyday, the political and the scientific 'meta-narrative of secularisation', the conditions of use and change among different varieties of such narratives, e.g. the 'Discontinuity/Rupture', the 'Continuity' and the 'Transposition', and their impact on politics related to models of political organisation and policies of religious accommodation (Koenig 2003: 70ff). Casanova 2005 (distinct from 1994) also applies this strategy. 'Secularisation' is not only clearly distinguished from 'modernisation' and all related connotations, but also from liberalism and democracy. This enables a comparative analysis of the various knowledge regimes in Europe and the US. In Europe, both among elites and ordinary people, the words 'normal', 'progressive', 'enlightened', 'modern' and the values of 'liberalism, universal human rights, political democracy, and tolerant and inclusive multiculturalism' are intrinsically linked to 'secularism' and actually identified with secularism (2005: 7ff), which results in 'illiberal' and 'intolerant secularism'.

21   Eisenstadt 1987, 1992, 2000; Flora 1999, Flora & Urwin (eds.) 1999; Madeley 2003; Spohn 2003, 2003a; Koenig 2003.

22   Weber 1972, chap. IX; Eisenstadt 1987. I follow Spohn's summary (2003: 326ff; see 2003a: 270-275; for the non-European world: 275-281).

23   For an analysis of the crucial structural distinctions, see: Madeley 2000, 2003: 13ff.

24   The Netherlands, Germany, Switzerland and also Canada (low cultic participation). As mentioned above, the Netherlands has been rapidly 'depillarised' and shows a fairly rapid decline of religious beliefs and practices, see Dobbelaere 1992, Crouch's 'paradox'. Patterns are clearly not ultra-stable, resistant against change or even break.

25   Martin has revised and modified his analysis of the Protestant and Latin patterns in 1990. For a criticism and discussion of the inherent problems of constructing types see Bader 2007a.

26   Bader 2007a for such a 'disaggregation of government.' Detailed comparative studies of religious governance are not available. Consequently, there is a dearth of empirical evidence and we simply do not know what different governments inside and among (nation) states have actually done and do when they govern religious diversity. Almost all available comparative studies focus only on legal rules and regulations.

27   *Disestablishment* directly presupposes 'strong establishment' of one Church, whereas *non-establishment* means that, in a (new) state, no Church is constitutionally or legally established. Yet 'strong establishment' is the relevant point of reference, at least indirectly. Non-establishment in the new American federal state is directed against established churches in some American states and in opposition to known forms and experiences of absolutist states and Caesaro-papist churches in Europe. In India, non-establishment and a constitutionally non-religious state has been a *conditio sine qua non* to prevent religious civil war, see Khilnani 1999, the different contributions

in Bhargava (ed.) 1998, Jacobsohn 2000, Rudolph & Rudolph 2000. Disestablishment also means quite different things, depending on whether it is directed against a strongly established church (e.g. the radically laïcist or secularist break in the French revolution mirroring 'Catholicism without Christianity' (Martin 1978: 24)) or religion (the radical disestablishment of Islam by Ataturk), or against weakly established churches (as in the Netherlands 1983 or Sweden in 2000). The differences between non-establishment, disestablishment and possible new establishments (e.g. 'plural establishment') should be kept in mind for the purposes of practical evaluation. Disestablishment itself is a crucially ambiguous idea (Modood 1996: 4). It may mean quite different things depending on the constitutional, legal and de facto status quo in a state. In addition, it may lead to quite different outcomes, as a comparison between the aggressive secularism of French republicans with American 'Godland' and his chosen people clearly shows, see Miller 1985: 233ff, Eisenach 2000.

28   At least six states – New Hampshire (till 1817), Connecticut (till 1818), New Jersey, Georgia, North and South Carolina and, depending on definitions, Massachusetts as well (till 1833) had established churches and plural establishment has seriously been discussed (Miller 1985: 10-45, three options for Virginia in 1784; see also: Handy 1976: 145). The New South Wales Church Act of 1836 is an Australian example of attempted pluralist establishment (Monsma & Soper 1997: 91f).

29   Ferrari (2002) elaborates the forms of cooperation between states and religious groups by detecting a pyramidal pattern of selective cooperation with three levels (10ff. for European countries). Monsma & Soper (1997) and Fetzer & Soper (2004) distinguish between three basic types: the strict church-state separation model, the established church model, and the pluralist or structuralist model. Fox (2006) tries to operationalise the extent of separation of religion and state (SRAS) and of government involvement in religion (GIR) by using five variables and a huge number of indicators or codes (546-555). 'Full SRAS' is 'separationism', whereas 'accommodation' means 'official SRAS and benevolent or neutral attitude toward religion' (545) or selective cooperation.

30   In France, religions are treated as a private affair and subjected to private associational law (Basdevant-Gaudemet 1995: 132), though not in the same way as other voluntary associations. On the one hand, the state has not treated religions as a strictly private affair but has restricted their associational freedom by intricate regulations (law of 1901; Bowen 2005, Bauberot 1998). In addition, the law of 1905 proscribes any direct financial help whereas many of their private charitable activities are able to obtain public money. On the other hand, religions are clearly privileged and, in spite of official non-recognition, religious communities are granted special status as cultic associations. There is no legal definition of religion. In practice, the courts and administrations decide; this situation is similar to that in the US.

31   Alsace-Lorraine is a 'concordat' department. In French Guyana and Saint-Pierre-et-Miquelon, the Roman Catholic Church is the only cult recognised by the state and, in Mayotte, it is the Republic that appoints Muslim legal specialists charged with implementing Islamic personal law. State subsidies to confessional schools and all attempts to unify and secularise the educational sector in the 1980s failed spectacularly (Peter 2004, Safran 2003: 443f; Willaime 2004: 176ff).

32   For the intricacies and inconsistencies of French rules and policies, see: Bowen 2005.

33   Recently, however, quite a lot of public money has gone into private religious schools, directly or indirectly (Minow 2000, Esbeck, chap. 10) as a consequence of voucher schemes and contracts. The US Supreme Court has declared that this is constitutional (Zelman v. Simmons-Harris 2002).

34   The actual problems are more pressing, the less open the systems are with regard to
     minority religions – the most pressing, obviously, in cases like Denmark and the
     'non-confessional' but 'Christian' instruction in England – the less alternatives in the
     form of 'ethics' or 'religious education' are available, see sect. 5.2.

35   For Germany, see: Robbers 1995: 72. Minow (2000: 1071) discusses related pro-
     blems of the availability of reproductive services (sterilisation) and assisted technol-
     ogy (artificial insemination, in vitro fertilisation), abortion, HIV, counselling, end-of-
     life choices in Catholic hospitals, particularly in small cities and rural areas.

36   For Austria, see Pötz 1995: 263ff. The same holds true in general for public media
     and cultural institutions, e.g. in Belgium (Torfs 1995: 28), Germany (Robbers 1995):
     representatives in boards of (semi-) public institutions (radio and television councils,
     etc.), Spain (mixed committees), Austria (Pötz 1995: 268f).

37   In this comparison, I do not include other aspects of church-state relations such as
     the admission and financing of religious ministers, the contested relationship be-
     tween civil and religious marriage (Robbers (ed.) 2001; see for Indonesia: Bowen
     1998) and the whole range of divergent state policies with regard to exemptions
     from compulsory military service, Sunday closings, working hours, prohibition of
     drugs and alcohol, dress, zoning, building and parking requirements (for the US,
     see: Galanter 1996, McConnell 1985, 1992; Pfeffer 1987, Hirsch 2000: 285ff for au-
     topsies), special admission rules (and education) for ministers of religion (Kraler
     2007).

38   This is contrary to Bouma's claim. At this level, 'global *government*' in a strict sense
     ('coercive isomorphism') is absent and convergence would have to result from a
     loosely structured 'world polity', from 'mimetic isomorphism' (imitation, best prac-
     tices), and from 'normative isomorphism' (Koenig 2003: 148ff, 156, 215ff) and/or
     from other modes of governance.

39   Robbers 2000. Massignon stresses the third aspect, the emergence of a 'concorda-
     tory Europe' that is 'pluralist with structural limits' (2003: 5), situated 'halfway be-
     tween the pluralist inter-denominational American model and the classic European
     model of a hierarchy of recognised religions'. In addition, Enyedi points to 'conver-
     ging tendencies between Europe and the US': 'Partly as a result of the policies pur-
     sued by the Bush administration, European-style state support for churches has at-
     tracted considerable interest. The irony is that while churches and politicians in the
     USA have started to embrace the idea of closer cooperation between church and
     state, in Europe, the principle of separation finds growing support among religious
     sectors.' (2003: 219; see also sect. 8.5). The more or less marked neglect of varieties
     of models of government of religious diversity in Europe vividly demonstrates one
     of the dangers of broad, normatively biased comparisons of two models known from
     confrontations between 'the' European model of capitalism and 'the' American mod-
     el.

40   If such a common institutional model of European regulation of religious diversity
     were to emerge, it would have to address at least three problems already signalled
     above: (i) the exclusion of small, new religious minorities; (ii) inequalities amongst
     the included, 'recognised' religions; and (iii) formal versus informal representation
     of organised religions at the level of European Governance Arrangements (EGAs)
     (sect. 8.6).

41   Koenig (2007) rightly focuses on 'identities and symbols' as strong countervailing
     tendencies (Casanova 2005: 7ff) but neglects or underestimates institutional and
     structural inertia.

Notes Chapter 2

1   Drawing on mounting criticism from liberal theologians (e.g. Thiemann, Wolter-storff, Neuhaus), from constitutional theorists (e.g. McConnell, Galanter, Laycock, Glendon, Segers, Lupu, Minow), political theorists (e.g. Monsma, Soper, Rosenblum) and critical liberal philosophers (e.g. Greenawalt, Carens, Tomasi) and post-modern philosophers (e.g. Fish, Neal, Connolly), its focus on principles (and the related underestimation of institutions, cultures, habits and virtues, traditions of judgment and action) and ideal models, its misguiding dichotomies, its shifts from 'model to muddle', its neglect of power asymmetries (Bader 1999a: 598-603, also for references to other critics): (i) The liberal political philosophers' focus on ideal models of well-ordered states, societies and ideally reasonable citizens is often combined with a quite unfortunate and unrecognised shift from *model to muddle*. Moreover, they do not tell us in detail how we move 'from there to here'. Principles that might be appropriate in an ideal world actually quite often stabilise inequalities if applied in an unmediated way. (ii) Some of the cherished liberal dichotomies are particularly misleading in our field: (a) private/public or market/state dichotomies block adequate descriptions of increasingly blurred boundaries and in-between situations (Hirst 1994, Minow 2000) and innovative normative thinking on alternative ways of governance of religious diversity instead of the old choice between (the ideology of) God's freest and biggest supermarket or statist religious corporatism. (b) The common links of the poles of the 'religious' with 'traditional, irrational, emotional, heteronomous, female, private' and of the 'secular' with 'modern, rational, reasonable, autonomous, male, public, state' during the formation of modern 'nation-states' (Koenig 2003: 59-75) is still plaguing normative liberal discussions of secularisation and 'public reason'. (iii) Its reproduction of the twin ideology of 'powerlessness of property' in the private sphere and 'propertylessness of power' (the myth of public power completely separated from the impact of structurally asymmetrical power relations in society) in the religious field. Liberal individualism and distrust towards collective rights, collective organisation and mobilisation hinders attempts by the negatively privileged to redraw the balance in all situations in which the predominant rules and practices systematically work in favour of privileged (religious or secular) majorities (para. 1.2.2.2 for this socio-logic of power asymmetries). Liberal strategies to individualise and privatise religion help to stabilise the privileges of majorities masked by a 'strictly neutral state' and 'religious-blind' rules.

2   In the sociology and history of knowledge from Marx, Mannheim and Bourdieu to the recent 'strong program' in science studies, in critical ethnic and racial studies, in recent feminism, in extensive criticism of 'Western' cultural imperialism, and in criticism of a-historical reason or simplistic evolutionism. I modify and extend Bourdieu's (2000) terminology and criticism (Bader 1988: 148ff; Van der Stoep 2004).

3   Føgelin 2003: 3ff. If my intent was only critical, I could bracket the following discussion. However, in a constructive perspective, I feel that I should give at least some indications of how to proceed.

4   Bader 1998, 2005e, 2006b; M. Williams 1998.

5   Harding 1990; Tully 2004.

6   See criticism by Bhaskar 1989. See Putnam's situated defence of pragmatist enlightenment versus either merely 'contingent' or 'scientistic': 'What goes missing in this dichotomy is precisely the idea ... that there is such a thing as the *situated* resolution of political and ethical problems ... that can be more and less *warranted* without being *absolute*' (2001: 47f).

7   The traditional theoretical strategies of establishing impartiality in moral and politi-
     cal philosophy – natural rights theories, classical and modern contractarianism and
     a hypothetical, monological constructivism – are particularly vulnerable to one or
     more of these fallacies and their methodological devices – an impartial contractor in
     an original position under the veil of ignorance, an impartial spectator, an ideal sym-
     pathiser or an impartial calculator of utility preferences – are more vulnerable than
     more dialogical conceptions, especially in more modest varieties ('nobody can rea-
     sonably disagree') though all share some remnants of cognitivist rationalism more
     or less hidden in 'reasonability' constraints. Habermasian strategies that explicitly
     criticise monological settings and demand actual instead of hypothetical dialogue
     can more easily avoid the dangers of 'parochial universalism' (Bell 1998: 568 vs.
     Brian Barry), particularly if they were freed from their quasi-transcendental founda-
     tions, their theoreticistic conceptions of reasons, and from claims that the conditions
     of ideal *herrschaftsfreien Diskursen* would be realised in actual discourses and that de-
     liberation would actually be completely separated from negotiation.

8   They all have to address the problem that these actual 'hermeneutic' dialogues do
     not take place under the ideal conditions of Habermasian discourses but under con-
     ditions of more or less serious power asymmetries, which have an impact on the
     availability of information, cognitive and normative framing and also on the compe-
     tencies of negatively privileged actors. Nevertheless, we have to accept their actual
     definitions and voices as an inevitable threshold for non-paternalistic forms of de-
     mocracy.

9   The claim of basic needs theories is contested: all human beings share a minimal
     common core of needs (some of them are shared with all mammals). This is the
     non-contingent core of (a) basic interests (needs are transformed into interests as
     soon as their satisfaction is (perceived to be) threatened by others), and of (b) basic
     rights (culture-dependent but increasingly also culture-transcendent articulations of
     basic needs in the original 'Western' language of rights. The justification of basic
     needs and basic rights by some moderate physiological and also historical anthropol-
     ogy (Bader & Benschop 1989 chap. III), however, is more 'common sense' and
     'down to earth' and seems less contested than more demanding justifications.

10   Bader 1997 and 2005d. For the EU: Schmitter 2000; Bader 2006; for basic income
     guarantees inside states: Kymlicka 2002: 83ff; Jordan & Düvell 2003: 138ff. For cor-
     porate social responsibility, see Whitehouse 2005.

11   Here, I neglect 'justificatory minimalism', which refers to the question of how to
     present and defend substantive moral minimalism in a culturally diverse and ethi-
     cally pluralistic world (Cohen 2004: 4). If the content of moral minimalism is not
     pre-given in nature and fixed but historically changing and culturally articulated,
     then theories appealing to natural law or Kantian notions of 'Reason' or recent trans-
     cendentalism will fail, as we might expect from our sketch of moderate universal-
     ism. Purely prudentialist theories will also fail to ground the moral nature of core
     values of minimalism and an independent secular political ethics may turn out to
     be too perfectionist and demanding. This seems to leave us with only two options:
     either a common ground strategy or the strategy of an 'un-foundational' political the-
     ory, focused not on justification but on legitimisation, and based on an 'overlapping
     consensus'. See sects. 3.2 and 3.3 for my discussion of first- and second-order secu-
     larism.

12   One could add a fifth level: a full-fledged 'ethos of pluralism' or a pluralist commu-
     nitarian ethics as proposed by Taylor, Bhargava, and Connolly. From levels i to v, but
     particularly from iii to v, we find a consecutive, progressive increase of thicker, more
     perfectionist and contested conceptions of a Good Life and of related, more demand-

ing conceptions of autonomy and toleration, accompanied by a diminishing concern to 'minimize the spill-over effects' (Tomasi 2002).

13   For informative debates on Cultural Rights, see: Hannum 1990; Poulter 1998; Koenig 2003. This development shows that more international 'consensus' is emerging on longer and more demanding sets of rights, adding moral force to attempts to change national or regional regimes not living up to these demanding moralities. Yet, there is ongoing and deep disagreement regarding the interpretation and weighing of civic, political, socio-economic and cultural rights.

14   Stressing subsistence rights is important against neo-liberal and libertarian attempts in general, but also against Kukathas' presentation of 'freedom of conscience' (2003: 15 and17) as the one and only most fundamental basic need or right.

15   I do not discuss whether the question of why it is morally appropriate for a liberal democratic state not to impose a strong nondiscrimination standard or democracy on every group and institution within states (even though that is the appropriate, required standard for many areas and aspects of public life in a liberal democratic state) is parallel to or analogue with the question of why it is appropriate to respect states that are not liberal democratic and not to expect them to adopt strong nondiscrimination standards and democracy in areas and aspects of their public lives where such standards do apply within liberal democratic states. And, if such a parallel exists, whether the reasons for granting respect would be the same in both cases? This issue created perhaps the most antagonism towards Rawls' Law of Peoples, though Rawls seems to reject the suggestion (by Kymlicka and others) of a strict parallelism. In my view, we can certainly ask comparable questions about what we think are appropriate minimal standards for groups and institutions within liberal democratic states and for all states, and what are appropriate methods for promoting compliance where it does not emerge of its own accord. However, neither the minimal standards nor the reasons for not simply enforcing compliance (where that seems feasible) have to be the same in the external and the internal cases.

16   I disaggregate and slightly revise Reich's treatment (2002, chap. 4; see also Kymlicka 2002: 228-244; Swaine 2005; Levey 2006a). For rhetorical reasons, I discuss the different notions of autonomy in reverse order to table 2.1.

17   Raz 1986; Richardson 1986; Macedo 1990, 1998: 60; 2000; Gutmann 1987; Gutmann & Thompson 1996; Hirst 1994; Kymlicka 1989, 1995, 2002; Levey 2006a.

18   Reich discusses three scenarios in which theorists could fail to deal with this tension adequately: (i) focusing only on respect (vs. Galston, Margalit and Halbertal, Kukathas); (ii) focusing only on exercise; (iii) showing respect only for the autonomous decisions of adults that 'potentially compromise the development of the capacity for autonomy in their children' (vs. Raz, Kymlicka but also against my own defence of possibilities for 'separate education' and exemptions).

19   Levey defends autonomy as rational revisablity (2006a: 2) but bases his argument against the imposition of liberal values on non-liberal minorities on the tensions between individual and collective autonomy that is inherent in the liberal value of autonomy itself (1997: 239-241).

20   Parekh 2000: 72; Galston 2002; Kukathas 2003; Tomasi 2004: 327-331; M. Williams 2005; Spinner 2005; Weinstock 2002; Cohen 2004: 212f.

21   They are certainly not confined to the 'West' but can be grounded in and argued for in many different cultural and religious traditions (Sen 2005 for India; Bary 1983 and Cohen 2004: 203-207 for a Confucian foundation; Bielefeldt 2000; Koenig 2003: 134f; WRR 2006: 132-139 for Islam). Criticism of a thicker moral autonomy would also expose conceptions of human beings as 'reason-giving and reason-receiving beings' that are too demanding (Forst 2006: 21; Cohen 2004). Certainly, there exists no 'human right to autonomy' in the legal sense, nor an explicit legal 'right to

revise their ends' (Kymlicka 2002: 237) apart from individual freedom of conscience. In addition, the meta-narrative of autonomy as a foundation of basic rights (see Dagger's argument that autonomy is 'the fundamental right' (1997: 35) from which all others flow; Griffin 2001: 311ff for 'personhood' and 'autonomy') is very much contested (Tasioulas 2002: 88-94 'personhood or pluralism'): a 'pluralist justification of paradigmatic human rights' and the language of basic needs is, in my view, preferable.

22   Obviously, one should not enforce compliance with high degrees of capability and exercise if this is impossible. A dilemma arises only when there is good reason to believe that some legal enforcement might be effective in promoting autonomy. And, even there, everyone should accept that one should not, for example, violate rights of religious freedom and require people to convert from some religion or abstain from any religion on the ground that this or any religion undermines autonomy. Conflict emerges over intrusions into religious practices and habits in the name of promoting practices and habits that are desirable from a comprehensive liberal autonomy perspective. This also qualifies what I mean by 'a laudable political ideal'. I do not see it as a good thing in itself but as an ideal that we are allowed to promote and encourage within the limits of minimal morality and of minimal liberal democratic standards, imposed by respect for others. In this interpretation, respect for others does not preclude the promotion of such an ideal altogether, see sect. 7.3.

23   See sect. 4.1 with Galanter 1960: 218ff; Kymlicka 2002: 230ff; Swaine 2006: 49ff) for an explicitly moderate-universalist defence of the three normative principles of liberty of conscience (rejection, affirmation and distinction).

24   Forst 2003; Hunter 2005 for Franck, Castellio, l'Hospital, Bodin, Erasmus, Coornhert, Grotius, Hobbes, Spinoza, Pufendorf, Thomasius, Locke and many others. 'Proto-liberals' (that is: neither liberal, let alone democratic) like l'Hospital, Hobbes and Pufendorf argued for state sovereignty and for state indifference but this need not (and in *cuius regio, eius religio* does not) include the full guarantee of individual tolerance or equal respect.

25   For Locke's ambiguous exclusion of Catholics and atheists, see: Macedo 1997: 63-65; Creppell 1996: 236f; Gutmann & Thompson 1996: 65ff; Richards 1986: 89-102; Forst 2006.

26   The right to exit is the bare minimum to be defended (vs. some Islamic doctrines and practices). As in the case of states, it cannot be fully compensated by internal voice. Yet my *non-infringement proviso* also applies here: stimulating (or even imposing) freedom of individual conscience and individual tolerance should not be allowed to override collective tolerance because absence of collective toleration seems to be the major evil.

27   The more substantive the interpretations of equality, the less anti-perfectionist they become. Stronger (e.g. republican or socialist) notions of democracy require more participation than thin 'liberal' ones, and also some 'democratization' of other fields (Cunningham 1987 and 2003; see sect. 6.2).

28   The more difficult it is to exit states compared with other organisations, the more important is effective voice, and effective voice means more than just aggregating votes, see sects. 6.2 and 7.4. More deliberative notions also imply thicker interpretations of the four democratic values of political equality, political freedom, autonomy and participation. Libertarian and 'thin' liberal conceptions are opposed to this drive.

29   See Bader 2007c for the shifts from controlling 'public reason' to deliberation to ethos. Libertarians (like Kukathas and Rosenblum), liberal pluralists (like Galston) and associative democrats resist this attitudinal drive of 'liberal democratic' congruency, see sect. 7.3-4. See sect. 10.3 for 'educational virtues' and 'civic minimalism'.

30   Associative democracy shares the libertarian distrust against majoritarianism in this
     regard, combined with liberal constitutional limitations of state sovereignty, but goes
     much further in proposals to delegate and differentiate sovereignty: see Part IV.

31   Then one has to explain why which moral standards should also be legal standards
     (moral obligations backed by legal obligations), which moral obligations may be le-
     galised and which should certainly not be legalised. The demanding values of com-
     prehensive liberalism, for example, cannot be meaningfully transformed into legal
     obligations.

32   The minimalist notion of 'gritting teeth toleration' defended by Levi's 'multicultural-
     ism of fear' may provide an insufficient basis for the maximum accommodations
     and exemptions I propose in Part III. My concept of differentiated morality, how-
     ever, allows me to use more demanding standards for evaluating policies provided
     that they do not infringe moral minimalism.

33   In debates on 'ratcheting up versus levelling down' labour standards or environmen-
     tal standards, one finds examples of 'California effects' without global or EU legal
     sanctions (Héritier, Vogel, Scharpf, Fung, Braithwaite and Drahos). See chaps. 7 and
     10 for the relation between civic minimalism and more demanding educational stan-
     dards and virtues. In my view, defending the minimalism of 'adequate education'
     need not be opposed to (as in Reich & Koski 2006) but can also be seen as a first
     step on the road to achieving greater equality of educational opportunities.

34   Walzer 1997; Rawls 1999; Williams 1998: 68, 180f; 2005; Kukathas 2003: 16f.
     Minimalist morality (Larmore 1996: 133) is not purely realistic or strategic. The im-
     portance of the normative, moral core of 'proto-liberal' versions of sovereignty, indif-
     ference and the proposed 'secularized legal and political institutions' tends to be lost
     by Hunter (2005) and Saunders (2005) by a misguided opposition to more demand-
     ing moralities. These 'secular states' (sect. 3.1) are moral, though minimalist ideals.
     Even subjects have not been treated as legal equals most of the time and, obviously,
     states did not show the required religious indifference.

35   Poulter 1998: 98ff. Interestingly, his 'virtually unqualified rights' (99) are co-exten-
     sive with my standards of minimal morality. 'Clashes between rights of roughly the
     same order of importance' (101) are the most difficult to resolve. See critically: Ren-
     teln 2004: 215f.

36   The satisfaction of basic needs, the granting of basic rights stressed by minimalism,
     is required to lead any life, fully independent from competing conceptions of a de-
     cent life, a satisfying life, a good life.

37   For my defence of associative democracy, the distinctions between (i) processes and
     policies, (ii) policies to shape the institutional environment and thereby stimulate vo-
     luntarism, and (iii) trying to directly impose voluntarism or 'autonomy' are crucial.
     The legal enforcement of comprehensive liberal standards requires a considered,
     stepwise, morally and prudentially convincing argumentation that is quite often ab-
     sent, e.g. in maximalist recommendations for 'democratic state schools' only, see
     chap. 10.

38   Bhargava sees that a clash between the thin values and 'small ideals' of minimal
     morality with 'ultimate values' or 'great ideals' 'has the potential of depriving people
     of living even a minimally decent existence, and ordinary life' (1998: 490) defending
     a minimalist version of the 'small ideals' (496, 511) that has the 'widest possible ap-
     peal, acceptable to both non-religious as well as religious people' also in non-Wes-
     tern societies. It 'does not presuppose a high degree of autonomy, full-blooded egali-
     tarianism or mandatory and intense political participation'. Like Raz, Taylor, and
     Connolly, however, he sees it as 'not fully satisfactory' (509) because it lacks a 'prop-
     erly political conception', i.e. a more 'communitarian' (510) 'politics of the common
     good' (537) and a pluralist ethics of deep diversity (510). The most original aspect of

his proposal is the explicit and well-considered contextualisation of the choice between (i) living together, which 'may be good enough in circumstances of deep and
open discord' (509), 'a good fallback strategy' or even 'the only available way' (511,
537) and (ii) 'under circumstances of deep diversity'(510), 'we need not to give up'
more demanding ideals of 'living together well' (see also 537ff on the 'life cycle' of
societies). See also Greenawalt 1995: 120; see sect. 9.8 for contexts.

39   The danger and temptation of crusading in the wrong ways by threatening and applying force on internal decent minorities compared with foreign states is much
greater because the usual prudential constraints limiting the use of force are absent.
If 'we' have the power and the means to enforce compliance, why not make use of
them?

40   This is criticised by Wilkins' 'third principle' of justice, requiring that 'any 'neutral'
rule which substantially burdens comprehensive doctrine(s) can be justified only if
it furthers a compelling state interest' (1997: 369), drawing on the 'three prong test'
in Lemon v. Kurtzman (1971) and on 'strict scrutiny' jurisdiction. Bader 1999a; Tomasi 2002, 2004. See for critical discussions of the 'three prong test': HLR Note
1987, Rosenblum 2000: 171ff.

41   For sex and gender, see: Minow 1990; for 'race': Gotanda 1991; for ethnicity: Bader
1997c, 1998.

42   He seems to agree with Hollinger (1996: 123f; see also Walzer 1997) that the 'application to religious affiliations of the ethnic-minority paradigm' (123) should be rejected. My rejection of religious state neutrality neglects neither important historical
differences between linguistic, ethno-cultural and religious pluralism (para. 6.4.1)
nor moral ones: it is not unjust for states to offer individuals incentives for linguistic
assimilation, but political attempts to promote religious homogeneity are clearly illiberal.

43   Handy 1976; Martin 1978: 21, 28, 36, 70, 284; Greenawalt 1995: 166ff; Casanova
1994 chap. 6; Connolly 1995, chap. 6; Eisenach 2000.

44   Bellah and Mooney. This story has been intrinsically connected to that of 'racial disestablishment', see Casanova 2005, sect. 8.5.

45   Miller 1985: 67f; Richards 1986: 118f; Thiemann 1996: 42f: Soifer 2000: 245ff; and
chap. 7 for criticism of the strict separation model, often indistinguishably related to
the strict neutrality metaphor.

46   For moral pluralists, this is not astonishing because the two clauses 'can easily work
at cross-purposes' (Thiemann 1996: 57) and cannot be 'consistently combined' (Valauri 1986). Galanter points out that '(t)he existence of competing and overlapping
principles can give courts and legislatures flexibility. Case law, after all, is among
other things a way of getting along with a plurality of principles which need not be
integrated in the abstract' (1966: 296) and opposes the respective use of 'separation,
neutrality, and accommodation' in 'unification strategies' (extensively documented in
HLR Note 1987: 1635ff), see sect. 4.1.

47   Glendon & Yanes 1991: 478; Thiemann 1996: 44f; Hirsch 2000: 291; Fish 1997.

48   Thiemann 1966: 45-55 for the Allegheny case; see HLR Note 1987: 1655ff and Tushnet 1986: 727ff for the quite similar Lynch vs Donelly case.

49   Bader 1999a: 604-607; Thiemann 1996: 60ff; Casanova 1994: 55ff; Galanter 1966:
292f; Tushnet 1986: 701f; Stoltenberg 1993; Laycock 1997; McConnell 1992; Monsma 1993; Lupu 1994; Smith 1995; Monsma & Soper 1997 and Tomasi 2004.

50   See HLR Note 1987 on 'perspective-dependence' (1647ff) and the recognition of
biases as a necessary precondition 'to transcend them rather than remaining in their
thrall' (1631).

51   Galanter 1966: 268, 279, 296; HLR Note 1987: 1609, 1621 and 1636; McConnell
1992; Monsma & Soper 1997; Minow 2000; Tomasi 2001, 200; Ferrari 2002. Un-

der conditions of religious diversity in modern welfare states, the *administrative* interference of the state is inevitably extensive and varied, and the degree of administrative discretion is fairly high (guided by general norms like 'public order', 'equity' and 'proportionality'), particularly if legislation is general or laws are supplemented by general executive orders. Even if guided by the idea of strict or formal neutrality, legislation and administration cannot be neutral in its effects under such conditions, and jurisdiction by administrative or constitutional courts would unfairly restrict freedom of religious exercise if guided by such a meta-legal principle (Monsma & Soper 1997).

52   'Symbolic accommodation' recognises that 'the principles of the Establishment Clause and our Nation's historic traditions of diversity and pluralism allow communities to make reasonable judgments respecting the accommodation of holidays with both cultural and religious aspects' (Justice Kennedy in the Allegheny case, see sect. 5.3. By equating religion with Christianity, however, it violates a fair though not fully equal treatment of religious minorities (Galanter 1966; HLR Note 1987: 1610, 1637f, 1640ff; McConnell 1992: 687; Thiemann 1996: 53f; Hirsch 2000).

53   See Bader 1998a: 436f for some educational, institutional and cultural proposals: open access or admission to law schools and a very roughly equal representation of students; replacing 'difference-blind' curricula with curricula that focus on and criticise structural power asymmetries and their impact on legal paradigms and traditions of interpretation and application of 'impartial rules'; selection procedures, allowing for a fair representation of relevant groups among judges in order to prevent the 'anomaly of rights or justice for blacks without black judges and lawyers'; sensitive professional ethical codes and, maybe even more important, internal control procedures by peer professionals and organisations; open and critical public debate among judges; external public criticism and control. See Van Dommelen (2003: 189-206) for fair representation of relevant groups among of supreme court justices. See Renteln 2004 for 'cultural defense'.

54   Our 'natural' capacity to distance ourselves from particularism – as moral and constitutional theorists, judges, politicians, citizens, and as scientists and professionals – seems to be very limited. It is stimulated by border crossings (the migrant, the stranger, the judge from outside) and, more importantly, by a considerable reduction in power asymmetries that helps in recognising the negatively privileged and 'others' as 'equals' (as Thukydides knew). The latter, in turn, very much stimulates the art of listening. In general, the translation of 'objectivity' to an ethos (and a subjective maxim) of scientists, of 'impartiality' into an ethos of judges, and of 'neutrality' into an ethos of administrators is obviously important but the institutional settings (the 'institutional cunning of reason') are paramount.

55   Following 'difference-blind principles' in the real world would then be an example of dangerous misplaced concreteness neglecting the difficult steps to explain how we can get from 'there' (ideal world) to 'here'. Kukathas's plea for 'politics of indifference' (2003: 15) is also vulnerable to this charge (in addition to his misguided replacement of 'justice' with 'authority').

56   I agree with Levey (1997, 2006) that justice as 'equality' does not work. Compared with his notion of 'acknowledgement and the signification of presence', however, I insist that symbolic acknowledgment has to be linked to relevant institutional representation in the political process, to institutional politics of presence (sect. 5.5, see Phillips 1995). Symbolic gestures are insufficient.

57   This can be understood as a modified use of Aristotle's characterisation of justice: treat equals equally and unequals unequally in proportion to their relevant differences (Bader 1998: 447-450). This carries with it a presumption as a baseline equal treatment that is broad enough to be endorsed by those with alternative theories of

justice, including even-handedness and neutrality, but it allows for differential treatment, provided the differences of those treated are 'relevant'. In turn, this shifts debates about general principles that lay down exceptionless rules for making exceptions to contextualised debates about appropriate policy, given the particular aims
that the justice-informed policy is supposed to achieve and the particular settings
and characteristics of the social groups and individuals in question.

58   Habermas 1992 (see my criticism 1993: 53ff). Greenawalt 1995: 115 and Rawls
     1999.

59   Conflicts between moral principles such as liberty and equality with regard to reli-
     gions are deepened by the fact that the inevitable trade-offs are themselves strongly
     contested. Strategies for reaching a consensus by moving 'deeper down' (towards
     foundations) or 'higher up' (towards meta-levels and second-order principles such as
     'agreement to disagree' or 'consent to dissent') fail to recognise that dissent is as ser-
     ious among ordinary people deliberating about moral and political issues as it is
     among judges of supreme courts, constitutional theorists and moral philosophers
     advocating foundational theories (Waldron 1993; Greenawalt 1995 Fish 1997; Neal
     1997; Murphy 2001; Parekh 2000: 304ff; Eisenach 2000; Shah 2000: 132ff; Spin-
     ner-Halev 2000: 142ff; Rosenblum 2001 and my earlier references in 1999: 617ff).

60   As universalist political philosophers become more context-sensitive, strong contex-
     tualists like MacIntyre or Walzer become more moderate, making some of their im-
     plicit context-transcendent moral criteria explicit (Shapiro 1999; Carens 2000,
     2004a).

61   Full-fledged non-contextualists defend absolutist universalism and reject even mod-
     est versions of moral pluralism. They stick to a deductionist or quasi-deductionist
     (instead of an analogical) application of moral principles in the sense that in all
     cases and contexts there is just one and only one moral solution and just one mo-
     rally permissible or required optimal institutional setting in every context. Finally,
     they accept moral intuitions only if they are derived from moral theory. They are
     clearly a dying race. The hard core seems to be not absolutism and deductivism but,
     instead, the rejection of moral pluralism and the insistence on one morally right an-
     swer only, as for example both Dworkin and Habermas do.

62   My interpretation of this institutionalist turn also implies an 'attitudinal turn' or,
     more generally, an analysis of the complementary or mutual interaction of princi-
     ples, institutions, cultures, habits and virtues, and good practices [6.1], see excellent:
     Willems 2003.

Notes Chapter 3

1   Modern capitalism could live without a Protestant Ethic (Weber's *caput mortuum*),
    and the religiously and philosophically indifferent state can do without secularism.
    Moreover, in the course of the development of configurations, strong oppositions
    and large trade-offs may relax and be transformed into smaller ones (e.g. liberty ver-
    sus equality; equality versus difference). The emergence of a certain threshold of so-
    cio-economic equality and 'equal opportunities' (e.g. in education) has been impossi-
    ble without a strong anti-liberal, socialist egalitarianism, intense struggles by the la-
    bour movement and a strong state, but they eventually found a broader 'ideological
    basis' (including social Christian, social liberal) and a new balance of competing
    principles of liberalism and egalitarianism could emerge (egalitarian liberalism or
    my preferred libertarian, democratic socialism). See chapter 10 for smaller trade-offs
    between diversity and equality in education and a less statist egalitarianism.

2   Differences in contexts are also highlighted by Greenawalt 1995: 130; HLR Note
    (1987: 1609, 1685 (*Mueller versus Allen*), 1730 (*Bradley* and *Lynch v Donelly*)), Weith-
    man, Taylor and Bhargava.

3   Brumberg & Diamond 2003; Minkenberg 2007; WRR 2006, chaps. 3 and 5.

4   Miller 1985: 347f; McConnell 1992: 741; Wolterstorff 1997. See also Maimon
    Schwarzschild, quoted in Greenawalt 1995: 99.

5   In my view, Muslim minorities do not present any credible threat to liberal democ-
    racy in Western states because the overwhelming majority of Muslim immigrants
    has moderate and completely legitimate claims to accommodate their religious
    needs (chaps. 5 and 8), and even orthodox and peaceful Muslim fundamentalists
    should not be unthinkingly associated with Islamicist terrorists.

6   See for Algeria: Kalyvas 2000 and Esposito 1996; for Malaysia: Meerschaut 2006;
    for Indonesia: Bowen 1998. Minkenberg 2007; Fox 2006.

7   The 'secular' character of the liberal-democratic state is also irrelevant in the case of
    elitist or anti-democratic classical liberalism and anti-liberal democratic majoritarian-
    ism – two other threats that are related to the compromise character of liberal de-
    mocracy, see sect. 2.2.

8   Sect. 1.3. Casanova (2005) distinguishes 'secularization' not only more clearly than
    1994 from 'modernization' and all related connotations but, as we have also seen
    from 'liberalism' and 'democracy'. In Europe, both among elites and ordinary peo-
    ple, 'normal', 'progressive', 'enlightened', 'modern' and the values of 'liberalism, uni-
    versal human rights, political democracy and tolerant and inclusive multicultural-
    ism' are intrinsically linked to 'secularism', actually identified with secularism (2005:
    7ff), resulting in 'illiberal' and 'intolerant secularism'. In the US, only academics in
    the social sciences and humanities are predominantly 'secularist' in this regard,
    whereas a vast majority of the population is non-secular.

9   Veer 1997. Nandy 1998: 298f; Madan 1998: 326ff and Chatterjee 1998: 345ff for si-
    milar arguments opposing the eulogy by Khilnani 1999. See more balanced views
    by Galanter, Bilgrami, Sen, Bhargava (all in Bhargava (ed.) 1998) and Bhargava
    2005; Eisenlohr 2006. In many recent Arab and North African authoritarian
    kleptocracies, the opposition against secularist elites and (nationalist or socialist) par-
    ties, and dependent 'modernization' policies from above is phrased in religious
    terms, and the ban of religious political parties (Tunisia, Baathist Syria) together
    with the export or external imposition of rule of law and democracy under the flag
    of 'secularism' makes secularism terminology completely counterproductive (George
    Joffé).

10 Given the important, but unspecified agreement on the substance of minimal or lib-
    eral-democratic morality and polities among Bhargava, Modood, Willaime and my-
    self, it seems that the main reasons why they stick to the secularism terminology
    are strategic. Modood wants to ally himself with the predominant secularist knowl-
    edge regime in England and he clearly draws a line between his position and reli-
    gious fundamentalists, whereas Bhargava wants to defend the decent and pluralist
    character of Indian 'secular' constitutionalism against anti-secularist Hindu (and
    emerging Muslim) fundamentalism. The reconceptualisation of *laïcité* as *laïcité plur-*
    ielle (or *ouvert, liberale, competent, de reconnaissance, d'intelligence, de maturité*) in oppo-
    sition to traditional concepts of *laïcité de combat* (or *ignorant, de separation, d'abste-*
    nance) by Willaime (2004, 2006), Bauberot and many French critics may also be de-
    fended as strategically prudent, given the predomination of secularist discourse.
    However, it reproduces important ambiguities by seducing or even forcing Muslim
    reformers into becoming defenders of 'secularism' (Peter 2004; Bowen 2004a). It
    also allows orthodox and fundamentalist Muslims to obfuscate, if not altogether
    hide, their position vis-à-vis the rule of law and democracy. See Willems (2004:

306ff) for an excellent criticism of the *'Verzerrungseffekte'* that are intrinsically linked to seeing recent conflicts in Germany *'nach dem kulturkampfanalogen Muster "Religion" vs. "'Säkularität'"*.

11   See Kalyvas 1996 for political parties. Promoting public education as 'secular education' created a religious counter-mobilisation in the 19th century as it does today (chaps. 5 and 10), and banning the headscarf also contributes considerably to the fundamentalisation of Muslims, see sect. 5.4.

12   Furthermore, more comprehensive 'pluralist versions of ethical secularism' (Bhargava) or 'ethos of pluralism' (Connolly) exclude all those who are not committed to demanding requirements of cultural pluralism or diversity. I think that thin, anti-communitarian, modestly libertarian associative democracy may not only be preferable to thicker versions of liberal democracy, particularly if these are imposed on dissenters, but also to perfectionist pluralist versions of ethical secularism and their contested praise of difference and diversity. Moreover, Bhargava blurs the distinction between the first two options, which are crucial for my defence of minimalism, and the more demanding ones that may or may not be morally recommendable and politically laudable.

13   Taylor 1998, Bhargava 1998. I drop the 'bare *modus vivendi*' mode (thorough disagreement on both political principles and grounds) because it is merely an unstable strategic truce, not a minimalist moral option that would require duties and self-restraint, even when a change in the balance of power would allow one to win the religious wars. 'Independent political ethics' 'requires *full agreement* on both political principles and the grounds for justifying them' (Richardson 1990: 10); the 'common ground strategy' can be seen as a 'constrained *modus vivendi*' (some agreement on minimalist principles), an overlapping consensus requires agreement on political principles but no shared grounds. In my presentation, I follow Taylor.

14   See Forst (2005: 13ff) for a concise presentation of Bayle's view.

15   For many contributions see Bauer & Bell (eds.) 1999. Recent Mauritian justifications of multi-ethnic and multi-religious nation building and policies of equitable co-existence are an excellent example, see Eisenlohr 2006.

16   This is the crucial difference between Rawls and Habermas (see their exchange in 1995) and Rawls (1999: 142) vs. Benhabib.

17   Taylor (1998: 51f) has rightly criticised the earlier versions of Rawls' OC and similar criticism is accepted by Rawls (preface 2. ed. PL; 1999: 141ff). Connolly's criticism completely ignores these important changes in Rawls' thinking. Even in Cohen's version (2004), I see (i) too much agreement; (ii) deliberation and reason are cut loose from negotiation and interests; (iii) content and reasonability constraints are maintained; (iv) the focus is on principles neglecting cultures, virtues, habits, and practices, and (v) he shares the narrow focus on 'membership/citizenship' characteristic for all deliberative democrats.

18   See Fox (2006: 537, 555, 561) for an empirical criticism of the 'idea that full SRAS is an essential element of democracy'. Taylor equates democratic and 'secular regimes' as opposed to 'non-secular or exclusionary regimes' (47) but insists that the separation of church and state 'that centerpiece of secularism' should not be confused with one formula, the 'complete disentanglement of government from any religious institutions' (see also Jacobsohn 2000, Bhargava 1998) because one formula would 'erect one background justification as supreme, and binding for all, thus violating the essential point of overlapping consensus. The US provides an unfortunate example of this.' (52). In the end, Rawls also accepts that 'the separation of church and state may appear to leave open the question whether church schools may receive public funds, and if so, in what ways' (1999: 145) starting to question 'strict separation' (see also Audi 1997: 38 'some kind of separation'). For Taylor, the 'inescapability of secu-

larism' (1998: 38ff; also Keane 2000: 8f) flows (i) from modern citizenship: from the nature of the modern democratic state which has to guarantee to all equal and autonomous members a direct, non-exclusionary access to democratic deliberation and decision-making. Yet, Taylor's interpretation of '*Immediatisierung*', shared by Bhargava, creates difficulties in understanding and positively evaluating modern 'intermediate organizations' under conditions of representative democracy (Bader 2007, 2007b; Part IV). (ii) It flows from the fact that legitimacy is 'no longer ... grounded in something other, something higher, than common action in secular time' (40, see also 2002; Keane 2000: 8f). 'This is why secularism, in some form, is a necessity for the democratic life of religiously diverse societies' (46, 47, 49). Indeed, a minimal threshold of cultural secularisation is presupposed, see sect. 1.2.

19   See similar: Cunningham 1987: 72ff. This does not restrict the means of influence to persuasion or reasonable deliberation but includes negotiation and fair compromises as well as positive and also negative sanctions, except violent sanctions.

20   Actual political communication is always top-down and bottom-up, is partly formal and partly informal, and takes place in at least three different arenas: formal politics (political communication amongst elites), the arena of social power (communication between parties, factions, interest organisations, NGOs, SMOs) and political communication amongst citizens. The unified public arena actually consists of differentiated arenas in which different publics compete (Dewey 1927 (1991), Young 1996). 'Reason' or emphatic 'discourse' and 'deliberation' are actually always mixed with 'power' and 'negotiation'.

21   See the excellent interpretation by Frankenberg & Rödel (1981: 95-235, 319-35). See also Richards 1986, part III. In opposition to strategies of administrative depoliticisation, the court is rightly very cautious regarding 'violence': criminal actions (violence against persons) are clearly banned. However, in cases of 'captive audience', freedom of political protest is more important than 'public order', and even 'violence against property' is not always outlawed right from the start.

22   This does not preclude specific legislation against religious hate speech (chap. 5; Koenig 2003; Ferrari 2002: 9f). Though balances in the US, Germany, India (Jacobsohn 2000; Galanter 1998) diverge, the right to free expression does not include a 'right to insult'.

23   'One (wo)man one vote' excludes all 'plural' or 'weighed' systems in political elections in opposition to all traditional exclusions on the basis of ascriptive discrimination (of women, blacks, ethnic and religious minorities) of class and income (workers, peasants, the poor) but also of 'education' as defended by classical liberals like J. S. Mill.

24   Section 2.2 and Bader 1991: 140-151; 1997: 158-170. See Cunningham (1987: 246ff; 2005: 71, 79) for the relationship between 'democracy and moral relativism', as distinct from 'ethical relativism'.

25   'The whole truth in politics' is, indeed, 'incompatible with democratic citizenship and the idea of legitimate law' (Rawls 1999: 138). Yet 'the zeal to embody the whole truth in politics is incompatible' (133) only if it refers to democratic *decision-making*: 'those who believe that fundamental political questions should be *decided* (my italics!) by what they regard as the best reasons according to their own idea of the whole truth – including their religious or secular comprehensive doctrine' (138). This, however, does not include his more demanding thesis that it would also require the exclusion of the competing 'whole truths' from *public talk in the 'public political forum'*. What it does include, though, is the requirement that legitimate law is 'politically (morally) binding' even if it is 'thought not to be the most reasonable, or the most appropriate by each' (137) because no unanimity or 'general agreement' can be expected, so majority decisions are inevitable the outcome of which is not 'true'

or 'correct' but 'reasonable and legitimate law' (1999: 168-170). For the time being, the acceptance of majority decisions and also a 'reasonable' public debate require that the 'zeal' be tempered by virtues of moderation. However, this is different from the much more demanding moral duty to exclude 'the whole truth as we see it' (1993: 218) from public talk, see Bader 2007c for extensive criticism.

26   Gill 2001 (following Tibi, Kepel, Olivier). Criticism of 'secularist fundamentalism' is scarce: Falk 1995: 68f, 242, Taylor 1998; Beckford 1987: 24ff and Miller 1985: 347f.

27   Cunningham 2005: 66f (not for philosophical, but for contingent historical reasons). Bruce also claims that 'the ultimately liberal and relativistic view that what everyone believed was equally true' has been the unintended consequence of 'removing the theologically justified coercion of the hierarchical church and permitting open access to the salvational truth' (2004: 7) by Protestantism. 'The irony of Protestantism is that it was its own impossible combination of an open epistemology and an insistence that there was only one truth that created pluralism', 2004: 10.

28   Dewey 1927; Barber 1988; Geuss 2002: 329ff. Non-foundationalism draws on a crucial distinction between 'foundation' and 'legitimation' in a cross-cultural, inclusive and democratic dialogue (Ingram 2004: 194ff).

29   This strategy of 'naturalization' to make the human-made look eternal, unchangeable and secure is the modern equivalent of declaring it 'sacred'. Both strategies are combined in 'sacred', 'inalienable', 'natural' human rights.

30   In this regard, non-foundationalism may mean fairly or fully independent from (i) competing ethical and meta-ethical foundations, and from competing (ii) epistemological, (iii) ontological, and (iv) metaphysical foundations. *Radical* non-foundationalism claims that we can put all these issues within brackets or be fully agnostic in this regard, because there is no need to look for any of the competing philosophical foundations of liberal democracy. More *moderate* non-foundationalism claims that a political philosophy underlabouring rights and democracy is compatible with all those competing foundations that are not directly at odds with democracy. It is more exclusive with regard to often unacknowledged implications of epistemological, ontological and metaphysical theories, and it is more open to strategies of developing theories in these fields that are more conducive to liberal or pluralist democracy, e.g. an ethical theory of deep diversity or an ethos of pluralism (like Taylor, Bhargava, Connolly), a pluralist epistemology (William James), or a multi-layered critical-realistic ontology (Putnam, Bhaskar).

31   Rorty 1997; see critically Bhaskar 1989: 146-179 and Putnam 2001: 41; Eisenach 2000: 149, Alexander 1993; Fish 1997.

32   Like other phrases, e.g. 'becoming unmanageable', this still wrongly implies that public debate could or should be in 'someone's hand'.

33   All critical historians and sociologists of religions and also all historically and sociologically informed critical theologians agree that the early phases of Christianity are seriously at odds with the selection, streamlining and dogmatisation of the early gospels into a misogynist New Testament by later Roman and Greek theocratic orthodoxies. The same is clearly also true for early *Islam*, see Ahmed 1992.

34   See the considered criticism of 'cultural or religious essentialism' (Picht, Huntington, Tibi) and its radical rejection by Bielefeldt 1998, chap. 5, 2000: 94ff.

35   These temptations are particularly strong in universal, monotheist, missionary religions like Christianity and Islam. 'Ethnic' religions like Hinduism or Confucianism and universal but non-theist religions like Buddhism do not exclude or even explicitly allow practitioners to also belong to other religious communities.

36   See Martin 1990 and Manow 2004 for the important distinction between Lutheranism and Calvinism, on the one hand, and radical Protestantism, on the other hand which prepared theoretical and institutional and organisational sources for modern

liberal democracy (Jellinek 2004). See Bruce's strong, exclusivist claim 'that there is a strong and non-accidental relationship between the rise of Protestantism and the rise of democracy', tolerance and pluralism (2004: 6), though the strongest links 'are unintended consequences', an 'ironic (and often deeply regretted) by-product'.

37 McConnell (2000: 93ff) discusses the three distinct Protestant ways to resolve the problem of citizenship ambiguity: Madison's radical liberal anti-majoritarianism; Jefferson's 'wall of separation'; Washington's 'salutary or happy accommodation'.

38 American bishops like Murray played an important role in the Catholic Aggiornamento.

39 In part IV, I present the specific advantages of Associative Democracy in this regard: (i) as a non-establishment option, it may help prevent the development of religious political parties; (ii) as a variety of Democratic Institutional Pluralism, it allows separate religious organisations in public life, religious political parties in particular and increases chances for medium- or long-term learning by fundamentalist religions running against their original intentions and purposes (lessons brought home by Kalyvas). Unfortunately, Kalyvas's analysis is misguided by uncritical secularist terminology: the 'confessional dilemma' (241) does not require 'secular organizations with secular priorities' (242) but organisational 'declericalization'. The required reinterpretation of Catholicism and redefinition of confessional identity should also not be conceived as 'a secular ideology' (247) and detachment from all religion (245). Finally, the 'politicization of religion contributed to the secularization of politics' (245, 260) only if one calls liberal democratic institutions and politics secular but then secularisation rules by definitional fiat, whereas the actual inclusion of (transformed) religious voices in the democratic political process makes the latter more plurivocal and less 'secular'.

40 Weber 1972, Eisenstadt 2000 and Unger 1987 III have clearly shown that the development of modern capitalism and of liberal democracies has been the result of a contingent configuration of constellations, not of any deep logic inherent in 'culture' or 'religion'. See also Stepan 2000: 44 against the 'fallacy of unique founding conditions'.

41 Obviously, the accommodation of Islam takes different forms, depending on the huge institutional variety of 'church-state-relations': Rath et al. 1996, 2001, Vertovec & Peach 1997, Koenig 2003, 2004, 2007; Peter 2004, Bowen 2004a, Grillo (ed.) 2004; Casanova 2005; Fetzer & Soper 2005 and Soper & Fetzer 2007; Sunier 2003; Mandaville 2001 for UK. See Casanova (2005) for the US. See for the relation between 'Islam' and 'Islams': Mandaville 2001: 54ff.

42 WRR 2004; Zürcher & Van der Linden 2004; WRR 2006 and Al-Azm for Arab countries, particularly for Hamas. Ahmad (2005) explains the transformation of the Jamaat-e-Islami in North India from Islamism to Post-Islamism, mainly as a consequence of its operation in a context of constitutional democracy compared to the authoritarian political systems in Algeria and Egypt that breed Islamism. In his comparison of the Catholic party in Belgium in the late 19th century and the FIS in Algeria, Kalyvas detected another nice paradox: 'In sum, the centralized, autocratic, and hierarchical organization of Catholicism allowed moderate Catholics to solve their commitment problem, while the absence of a comparable structure in Algeria contributed to the inability of the moderate FIS leadership to credibly signal its future intentions. It is indeed ironic that Islam's open, decentralized, and more democratic structure eventually contributed to the failure of democratization, while the autocratic organization of the Catholic Church facilitated a democratic outcome' (2000: 390).

43   See Forst 2005: 12f for 'Locke's fear'. See Delfiner (without year: 316ff); McConnell
      (2002: 90-93) and Segers & Jelen (1998, Part Two). Jelen generally treats religion as
      'something of a dangerous stranger to democratic politics' (3) and Seeger reproduces
      the exact, generalized mirror image. For recent German versions, see: Willems
      2004: 310ff.

44   For the first powerful refutation in the Western tradition, see: Pierre Bayle's *Pensées*
      (1683) with the courageous idea that a 'society of atheists' would be possible – and
      possibly be even more peaceful than religious societies' (Forst 2005: 13). Much ear-
      lier, Michel de l'Hospital has already stated that 'it is possible to be a citizen without
      being a Christian' (quoted in Saunders 2005: 6). Audi 1989: 290f, Shaw 1999: 635,
      647 versus Kant's position; Rawls with Madison versus Henry (1999: 164f).

45   Hastings 1996: 41ff; Rosser-Owen 1996: 83). See Richards (1986: 95, 111f) against a
      similar defence of the 'multiple establishment' in Virginia 1776 by Patrick Henry
      and Richard Henry Lee ('to preserve public morality in the state'). HLR Note 1987:
      1613 – 19. See Willems (2004: 313f) for a criticism of German version of *'(zivil-)reli-
      giöse Begrenzungsformeln des Politischen'*.

46   The related claim that priority for democracy would be unfair because 'secular citi-
      zens (but not religious citizens – V.B.) are able to lead whole and integrated lives'
      (Parekh 1996) is untenable because secular citizens themselves may also hold more
      comprehensive 'secular' moral theories and conceptions of a good life. In my view,
      the whole idea that public or political debate should help citizens to lead whole and
      integrated lives in modern societies is incompatible with any conceivable version of
      political deliberation in modern, differentiated and culturally deeply diverse state so-
      cieties (see also Rosenblum's rejection of 'integralism' charges (2000: 15-21).

Notes Chapter 4

1   This article is much clearer than the First Amendment phrasing. See the detailed
      discussion in Ferrari 2002: 7-11 for ECHR and the different wordings in constitu-
      tions of the Member States of the EU, see also Monsma & Soper 1997 for Dutch,
      German and Australian versions. Koenig (2003: 153ff) presents the debates, declara-
      tions and covenants at the global level (UN, 130ff) and regional levels (ECHR, Amer-
      ican Charter (ACHR) and African Charter (ACHPR).

2   Koenig has shown (2003: 133-145) that, in the first phase (1945-1966) of debates, de-
      clarations and covenants at the UN level, a strictly individual interpretation of reli-
      gious freedom was predominant. In the second phase (1966-1989), a more collec-
      tive interpretation was added (equal treatment, nondiscrimination has been very
      much expanded), which involves the positive duties of states. In the third phase
      (since 1989), minority protection (including religious minorities) has strengthened
      the *'kollektivrechtliche Interpretation'*.

3   UD Art. 18 explicitly includes the right to exit and the 'freedom to change his reli-
      gion or belief'. Due to massive resistance by Muslim states, it has not been included
      in ICCPR, Art. 18. According to classical Islamic law, this is a crime (*irtidad, murtad*)
      that has to be punished with death (and civil death) according to the four most im-
      portant Sunnite law schools (*Shafii, Hanafi, Maliki, Hanbali*). For an overview, see:
      WRR 2006: 123-127.

4   Both at the European level (sects. 1.3.3.2 and 1.3.3.9) and the UN level, it has been
      the common understanding that 'neither the establishment of a religion nor the re-
      cognition of a religion or a belief by a State nor the separation of Church from State
      shall by itself be considered religious intolerance or discrimination on the ground of
      religion or belief' (Draft Convention UN-CHR (1967), Art 1(d)).

5   Laycock, among many others, criticises this interpretation but he also claims, in a strategic move (1997: 73f), that it would not be the dominant opinion (criticising the 'no-aid-theory' and its 'base-line': government inactivity but defending the 'nondiscrimination-theory' and its baseline: equal treatment or even-handedness).

6   From a strictly anti-perfectionist standpoint of justice, the state has certainly no positive obligation to finance new church buildings, to reconstruct old ones or to subsidise or aid religions financially in any way. The state is also not obliged to fund national heritage programmes or to subsidise the high arts (symphony orchestras, theatres, museums). But if it does, as nearly all existing liberal-democratic states did and continue to do, equality before the law requires that it does so equally or even-handedly – e.g. not privileging 'old-comers' (in a broad sense 'established' religions) to the disadvantage of new minority religions.

7   See Swaine 1996, 2001, 2006; Spinner-Halev 2000 for old, encompassing religions; Robbins 1987: 137ff, Rosenblum 1998: 98ff for 'new' totalistic sects.

8   The relevant cases in the US are: *EEOC vs. Southwest Baptist Theol. Sem; Bob Jones University v. United States; Goldsboro Christian Schools, Amos.* For divergent interpretations, see: Pfeffer 1987; Kelley 1987; Robbins 1987; McConnell & Posner 1989; Rosenblum 1998: 79ff; Spinner-Halev 2000, chap. 7. and Cole Durham 2001: 701ff. See also Minow (2000: 1080ff) and Tomasi (2004: 334ff) who, unfortunately, are not aware of traditions and experiments of associational welfare provision as defended by AD, see sect. 6.3. In many European countries, core personnel of churches has a special legal status: for Belgium: Foblets & Overbeke 2002: 114; for Italy: Ferrari 1995: 191f; for Austria (Pötz 1995: 271f). Yet, in all countries, and increasingly so, the legal treatment of religion-related and non-religious personnel is subsumed to labour law and collective agreements.

9   See for many: Okin 1989; Jean Cohen 2001 and Minow 2000: 1080f.

10   Serious difficulties arise in cases in which FBOs and political parties claim that, e.g. racist or genderist discrimination belongs to the core of their beliefs (see below), i.e. when religious and racist or sexist discrimination are intrinsically intermingled.

11   The state's aim is not 'funding discrimination'. Rather, 'the government is funding social services for the poor and needy' and effective and efficient provision of care and social services. FBOs, not governments, are 'discriminating on the basis of religion in its staffing decisions' but so do 'environmental organizations favoring employees devoted to environmentalism'. This is 'not intolerant or malicious' (Esbeck 2004; see Esbeck et al. (2004: 192): The 'aim is not to grant religious preferences but to stop discrimination against social involvement by churches, synagogues, mosques, and other faith-based groups of all kinds'.

12   Racist legitimisations of exclusion are obviously incompatible with the universal core of Christendom (and Islam) and these beliefs and practices should be criticised in public. However, if the authorities of sects that do not ask for public money stick to their interpretations and if this is done according to the established decision-making procedures, the state should not legally interfere to change these beliefs or dismiss these authorities.

13   The US Supreme Court has not only allowed racist exclusion from membership but also a fairly high amount of illiberal and anti-democratic treatment of members of religious associations. For historical reasons (holocaust), the *Bundesverfassungsgericht* in Germany is much more interventionist in this regard (as in cases of balancing anti-discrimination and freedoms of political communication), striking a different balance.

14   See Basdevant-Gaudemet (1995: 147f) for hiring and firing in France (difference between school and hospital); Casey (1995: 176) for the dismissal of a catholic teacher in Ireland; Ferrari (1995: 198f) for all *'Tendenzorganisationen'* in Italy. The Spanish

Constitutional Court (1981) clearly specified that teachers 'are not entitled to direct open or surreptitious attacks' (Glenn & Groof 2002: 507f); Bijsterveld (1995: 242f) for a change in the direction of detailed case law in the Netherlands. See the detailed discussion of the AWGB, art. 5.2 c and Art. 7.2 in Assscher-Vonk, Groenendijk (eds.) 1999: 170-178, 187-192; see Vermeulen 2004: 43f. See Robbers (1995: 72) for Germany; Minow (2000: 1090) for divergent rulings in cases of gender discrimination in New York and San Francisco.

15   Faith-based hospitals are not allowed to select patients in Europe and the US in general, particularly not in small cities or rural areas where they may be the sole health-care providers.

16   Minow discusses all three problems, particularly the potential unfairness of publicly financed huge non-profits competing with small private for-profit service providers (2000: 1084f).

17   Moore 2005: 292; Mahajan 2005 and Levy 2000: 17. Maier 2004: 33f; Poulter 1998 and Renteln 1990, 2004: 202ff. Ultra-orthodox interpretations and practices of shari'a criminal offence laws, such as the cutting-off of hands for theft, crucifying for robbery and stoning for adultery that are subject to highly contested 'traditional' Islamic rules of evidence are clearly incompatible with this minimalist core of morality, see WRR 2006: 123ff for hadd crimes and punishments in Muslim-majority countries. See Peters 2003 for some West-African countries such as Nigeria. In Malaysia, two radical Islamic provinces (Kelantan (1993) and Terengganu (2002)) introduced hudud law, but the laws have not yet been applied because the federal government judges them to be unconstitutional (court case is pending) (Meerschaut 2006). Yet, these interpretations and practices are also vehemently criticised within the Islamic tradition; see the recent Topkapi declaration and Tariq Ramadan's proposal of a 'worldwide moratorium' based on the hope that this can be plausibly and convincingly shown from 'within' instead of being 'imposed' by the West.

18   It is important to repeat that organised religions, publicly recognised religions in particular, make such scrutiny and external interference much easier, compared with unorganised, 'invisible' sects.

19   Hoekema 2001: 170-172. For alternative forms of sentencing and conflict-mediation, see: Shachar 2001: 160ff; Sheleff 2000, ch. 14 Cultural Defence; Hoekema 2004 for Alevites in the Netherlands; Renteln 2004 for a strong case in favour of a formal, partial cultural defence.

20   Coene & Longman (eds.) 2005. By the way, FGM (female genital mutilation) is not prescribed by 'Islam'. It is an ethno-cultural practice of some African tribes also practiced by Christians.

21   Reynolds v. US. See Sheleff 2000: 330-353; Meerschaut 2006 for the variable treatment in Hindu and Chinese customary law compared with Islamic family law in Malaysia. Parekh (2000: 282-292) rightly criticises myopic and hypocritical apologies of modern monogamy (i.e. actual serial polygamy) but still sees monogamy as the appropriate form of a good life. Similarly, in the heated debate on 'arranged marriages', one should focus on 'marriage under duress' (Phillips & Dustin 2004; Renteln 2004: 122ff) instead of importing culturally specific – very much contested – notions and practices of romantic love and idealised notions of total free choice of spouses into 'universal morality' and modern criminal law.

22   For Hindu and Muslim law in India, see: Mahmood 1983; Sen 1995; Galanter 1998: 245-249 vs. Smith 1998: 226; Nussbaum 1997 and 2000: 168ff, 212ff; Rudolph & Rudolph 2000 and Mahajan 2005. See Bowen 1998 for Indonesia; WRR 2006: 127ff-152.

23   See briefly Bader 1998a: 201ff; for Germany and France: Maier 2004.

24   Okin 1997, 2005 for many.

25 Phillips 2005 and Mahajan 2005 focus on strategic dilemmas of minority religions. Reitman 2005 gives clear priority to equality between the sexes and proposes accommodation for purely strategic reasons.

26 For similar strategies to split the issues and areas, see: Smith 1998: 205; Rudolph & Rudolph 2000 and Nussbaum 2000: 217.

27 Spinner-Halev has pointed out that she 'fails to distinguish between oppressed and non-oppressed groups' (2001: 93). The cultural and structural minority position of 'Indian and Israeli Muslims and Native Americans' should also clearly make a normative difference compared with 'Jewish family law in Israel'.

28 The difference between newly recognised and institutionalised religious family law (as a consequence of immigration) and recognised 'established' institutions is clearly important, as the example of the recently rejected (September 2005) attempts to recognise a private Islamic arbitration tribunal in Ontario shows. See Shachar 2005: 61-69 for a short criticism and 73-77 for institutional proposals in the perspective of a joint governance approach.

Notes Chapter 5

1   The tension between the 'universalism' of the societal requirements of modernity (stylised by ideologies of modern professionalism) and the political requirements of democracy on the one hand, and the particularism of the nation state and national unity, on the other hand, has been inherent right from the start. Yet, it has been much more difficult to defend or present national culture and identity as neutral and universal, see Bader 1995a, 1997b, 1999 (vs. Nussbaum and Viroli).

2   Kymlicka 1995; 2002, chap. 8. For a sharp criticism of both liberal (Callan, Gutmann, Macedo) and multicultural civic schooling, see: Murphy 2004; Reich 2002. See Williams' criticism of Macedo (2003: 214-223); Parekh 2000: 224ff and McAndrew 2003.

3   Hard cases have the advantage that they stimulate debates on the exact limits of liberal accommodation. In cases of some *isolationist* religious minorities, like the Amish, the associational freedoms of religion conflict seriously with individual religious freedom of children and other basic human rights such as equal treatment of the sexes and equal opportunity for all. As the *Yoder* case shows (Spinner-Halev 2000), the possibilities and limits to liberal accommodation involve hard issues such as years of mandatory education, minimal curriculum, exit options of children, sex equality and basic versus best interests. Most Muslim groups in Western societies, however, only claim modest exemptions. Most fundamentalist but peaceful religious minorities (Stoltenberg 1993 for the famous *Mozert* case) oppose 'exposure' to 'modern', 'secular' or 'liberal' ways of living, particularly sexuality and (exclusive) teaching of evolutionary biology; see sect. 7.3 for my general lines of resolution. A dramatised focus on 'weird' schools may also be strategically misleading, see sect. 10.

4   See Murphy 2004 for examples of subordinating history teaching to 'some civic agenda' (248ff). Obviously, this is not a peculiarity of American civic schooling. Murphy is right in criticising charges that schooling that focuses on knowledge and skills without explicitly teaching civic virtues would be 'a-moral' (244f) and also in defending the moral character of his 'developmental hierarchy' of 'intellectual virtues' of 'truth-seeking'. In addition, he admits that there is a tension between civic and intellectual virtues (see also Eisgruber 2002) but he uncritically assumes that intellectual virtues would be uncontested and culturally neutral.

5   See Glenn 2004: 341 for the ruling of the ECHR in the *Kjeldsen* case.

6   The phrase is often used to demarcate them (in the German context by Pfaff 2000, quoted in Fetzer & Soper 2005: 112). The Ontario Court of Appeal elaborated the differences between indoctrination and education in eight points: may sponsor the study but not the practice of religion; may expose but not impose; instruction versus indoctrination; educate about all religions, not to convert to any one religion; academic and devotional; inform and conform (Glenn & Groof 2002: 148). Willaime 2004: 166ff.

7   See Akhtar in *The Muslim Parent's Handbook* (1993: 6, quoted in Fetzer & Soper (2005: 41). See also Koenig (2003: 167ff) & Modood (2005) for criticism of the neglect of religion in the British 'race- and ethnic relations' MC paradigm by Muslim organisations, by the CRE 1992, by HRC and by European institutions like the CDMG (1991) and ECRI (211ff).

8   Professional teachers associations have most fiercely resisted claims for religious accommodation and for separate religious schools (see Fetzer & Soper for Britain (2005: 46) and Peter 2004 for France (see, however, Bowen 2006: 120ff and note 48).

9   Birmingham syllabus 1962. Rath et al. 1996: 218-228; Grillo 1998: 207-212; Parekh 2000: 254ff; König 2003: 169ff and Fetzer & Soper 2005: 38-46.

10   In Austria, there have been no alternative ethics courses and it appears that students (or their parents) could easily opt out without having to take alternative courses (Pötz 1995: 265f). Hamburg and North Rhine-Westphalia offered alternative courses (Fetzer & Soper 2005: 113f). Berlin-Brandenburg tried to resolve the problem of Islamic instruction by introducing new obligatory courses '*Lebensgestaltung – Ethik – Religion (LER)*', provoking massive resistance from churches and Christian Democrats and eventually contributing to a further pluralisation of religious instruction (Koenig 2003: 207).

11   The facts that not many Muslim organisations in England seem to complain (or at least do not openly oppose) the daily act of collective worship, and that the latter focuses 'on the moral aspect that is shared among religions' (Griffith, quoted in Fetzer & Soper 2005: 40) should not be misunderstood as an indication of the moral fairness of pragmatic accommodation policies, not even from their own perspective. It is better to see it as strategic accommodation, as 'learning to live with', maybe eventually even as a comparative '*amor fati*'. From the perspective of relational neutrality and even-handedness, they do not live up to what morality minimally requires.

12   See Delfiner for Switzerland. In this regard, even the cherished republican ceremonies of saluting the flag or singing national anthems to stimulate 'national identity' are easier to defend. Often, they are combined (Bader 1995: 85f; Koenig 2003 for religious-national identity politics).

13   Since 1975–1976 more than 700 Muslim teachers in Belgium provide two hours per week of Islamic instruction in governmental schools. 'This has meant that calls for Islamic schools ... have been muted' (Merry & Driessen 2005: 414). The establishment of the only Islamic primary school has been linked to the refusal to make a provision for Islamic instruction by two municipalities in Brussels.

14   Herrick (1996: 50) from a 'secular humanist' position. Muslim organisations have immediately and rightly criticised the 'secularist' approach to religious education (Dwyer & Meyer 1995: 44).

15   The fear of divisiveness and disintegration has been refuted by the Catholic bishop of Leeds: 'The experience of my own community (which has been a persecuted minority) is that having our own school within the state system helped us to move out of our initial isolation so as to become more confident and self-assured. The effect of the separate schools has been integration not divisiveness' (*Times Educational Supplement*, 4 January 1991). See sect. 10.4.

16 The Council of Europe, drawing on an extensive interpretation of the right to religious freedom and minority protection, has rightly criticised British liberal pragmatism, German corporatism and French secularist republicanism in this regard for not living up to the moral and legal minimum (ECRI reports: Koenig 2003: 187f and 212). See the 5th policy recommendation of ECRI (COE Doc. CRI (2000). See sect. 8.6 for the danger of institutionally pluralist regimes to continue majority bias, and sect. 10.1 (with Vermeulen 2004, Groof 2004).

17 The 2005 report by the Dutch school inspection service of Muslim primary schools offered little support to the dramatised but uninformed debates in the media and parliament (sect. 10.4 for comparative evidence).

18 See the *Nyazi v. Rymans Ltd* or *Ahmad versus ILEA cases* (even-handedly treated by Parekh 1995: 65ff). Flexibilisation of working time schedules in recent capitalist corporations increases the opportunities for such accommodations.

19 The ideologies of culturally 'neutral modernity', 'secularism', and 'professionalism' have been strong, not only in education but also in post-WW II sociology of organisation. Recently, due to work by various anthropologists of organisation, it is increasingly obvious that cultures of seeing, doing and organising things in 'modern' organisations are rife with majority bias. To counter this bias in the education of professionals, in the respective arts and sciences of organisation and management, as well as inside organisations, moral demands and critical reflection are not enough. One needs ethno-religiously interested counter-experts and a culturally diversified managerial and professional staff in armed and police forces, public administrations, private production and service organisations providing social services and all kinds of care, and education to check the 'professional mind-set' (Minow 2000: 1090f). See for human service organisations: Gastelaars 1997; Meerman 1999.

20 The decision by the German Federal Administrative Court that the only way Fereshta Ludin, as a public employee, 'could fulfil her duty to be religiously neutral is to remove her hijab during class,' has been ambiguously overruled by the *BverfG* (Fetzer & Soper 2003: 115f), stimulating legislation by *Bundesländer* (Bayern, Baden-Württemberg, Hessen, Saarland) that ban the hijab and at the same time allow crosses in classrooms (Berghahn & Rostock 2006). In addition to violations of religious freedom, in the case of teachers, the ban also violates principles of nondiscrimination and equal treatment. The French state is at least in principle 'more consistently wrong' with regard to 'ostensible religious signs', see sect. 5.4. Saharso 2004 for opposite rulings in the Netherlands.

21 Saharso & Verhaar 2004; Maris 2004 for the Dutch case, the ruling by Commissie Gelijke Behandeling and by the courts. I would even allow imaginative tinkering with *'toga and barret'* to symbolise embedded impartiality instead of reproducing myth and ideology of 'difference-blind' judicial impartiality in its symbolic manifestations. The argument, though, is more plausible in the case of judges (uniform requirements in all countries and also in European and International Courts) than with the cases involving teachers. Contextualised morality requires discussing field-specific and organisation-specific arguments in different polities (schools are not hospitals, courts, police or military forces or public administration) and France is not Turkey.

22 Dassetto 2000: 36ff for Europe; Fetzer & Soper 2005: 46ff for Britain (in 2003: one mosque or prayer room for every 1,071 Muslims), 87-90 for France (one of every 3,333 Muslims), 117-120 for Germany (one of every 1,458 Muslims). See comparative case study by Maussen 2007.

23 See comparatively: Moskos & Chambers 1992 for traditional exemptions from military and compulsory civil service. For the jurisdiction of the US Supreme Court: Galanter 1996: 226, 231f, 246f. McConnell 1985, 1992 and Pfeffer 1987: 103ff. The ac-

commodation of cemeteries has been fairly easy in the Netherlands and extremely restrictive or even absent in Sweden or France (Bowen (2006: 43-48) for a short documentation of the fairly absurd debates whether ground and/or graves of cemeteries are 'private' or 'public').

24   Yet the choice is constrained, because in deeply religiously divided societies it is not just a matter of prudence to have special laws.

25   Art 4 (2) Declaration 1981: 'All States shall make all efforts to enact or rescind legislation where necessary to prohibit any such discrimination..' (quoted in Koenig 2003: 138). The CRE has massively criticised Britain and has recommended 'that a specific law against incitement to religious hatred should be introduced and a law against religious discrimination should be given further serious consideration'. (Koenig 2003: 179f). The British case is particularly informative because anti-discrimination laws did not include religious discrimination and the blasphemy law discriminated against Islam.

26   Again, the British case demonstrates bad practice. See for Patten's reaction to Muslim demands for treating Islam equally to the Anglican Church in the existing blasphemy law: Koenig 2003: 175f; see extensively Parekh 2000: 260ff and briefly Fetzer & Soper 2005: 37f, 59.

27   Both the proposal by the Dutch Minister of Justice, Donner, to reformulate Dutch blasphemy law in 2004, and the aggressive secularist reactions in parliament to get rid of the law are examples of these kinds of bad, untimely and discriminatory practices.

28   This proposal by the Stasi commission, intended to demonstrate that the new interpretation of laïcité is really pluralist (in opposition to the old laïcité en combat), has remarkably not really been discussed and rejected immediately in political circles.

29   See Levey's proposal to institute 'a new public holiday in honour of all religious and cultural minorities' (2006: 365) to signify their presence which is not explicitly linked to institutional politics of presence (chap. 2: note 59).

30   India has about 17 gazetted (mandatory) holidays. Three are secular: Republic day, Independence day and Gandhi jayanti (the Mahatma's birthday). Religions that have officially recognised holidays are Hinduism, Islam, Christianity, Sikhism, Jainism and Buddhism. In addition, all government, public school and university employees can choose any two from a list of 32 religious festivals. These are called restricted holidays and are optional. In brief, everyone has 19 holidays a year (17 for everyone and two personal choices from a list of 32) (personal communication by Rajeev Bhargava).

31   See König 2003: 58ff and 77-83 for religious symbols of territorialised states and nations and recoding and instrumentalising religion by nation states.

32   Modood 1996, Parekh 2000, König 2003: 92, 175f, 179f, Fetzer & Soper 2005. Yet, proponents of pluralising establishment such as Modood or Parekh do not answer the question of why the symbolic recognition of Christianity and other organised religions without constitutional establishment (as in non-constitutional pluralism) is not enough? Symbolic recognition without constitutional establishment may achieve the same ends in much better ways.

33   Here, the difference between the American 'liberal assimilationist' version of separationism (defended by Hollinger 2003 as a model for all European states) and the French 'republican assimilationist' version is most outspoken. See sect. 8.5 along with Casanova 2005.

34   Jézéquel 1999: 89f, quoted from Fetzer & Soper 2005: 79. See briefly Fetzer & Soper 2005: 78ff; Bowen 2006 and Maier 2004: 23ff.

35   I quote from an extensive e-mail correspondence between Carens, Weil, Bauböck, Spinner and others in February 2004. See also criticism by Bowen 2004, 2004a.

36   I personally doubt whether the shaky distinction between 'visible' signs that are al-
     lowed (otherwise, the violation of ECHR, Art. 9 would be too evident) and *'signe os-
     tensible'*, claimed to be judged 'objectively', would survive critical legal scrutiny. I also
     have serious doubts whether the ECHR ruling (29 June 2004) is in line with the let-
     ter, or at least with the spirit, of European Law because the Strasbourg Court as well
     as the EP have consistently criticised the Turkish version of the 'secular state' for vio-
     lating basic religious freedoms. Yet, for a contextualised moral theory, contexts and
     facts matter: the Turkish ban might seem more plausible because the 'perceived'
     threat by 'Muslim fundamentalists' might be much stronger than in France (see,
     however, Zürcher & Van der Linden (2004) and many others, arguing that Turkey
     has changed dramatically over the last twenty years).

37   The need for a law, then, reflects 'a weakness on the part of the French state, namely
     an inability to effectively exercise its (legal – V.B.) monopoly over the use of vio-
     lence.' (Carens) The choice of an indirect means to protect Muslim girls who do not
     want to wear the *hijab* against the (threat of) physical coercion reflects the fact that
     the state is unable to directly protect them. It is particularly inappropriate, because it
     does not even attempt to tackle the problem of protecting the basic rights of minors
     inside families or communities (sect. 7.3 for my proposals).

38   Pluralising public education and introducing fair chances for Muslim religious in-
     struction may reduce the demand for Muslim schools (Bauböck 2004) but does not
     morally legitimise the ban of the *hijab* in public schools.

39   Martin 1978; Willaime 1986: 164 ('syncretism of laicist and Catholic culture'); König
     2003; Safran 2003, 2004.

40   This is the case particularly if one takes into account that huge social and cultural
     pressures are working towards cultural assimilation anyway (Zolberg 1997: 150f),
     even in cases where organised ethnic and religious minorities actively try to resist
     assimilation.

41   Fetzer & Soper, König, Rath et al., Safran & Bowen come to the same conclusion. It
     is ironic that even Britain's weak establishment, the most 'monopolistic' version of
     religious institutional pluralism, does better than France (see also the conclusion of
     a comparison of Muslim prison chaplains in France and Britain by Beckford 2005).
     For these reasons, it seems likely that an official recognition in the *European Draft
     Convention*, that European history, culture and institutions have been deeply formed
     by Christianity – as proposed by Christian politicians and most explicitly defended
     by Joseph Weiler but turned down eventually – would not have hindered actual plur-
     alisation of cultural practices and symbols, at least not any more than neglecting this
     fact and proclaiming neutrality.

42   See Safran 2003 for an informative comparison of France and the US, demonstrat-
     ing the differences between these two varieties of 'strict separation'. Both however
     share the highly symbolically and dramatised defence of 'common public education'
     (Rosenblum 2002: 150f, 167; 10.1).

43   See Casanova (2005: 7ff) for French and also European illiberal secularism (vaguely
     Christian, cultural European identity), resistance to accommodation of symbols and
     opposition to Turkish membership of the EU. 'Europe, rather than Turkey is actually
     the "torn country"'.

Notes Chapter 6

1   All liberal theories of morality, together with 'liberal morality' itself, are indiscrimi-
     nately said to have five crucial shortcomings. (i) They are accused of 'mono-Kantian-
     ism and *mono*-secularism' and 'unitarianism' (just like their counterpart: 'mono-the-

ism', 1999: 11). In addition, they are criticised as 'command morality' (1995: 181): the 'commands ... of practical reason, or communicative competence' (1999: 13) 'must set the authoritative matrix of public life' (1999: 6), and it is suggested that liberal philosophers try to 'occupy such a place of unquestioned authority' (1999: 33, 38). (ii) They are said to use uncritical concepts of 'reason' neglecting its 'normalizing', 'disciplining', 'excluding', 'encapsulating' powers, or its 'violence'. (iii) Liberal theories and (even moderately universalist) liberal morality are inherently 'closed': 'fixed set of rules', 'crystallized codes', 'retrospective', 'backward looking', 'ex post'. All 'registers of justice' are inherently conservative, unable to deal with the ambiguity of morality, denying development and renewal of morality (1995: 185f, 232). (iv) Principles or 'codes' of liberal morality are not determinate enough and 'recourse to the porous rules of a ... public procedure, reason or deliberation are insufficient' (2004: 87; 2000: 614, 1995: xvi). (v) Liberal morality is also insufficient because it either 'ignores' the 'visceral register of subjectivity and inter-subjectivity', 'visceral aptitudes' and 'visceral judgment', or 'it disparages it in the name of a public sphere in which reason, morality, and tolerance flourish' (199: 3, see 25ff, 163ff); by which it 'forfeits some of the very resources needed to foster a generous pluralism'.

Connolly's own 'ethos of pluralization' is ambiguously caught between a full rejection of liberal morality, principles and rights and their replacement by a 'postmodern', 'post-liberal' ethos on the one hand and, on the other hand, by the possibility of productive complementarity that is not further elaborated (Bader 2006 on website).

2   Concepts are contested. I use a broad, anthropological, dynamic, heterogeneous concept of culture(s) (Bader 1995: 94ff; 2001). Habits or attitudes are conceived as 'embodied' cultures and cultures as 'objectified' habits (Bader 1991, chap. 3). I take virtues to be a combination of specific competencies and motivations to think and act in a normatively praised way (Christis 1998: 283-297: virtues cannot be reduced to competencies only, let alone to moral competencies or cognitive competencies. They also require a motivational commitment or readiness to use competencies that is more or less deeply embedded in 'attitudes', 'character' or 'personality'.) Culture(s), habits and virtues together do not determine but structure practical judgment and action. Thus, in the medium or long terms, they are influenced by traditions of good judgment and practices, and obviously by institutions as well. Here, I bracket all the links of virtues with institutions, culture(s), and practices, focusing only on virtues and on political virtues in particular (Bader 1997: 786 for 'political' virtues, and note 51 on social, economic, professional virtues).

3   Liberal-democratic virtues are clearly distinct from aristocratic or other elitist virtues in non-democratic polities, but also from classic and modern civic-republican virtues, which are explicitly perfectionist and informed by a theory of the good life that should be supreme. They are also distinct from classic liberal virtues that are implicitly or explicitly elitist.

4   See Walzer's excellent treatment of the 'different attitudes of toleration' (1997: 10ff), stressing minimalism and highlighting the paramount importance of 'regimes' or institutions of toleration compared with principles and virtues of tolerance. See Kymlicka 2005 for tensions between principles and institutions of Multiculturalism and the perfectionist ideal of demanding 'intercultural citizenship', the respective virtues, and some counterproductive effects of the latter, see sect. 9.6.

5   Gutmann 1994: 24 & Macedo 1991: 267, 269, 272ff for the dialectic of civil mutual respect and personal self-conceptions. See Van den Berg (2004) for a very sober version. See chap. 10 for education.

6   Feminist approaches explicitly pluralise 'public reason', becoming increasingly agonistic: Benhabib 1996, 2003 and Devreux 2005. See Valadez 2001 and Tully 1999,

2005 for increasingly agonistic theories of ethno-national diversity. See Mouffe (2000) in the 'post-Marxist' tradition.

7   Bader 2001d: 203; see also Murphy 2004: 265, 233. See above for: institutional rules of public talk that discipline presented reasons much more effectively than reason restraints; institutional learning of liberal democracy by religious parties through the institutional logic of competitive democratic party systems; learning toleration by living under effective regimes of toleration that guarantee minimally tolerant everyday interactions.

8   See Warren 2001 for short summaries and extensive criticism of social scientists. Recently, many liberal political philosophers (Macedo, Galston, Rawls, Audi) have stated that 'private' or 'social' associations such as churches and sects contribute significantly to the development of civic and political virtues (Bader 1997, note 8 for criticism). Associative democracy has a better record as a 'Seedbed of Virtues' and also for the 'Transformation of Politics' (Cohen & Rogers 1992, Hirst 1994, Bader 1998b, 1999b) but should not reproduce undifferentiated optimism.

9   See Warren's systematic analysis of the developmental democratic effects of associations. 'In Rosenblum's terms, the primary moral effect of association is the experience of reciprocity built on mutual expectations of performance. Insofar as association has a voluntary dimension, reciprocity is the basic sociological building block of cooperation. That is, there is a generic 'democracy of everyday life' built into association, albeit in segmented and pluralised ways. There is no necessity, of course, that such relationships will generalise, but they may provide developmental experiences upon which civic virtues might be built. One is trust, at least when combined with its reciprocal virtue, *trustworthiness*' (2001: 74). Other effects are contributions to 'self-respect' that 'also enables the *recognition* of others' (75, my italics).

10 See Walzer above and Bader 2003c: 152f. Estlund has shown that high degrees of voluntarism are a mixed blessing in this regard because they can actually go hand in hand with high degrees of demographic segregation, whereas compulsion (in the Army and particularly in workplaces) can create important 'bridging ties' across class and ascriptive cleavages , and also civic virtues. These ties may be thinner than the traditional thick 'bonds of sameness' or 'bonding ties' but they are more appropriate in culturally diverse societies (2003: 20 and Conclusion).

11 See Hayward's (2003) criticism of claims by Jacobs, Dahl and Dagger of deeply beneficial effects of democratic '*city-cenship*'. See Estlund (2003: 74ff) for a critical reading of the contact hypothesis. See also Soroka, Johnston & Banting 2004: 50f.

12 The mode of formal recognition is variable but merely 'private pluralism', interest-group pluralism or 'social, but not political' pluralism in civil society (Rawls 1993) is not enough (Tamir 1993: 72, 1997; Eisenberg 1995: 17; Williams 1998: 67f; Bader 1999a).

13 Bader & Benschop 1989: 258ff; Hirst 1989: 11ff, 1990: 105ff; Bader 1995a: 211ff; Lijphart 1984: 30 and Eisenberg 1995: 64ff.

14 For a short analysis of conceptual and theoretical traditions and of the overlaps of the three types of IP: Bader 2003c: 35ff; see also Schmidt 2006: 224ff.

15 See Bader 2007b and Schmidt 2006 for an analysis of the many dilemmas inherent in multi-layered and multi-level polities. Unfortunately, little use has been made thus far of neo-institutionalist studies in the social sciences for research of 'multicultural' or religious representation.

16 The first detailed institutional designs and practical experiments with 'economic, industrial or social democracy', with democratic functional representation can be found in the socialist labour movement, particularly in Austro-marxism (Bauer, Renner, Adler), in developing labour law (Sinzheimer, Renner, Klare), in Guild-Socialism (Cole), in Laski's political pluralism, and later in democratic neo-corporatism

(Schmitter, Lehmbruch, Streeck). Originally, their focus was the representation of labour and capital/management but in socialist experiments around 1900, consumers and clients were already integrated and many attempts were later made to include occupational and professional representation and also 'non-productivist' interests.

17   Territorial concentration plays a role regarding three distinct problems: (a) Minorities in a polity can be majorities at a territorial meso-level (regions across state borders or states or provinces within federal states). If this is the case, territorial federalisation may be feasible to address problems of First Nations or national minorities. (b) If ethno-religious or national minorities do not form numerical majorities at this meso-level (and in this sense can be characterised as 'territorially dispersed minorities'), there are still minimal thresholds of territorial concentration required for their own separate associations or organisations in order to make possible the 'parallel existence of self-governing communities sharing the same space but applying rules in matters of community concern to their members' (Hirst 2001: 23). (c) Distinct from such situations of 'mutual extra-territoriality' are situations in which specific ethno-religious, national, but also broader ascriptive, gender minorities form numerical majorities on a micro-level. This local concentration of gay communities, of retired people, of religious sects or of ethnic immigrants in neighborhoods or villages enables the formation of regimes of 'territorial micro-governance'. These local majorities may be very rich and powerful ('gated communities') or ghettos of the very poor and powerless.

18   See proposals for European Governance Associations (EGAs) by Schmitter 2000; Bader 2006, 2007b.

19   Kymlicka 1995, 2001: 348ff; Carens 2000, Williams 1998: 204; Levy 2000; Ingram 2004 and Valadez 2001.

20   See Eisenberg's criticism (1995: 20ff) that applies also to Hollinger (1996: 116-125), Kymlicka (1995: 3) and Walzer (1997). The illusory claim of free choice and freely shifting involvements is very often, traded as the characteristic sign of 'Postmodernism'.

21   See Warren 2001: 96ff and, for the normative consequences: Scheffler 2001 and Bader 2005c.

22   Normatively richer theories of self-development should distinguish between constitutive and contingent aspects of identity and oppose the 'communitarian' reduction of self-development to mere socialisation: neither biology nor history is destiny.

23   Thus, ascriptive groups might not share any cultural practices (which means they may not form cultural communities) and they might not develop any positive group identity: purely negative collective identities (being aware of the fact that they are ascriptively categorised by others and fighting against this specific – or against all – ascriptive inequality) may be a sufficient condition for organising and mobilising as a conflict group.

24   See, for example, Galanter's criticism of imposing definitions of 'religions that favour private and voluntary observance' (1998: 283) on Hinduism that is spilt between 'born a Hindu' (273) and 'membership by initiation' (276).

25   One cannot usually change one's sex, age or skin colour (although one can undergo a sex-change operation) but someone can change one's language, religion and 'nation'. Exit from a non- or involuntary group is always possible, but with varying degrees of difficulty.

26   See Parekh (1994: 204f, 2000) for the two dangers of assimilationist liberalism: the 'religionization of culture' and/or the ethnicisation of culture. See Bader 2003c: 146ff for the preferred option of self-definition of belonging, its limits, and how to avoid the dangers of inevitable 'categorisation' implied in all versions of democratic institutional pluralism, the 'pillarised' versions in particular.

27   We should also note that religious categorisation does not presuppose any shared re-
     ligious practices (Bader 2001) and that protest against religious categorisation/discri-
     mination is an important option. Fully assimilated 'liberal Jews' in the United States
     (Wasserstein 1996) or the Netherlands (Solinge & de Vries (ed.) 2001) that do not
     share any religious practices and are not part of a Jewish religious community, and
     many recent immigrants categorised as 'Muslims' who may be completely 'secu-
     larised' have excellent reasons to protest against anti-Semitism and Islamophobia.

28   This is certainly true in cases of 'ethnic religions'. The process in which 'universal'
     religions such as Christianity and Islam have disentangled themselves from original
     ethnic cores has been long and difficult. See sect. 8.5 for the huge 'ethno-national'
     diversity of 'Muslims in the West'. See Martin (1978: 30, 40, 43, 52f, 77-82) for the
     tricky two-way relationship of linguistic, ethnic, and religious cultures and identities.
     For the chequered relations between 'nations' and 'religions', see: A. Smith 1981; Ba-
     der 1995: 85f; Safran 2003).

29   To mention another case: 'The popular view in the West that Female Genital Mutila-
     tion is a 'Muslim' practice is doubly incorrect: FGM is practised by Christians, Jews
     and animist as well as Muslims in parts of sub-Saharan Africa, and is strongly dis-
     avowed by many Muslim leaders. Yet this popular perception is very strong' (Kym-
     licka 2005).

30   Sect. 2.4 versus Kymlicka 1997: 21. If one takes language as the core of ethno-na-
     tional culture, as becomes increasingly clear in Kymlicka's later writings, it is possi-
     ble for a state to have at the very least more than one established or official lan-
     guage. This very much resembles 'plural establishment'. And the weak version of
     'deism' that goes hand in hand with constitutional separation in the US can easily
     be compared with the necessary 'partial establishment of culture'. At the very least,
     the differences between 'religion' and (i.e. ethno-national) 'culture' would be less
     sharp than Kymlicka assumes. König 2003: 15, 35 (criticising Joppke; see also Jansen
     2006, chap. 2).

31   For these two options, see also Poulter (1998: 11ff) and Renteln 2004: 13ff.

32   Bader 1995: 49ff and 146f. In my view, my model is more productive than those of
     Grillo (1998: 5), Crouch (1999: 288ff: 'segregation, assimilation, integration'), or Va-
     ladez (2001: chap. 6, 7: 'accommodationist, autonomist, secessionist' groups).

33   Walzer explicitly allows only 'two forms,' 'versions' of toleration (1997: 84f, 91) or
     'central projects of modern democratic politics': individual assimilation (my cell 1:
     assimilation in a project of democratic inclusiveness) and group recognition (my cell
     2: group recognition in a project of institutional separation). We certainly agree that
     these two projects cannot be easily combined (86f) and that they show divergent
     tendencies. However, the two realistic utopias (cells 3 and 4) cannot be ruled out *a li-
     mine* by declaring them impossible. It is particularly disappointing that Walzer as-
     sumes the regime of 'consociation' to be inherently 'elitist' and necessarily based on
     enforced assimilation of closed 'communities of fate'. If 'individual autonomy' and
     'group autonomy' cannot be reconciled (87, 91), then only some vague 'postmoder-
     nist project of toleration' (87ff) seems to present a promising alternative (see for si-
     milar 'postmodernist' lyrics: Hollinger 1996: 116-125). Colin Crouch's discussion of
     'sociological liberalism' (2000: 33ff, 195, 291) suffers from similar limitations, and
     the same unfortunately holds for Parekh's three models (2000: 199ff: 'procedural-
     ist,' 'civic assimilationist,' 'millet').

34   Contrary to Max Weber, Ottoman rule is not a good example of 'patrimonialism' but
     represents political arrangements of a constitutional nature 'resting to a considerable
     extent on negotiated solutions and popular acceptance' (Adanir 2000: 7f). The ob-
     vious legal inequality between Muslim and non-Muslim has been moderated in
     practice by many tax exemptions (12ff) and by legal equality before the *kadi*. In so-

cio-economic terms, the Turkish majority had no advantages and even careers in the armed forces and state administration have been wide open to minorities (Adanir 2002).

35 Kymlicka uses the millet system to highlight his distinction between two principles of tolerance: 'individualist' (principles of individual autonomy, individual freedom of conscience, of heresy, apostasy) in his model of 'liberal societies' versus collective or communal principles (autonomy and self-government). His focus on principles masks the facts that, (i) in practice, quite a lot of scope for dissent (1995: 82, 157f, 162f, 231) within millets can be found, (ii) some religions effectively evaded 'being squeezed into clear-cut millets' (it is not sufficient to say that millets have been 'further subdivided into various local administrative units usually based on ethnicity and language' (156), (iii) the interpenetration of millets and local/territorial autonomy allowed for much more mixing and more practical individual choice (actual exit options limiting the hold of theocratic leaders). By the way, his 'liberal societies' have been textbook utopias in the centuries in which the millet system actually existed (comparing model with muddle). Walzer discusses the millet system as an example of toleration and peaceful coexistence in multi-national empires (1997: 17f, 40, 67), focusing more on actual practices, motivations and institutions of toleration than on the principle of tolerance. But he does not fully use the chances of this approach. Instead, he also reproduces the dichotomous picture of two opposed models (67), overlooks territorial units completely, overestimates compartmentalisation and homogeneity (only in the imperial capitals some 'neutral space' is allowed for lonely dissidents and heretics, cultural vagabonds, intermarried couples' (16) and presents a stark tension and choice between individual or collective autonomy, not only in the millet system but generally. See similarly Parekh 2000: 205f.262.

36 Kalyvas 2003; Birtek 2006. See section 9.8 for external conditions. See John 2001 and Adanir 2000 for comparisons with the Habsburg Empire. 'Neutrality' and 'more evenhanded rule' is, more in general, an important aspect of the 'imperial version of multiculturalism' (Walzer 1997: 17).

37 Nearly a century later, the potential transition from the multi-national regimes of the Soviet Empire and of Yugoslavia to democratic multi-national federations has also tragically failed (Brubaker 1995 and Adanir & Faroqhi (eds.) 2002).

38 See Cohen & Rogers 2002; Hirst 1994, chap. 2 and 3; Bader 2001a, 2001c, and Cohen & Sabel 2002 for a vivid defence against traditional charges. See also a short summary in Bader 2003: 282f.

39 Figgis 1914: 67ff, 87f (Hirst 2000) and see Glendon & Yanes 1991: 534ff for Catholicism; Kuyper, Miller 1985: 272ff and Skillen 1994: 249f. for Calvinist 'souvereiniteit in eigen kring'.

Notes Chapter 7

1 Monsma and Soper (1997) use their model mainly 'to classify the five countries', whereas I focus more explicitly on the normative evaluation of institutional designs and policies. In addition, my model is explicitly multidimensional and distinguishes three relevant varieties of institutional pluralism from institutionally monist types blurred in Monsma and Soper's 'established church' model. Bhargava makes 'establishment' more complex by adding establishment of one or many religions (2005: 5ff). However, in his presentation of the 'Indian model', he tends to overestimate the constitutional dimension and neglects PE and also NOCOP, where official status is given but is not constitutionalised.

2   Compared with the general types of incorporation of ethno-religious minorities (Figure 7.1) these models are exclusively focused on religious diversity. Furthermore, they are more fine-grained (distinguishing constitutional, legal, administrative, political and cultural dimensions, which may and actually do diverge) and they are exclusively normative. I also exclude strategies of religious minorities in response to ideals and predominant policy models. The construction of the models, however, follows the same general logic (how state institutions and policies should respond to cultural and religious diversity; institutional monism vs. pluralism; degrees of cultural pluralism), which explains some overlap. NEPP follows the logic of inclusion (cells 1 and 3 in figure 7.1), and the USA and France. The states meant to exemplify these predominant models may be either on their way to become more 'Post-Christian' and relationally neutral (moving forward to cell 4) or move back to cell 1. The three varieties of religious institutional pluralism all follow the logic of (degrees of) institutional separation, and the respective states meant to be guided by these models (e.g. the Netherlands) are somewhere on their way from cell 2 (corporatist or pillarised NOCOP) either to the realistic utopia of AD (cell 3) or to the realistic utopia of cell 4, or back to cell 2 or even 1. This indicates at least two important points. First, one has to handle with care the empirical references (the distance between ideals, empirically predominant policy models and actual institutions and policies is bigger than the examples suggest). Second, the future path of institutions and policies is not determined or closed but open and unpredictable to a certain degree.

3   Religious institutional pluralism can strengthen religious minorities in their opposition against enforced assimilation by majorities and especially by the state, increasing the chances to reproduce or transform religious practices on their own terms, if they wish so (Walzer 1997: 69ff; Spinner-Halev 2000: 7, 20, 40).

4   The most vivid defenders of fairly unlimited 'church autonomy' can be found in the Catholic and orthodox Calvinist tradition.

5   It is 'no accident that pragmatists, civic republicans, anti-foundationalists, historicists and postmodernists in academia' substantially agree with 'religious evangelicals, liberal nationalists, and pluralist communitarians in attacking prevailing church-state jurisprudence' (Eisenach 2000: 111, 115). However, the common critical core of this coalition of strange bedfellows directly evaporates if one looks more closely. Their critical diagnosis is not the same (e.g. nostalgic neo-conservative diagnosis of 'modernity' versus justice-based criticism) and their institutional and policy alternatives differ widely, ranging from neo-Hobbesian or Schmittian decisionism (Fish, Alexander) via Rorty's ironic tribalism to Benjamin Barber's and Hilary Putnam's non-ironic democratic pragmatism to my plea for AD.

6   Reich 2002a: 3. This is the pedagogic counterpart (sect. 10.2) of the general notion of limited, divided and delegated sovereignty or authority.

7   These basic rights (sect. 2.2) are under-determined: what basic education includes, for example, cannot be determined independently from the stage of historical and societal development and the situation of specific minorities like isolationist religious minorities, nomadic minorities or indigenous peoples: how many years of mandatory education? Education in 'public' schools or within ethno-religious communities? Scope and degree of exemptions? It is the counterpart of the under-determinacy of 'autonomy', see chap. 10.

8   The consequences of taking children out of native, tribal and isolationist families and groups are far more serious than in other ethno-religious minority cases, making outplacement a morally and prudentially almost impossible option. I also think that an inter-culturally defensible concept of a basic interest of children developing into autonomous adults (Reich 2005, Shapiro 1999: 72, 85-88) should be even more minimalist in order to prevent the imposition of still fairly thick liberalism: 'autono-

mous' according to the conceptions of the respective communities as long as they are compatible with minimal morality.

9   See Shapiro 1999 for a clear demonstration of the different weights in different countries as well as the historical shifts within the US.

10 See sects. 8.5 and 8.6 for the selective affinity of AD and the idealised US model of religious denominationalism.

11 'The degree of nonvoluntariness can be represented by the costs to individuals of exiting the association' (Warren 2001: 99, see 99-103). See also Okin 2005 for criticism of Raz, Galston, Kukathas.

12 It may even be legitimate for certain minorities to make exit very costly in cases of common property of land (many native people) or more generally (e.g. Hutterites). Even then, it is possible to work out options that safeguard high degrees of communal autonomy without completely sacrificing individual exit options, as Spinner-Halev (2000: 77f) has convincingly shown. This seems to be much more promising than generalised statements like 'the whole exit strategy ... fails' (Weinstock 2002: 12, 19) and to discard exit in favour of 'individual well-being'.

13 See Swaine (2001, 2004, 2006) for a liberal justification of such a policy for theocratic communities.

14 The Amish, Hutterites, Mennonites or Chassidim in the US, and ultra-orthodox Jews in Israel are the strongest defenders of 'strict separation' of state and religion. They do not ask or accept any public money and just want to be left alone and engage in politics only if this 'splendid isolation' is threatened.

15 Rosenblum has pointed out the 'unintended liberal consequences' of such litigation by religious groups for their self-definition: 'the moral education of membership in a group that asserts rights should not be overlooked, particularly when it appears to be in tension with the groups' own norms' (1998: 103-108). See also Swaine 2001: 318 and Tomasi 2001: 43f, unfortunately neglected by Levey 2006.

16 Overruling 'decisions' taken on the basis of institutional settings would be obviously incompatible with any institutionalisation of pluralism.

17 Standards, operationalisation and measurement are contested (Bader & Engelen 2003: 385f).

18 The appropriate modes of representation for different types of minorities in the political process in divergent contexts are largely unexplored research themes. AD certainly does not provide a ready-made blueprint to answer urgent questions such as: which religions should be represented in which ways, in which fields, regarding which issues? No generally applicable answers can be expected.

19 In the UK, the weakly established Anglican Church has reserved seats in the House of Lords as a remnant of strong establishment. Proponents of PE consequently require seats for old and new minority religions (Catholics, Jews and Muslims) but this is a rather exceptional situation.

20 Defenders of liberal, republican and deliberative democracy all seem to think that it would be sufficient to stress the normative 'openness' of the political process, or that general measures to increase it would be sufficient.

21 Practices of obligatory information, for example, that exceed general information rights and legislation and specify that authorities (whether public or private) have to inform minorities on specific issues (as in the German *Betriebsverfassungsgesetz*) have not entered political philosopher's proposals.

22 See Williams (1998: 208-212) for other minorities.

23 Obviously, the voices of other relevant minorities, e.g. humanists, deserve the same or similar institutional backing and representation. The difficult problem here, as in all other cases, is who should be present (see chap. 8 for trade-offs). Selectivity in public hearings is fairly low but much higher in 'Ethics Councils'.

24 None of these measures reduce voice to final say, but all have an impact when it comes to 'listening' and perhaps even to initial bargaining and deliberation. There are many existing or imaginable ways of strengthening voice (along with loyalty, as is always hoped for) that have been neglected in debates focused on group rights and vetoes. These options may be particularly important for those minorities who do not strive for a broad scope of institutional pluralism or autonomy, but seek more voice in specific issues and fields they define as crucial. The prototype of polity-wide consociationalism has not stimulated the elaboration of all possibilities of power sharing in specific fields, and the legalistic focus of the group rights discussion has blocked the possibility of taking more flexible practices of minority representation into account (the pre-occupation with 'group rights' shares the legalist and constitutionalist bias of American politics). Political scientists like Lijphart and Horowitz avoid these legalistic pitfalls more easily.

25 Hirst 1994: 24,56ff, 176, 201f; Bader 1998a: 195-200; Bader 2001a: 38ff; 2001b: 195-198.

26 Recently, the representation of relevant stakeholders has been guaranteed by law in many countries, see sect. 10.6 for education. AD does not need to be invented from scratch.

27 See Dewey 1927, Benhabib 1996, and Bartholomew 1999 for thicker, more interactive and pluralist, less abstract, unitary and anonymous conceptions of public(s).

28 Hirschman 1978; Carens 1987, Bader 2005d. This is the structural reason why voice or political democracy in territorially-bound units (polities, states) is more important than in organisations based on formally free or voluntary membership.

29 Both 'equal' respect and concern and opportunities for democratic internal participation for dissenting minorities (e.g. women) are absent in the cases of undemocratic and illiberal religions.

30 See Deveaux (2005: 353-360) for negotiations, consultations and hearings in the 'Harmonization of the Common Law and the Indigenous Law' sponsored by the South African Law Commission. In comparing experiences of Parsi, Christian and Muslim personal law reform in India, Mahajan has shown that voice is not always necessary (the Parsi case), that it has to be organised (2005: 109, the Christian case) and that the status of minority community members as citizens has to be secure (the case of the failure of attempts to make personal Muslim laws more just for women). See Shachar 2005 for the poor consultation process in the attempts to establish a private Islamic arbitration tribunal (Dar-ul-Quada) in Ontario.

31 Particularly promising in this regard would be Shachar's 'transformational accommodation' (2001: 118-126) approach because of its high degree of institutional and legal detail. It is supposed to avoid the disadvantages of the other joint governance approaches (federal, temporal, consensual and contingent accommodation). On the face of it, my approach looks similar to the contingent accommodation model in which 'the state yields jurisdictional autonomy to nomoi groups in certain well-defined legal arenas, but only as long as their exercise of this autonomy meets certain minimal state-defined standards. If a group fails to meet these minimal standards, the state may intervene in the group's affairs.' (109). However, I place this minimally required state intervention within the framework of AD, and this enables me to resolve the main difficulties mentioned by Shachar: (i) who defines the minimal standards? How are they defined, interpreted and applied? (115f) AD provides for an excellent means for challenging majority bias disguised as 'modern' or 'neutral'. (ii) Intervention 'requires a complex regulatory regime' (110, inspections of actual performance and compliance). AD combines self-regulation and self-scrutiny with public scrutiny and gives associations an important role not only in standard setting but also in control regimes. (iii) Given the power asymmetries, 'it is hard to see how this

(analytically attractive) model of mutual 'mirror-image policing' can be applied in practice' (112). AD tries to precisely redress these power asymmetries (and does so much more effectively than Shachar's 'transformational accommodation' model). (iv) It 'relegates individual group members to a more passive position' (whistle-blowers). AD not only provides important exit options for minorities within minoritie, it also enables organised voice inside religious associations. (v) The most crucial interests of 'vulnerable group members' would not be 'maximised'. In my view, the combination of actual voluntarism, real exit options and critical public scrutiny does a lot to protect vulnerable minorities. In contrast, transformational accommodation encounters difficulties in explaining why traditionalist leaders should not choose to ostracise, exclude and excommunicate critical voices inside (124f, but see 139, 143). Also, it shares the problem with associative democracy of how to respond to the trade-off between (threat of) exit and voice. Her example of how transformative accommodation works in education (154ff) shows how little space for accommodation is actually created. Intending to avoid both the pitfalls of the idealised American 'strict separationist' approach and a 'separate but equal school system' (155) she thinks that the German (and the Austrian) system of *religious instruction* in public schools would provide the best available option, see also Bauböck 2002. Compared with an AD educational system (chap. 10), her preference is fairly traditionalist republican, neglecting the strongly majoritarian religious or strongly secularist bias of presumed 'neutral' curricula and pedagogy in government schools, see sect. 5.2. Pluralisation stops short before the gates of the 'same general curriculum which is developed, implemented, and supervised by the state in its sub-matter authority' (157). Minority schools, which are subject to the same standards and public scrutiny as all schools, are viewed with generalised suspicion whether parents and students are choosing them freely, like in AD, or are given no choice by 'separate but equal' *Jim Crow* laws.

32 Swaine 2001: 328f: exit requirements, educational and human rights requirements, zones of legal autonomy discriminating between civil matters and criminal areas, etc. Spinner-Halev's treatment of conservative religions within the confines of citizenship also stresses exit rights and options (2000: 57, 63, 70ff); no physical harm to members (torture of girls); basic health care, no marriage before the age of consent and educational requirements. However, his interpretation of the first principle of 'non-intervention' is clearly much weaker than Swaine's semi-sovereignty or my defence of associational autonomy. In addition, his care for 'support for healthy mainstream liberal society' (205) allows for fairly anti-accommodationist sweeping generalisations (208ff). Kymlicka's interpretation of minimal autonomy is also much thicker than mine (2002: 228-244) and this is more strongly the case in Levey's contributions (1997, 2001, 2006) and in Nussbaum's 'principle of moral constraint' (2000: 190ff). Its more restricted 'political use' already legitimises strong and deep policies of liberal-democratic congruence because the full list of rights is included in the 'protection of the central capabilities' constituting a 'compelling state interest' (2000: 202). Consequently, not much space for accommodations is left. Eventually, the more expansive 'social use' of the principle of moral constraint legitimises thick perfectionist and paternalist policies (82ff, 88, 92, 194ff; see similar: Ingram 2003). Clearly, the range of 'minimal requirements of liberal democracy' is as large and contested (Moore 2005: 282ff, 27) as is the question of the most satisfying theoretical approach (see the contributions in Cohen, Howard & Nussbaum (eds.) 1999).

33 This presupposes a fairly strong state, a peculiar dilemma for AD (Bader 2001a: 56). Appropriate socio-economic policies cannot be addressed here.

Notes Chapter 8

1   Both tendencies are stronger in states with dense and deep systems of legal regula-
     tions (as in the Netherlands) but can be softened by practices of condoning instead
     of (always only attempted) strict law enforcement.

2   Bader 2007a; empirically Koopmans & Stratham 2000; for Muslim leaders in Eur-
     ope: Klausen 2005.

3   See para. 1.3.3.3 for this 'pyramidal pattern' of privileges and corresponding regula-
     tions. The scale runs from non-registration, non-recognition and non-establishment
     to establishment in terms of highest/lowest formal church autonomy. It is superim-
     posed by the pyramidal pattern of selective and gradational cooperation for 'selective
     cooperation countries'. I disagree slightly with Ferrari 2005: 7 in two regards: first,
     selectivity and gradualism are not limited to 'the European pattern' but also charac-
     terise the US, which also does not provide 'a general equality among all religious
     communities'. In my view, the main difference lies in the presence or absence of in-
     stitutionalised, selective cooperation. Second, Ferrari deals with the two dilemmas in
     terms of 'compatibility' (with the state's lack of competence on religious matters and
     with the principle of equality). I am also interested in the question of whether and
     how the different regimes are conducive to substantive autonomy and equality, i.e.
     how they try to resolve the tricky normative trade-offs involved.

4   See Bader (1991: 243-246) for criticism of the respective 'iron laws' and the illusions
     of the one-best organisational model that would fit all contexts. Large churches like
     the Roman Catholic, Lutheran or Anglican are clearly more vulnerable to these ten-
     dencies.

5   Institutionalised negotiations add external pressures on internal control and disci-
     pline of constituency and members, they strengthen the internal power position of
     religious leaders (they gain external resources such as recognition, social relations,
     external legitimacy, decisions over granted external money), and they increase time
     pressure on internal democratic decision-making.

6   Given serious structural power asymmetries between (secular or religious) majori-
     ties and minorities, how can religious minorities prevent reactive essentialism (the
     purification of cultures or religions) and the silencing of dissenting voices, without
     being prey to the strategies of divide and rule often successfully used by majorities
     (and 'their' state)? This is indeed a structural, strategic dilemma for all minorities
     (Bader 1991, chap. 10) that cannot be resolved by 'strategic essentialism' (Bader
     2001: 264ff). This dilemma exists in all regimes of government of religious diversity
     but it is sharpened by corporatist institutions and by the wrong, rigid variety of Mul-
     ticulturalism Policies, sharply criticised by Baumann, Hollinger or Barry (see Bader
     2006b for criticism).

7   For a brief analysis, see: Bader 2006, 2007b.

8   Huge numbers in France, the UK, Germany and the Netherlands. Muslims in the
     UK came mainly from the Indian subcontinent, in Germany from Turkey, in France
     from the Magreb. The density of transnational networks and ties with countries of
     origin differs and different main states from the regions of origin try to influence
     developments (e.g. Diyanet in Germany; Morocco, Tunisia, Algeria and Saudi Arabia
     in France; Morocco and Turkey in the Netherlands).

9   Like the French administration, the Belgian administration played an active part in
     the elections for a constituent assembly in 1998 (which then appointed an executive
     committee, recognised in May 1999) 'creating a special commission to check the
     conduct of the elections, validating the results and sustaining all the costs of the
     election procedure. However, in addition 'over half of the members designated to
     take part in the executive committee were rejected by the Ministry of Justice as they

were considered to be of an excessively radical orientation' (Ferrari 2005b: 12-14), and the constituent assembly was dissolved in 2004 before its natural term of office had expired (2009).

10   See Peter (2004: 7-15, 20f) and Bowen (2004) for the impacts of these attempts to create a 'moderate', anti-fundamentalist, republican, individualised and subjectivised 'Islam de France' on discourses and claims by Muslim intellectuals and leaders.

11   Following the pattern of Jewish and Protestant federations. This option is also defended by Modood for the UK (2005: 21f).

12   Ferrari 2005b: 17. In addition to my arguments against the emergence of one 'concordatory Europe' (Massignon 2003, see para. 1.3.3.9), one would have to recognise differences in the organisational and representational structures of the divergent religions (e.g. the KEK (Council of European Churches), the COMECE (Commission of European Bishop Conferences), the EHF (European Humanist Federation) at the EU level.

13   This structure is typical for all churches before the development of welfare states, but even more so for all ethnic immigrant churches (chap. 4). In the US, due to absent or poor welfare state arrangements, this congregational structure is much more important for immigrants. In general, mosques are particularly apt for this task.

14   Casanova 2005: 28. In NEPP, the symbolic representation of religious pluralism and relational state neutrality is more informal and ad hoc because no clear, formalised representational structure exists (which religions, whom to choose as representative?). In existing NOCOPs, the symbolic representation of religious pluralism and relational state neutrality is formalised but unduly restrictive. AD hopes to achieve a better balance also in this regard, but this aspect is not dealt with extensively here for reasons of space (see indications in sect. 5.4).

15   AD is situated between existing American denominationalism and existing regimes of selective cooperation. It shares with American denominationalism the importance of high degrees of voluntariness of (religious) associations, the preference for internally democratic structures, the avoidance of state sanctioning from above and the preference for building associations from below and in free rivalry with others. However, when it comes to answering the difficult questions of 'how to come from here to there?', it may be easier to start from existing NOCOPs and the urgent requirements for change 'to keep up with the times' (Ferrari 2005a: 8f). This makes this question practically and strategically all the more urgent.

16   Generally against the state crafting of associations from above: Hirst's criticism (1992: 473-477) of Cohen & Rogers; Bader 2001a: 42, 55-60.

17   They require and also stimulate frame reflection, a thorough revision of cognitive and normative patterns (Hoekema 2001; Parekh 2000: 331ff; Zinterer 2000).

18   See Ferrari's (2005a: 9) fourth requirement 'to reduce the degree of discretionary power enjoyed by public authorities in establishing the level to which each religion can have access by ensuring an effective system of claims against the decisions of the executive powers.'

19   See Ferrari's second requirement: '(i)ndispensable to maintain a certain proportion between the collaboration and support that the State offer to the various religions: if the range between those placed at the lower levels and at the higher levels is too wide, not only does equality suffer, but so does individual religious freedom.' (2005a: 9). See also Kraler 2007 for special admission rules for ministers of religions and for education of Imams.

20   See Ferrari's third requirement: 'The mobility of religious faiths throughout all the levels of the pyramid' must be guaranteed. The model 'must be open to the transformations of history: a constant correspondence between social reality and legal reality is essential' (2005a: 9). Yes, but how?

21 Staff of eight at COMECE Brussels office, six at KEK, and two at EHF, resulting in disparities in access to information and influence on decision-making in the Commission preparing directives. See also Willaime 2004; Koenig 2003 (and 2006: 18ff for more details on the weakness of Muslim organisations at EU level).

22 Structural inequalities and power asymmetries may restrict the freedom of minorities to define their interests, identities, self-respect and motivation to participate and their strategic options (Bader 2003c: 147) or to do so more autonomously. In my view, AD accepts these stepwise increasing thresholds of agency, will and organisational capacity as the inevitable price to be paid for non-elitist or non-paternalist forms of group representation (the state may invite them and create options but should not try to organise and demand or impose representation). In addition, if the processes of societal and cultural secularisation and *glocalisation* would not only undermine the rigid 'corporatist' systems of selective cooperation but also the minimally required collective, organisational capacity, as some sociologists predict (sect. 1.2), this would also undermine associative religious governance. Yet this is not a problem for AD, because it is justice-based and not about perfectionist conservationism. If most religions were to lose the will to be politically present and represented even if institutional opportunities are available and fair, so be it.

23 It is also important that a seat at the tables should not go hand in hand with additional monetary privileges: faith-based educational providers should be fairly and indiscriminately financed whether they are represented or not. The relevant analogy to exclude additional material unfairness would be the German five per cent clause for parties represented in parliament: parties below this threshold are indiscriminately publicly financed (according to the percentage of votes) in order to prevent additional material discrimination.

24 See Bader (1991: 291-298) for strategic dilemmas of resource-poor groups.

25 This is another, insufficiently recognised trade-off related to the balance between 'church autonomy' and external public scrutiny. However, a differentiated application of co-determination systems instead of imposing one model of democratic corporate governance on all may undermine existing, more developed models, as the case of *Societas Europeana* recently demonstrates.

26 Bader 2006 and 2007b, based on proposals by Phil Schmitter, Jörges & Nyer and others.

27 Casanova (2005: 12ff) rightly criticises the strong exclusionary tendencies of existing NOCOPs in Europe, but sketches a too rosy picture of the American constitutional model and denominationalism (23, 26-28).

Notes Chapter 9

1 If this is still unacceptable for determined ethno-religious secessionist movements, secession may in some cases (Bauböck 2000) be the only practicable and legitimate alternative to IP and to integrationist repression. Yet, the tragedies in Northern Ireland, the Balkans and on the Indian subcontinent vividly demonstrate that secession often ends in nightmares.

2 See Hirst (1994: 56f) for thin but strong forms. See my criticism: 2001d: 189f. See empirically for Canada: Jedwab (2005) and Biles, Tolley & Ibrahim (2005).

3 See contributions in Van Parijs (ed. 2004), Banting & Kymlicka 2005, Bader 2005d, 2006.

4 Again, voluntary participation is a better precondition for the development of civic and democratic virtues and inter-communal interactions. However, legal voluntariness of voting and party membership (stressed by Hirst & Rosenblum) should not

make us blind to the limits of free choice in cases of serious ascriptive cleavages and serious strategic dilemmas (Horowitz 1985: 298, 324ff, 344, 353f; Williams 1998: 205ff).

5   Fashionable 'management of diversity' policies (all individuals are so 'different' but ascriptive groups remain so unequal) tend to be fairly unsuccessful if not extended into minority-inclusive democratic corporate governance policies, see also Estlund 2003: 142-144, and chap. 9.

6   The irony and dialectics of this argument by Estlund is absent from civil society debates and also not clearly seen by Rosenblum and Warren. Compulsion in the Army (Estlund 2003: 75) and in workplaces may have much neglected beneficial effects if it is not too harsh (as usually in prisons). Mandatory government education, however, is legally proscribed (10).

7   For policies to prevent reproduction of 'dead end jobs' and 'dead end markets', see: Engelen 2003 and Rath 2004.

8   Territorial concentration and direct physical interaction seem to be a condition of retaining and transforming cultures even under conditions of the World Wide Web: transforming mosaics of collective cultures versus individualising 'melting pots'. As in education (chap. 10), less 'internal' cultural or religious diversity may be more conducive to more overall diversity in societies.

9   Actually, voluntarism fosters residential self-segregation of the 'white rich' (see also Estlund 2003: 8, 64ff, 130) and reactive self-segregation of minorities (67f).

10   Berg 2003, Bader 2006a for more agonistic versions of recognition.

11   Policies to 'enforce' or 'impose' inter-communal mingling in recreational activities, in friendship, mating, marriage or religious practices are so clearly incompatible with basic civil liberties that nobody dares to defend them, although an increase in these mixings actually has the most profound effects in terms of respect toleration (Hollinger 2003a and Estlund 2003 for the US).

12   Nordlinger's claims (1972: 32) are thoughtfully rejected by Sisk 1996: 70.

13   See Bader 2001 for documentation and refutation of this criticism; See 2005: 86ff for the real dilemmas of MCP and ways to resolve them more productively.

14   See recent diatribes against multiculturalism in the Netherlands and the external intervention into these debates on the Blok committee report by exporters of a stylised French Republican model (Giles Kepel) or an English 'diversity' model (Trevor Phillip). Now that Paris has been in flames, French-style republicans have a lot of food for thought.

15   See extensively: Bader (1991, specified for 'ethnic' conflicts: 1995). See Lijphart's favourable conditions (1977: 54; 1985; 1991: 497ff).

16   See generally Gurr (1993), Horowitz (1985) and G. Smith (2000). In addition, arguments against DIP, referring to the Break Down of the Soviet Union or Yugoslavia (Offe 2000 and many others) are not persuasive against the further development of DIP in established democracies like Canada or the Netherlands (para. 6.4.2: from cell 2 to 4 in figure 7.1). The transitions from non-democratic IP (like South Africa) to DIP and AD seem to be easier than from monist types of non-democratic government (Lijphart 1985). See Junne & Verkoren (eds.) (2005: 308, Table 17.1) for a holistic approach in the associationalist spirit to post-conflict development.

17   See, however, Frey 2004. Yet, one should be aware of the fact that these arguments can be (and have been) easily extended against any type of liberal-democratic polity in favour of autocracy. In addition, one should be aware of the self-fulfilling prophecy of the logic of distrust and escalation in some readings of si vis pacem para bellum. It is enough to reject the general charge here that AD would only be feasible under normal conditions or 'in good weather'. Yet I share the objection that it is vulnerable in very 'rough weather'. I bracket the discussion of other important contex-

tual factors here as minority-majority relations, dynamics of escalation, coincidental events, timing and also broad background conditions (see briefly Bader 2003c: 155f).

Notes Chapter 10

1   Weak states have been unable to realise mandatory education and very much depends on religious non-governmental schools (in European history) and/or private non-governmental providers (many recent African states). It also seems safe to say that a certain minimal threshold of equal educational opportunities for all children requires a fairly strong sector of governmental education. However, if this threshold is eventually realised, states can reduce their role as educational providers.

2   See for Canada: Campbell 2004: 187, 203. I also resist the temptation to use highly aggregated country templates (e.g. France (near the civic republican pole), the Netherlands ('unique' (Wolf & Macedo 2004: 68) near the pluralist pole) and the US in between (Galston 2004: 318ff), or European regimes ('colossal, excessive' regulation) versus the US (Witte 2004: 365; Garnett 2004: 332), or European regimes (state, regulation) vs. US (constitutional freedoms, choice, civil society) because they tend to reproduce mythical pictures of integrated educational systems preventing the discussion of the pros and cons of practices regarding specific issues from which we are better able to learn.

3   Wolf & Macedo 2004: IX; Justice Brennan (quoted in Garnett 2004: 325), and Justice Stevens (quoted in Campbell 2004: 188). For 'ghost stories to frighten the gullible' in the US, see Glenn 2004: 343; Garnett 2004: 326 and Witte 2004: 355. For Ontario's human rights commissioner, see Campbell 2004: 187, 203. Similar dramatised accusations, guided by moral and political panics, were recently raised in the Netherlands against Muslim schools, see Shahid & Koningsveld 2006; Driessen & Merry 2006.

4   In the US, the judicial oversight and legal battles are much stronger whereas in European countries discretion for democratic legislation is greater. Classic liberals (McConnell 2004: 134) are suspicious whereas civic republicans and proponents of 'democratic education' (Gutmann 2004, Rosenblum 2004) favour more discretion.

5   McConnell's confrontation of liberalism versus democracy suggests otherwise (2002: 102). Particularly misleading (Macedo 2002: 8) are his statements that it is 'time to discard the notion of democratic control'. However, in my view, even he does not make such a choice.

6   Glenn & Groof 2002; Witte 2004: 358. McConnell is not as outspoken and is rightfully criticised by Rosenblum 2004: 154f.

7   See Wolf & Macedo 2004: 23f for Garnett & Glenn. Choice is always translated as 'parents choice' by Glenn & Groof 2002. They also play the 'either state or family and parents' and the 'final authority' game (2002a: 71f) and vote for parental and familial authority.

8   This is criticised by Dwyer 2002; Reich 2002, 2006 and also Gorard 2004: 164. Pupils are mostly treated as objects whose legitimate (basic or best) interests have to be cared for by either parents or governmental educational authorities (Macedo 2002: 14f; Gutmann 2002: 26; 28f; Wolf & Macedo 2004: 8). The voices of maturing students and their representatives are rarely taken seriously. They are also absent from Rosenblum's discussion (2002: 152, 166).

9   This is more clearly pointed out by McConnell than Gutmann recognises (2002: 28f) but even beyond the requirements of civic minimalism, parental authority cannot and should not be 'supreme'. See the appropriate balance established by Justice

La Forest of the Canadian Supreme Court (in *B (R) v Children's Aid Society of Metro-politan Toronto*) quoted in Glenn & Groof (2002: 150).

10   Alberta School Law 1999 c 28 s3 (Glenn & Groof 2002: 177f; for Norway: 411). See Harris 2004: 105 for England and Wales. Part of the core is clearly to prevent racism and authoritarianism (Glenn & Groof 2002: 6, 577). See Harris (2002: 113) for the ruling of the ECHR on corporal punishment in *Campbell and Cosans v. United Kingdom* (4.4).

11   See Glenn & Groof 2002: 582f for Sweden; Reuter (2002: 218f) for Germany. Both within states and in a comparative perspective, the crucial question remains: '*which* civic virtues?', see Galston 2002: 321.

12   The ban on *anti-racism* in laws and regulations is much stronger and clearer than the requirement to teach *sex and gender equality*, partly because many religions learned only fairly recently to oppose sexism and genderism and some orthodox in-terpretations of Christianity, Judaism and Islam still resist learning their lessons, while only some weird, racist Protestant fundamentalists (e.g. the American South-ern Presbyterian Church) teach racist versions of Christianity.

13   Dijkstra et al. 2004: 71ff: 'non-public schools are generally more effective in their teaching than are public schools'. The most important reasons for this are 'better educational administration, stronger value-oriented relationship(s) among parents and schools, and more deliberate self-selection process', clearly not 'social segrega-tion' or selection of better-qualified student body (72). Wolf & Macedo 2004: 21ff; Campbell 2004: 208; Dronkers 2004: 287ff, 306ff and Glenn 2004: 340, 344. All evidence is contested but the onus lies clearly on those who claim the opposite.

14   Campbell 2004: 189 for Canada (Fraser & Friedman report); Dronkers 2004 for Eur-opean countries.

15   Dijkstra et al. (2004: 81). 'It is increasingly argued that religious, especially Catholic, schools not only provide more effective learning environments but also offer a more effective civic education' (Dronkers 2004: 287, 295f (for Belgium), for France (297), for some German *Länder* (302). See the strong claims by McConnell (2002: 125-128); Campbell 2004: 210 for the results of the IEA study of the effects of civic edu-cation in 24 nations.

16   Glenn & Groof 2002: 584; Macedo 2002: 10; McConnell 2002: 120, 130-133; Gut-mann 2002: 173; Dronkers 2004: 308; Wolf & Macedo 2004: 14 and Gorard 2004: 143ff, see his table 5.1: Class 'Segregation Index' for all EU countries.

17   Galston 2002, Glenn & Groof 2002. School desegregation depends on housing de-segregation, which, compared with workplace segregation, is much more difficult to police. Individual white home owners' decisions to flee or avoid mixed neighbour-hoods 'are not even open to legal challenge' (Estlund 2003: 65f).

18   Apart from radical Jacobins and state socialists, no one seems to defend this. How-ever, socialist and social-democratic education policies also strongly favoured govern-mental schools and the extremely low percentage of non-governmental schools in Finland, Sweden and Norway is a testimony of this heritage.

19   See Meuret 2004 for France; McConnell 2002 for the *USA vs. Galston* 2002: 322.

20   Glenn & Groof 2002: 5; Vermeulen 2004: 49; Gorard 2004: 148 and Glenn & Groof 2002: 585f.

21   Religious schools are permitted to reject students only if there is a 'compelling legiti-mate interest' (Vermeulen 2004: 45) and if they consistently apply religious criteria (37 for the Netherlands). See Glenn & Groof 2002: 171f and 2002a: 149f for the Eur-opean Court. See the *Maimonides* case (1988) for difficulties stemming from the overlap of ethnic and religious criteria.

22   McConnell 2002: 131; Campbell 2004: 208; Glenn & Groof 2002: 17.

23 Cases of massive overlap in the sense of 'mono-religious and mono-ethnic' (Vermeulen 2004: 53) under-class schools are obviously of particular concern (see also Glenn & Groof 2002a and Dronkers & Levels 2005).

24 See McConnell 2002: 129 for a refutation of the civic-republican argument 'that common schools are worth the increased divisiveness, hegemony, and mush because of the supreme value of having children educated in diverse classrooms, with students of different racial, cultural, socio-economic, and religious backgrounds.' See also Macedo 2002: 17; Galston 2002.

25 McConnell 2002: 122ff; Wolf & Macedo 2004: 24; Glenn & Groof 2002: 24, 164.

26 Vermeulen 2004: 38 ('probably do not oblige states to fund') and Glenn & Groof 2002: 578, and 2002a: 245ff for emerging European law and jurisdiction (Glenn & Groof 2002: 578 'emerging as an international legal norm'). See particularly the *Lüster Resolution* of March 1984 of the EP, Art. 9 (Glenn & Groof 2002a: 265). The legal situation in the US after Zelman is open: Galston 2004: 321f, Garnett 2004: 324; McConnell 2002: 120. My understanding of 'fairly equal funding' is compatible with new 'adequacy' standards increasingly used by US courts and does not require fully equalising per-pupil expenditures across states, and districts in governmental and non-governmental schools (Liebman & Sabel 2003: 24ff).

27 For country studies, see: Macedo & Wolf 2004, for comparative analysis: Glenn & Groof 2002: 578f, 584ff, chart 2 and 2002a, chap. 9.

28 See para. 1.3.3.6 for an extremely rough sketch of the 'market share' of student enrolment in non-governmental, religious schools. See Wolf & Macedo (eds.) 2004 and Glenn & Groof 2002 for more detailed information.

29 Only Bulgaria, Greece, Iceland, Italy, Luxemburg, Portugal, Russia, Scotland and Switzerland do not (Glenn & Groof 2002a: chart 2, row 5). See also Fase 1994 and Bader 1998a: 195-199, 210f.

30 Most transparently in the Danish taximeter system that comprises four grants: a basic grant (lump sum), a teaching grant, an administration/operations grant and a building grant, based on the actual levels of verified number of enrolled pupils (Glenn & Groof 2002: 190).

31 Complexity and lack of transparency of existing systems of public funding (Leenknegt 1997, 223ff) are the outcome of fierce historical struggles and highly sensitive, negotiated arrangements that are difficult to change. Yet clear and transparent principles, standards, rules, procedures and practices of funding are preferable because they would enable more stability and predictability for educational providers, they provide better chances for judicial appeal against unfair administrative discretion of governmental authorities, and they contribute to an open, well-informed public debate and political decision-making.

32 Ontario had a fully equally funded, quasi-public Catholic system but did not provide financial support for 'private religious schools'. This was brought before the court in 1996 in *Adler v. Ontario* but the court decided that the Canadian Constitution would allow this. In 1999, the UNHCR ruled that this was in violation of the ICCPR (Campbell 2004: 201ff; Glenn & Groof 2002a: 154ff). In 2001, a new tax credit system was introduced.

33 Glenn & Groof 2002a: 186f for Sugerman, Jencks et al.); my criticism of Hirst's proposal: Bader 2001a: 46f, 2001b: 192f, 197). Today, I would emphasise more clearly that voucher financing should not replace but supplement other diverse forms of direct public financing.

34 See Bader 1998a: 195ff for a brief overview of attempts to pluralise governmental schools in Western European countries. Today, I would like to highlight the important role of a diverse non-governmental sector for the overall pluralisation of educational regimes and that certain minimum standards should be required in both sec-

tors to live up to basic requirements of living in a democratic and culturally widely diverse society. More demanding pluralisation of ethos and content of education should not be imposed but should convince parents and students by way of attractive examples.

35   Both in Europe (Vermeulen 2004: 34f) and in the US (Galston 2004: 319ff for *Meyer* 1923; *Farrington* 1927; Glenn 2004: 342 for *Pierce* 1925; Glenn & Groof 2002: 245 for *Ohio v. Wishner*. See Campbell (2004: 203) for Canada.

36   Garnett (2004: 324f vs. 'ideological commandeering'); see Glenn & Groof 2002: 591; 2002a: 247.

37   In the Netherlands, *vrije scholen*, and in England and Wales, independent schools (Harris 2004: 102f, Leenknegt 1997: 107ff) are exempted from regulation, inspection and control. See Groof 2004: 166 for Belgium.

38   Witte (2004: 366). My version of AD, even more so than Paul Hirst's, focuses on this core of minimal financial accountability.

39   Belgium (Groof 2004: 176), the Netherlands (Vermeulen 2004: 46), Sweden, Denmark and Finland (Glenn & Groof 2002: 589). For the interesting experiment with the 'National Core Curriculum Bank' in Hungary, see Glenn & Groof 2002: 588.

40   For instance 'music and drama' (*Talmud Torah School* case; Harris 2004: 103f, 109f) or sex education (*Kjeldsen* case; Harris 2004: 109, 112).

41   This should not be misunderstood as an argument against obligations for schools to provide information on (i) admission of students; (ii) curriculum and pedagogy, (iii) student achievements, (iv) expenditure and financial information (Witte 2004: 363f). The public ranking of schools is more contested and proscribed in Denmark and Sweden.

42   Norway seems to still be free of any inspections (Glenn & Groof 2002: 593) and also of standard testing until the end of compulsory education (401f).

43   See the rulings of the ECHR in the *Kjeldsen case* (Glenn 2004: 341) and of the Spanish Constitutional Court in 1985 (Glenn & Groof 2002: 503f). Remarkably, the issue is almost completely neglected in the theoretical literature (e.g. Wolf & Macedo 2004: 15f).

44   The Flemish Education Council (*Onderwijsraad*) is composed of 'representatives of networks (i.e. recognised umbrella organisations of religious or philosophical and communal providers), trade unions, parents, students, economic and social experts, ministry officials'. Parents' and students' associations are supported by government. Half the Educational Inspectorate (*Onderwijsinspectie*) is composed of official government networks and half from the subsidised private educational networks, and this 'equal representation in the inspectorate corps is intended to guarantee objectivity' (Groof 2004: 177). In Denmark, non-governmental schools also participate in selecting inspectors (Glenn & Groof 2002: 593).

45   Some elements of associational standards setting and monitoring are also developing in American reforms of governmental education in opposition to misleading dichotomies of either 'top down' centralisation (Liebman & Sabel 2003: 31-38) or 'bottom up', grass-roots driven, anti-institutional, teacher-centric 'new localism' (39ff). The kernels of this kind of new approach to school governance are layered regimes of standards setting and monitoring, which provide fair amounts of autonomy for states, districts, schools and teachers (see 71ff for the development of the Texas Assessment of Academic Skills), which involve all of the relevant stakeholders in standard setting, monitoring (see 73 for the Texas School Improvement Initiative), insisting on the pivotal importance of internal compared to external accountability (134), shift the focus from sanctions to incentives, and introduce new ways to compare and learn from best practices and feedback among the different levels (see also Sabel 2004). Unfortunately, Liebman and Sabel bracket non-governmental schools com-

pletely and are in danger of reproducing the secularist bias of the new professionalism in education.

46   In the Netherlands this is between 200 to 300 pupils; in Norway 16; in Denmark 12
     pupils in the first, 20 in the second, and 28 from the third year of operation (Glenn
     & Groof 2002: 188).

47   In Belgium, the 'legal representatives of each recognized philosophical or religious
     community themselves organize the pedagogic inspection' (Groof 2004: 172).

48   See the Dutch Education Participation Act 1992 (Vermeulen 2004: 51; Leenknegt
     1997: 205ff); for England and Wales (Harris 2004: 119); for Denmark (Glenn &
     Groof (2002: 186, 188). In Spain, a democratic composition of school councils is
     prescribed by law and has greatly contributed to the loss of a sizeable part of the
     Catholic Church's previous control (Glenn & Groof 2002: 500).

49   See Groof 2004: 171) for qualified exemptions from co-determination in Belgium,
     and Leenknegt 1997: 201-210 for the Netherlands.

50   Orthodox religious minority schools try to extend their criticism of liberal-demo-
     cratic morality and virtues into the selection of teachers. Controlling actual teaching
     practices from the outside, particularly against the resistance of teachers, parents,
     school heads and associations of providers, is much more difficult if the internal or-
     ganisation of schools is not open, transparent and democratic (see chap. 7 for the
     difficult trade-off between autonomy and democracy; see also Eisgruber 2002: 59,
     70, 82; Rosenblum 2002: 154). In addition, control is then limited to *minimum* stan-
     dards and cannot induce more demanding, better performances.

51   Today, I have changed my generalised preference for public schools. Still, I believe
     that 'Democratic control, inspection and effective impact on changes of curricula,
     materials, methods and practices of teaching should ... be the litmus test' (Bader
     1998a: 200). However, I am now not generally 'convinced that semi-public and pub-
     lic institutions imply fewer obstacles in this regard'. If, and to the degree to which it
     is true that teachers in public schools are more committed liberal democrats, that
     textbooks and teacher's guides are better in public schools and, in addition, are more
     adequately implemented in teaching practice, this would be an important advantage
     of governmental schools. However, this should not simply be presumed but made
     plausible by comparative empirical evidence. In a personal communication, Frank
     Cunningham provides such evidence from his first-hand experience with developing
     philosophy courses, textbooks and teacher guides for 'public' (secular) and 'separate'
     (Catholic) schools in Ontario.

52   Gutmann (2002: 30, 41, 171) and Rosenblum (2002: 152f vs. 'government in the sin-
     gular', stressing the 'tug of war' among governmental authorities) rightly refute this
     charge.

53   Canada's provinces provide widely divergent 'multiple templates', 'laboratories'
     (Campbell 2004: 190ff) or a 'patchwork quilt' (Glenn & Groof 2002: 141).

54   Decentralisation is however not the same as actual autonomy. Switzerland has one
     of the most decentralised educational systems, but allows almost no autonomy for
     schools due to detailed, specified systems of regulation (Glenn & Groof 2002: 533f).
     Denmark is less decentralised but gives a huge amount of autonomy to the schools.

55   For the US, see Glenn & Groof 2002: 539ff; for Canada, Campbell 2004; Glenn &
     Groof 2002: 141ff, Australia (Glenn & Groof 2002: 9ff). New Zealand (377ff); Eng-
     land and Wales (Harris 2004; Gorard 2004); even Italy (Ribolzi 2004).

56   As in Italy (Ribolzi 2004), France (Meuret 2004) and also in some civic-republican
     defences of public schools in the US (astonishingly also by Rosenblum 2002: 150).

57   Markedly different to classical liberal criticism of mandatory state education (W. van
     Humboldt, J.S. Mill) and state paternalism. Gutmann, for example, does not give
     much substance to her claim that democratic education 'defends a mixed system of

private and public schooling' (2002: 171). Reich (2006: 20f) is much clearer in this regard: 'At least in principle, public, private, religious and even home schools can be successful in achieving the right ethos and common educational vision of the ideal of common schooling'.

58 Glenn 2004, Glenn & Gorard 2002a.

59 As in England and Wales 1997 (Harris 2004: 102). Liebman and Sabel also insist that new forms of school governance are not just a 'hybrid' of traditional hierarchy or markets (2003: 9), e.g. they involve new public-private infrastructures for professional development (59) and private (Just for Kids (75) and semi-public initiatives (Dana Centre).

60 See sect. 9.1; see Galston 2004: 317 for English pluralism. In the Christian tradition: Protestant *souvereinteit in eigen kring* and catholic *subsidiarity*. See also Glenn & Groof 2002a: 104f, Glenn 2004: 347; McConnell 2002.

61 For 'bootstrapping' in education, see: Liebman & Sabel (2003: 135); for mixed pension regimes: Engelen 2003.

References

Abou El Fadl, K. (2001), *Speaking in Gods Name*. Oxford: Oneworld Publications.
— et al. (eds.) (2002), *The Place of Tolerance in Islam*. Boston: Beacon Press.
Adanir, F. (2000), 'Religious Communities and Ethnic Groups under Imperial Sway'. ENCS Conference paper, Bremen 18-21 May.
— (2002), 'The Formation of a 'Muslim' Nation in Bosnia-Herzegovina', in Adanir, F. & S. Faroqhi (eds.), 267-304.
— & S. Faroqhi (eds.) (2002), The Ottomans and the Balkans. Leiden: Brill.
— (2002), 'Introduction', in F. Adanir & S. Faroqhi (eds.), 1-56.
Ahmad, I. (2005), 'From Islamism to Post-Islamism'. Ph.D. thesis, University of Amsterdam.
Ahmed, L. (1992), Women and Gender in Islam. New Haven: Yale University Press.
Ahonen, P. (April 2000), *A Minority State-Church in a Liberal Democracy*. Copenhagen: ECPR, 14-19.
Alexander, L. (1993), 'Liberalism, Religion, and the Unity of Epistemology'. *San Diego Law Review* 30: 763-797.
Anderson, J. (ed.) (2004), *Religion, Democracy and Democratization*. Special Issue of *Democratization*. New York and London: Taylor & Francis.
Asad, T. (1993), *Genealogies of Religion*. Baltimore: Johns Hopkins University Press.
— (2003), Formations of the Secular. Stanford: Stanford University Press.
Asscher-Vonk, I, & Groenendijk, C. (1999), *Gelijke behandeling: regels en realiteit*. The Hague: Sdu.
Audi, R. (1989), 'The Separation of Church and State and the Obligations of Citizenship'. *Philosophy and Public Affairs*, 18: 259-296.
— (1991), 'Religious Commitment and Secular Reason: A Reply to Prof. Weithman'. *Philosophy and Public Affairs*, 20/1: 66-76.
— (1997), 'The State, the Church, and the Citizen', in P. Weithman (ed.) *Religion and contemporary liberalism*. Notre Dame: University of Notre Dame Press, 38-75.

Bader, V. (1988), 'Macht of waarheid?' *Kennis en Methode* 12/2: 138-157.
— (1991), *Kollektives Handeln. Protheorie sozialer Ungleichheit und kollektiven Handelns, Teil II*. Opladen: Leske+Budrich.
— (1991a), 'The Constitution of Empowered Democracy: Dream or Nightmare?' in R. de Lange & K. Raes (eds.) *Plural Legalities. Critical Legal Studies in Europe*. Nijmegen: Ars Aequi Libri, 118/6-134/22.
— (1993), '*Viel Geltung und immer weniger Faktizität*', in H. Ganßmannand S. Krüger (eds.) *Produktion, Klassentheorie*. Hamburg: VSA, 50-78.
— (1995), *Rassismus, Ethnizität und Bürgerschaft*. Münster: Verlag Westfälisches Dampfboot.
— (1995a), 'Citizenship and Exclusion.' *Political Theory* 23: 2: 211-246.
— (1997), 'The Arts of Forecasting and Policy Making', in V. Bader (ed.) *Citizenship and Exclusion*. London etc.: MacMillan 153-172.
— (1997a), 'Fairly Open Borders', in V. Bader (ed.) *Citizenship and Exclusion*. London etc.: MacMillan, 28-62.

— (1997b), 'The Cultural Conditions of Trans-National Citizenship', *Political Theory* 25/6: 771-813.
— (1997c), 'Ethnicity and Class: a proto-theoretical mapping-exercise', in W. Isajiw (ed.) *Comparative Perspectives on Interethnic Relations and Social Incorporation*. Toronto: Canadian Scholars' Press, 103-128.
— (1998), 'Dilemmas of Ethnic Affirmative Action', *Citizenship Studies* 2/3: 435-473.
— (1998a), 'Egalitarian Multiculturalism', in R. Bauböck & J. Rundell (eds.) *Blurred Boundaries*. Ashgate: Aldershot, 185-222.
— (1999), 'For Love of Country'. *Political Theory* 27/3: 379-397.
— (1999a), 'Religious Pluralism. Secularism or Priority for Democracy?' *Political Theory* 27/5: 597-633.
— (1999b), 'Citizenship of the European Union.' *Ratio Juris* 12/2: 153-181.
— (2001), 'Culture and Identity. Contesting Constructivism'. *Ethnicities* 1/2: 251-273.
— (2001a), 'Problems and Prospects of Associative Democracy', in P. Hirst & V. Bader (eds.) *Associative Democracy – the real third way?* CRISPP 4/1: 31-70.
— (2001b), 'Associative Democracy and the Incorporation of Ethnic and National Minorities', in P. Hirst & V. Bader (eds.) *CRISPP* 4/1: 187-202.
— (2001c), 'Introduction', in *CRISPP* Vol. 4/1: 1-14.
— (2001d), 'Institutions, Culture and Identity of Trans-National Citizenship', in C. Crouch & K. Eder (eds.) *Citizenship, Markets, and the State*. Oxford: Oxford University Press, 192-212.
— (2001e), 'Cohesion, Unity and Stability in Modern Societies', in A. van Harskamp & A. Musschenga (eds.) *The Many Faces of Individualism*. Leuven: Peeters: 107-132.
— (2003), 'Religious Diversity and Democratic Institutional Pluralism'. *Political Theory* 31/2: 265294.
— (2003a), 'Religions and States', in *Ethical Theory and Moral Practice* 5/1: 55-91.
— (2003b), 'Taking Religious Pluralism Seriously', in *Ethical Theory and Moral Practice* 5/1: 3-22.
— (2003c), 'Democratic Institutional Pluralism and Cultural Diversity', in D. Juteau & C. Harzig (eds.) *The Social Construction of Diversity*. Berghahn, 131-167.
— (2005), 'Dilemmas of Multiculturalism', in *Canadian Diversity/Diversité Canadienne* 4/1: 86-89.
— (2005a), 'Introduction: The Future of Multiculturalism'. *Canadian Diversity/Diversité Canadienne* 4/1: 9-11.
— (2005b), 'Associative Democracy and Minorities Within Minorities', in A. Eisenberg & J. Spinner (eds.) *Minorities Within Minorities*. Cambridge: Cambridge University Press, 319-339.
— (2005c), 'Reasonable Impartiality and Priority for Compatriots'. *Ethical Theory and Moral Practice* 8: 3-105.
— (2005d), 'The Ethics of Immigration'. *Constellations* 13/3: 331-361.
— (2005e), Ethnic and Religious State Neutrality: Utopia or Myth? in H. Sicakkan & Y. Lithman (eds.) *Changing the Basis of Citizenship in the Modern State*. New York, Queenston: Edwin Mellen, 161-198.
— (2006), 'Building European Institutions', Forthcoming in S. Benhabib & I. Shapiro (eds.) (2007) *Identities, Affiliations, and Allegiances*. Cambridge: Cambridge University Press, 113-135.
— (2006a), 'Misrecognition, Power, and Democracy', in B. van den Brink & D. Owen (eds.) (2007) *Recognition and Power*. New York: Cambridge University Press, 238-269.
— (2006b), 'Defending Differentiated Policies of Multiculturalism'. Forthcoming in J. Biles & P. Spoonley. (eds.) *National Identities*. Special Issue of *Canadian Ethnic Studies* 9/3, September 2007.
— (2006c), 'Religions and the Myth of Secularization'. http://home.hum.uva.nl/oz/baderv.

— (2007), 'Artikel: (Staats-)Bürgerschaft'. Forthcoming in S. Gosepath et al. (eds.) *Handbuch der Politischen Philosophie und Sozialphilosophie*. Berlin: Walter de Gruyter.

— (2007a), 'Regimes of Governance of Religious Diversity in Europe. Introduction'. forthcoming in *JEMS* 33/6, Special Volume *State Governance of Islam in Europe*.

— (2007b), 'Komplexe Bürgerschaft'. Forthcoming in S. Zurbuchen (ed.) *Bürgerschaft und Migration*. LIT: Münster, 53-135.

— (2007c), 'Secularism, Public Reason or Moderately Agonistic Democracy?' Forthcoming in G. Levey & T. Modood (eds.).

— (2007d), 'Religions, Toleration, and Democracy' Paper for ECPR workshop in Pisa, 6-8 September.

— & A. Benschop (1989), *Ungleichheiten. Protheorie sozialer Ungleichheit und kollektiven Handelns. Teil I*. Opladen: Leske+Budrich.

— & E. Engelen (2003), 'Taking Pluralism Seriously', in *Philosophy and Social Criticism*, 29/4: 375-406.

— & Saharso, S. (2004), 'Contextualized Morality and Ethno-religious Diversity. Introduction'. *Ethical Theory and Moral Practice* 7/2: 107-115.

Banting, K. & Kymlicka, W. (2005), 'Multiculturalism and the Welfare State'. Canadian Diversity 4/1: 103-107.

Barber, B. (1984), *Strong Democracy*. Berkeley, etc.: University of California Press.

— (1988), *The Conquest of Politics*. Princeton: Princeton University Press.

Barbier, M. (1995), *La laïcité*. Paris L'Harmattan.

Barry, B. (2001), *Culture and Equality*. Cambridge: Polity Press.

Bartholomew, A. (1999), *Does a Deliberative Approach to Problems of Group Differentiated Rights 'Make All the Difference?'* Unpublished manuscript.

Bary, T. de (1983), *The Liberal Tradition in China*. Hong Kong: Chinese University Press.

Basdevant-Gaudemet (1995), 'Staat und Kirche in Frankreich', in Robbers (ed.), 127-158.

Bauberot, J. (1998), 'The Two Thresholds of Laïcization', in R. Bhargava (ed.), 94-136.

Bauböck, R. (1994), *Transnational Citizenship*. Avebury: Aldershot Press.

— (2002), Paradoxes of self-determination and the right to self-government. Vienna: IWE.

— (2002a), Cultural minority rights in public education? in A. M. Messina (ed.) *West European Immigration and Immigration Policy in the New Century*. Westport: Prager, 161-189.

— (2004), 11 February, e-mail to P. Weil et al.

Bauer, J. & Bell, A. (eds.) *The East Asian Challenge for Human Rights*. Cambridge: Cambridge University Press.

Beckford, J. (1987), 'The Restoration of Power to the Sociology of Religion, in T. Robbins & R. Robertson (eds.), 13-38.

— (1993), 'States, Governments, and the Management of Controversial New Religious Movements', in E. Barker et al. (eds.) *Secularization, Rationalism, and Sectarianism*. Oxford: Clarendon Press, 125-144.

— (2005), 'Muslims in the Prisons of Britain and France'. *Journal of Contemporary European Studies* 13/3, 125-144.

Beitz, C.R. (1989), *Political Equality*. Princeton: Princeton University Press.

Bell, D. (1998), 'The Limits of Liberal Justice', in *Political Theory* 26/4, 557-582.

Benhabib, S. (1996), 'Deliberative Rationality and Models of Democratic Legitimacy', in Behnhabib (ed.) *Democracy and Difference*. Princeton: Princeton University Press.

— (2002), *The Claims of Culture*. Princeton: Princeton University Press.

Berg, P. van den (2004), 'Be Prestige-Resilient!', in *Ethical Theory and Moral Practice* 7/2: 197-214.

Berghahn, S./Rostock, P. (2006), 'Cultural Diversity and Gender Equality – The German Case'. Conference Paper, Amsterdam Free University, 8-9 June.

Berry, J. et al. (2006), *Immigrant Youth in Transition*. Mahwah: Lawrence Erlbaum Association.

Bhargava, R. (ed.) (1998), *Secularism and its Critics*. Oxford: Oxford University Press.
— (1998), 'Introduction', in Bhargava (ed.), 1-30.
— (1998a), 'What is Secularism For?', in Bhargava (ed.), 486-542.
— (2005), 'Political Secularism'. Forthcoming in G. Levey & T. Modood (eds.) (2007).
Bhaskar, R. (1986), *Scientific Realism and Human Emancipation*. London: Verso.
— (1989), *Reclaiming Reality*. London: Verso.
Bielefeldt, H. (1998), *Philosophie der Menschenrechte*. Darmstadt: Wissenschaftliche Buchge-sellschaft.
— (2000), '"Western" versus "Islamic" Human Rights Conceptions?', in *Political Theory* 28 (1): 90-121.
Bijsterveld, S. C. van (1995), 'Staat und Kirche in den Niederlanden', in G. Robbers (ed.), 229-250.
Biles, J. et al. (2005), 'Does Canada have a Multicultural Future?' in *Canadian Diversity* 4: 1, 23-28.
Bilgrami, A. (1994), 'Two Concepts of Secularism', in *Economic and Political Weekly*, 9 July, 1749-1765.
— (1998), 'Secularism, Nationalism, and Modernity', in Bhargava (ed.), 380-417.
Birtek, F. (2006), 'From Affiliation to Affinity'. Forthcoming in S. Benhabib & I. Shapiro (eds.) *Identities, Affiliations, and Allegiances*. Cambridge: Cambridge University Press.
Bouma, G. (1999), 'From Hegemony to Pluralism', in *Australian Religion Studies Review* 12/2: 7-27.
— (2004), 'A Comparative Study of the Successful Management of Religious Diversity: Melbourne and Hong Kong', in *International Sociology* 19 (1): 5-24.
Bourdieu, P. (1987), 'Sociologues de la croyance et croyance de sociologues', and 'La dissolu-tion du religieux', in *Choses dites*. Paris: Éditions de Minuit, 106-123.
— (2000), *Pascalian Meditations*. Cambridge: Polity Press.
Bovens, M. (1993), 'Babel binnen het recht', in N. Huls N. & H. Stout (eds.) *Recht in een mul-ticulturele samenleving*. Zwolle: Tjeenk Willink, 159-172.
Bowen, J. (1998), *Islam, Law and Equality in Indonesia*. Cambridge: Cambridge University Press.
— (2004), 'Does French Islam Have Borders?' in *American Anthropologist* 106 (1): 43-55.
— (2004a), 'Beyond Migration: Islam as a Transnational Public Space', in *Journal of Ethnic and Migration Studies*, 30 (5): 879-894.
— (2004b), 'Muslims and Citizens', in *Boston Review*, February/March, 31-35.
— (2006), *Why the French Don't Like Headscarves*. Princeton: Princeton University Press.
— (2007), 'Europeanising the Governance of Religious Diversity'. Forthcoming in *JEMS* 33/6.
Brake, W. ter (2004), Religious War and the Cultural Politics of Peace. Unpublished manu-script.
Brubaker, R. (1996), *Nationalism reframed*. Cambridge: C Cambridge University Press.
— (2004), 'The Return of Assimilation', in *Ethnic and Racial Studies* 2004: 4, 531-548.
Bruce, S. (1992), 'Pluralism and Religious Vitality', in S. Bruce (ed.), 170-194.
— (2004), 'Did Protestantism Create Democracy?', in J. Anderson (ed.), 3-20.
— (2005), *Politics and Religion*Cambridge: Polity Press.
Brumberg, D. & Diamond, L. (2003), Introduction, in Diamond (ed.), ix-xxvi.

Cahill, D. et al. (2004), *Religion, Cultural Diversity and Safeguarding Australia*. Canberra: Commonwealth of Australia.
Campbell, D. (2004), 'The Civic Implications of Canada's Education System', in P. Wolf & S. Macedo (eds.), 187-212.
Canas, V. (1995), 'Staat und Kirche in Portugal', in Robbers, G. (ed.), 281-302.

Caney, S. (2001), 'Cosmopolitan Justice and Equalizing Opportunities', in *Metaphilosophy* 32: 1/2, 113-134.

Carens, J. (1987), 'Aliens and Citizens: the case for open borders', in *Review of Politics* 49/2, 251-273.

— (1997), 'Two Conceptions of Fairness', in *Political Theory* 25: 6, 814-820.

— (2000), *Culture, Citizenship, and Community*. Oxford: Oxford University Press.

— (2004), 6, 9 February, e-mail to P. Weil et al.

— (2004a), 'A Contextual Approach to Political Theory', in *Ethical Theory and Moral Practice* 7, 117-132.

— & M. Williams (1998), 'Muslim Minorities in Liberal Democracies', in R. Bhargava (ed.), 137-176.

Casanova, J. (1994), *Public Religions in the Modern World*. Chicago and London: University of Chicago Press.

— (2005), 'Immigration and the New Religious Pluralism'. Paper Symposium: Religion and Multicultural Citizenship, Sydney 11-13 July. Forthcoming in T. Banchoff (ed.) *Democracy and the New Religious Pluralism*. Oxford: Oxford University Press, Spring 2007.

Casey (1995), 'Staat und Kirche in Irland', in G. Robbers (ed.), 159-184.

Chatterjee, P. (1998), 'Secularism and Tolerance', in R. Bhargava (ed.), 345-379.

Chaves, M. & Cann, D. (1992), 'Regulation, Pluralism, and Religious Market Structure', in *Rationality and Society*, 4: 272-290.

Christis, J. (1998), *Arbeid, Organisatie en Stress*. Amsterdam: Het Spinhuis.

Coene G. & Longman, C. (2005), 'Ten Geleide', in G. Coene & C. Longman (eds.) *Eigen emancipatie eerst?* Gent: Academia Press, 1-28.

Cohen, J. (2004), 'Minimalism About Human Rights: The Most We Can Hope For?' in *The Journal of Political Philosophy* 12/2, 190-213.

— (ed.) (1999), *Is Multiculturalism Bad For Women?* Princeton: Princeton University Press.

Cohen, J. & Rogers, J. (1992), 'Secondary Associations and Democratic Governance', in *Politics and Society*. 20/4: 391-472.

Cohen, J. & Sabel, C. (2002), Directly-Deliberative Polyarchy. Website Charles Sabel: http://www2.law.columbia.edu/sabel/papers/DDP.html

Cohen, J. L. (2001), 'Personal Autonomy and the Law', in B. Rössler (ed.) *Privacies*. Stanford: Stanford University Press, 73-97.

Cole Durham, Jr., W. (2001), 'The Right to Autonomy in Religious Affairs', in G. Robbers (ed.) *Church Autonomy*. Frankfurt am Main: Peter Lang, 683-714.

Connolly, W.E. (1995), *The Ethos of Pluralization*. Minneapolis: University of Minnesota Press.

— (1999). *Why I am not a Secularist*. Minneapolis: University of Minnesota Press.

— (2005), *Pluralism*. Durham, NC: Duke University Press.

Creppell, I. (1996), 'Locke on Toleration', in *Political Theory* 24/2: 200-240.

Crouch, C. (2000), *Social Change in Western Europe*. Oxford: Oxford University Press.

Cunningham, F. (1987), *Democratic Theory and Socialism*. Cambridge: Cambridge University Press.

— (2003), *Theories of Democracy*. London and New York: Routledge.

— (2005), 'The Conflicting Truths of Religion and Democracy', in *Social Philosophy Today* 21: 65-80.

Dagger, R. (1997), *Civic Virtues*. New York: Oxford University Press.

Davie, G. (1996), 'Contrastes dans l'héritage religieux de l'Europe', in G. Davie et al. (eds.) (1996), *Identités religieuses en Europe*. Paris: La Découverte, 43-64.

Delfiner, H. (without year, 1966), *Church state relations and religious instruction in the public elementary schools of Switzerland, West-Germany and the United States*. Ph.D. thesis.

Deveaux, M. (2005), 'A Deliberative Approach to Conflicts of Culture', in A. Eisenberg & J. Spinner (eds.) *Minorities Within Minorities*. Cambridge: Cambridge University Press, 340-362.

Dewey, J. (1927), *The Public and Its Problems*. Athens: Swallow Press.

Diamond, L. et al. (eds.) (2003), *Islam and Democracy in the Middle East*. Baltimore: Johns Hopkins University Press.

Dyke, V. van (1995), 'The Individual, the State, and Ethnic Communities in Political Theory', in W. Kymlicka (ed.). *The Rights of Minority Cultures*. Oxford: Oxford University Press, 31-56.

Dijkstra, A., Jonkers, J. & Karsten, S. (2004), 'Private Schools as Public Provisions for Education: School Choice and Market Forces in the Netherlands', in P. Wolf & S. Macedo (eds.), 67-90.

Dobbelaere, K. (1992), 'Church Involvement and Secularization', in E. Baker et al. (eds.) *Secularization, Rationalization and Sectarianism*. Oxford: Clarendon, 19-36.

Dommelen, E. van (2003), *Constitutionele Rechtspraak vanuit rechtsfilosofisch perspectief*. Boom Juridische Uitgevers.

Dronkers, J. (2004), 'Do Public and Religious Schools Really Differ?', in P. Wolf & S. Macedo (eds.), 287-313.

— & Levels, M. (2005), 'Migranten en school segregatie in hoogontwikkelde landen', in S. Karsten et al. (eds.) *Grenzen aan de maakbaarheid*. Antwerp and Apeldoorn: Garant.

Driessen, G. & Merry, M. (2005), Islam and schools: The Dutch experience, in (CIPMO), *Islam in Europe. European Islam*. International conference on Islam. Milan, Italy, 22-23 June.

Dübeck, I. (1995), 'Staat und Kirche in Dänemark', in G. Robbers (ed.), 39-60.

Dworkin, R. (1977), *Taking Rights Seriously*. London: Duckworth.

Dwyer, J. (2002), 'Changing the Conversation about Children's Education', in S. Macedo & Y. Tamir (eds.), 314-357.

Eisenach, E. J. (2000), The Next Religious Establishment. Lanham etc.: Rowman & Littlefield.

Eisenberg, A. (1995), Reconstructing Political Pluralism. Albany: State University of New York Press.

— (2005), 'Identity and Liberal Politics', in A. Eisenberg & J. Spinner (eds.), 249-270.

Eisenlohr, P. (2006), 'The politics of diaspora and the morality of secularism: Muslim identities and Islamic authority in Mauritius', in *J. Roy Anthropological Institute* 12, 305-412.

Eisenstadt, S. N. (1987), *The European Civilization in Comparative Perspective*. Oslo: Scandinavian University Press.

— (2000), *Die Vielfalt der Moderne*. Velbrück: Weilerswist.

Eisgruber, C. (2002), 'How Do Liberal Democracies Teach Values?', in S. Macedo & Y. Tamir (eds.), 58-86.

Elfstrøm, G. (1990), *Ethics for a Shrinking World*. Houndsmill and London: MacMillan.

Engelen, E. (2000), *Economisch burgerschap in de onderneming*. Amsterdam: Thela Thesis Pub.

— (2003), 'How to Combine Openness and Protection?', in *Politics and Society* 31: 4, 503-536.

— (2004), 'Associatief-democratische dromen over verplaatste politiek', in E. Engelen & M. Sie (eds.), 307-338.

— & Sie, M. (2004), 'Democratische vernieuwing', in E. Engelen & M. Sie (eds.) *De staat van de democratie*. Amsterdam: Amsterdam University Press, 17-38.

Enyedi, Z. (2003), 'Conclusion: Emerging Issues in the Study of Church-State Relations', in J. Madeley & Z. Enyedi (eds.), 218-232.

Esbeck, C. (2001), 'A Typology of Church-State Relations in Current American Thought', in Lugo (ed.) *Religion, Public Life, and the American Polity*. Knoxville: University of Tennessee Press, 336.

— & Carlson-Thies, S. et al. (2004), *The Freedom of Faith-Based Organizations to Staff on a Religious Basis*. Washington DC: Center for Public Justice.

Esposito, J. & Voll, J. (1996), *Islam and Democracy*. New York and Oxford: Oxford University Press.

Estlund, C. (2003), *Working Together*. Oxford and New York: Oxford University Press.

Etzioni, A. (1996), *The New Golden Rule*. New York: Basic Books.

Falk, R. (1995), *On Humane Governance*. Cambridge: Polity Press.

Ferrari, S. (1995), 'Staat und Kirche in Italien', in G. Robbers (ed.), 185-210.

— (2002), 'Islam and the Western European Model of Church and State Relations', in W. Shadid & P. Koningsveld (eds.), 6-19.

— (2005), 'The legal status of Muslims in Western Europe'. Unpublished manuscript.

— (2005a), The Secular State and the Shaping of Muslim Representative Organizations in Western Europe. Unpublished manuscript.

— & Bradney, A. (eds.) (2000), *Islam and European legal Systems*. Ashgate: Aldershot.

Fetzer, J.S. & Soper, J.C. (2004), *Muslims and the State in Britain, France and Germany*. Cambridge University Press.

Figgis, J.N. (1914), *Churches in the modern state*. London etc.: Longmans, Green and Co.

Fish, S. (1997), 'Mission Impossible' in *Columbia Law Review* 97: 8, 2255-2333.

Flathman, R.A. (1998), 'It All Depends...', in *Political Theory* 26: 1, 81-84.

Flora, P. & Urwin, D. et al. (1999), 'State Formation, Nation-Building and Mass Politics in Europe'. Oxford: Oxford University Press

Føllesdal, A. (1997), 'Do welfare obligations end at the boundaries of the Nation-State?' in Koslowski & Føllesdal (eds.) *Restructuring the Welfare State*. Berlin: Springer Verlag, 1997, 145-163.

Fogelin, R. (2003), *Walking the Tightrope of Reason*. Oxford and New York: Oxford University Press.

Forst, R. (2004), 'The Limits of Toleration', in *Constellations* 11/3: 3, 12-25.

— (2006), '"To tolerate means to insult": Toleration, recognition, and emancipation', in B. van den Brink & D. Owen (eds.) (2007) *Power and Recognition*. Cambridge: Cambridge University Press, 215-217.

Fox, J. (2006), 'World Separation of Religion and State Into the 21st Century', in *Comparative Political Studies* 39/5: 537-569.

Frankenberg, G. & Rödel, U. (1981), *Von der Volkssouveränität zum Minderheitenschutz*. Frankfurt: EVA.

Frey, B. (2004), *Dealing With Terrorism – Stick or Carrot?* Cheltenham and Northampton: Edward Elgar.

Fung, A. (2003), 'Associations and Democracy', in *Annual Review of Sociology* 29, 515-539.

Fung, A. & Wright, E. O. (2001), 'Deepening Democracy: Innovations in Empowered Participatory Governance', in *Politics and Society* 29/1: 5-41.

Galanter, M. (1966), 'Religious Freedoms in the United States: A Turning Point', in *Wisconsin Law Review*. Spring, 217-296.

— (1998), 'Secularism, East and West', in R. Bhargava (ed.), 234-267.

— (1998a), 'Hinduism, Secularism and the Indian Judiciary', in R. Bhargava (ed.), 268-297.

Galston, W. (1991), *Liberal Purposes*. Cambridge, MA: Cambridge University Press.

— (2002), *Liberal Pluralism*. Cambridge: Cambridge University Press

— (2004), 'Civic Republicanism, Political Pluralism, and the Regulation of Private Schools', in P. Wolf & S. Macedo (eds.), 315-323.

Garnett, R. (2004), 'Regulatory Strings and Religious Freedom', in P. Wolf & S. Macedo (eds.), 324-338.

Gastelaars, M. (1997), *'Human Services' in veelvoud*. Utrecht: SWP.

Geuss, R. (2002), 'Liberalism and its Discontents', *Political Theory* 30/3: 320-338.

Gill, A. (2001), 'Religion and Comparative Politics', in *Annual Review of Political Science* (4): 117-138.

Glendon, M.A. & Yanes, R.F. (1991), 'Structural Free Exercise', in *Michigan Law Review* 90: 3, 477-550.

Glenn, C.L. (2000), The Ambiguous Embrace: Government and Faith-Based Schools and Social Agendas.

Glenn, R. (2004), 'School Choice as a Question of Design', in P. Wolf & S. Macedo (eds.), 339-354.

—   & Groof, J. de (2002), *Finding the Right Balance. Freedom, Autonomy and Accountability in Education* vol. I. Utrecht: Lemma Publishers.

—   & Groof, J. de (2002a), *Finding the Right Balance* vol. II.

Goodin, R. & Tilly, C. (eds.) (2006), *The Oxford Handbook of Contextual Political Analysis*. Oxford: Oxford University Press.

Gorard, S. (2004), 'School Choice Policies and Social Integration: The Experience of England and Wales', in P. Wolf & S. Macedo (eds.), 131-156.

Gotanda, N. (1991), 'A critique of "Our Constitution is Color-Blind"', in *Stanford Law Review*, 44: 1, 1-68.

Gray, J. (2000), *Two Faces of Liberalism*. Cambridge: Polity Press.

Greenawalt, K. (1995), *Private Consciences and Public Reasons*. Oxford: Oxford University Press.

—   (2000), 'Five Questions about Religion Judges Are Afraid to Ask', in N. Rosenblum (ed.) *Obligations of Citizenship and Demands of Faith*. Princeton etc.: Princeton University Press, 196-244.

Griffin, J. (2001), 'First Steps in an Account of Human Rights', in *European Journal of Philosophy* 9/3, 306-327.

Grillo, R. D. (1998), *Pluralism and the Politics of Difference*. Oxford: Clarendon Press

—   (ed.) (2004), *Islam, Transnationalism, and the Public Sphere in Western Europe*, *JEMS* 30/ 5.

Groof, J. de (2004), 'Regulating School Choice in Belgium's Flemish Community', in P. Wolf & S. Macedo (eds.), 157-186.

Guillaumin, C. (1995), *Racism, Sexism, Power and Ideology*. London: Routledge.

Gutmann, A. (1987), *Democratic Education*. Princeton: Princeton University Press.

—   (2000), 'Religion and State in the United States', in N. Rosenblum (ed.), 127-164

—   (2002), 'Civic Minimalism, Cosmopolitanism, and Patriotism', in S. Macedo & Y. Tamir (eds.), 23-57.

—   (2002a), 'Can Publicly Funded Schools Legitimately Teach Values in a Constitutional Democracy?', in S. Macedo & Y. Tamir (eds.), 170-191.

—   & Thompson, D. (1996), *Democracy and Disagreement*. Cambridge and London. Belknap Press of Harvard.

Habermas, J. (1992), *Faktizität und Geltung*. Frankfurt: Suhrkamp.

—   (1995), 'Reconciliation through the Public Use of Reason', in *Journal of Philosophy* 92/3: 109-131.

—   (2001), *Glauben und Wissen*. Frankfurt: Suhrkamp.

Hacker-Cordon, C. (2003), *Global Injustice and Human Malfare*. Unpublished Ph.D. thesis. Yale University.

Handy, R. T. (1976), *A History of the Churches in the United States and Canada*. Oxford: Clarendon Press.

Hannum, H. (1990), *Autonomy, Sovereignty, and Self-Determination*. Philadelphia: University of Pennsylvania Press.

Harding, S. (1990), *Whose science? Whose Knowledge?* Open University Press.

Harris, N. (2004), 'Regulation, Choice, and Basic Values in Education in England and Wales', in P. Wolf & S. Macedo (eds.), 91-130.

HRL = Harvard Law Review Note (1987), 'Developments in the Law: Religion and the State'. *Harvard Law Review*, 100: 1606-1781.

Hayward, C. (2003), 'Binding Problems, Boundary Problems'. Paper Yale October 2003, forthcoming in S. Benhabib & I. Shapiro (eds.) (2007).

Heikkilae, M., Knuutila, J. & Scheinin, M. (1995), 'State and Church in Finland', in Robbers (ed.), 279-294.

Hervieu-Léger, D. (1986), *Vers un nouveau christianisme?* Paris: Cerf.

— (1996), 'La religion des Européens' in Davie, G. et al. (eds.) *Identités religieuses en Europe*. La Découverte: Paris, 9-24.

Hirsch, H.N. (2000), 'Let Them Eat Incidentals', in N. Rosenblum (ed.), 280-293.

Hirschman, A. (1970), *Exit, Voice, Loyalty*. Cambridge: Harvard University Press.

— (1978), 'Exit, Voice, and the State', in *World Politics* 31/1, 92ff.

Hirst, P. (ed.) (1989), *The Pluralist Theory of the State*. London: Routledge.

— (1994), *Associative Democracy*. Cambridge: Polity Press.

— (2001), Comment. Amsterdam workshop.

— (2000), 'Figgis, Churches and the State', in D. Marquand & R. Nettler (eds.) *Obligations of Citizenship and Demands of Faith*. Princeton etc.: Princeton University Press, 104-120.

— & Bader, V. (eds.) (2001), *Associative Democracy: The Real Third Way*. London: Frank Cass.

Hoekema, A. (2001), 'Reflexive Governance and Indigenous Self-Rule: Lessons in Associative Democracy?' in P. Hirst & V. Bader (eds.), 157-186.

— (2004), *Rechtspluralisme en Interlegaliteit*. Amsterdam: Vossius Pers UvA.

— et al. (1998), *Integraal bestuur*. Amsterdam University Press.

Holder, C. (2005), 'Self-Determination as a Basic Human Right', in A. Eisenberg and J. Spinner (eds.) *Minorities Within Minorities*. Cambridge: Cambridge University Press, 294-318.

Hollinger, D. (1996), *Post-Ethnic America*. New York: Basic Books.

— (2003), 'Religious Disestablishment in Western Europe', in *Responsive Community* Spring, 25-30.

— (2003a), 'Amalgamation and Hypodescent,' in *American Historical Review*, December, 1363-1390.

Honig, B. (1999), 'My Culture Made Me Do It', in J. Cohen (ed.).

Horowitz, D. (1985), *Ethnic Groups in Conflict*. Berkeley: University of California Press.

— (1991), 'Ethnic Conflict Management for Policymakers,' in J. Montville (ed.) *Conflict and Peace-Making in Multiethnic Societies*. New York: Lexington, 115-130.

— (1991a), 'Making Moderation Pay', in J. Montville (ed.), 451-475.

Hunter, I. (2005), 'The Shallow Legitimacy of Secular Liberal Orders'. Forthcoming in G. Levey & T. Modood (eds.) (2007).

Iban, I.C. (1995), 'Staat und Kirche in Spanien', in G. Robbers (ed.), 99-126.

Ignatieff, M. (2004), *The Lesser Evil*. Edinburgh: Edinburgh University Press.

Ingram, D. (2004), *Rights and Fulfillment in the Era of Identity Politics*. New York etc.: Rowman & Littlefield.

Israel, J.I. (1995), *The Dutch Republic*. Oxford: Clarendon.

Jacobsohn, R.J. (2000), 'By the Light of Reason', in N. Rosenblum (ed.) *Obligations of Citizenship and Demands of Faith*. Princeton etc.: Princeton University Press, 294-320.

Jansen, Y. (2006), *Stuck in a Revolving Door*. Ph.D. thesis, University of Amsterdam.

Jedwab, J. (2005), 'Neither Finding nor Losing Our Way', in *Canadian Diversity* 4: 1, 95-102.

Jörges, C. (1999), 'Bureaucratic Nightmare, Technocratic Regime and the Dream of Good Transnational Governance', in C. Jörges & Vos (eds.), 3-18.

— (1999a), 'Good Governance' Through Comitology? in Jörges & Vos (eds.), 311-338.

John, M. (2000), 'National Movements and Imperial Ethnic Hegemonies in Austria 1867-1918. ENCS Conference Paper, Bremen, 18-21 May.

Jones, C. (1999), *Global Justice*. Oxford University Press: Oxford.

Joppke, C. & Morawska, E. (eds.) (2003), *Toward Assimilation and Citizenship*. New York: MacMillan.

Jordan, B. & Düvell, F. (2003), *The Boundaries of Equality and Justice*. Cambridge: Polity.

Junne, G. & Verkoren, W. (eds.) (2005), *Postconflict Development*. London: Lynne Rienner, Boulder.

Juteau, D. (1999), *L'ethnicité et ses frontières*. Montreal: Presses de l'Université de Montréal.

Kalyvas, S. (1996), *The Rise of Christian Democracy in Europe*. Ithaca etc.: Cornell University Press.

— (2000), Commitment Problems in Emerging Democracies', in *Comparative Politics* July: 379-398.

— (2003), Comments on Bader's paper 'The More Inclusion, the Less Motivation?' 5 October, Yale University.

Keane, J. (2000), 'Secularism?', in D. Marquand & R. Nettler (eds.) *Religion and Democracy*. Oxford: Blackwell, 5-19.

Kelley, D.M. (1987), The Supreme Court Redefines Tax Exemption, in T. Robbins & R. Robertson (eds.), 115-124.

Kepel, G. (1996), *Allah in the West*. Cambridge: Polity Press.

Khilnani, S. (1999), *The Idea of India*. New York: Farrar, Straus and Giroux.

Klausen, J. (2005), *The Islamic Challenge: Politics and religion in Western Europe*. London: Oxford University Press.

Koenig, M. (2003), *Staatsbürgerschaft und religiöse Pluralität in post-nationalen Konstellationen*. Marburg: Ph.D. thesis, Marburg University.

— (2004), 'Öffentliche Konflikte um die Inkorporation muslimischer Minderheiten in Westeuropa'. *Journal für Konflikt- und Gewaltforschung*, 6/6: 85-100.

— (2006), 'Incorporating Muslim Migrants in Western Nation States', in *Journal for International Migration and Integration* 6/2, 219-234.

— (2007), 'Europeanising the governance of religious diversity', forthcoming in *JEMS* 33/6.

Koopmans, R. & P. Stathman (eds.) (2000), *Challenging Immigration and Ethnic Relations Politics*. Oxford: Oxford University Press.

Korver, A. & Wilthagen, A. (2002), 'Werkdadig', in J. Outshoorn (ed.) *De bindende werking van concepten*. Amsterdam: Aksant 97-135.

Kraler, A. (2007), 'The Political Accommodation of Immigrant Religious Practices'. forthcoming in *JEMS* 33/6.

Kukathas, C. (1998), 'Liberalism and Multiculturalism: The Politics of Indifference', in *Political Theory* 26/5: 686-699.

— (2003), *The Liberal Archipelago*. Oxford: Oxford University Press.

Kymlicka, W. (1995), *Multicultural Citizenship*. Oxford: Oxford University Press.

— (1997), *States, Nations and Cultures*. Assen: Van Gorcum.

— (1997a), 'Liberal Complacencies', in *Boston Review*, Winter.

— (2001), *Politics in the Vernacular*. Oxford: Oxford University Press.

— (2002), *Contemporary Political Philosophy*. (2nd ed.). Oxford: Oxford University Press.

— (2005), 'The Uncertain Futures of Multiculturalism', in *Canadien Diversity* 4/1: 82-85.

— (2005a), 'Multicultural States and Intercultural Citizens'. Dutch translation in B. v. Leeuwen & R. Tinnevelt (eds.) *De multiculturele samenleving in conflict*. Leuven: Acco, 55-77.

Lash, K. (2001), 'Five Models of Church Autonomy', in G. Robbers (ed.), 303-319.

Laycock, D. (1997), 'The underlying unity of separation and neutrality', in *Emory Law Journal*, 46/1: 43-74.

Leenknegt, G. (1997), *Vrijheid van Onderwijs in 5 Europese Landen*. Deventer: Tjeenk Willink.

Leezenberg, M. (2001), *Islamitische Filosofie*. Amsterdam: Bulaaq.

Lefort, C. (1999), *Fortdauer des Theologisch-Politischen?* Vienna: Passagen Verlag.

Leggewie, C. (1993), *Alhambra*. Reinbek: Rowohlt.

Leiprecht, R. & Lutz, H. (1996), 'The Dutch Way', in Gstettner, P. & Auernheimer, G. (eds.) *Jahrbuch für Pädagogik*. Frankfurt, 239-262.

Levey, G. (1997), 'Equality, Autonomy, and Cultural Rights', in *Political Theory* 25/2: 215-248.

— (2006), 'Symbolic Recognition, Multicultural Citizens, and Acknowledgement', in *Australian Journal of Political Science* 41/3, 355-370.

— (2006a), 'Identity and Rational Revisability', in I. Primoratz A. & Pavkovic (eds.) *Identity and Self-Determination*. Aldershot: Ashgate.

— & Modood, T. (eds.) (2007), *Secularism, Religion, and Multicultural Citizenship*. Cambridge: Cambridge University Press.

Levy, J. (2000), *The Multiculturalism of Fear*. Oxford: Oxford University Press.

Liebman, J. & Sabel, C. (2003), *A Public Laboratory Dewey Barely Imagined: The Emerging Model of School Governance and Legal Reform*. On Charles Sabel's Website: http://www2.law.columbia.edu/sabel/papers/deweySAE3NYUEDITjslcfsedi.doc

Lijphart, A. (1968), *The Politics of Accommodation*. Berkeley: University of California Press.

— (1977), *Democracy in Plural Societies*. New Haven: Yale University Press

— (1984), *Democracies*. New Haven and London: Yale University Press.

— (1985), *Power-Sharing in South Africa*. Berkeley: IIS, UC Berkeley.

— (1991), 'The Power-Sharing Approach', in J. Montville (ed.) *Conflict and Peace-Making in Multiethnic Societies*. New York: Lexington, 491-509.

— (1995), 'Self-Determination versus Pre-Determination in Powersharing Systems', in Kymlicka, W. (ed.) *The Rights of Cultural Minorities*. Oxford: University Press, 275-287.

Lind, M. (1995), *The Next American Nation*. New York: Free Press.

Luckmann, T. (1967), *Invisible Religion*. New York: MacMillan.

Luhmann, N. (1977), *Funktion der Religion*. Frankfurt am Main: Suhrkamp.

— (2001), *Die Religion der Gesellschaft*. Frankfurt am Main: Suhrkamp.

Lustick, J. (1979), 'Stability in Deeply Divided Societies: Consociationalism versus Control'. *World Politics* 31, 325-344.

Macedo, S. (1991), *Liberal Values*. Oxford: Oxford University Press.

— (1997), 'Transformative Constitutionalism and the Case of Religion', in *Political Theory*, 26/1: 56-80.

— (2000), *Diversity and Distrust*. Cambridge etc.: Harvard University Press.

— (2002), 'Introduction', in S. Macedo & Y. Tamir (eds.), 1-22.

— & Tamir, Y. (eds.) *Moral and Political Education*. NOMOS 43, New York University Press.

— & Wolf, P. (2004), 'Introduction: School Choice, Civic Values, and Problems of Policy Comparison', in P. Wolf & S. Macedo (eds.), 1-30.

Madan, T.N. (1998), 'Secularism in Its Place', in R. Bhargava (ed.), 297-320.

Madeley, J. (2003), 'Towards an Inclusive Typology of Church-State Relations in Europe'. ECPR Copenhagen, 14-19 April 2000. Shorter version published as: 'A Framework for the Comparative Analysis of Church-State Relations in Europe', in J. Madeley & Z. Enyedi (eds.), 23-50.

— (2003a), 'European Liberal Democracy and the Principle of State Religious Neutrality', in J. Madeley & Z. Enyedi (eds.), 1-22.

— & Enyedi, Z. (eds.) (2003), *Church and State in Contemporary Europe*. London: Frank Cass.

Mahajan, G. (2005), 'Can intra-group equality co-exist with cultural diversity?' in A. Eisenberg & J. Spinner (eds.) *Minorities Within Minorities*. Cambridge: Cambridge University Press, 90-112

Maier, S. (2004), 'Multicultural Jurisprudence'. Council of European Scholars Conference, Chicago, 11-13 March.

Mandaville, P. (2001), *Transnational Muslim Politics*. London and New York: Routledge.

Manow, P. (2004), 'The Good, the Bad, and the Ugly'. MpfG Working Paper 04/3, September.

Mansbridge, J. (1992), 'A deliberative perspective on neocorporatism', in *Politics and Society* 20: 4, 493-506.

Markoff, J. & Reagan, D. (1987), 'Religion, the State and Political Legitimacy in the World's Constitutions', in T. Robbins & R. Robertson (eds.), 161ff.

Marquand, D. & Nettler, R. (eds.) (2000), *Religion and Democracy*. Oxford: Blackwell.

Marramao, G. (1992), 'Säkularisierung', in *Historisches Wörterbuch der Philosophie*, Band 8. Schwabe + Co. Basel.

Martin, D. (1978), *A General Theory of Secularization*. New York: Harper & Row.

— (1990), *Tongues of Fire*. Oxford: Basil Blackwell.

Marty, M. & Appleby, S. (eds.) (1991), *Fundamentalism Observed*. Chicago, London: University of Chicago Press.

Massignon, B. (2003), Regulation of religious diversity by the institutions of the EU (http://www.hartsem.edu/sociology_online_articles_massignon.html).

Maussen, M. (2007), 'Constructing Mosques: Negotiating Islam and Cultural Diversity in the Netherlands and France (1900 - 2004)'. Ph.D. thesis, University of Amsterdam.

Mayer, A. (1999), *Islam and Human Rights*. Boulder, CO: Westview Press.

Mazower, M. (2005), *Salonica*. London, New York, Toronto and Sydney: Harper Perennial.

McAndrew, M. (2003), 'Should National Minorities/Majorities share common institutions or control their own schools', in C. Harzig & D. Juteau et al. (eds.) *The Social Construction of Diversity*. New York and Oxford: Berghahn, 186-211.

McConnell, M. (1992), 'Accommodation of Religion', in *George Washington Law Review* 60: 3, 685-742.

— (2000), 'Believers as Equal Citizens', in N. Rosenblum (ed.) *Obligations of Citizenship and Demands of Faith*. Princeton etc.: Princeton University Press, 90-110.

— (2001), 'Old Liberalism, New Liberalism, and People of Faith', in M. McConnel, et al. (eds.) *Christian Perspectives on Legal Thought*. New Haven: Yale University Press.

— (2002), 'Educational Disestablishment', in S. Macedo & Y. Tamir (eds.), 87-146.

— & Posner, R. A. (1989), 'An Economic Approach to Issues of Religious Freedom', in *University of Chicago Law Review* 65: 1, 1-60.

McLean, D. (1995), 'Staat und Kirche im Vereinigten Königreich', in T. Robbers (ed.), 333-350.

Meerman, M. (1999), *Gebroken Wit*. Amsterdam: Thela Thesis.

Meerschaut, K. (2006), *Diversiteit en Recht*. Ph.D. thesis, Vrije Universiteit Brussel.

Merry, M. & Driessen, G. (2005), 'Islamic schools in three western countries'. in *Comparative Education* 41/4, 411-432.

Messner, F. (1999), 'La Législation culturelle des pays de l'Union européenne', in F. Champion & M. Cohen (eds.) *Sectes et démocratie*. Paris, 331-358.

Meuret, D. (2004), 'School Choice and its Regulation in France', in P. Wolf & S. Macedo (eds.), 238-267.

Miller, D. (1995), *On Nationality*. Oxford: Oxford University Press.

— (2007), *National Responsibility and Global Justice*. Forthcoming. Oxford: Oxford University Press.

Miller, W. L. (1985), *The First Liberty*. New York: Alfred A. Knopf Inc.

Minkenberg, M. (2003), 'The Policy Impact of Church-State Relations: Family Policy and Abortion', in J. Madeley & Z. Enyedi (eds.), 195-217.

— (2003a), 'Staat und Kirche in westlichen Demokratien', in M. Minkenberg & U. Willems (eds.), 115-138.

— (2007), 'Democracy and religion today'. Forthcoming in *Journal of Ethnic and Migration Studies*, 33/60.

— & Willems, U. (eds.) (2003), 'Politik und Religion', in *PVS Sonderheft* 33/2002, June 2003.

Minnerath, R. (2001), 'Church Autonomy in Europe', in G. Robbers (ed.) *Church Autonomy*. Frankfurt am Main: Peter Lang, 381-394.

Minow, M. (1990), *Making All the Difference*. Ithaca: Cornell University Press.

— (2000), 'Partner, not Rivals?', in *Boston University Law Review* 80: 1060-1094.

Modood, T. (1996), 'Introduction', in T. Modood (ed.) *Church, State and Religious Minorities*. London: Policy Studies Institute.

— (2001), Comment. Religious Pluralism Workshop. Amsterdam, 29 June.

— (2005), 'Muslims, Religious Equality and Secularism'. Forthcoming in G. Levey & T. Modood (eds.) (2007).

— (ed.) (1996), *Church, State and Religious Minorities*. London, Policy Studies Institute (contributions by Tariq Modood, Bhikhu Parekh, Anne Phillips, Jim Herrick, Sylvia Rothschild, Dharmchari Kulananda, Daoud Rosser-Owen).

Monsma, S. & Soper, C. (1997), *The Challenge of Pluralism Church and State in Five Democracies*. Lanham, New York, etc.: Rowman & Littlefield.

— (2006), *Faith, Hope & Jobs*. Washington, DC: Georgetown University Press.

Moore, M. (2005), 'Internal Minorities and Indigenous Self-Determination', in A. Eisenberg & J. Spinner (eds.) *Minorities Within Minorities*. Cambridge: Cambridge University Press, 271-293.

Moore, R.L. (1994), *Selling God*. New York and Oxford: Oxford University Press.

Mortanges, R. & Tanner, E. (eds.) (2005), *Kooperation zwischen Staat und Religionsgemeinschaften nach Schweizerischem Recht*. Zurich etc.: Schulthess.

Mouffe, C. (2000), *The Democratic Paradox*. London: Verso.

Moskos, C. & Chambers, J.W. II (eds.) (1993), *The New Conscientious Objection*. New York and London: Oxford University Press.

Müller, A. (2005), 'Ist der freiheitliche Staat auf vorpolitische Ressourcen des Religiösen angewiesen etc.?' in R. Mortanges & S. Tanner (eds.), 35-90.

Murphy, J. B. (2004), 'Against Civic Schooling', in *Social Philosophy and Policy Foundation*, 221-265.

Nandy, A. (1998), 'The Politics of Secularism and the Recovery of Religious Toleration', in R. Bhargava (ed.), 231-344.

Neal, P. (1997), *Liberalism and its Discontents*. Houndsmill etc.: MacMillan.

Nordlinger, E. (1972), *Conflict Regulation in Divided Societies*. Cambridge: Harvard Univ. Press.

Novotny, H. et al. (2001), *Re-Thinking Science. Knowledge and the Public in an Age of Uncertainty*. Polity Press: Cambridge.

Nussbaum, M. (1997), 'Religion and Women's Human Rights', in P. Weithman (ed.), 93-137.

— (1999), *Sex and Social Justice*. New York etc.: Oxford University Press.

— (2000), *Women and Human Development*. Cambridge: Cambridge University Press.

— (2000a), 'Religion and Women's Equality: The Case of India', in N. Rosenblum (ed.), 335-402.

Offe, C. (1998), 'Homogeneity and Constitutional Democracy', in *Journal of Political Philosophy* 6/2: 113-141.
— (1998a), 'Designing Institutions in East European Transitions', in R. Goodin (ed.), *The Theory of Institutional Design*. Cambridge: Cambridge University Press, 199-226.
Okin, S. (1989), *Justice, Gender and the Family*. New York: Basic Books.
— (1997), 'Is Multiculturalism Bad for Women?', in *Boston Review*, Winter. http://www.bostonreview.net/BR22.5/okin.html
— (2002), 'Mistresses of Their Own Destiny', in *Ethics* 112/2: 205-230.
— (2005), 'Multiculturalism and Feminism: No Simple Question, No Simple Answers', in A. Eisenberg & J. Spinner (eds.) *Minorities Within Minorities*. Cambridge: Cambridge University Press, 67-89.
Otterbeck, J. (2004), 'The Legal Status of Islamic Minorities in Sweden', in Aluffi & Zincone (eds.) *The Legal Treatment of Islamic Minorities in Europe*. Leeuven: Peeters.

Parekh, B. (1994), 'Cultural Diversity and Liberal Democracy', in D. Beetham (ed.) *Defining and Measuring Democracy*. London etc.: Sage, 199-221.
— (1996), 'Religion in Public Life', in T. Modood (ed.), 16-23.
— (2000), *Rethinking Multiculturalism*. Houndsmill etc.: MacMillan.
— (2005), 'Principles of a Global Ethic', in J. Eade & D. O'Byrne (eds.) *Global Ethics and civil society*. Ashgate: Aldershot Press, 15-33.
Parijs, P. V. (ed.) (2004), *Cultural Diversity versus Economic Solidarity*. De Boeck: Brussels.
Pauly, A. (1995), 'Staat und Kirche in Luxemburg', in G. Robbers (ed.), 211-228.
Penninx, R. & Schovers, M. (2001), *Bastion of bindmiddel?* Amsterdam: IMES Essays.
Peter, F. (2004), 'Crisis of Laïcité and Reformist Discourses in France'. Unpublished manuscript,. Leiden: ISIM.
Peters, R. (1998), 'Islamic law and human rights', in *Recht van de Islam* 15: 7-24.
— (2003), *Islamic Criminal Law in Nigeria*. Ibadan: Spectrum.
Pfaff, S. & Gill, A. (2006), 'Will a Million Muslims March? Muslim Interest Organizations and Political Integration in Europe', in *Comparative Political Studies* 39/37: 803-828.
Pfeffer, L. (1987), 'Religious Exemptions', in T. Robbins & R. Robertson (eds.) *Church-State Relations*. New Brunswick etc.: Transaction Inc., 103-114.
Phillips, A. (1995), *The Politics of Presence*. Oxford: Clarendon.
— (1996), 'In Defense of Secularism', in T. Modood (ed.), 23-30.
— (2005), 'Dilemmas of gender and culture', in A. Eisenberg & J. Spinner (eds.) *Minorities Within Minorities*. Cambridge: Cambridge University Press, 113-134.
— & Dustin, M. (2004), 'UK initiatives on forced marriage: regulation, dialogue exit'. *Political studies* 52, no. 3, 531-551.
Plesner, I. (2001), 'State Church and Church Autonomy in Norway', in Robbers, G. (ed.) *Church Autonomy*. Frankfurt am Main: Peter Lang, 467-484.
Poulter, S. (1998), *Ethnicity, Law, and Human Rights*. Oxford: Clarendon Press.
Pötz, R. (1995), 'Staat und Kirche in Österreich', in G. Robbers (ed.), 251-280.
Putnam, H. (2001), *Enlightenment and Pragmatism*. Assen: Van Gorcum.

Rath, J. et al. (1996), *Nederland en zijn Islam*. Amsterdam: Spinhuis.
— (2001), *Western Europe and its Islam*. Leiden: Brill.
— & Kloosterman, C. (eds.) (2003), *Immigrant Entrepreneurs*. Oxford: Berg.
Rawls, J. (1971), *A Theory of Justice*. Cambridge, MA.: Harvard University Press.
— (1993), *Political Liberalism*. New York: Columbia University Press. Preface 2nd edition 1996.
— (1995), 'Reply to Habermas', in *Journal of Philosophy* 92/3: 132-180.
— (1999), *The Law of Peoples*. Cambridge: Harvard University Press.
Raz, J. (1986), *The Morality of Freedom*. Oxford: Oxford University Press.

Rehrmann, N (2000), 'A Legendary Place of Encounter'. ENCS Conference Paper, Bremen 18-21 May.

Reich, R. (2002), *Bridging Liberalism and Multiculturalism in American Education*. Chicago: University of Chicago Press.

— (2005), 'Minors Within Minorities', in Eisenberg, A. & Spinner, J. (eds.) *Minorities Within Minorities*. Cambridge: Cambridge University Press, 209-226.

— (2006), 'Common schooling and educational choice'. Unpublished manuscript.

— & Koski, W. (2006), 'The State's Obligation to Educate: Adequate Education or Equal Education?', Manuscript for rethinking *Rodriguez*.

Reitman, O. (2005), 'On Exit', in A. Eisenberg J. & Spinner (eds.) *Minorities Within Minorities*. Cambridge: Cambridge University Press, 189-208.

Renteln, A.D. (1990), *International Human Rights*. Newbury Park, London: Sage.

— (2004), *The Cultural Defense*. Oxford: Oxford University Press.

Reuter, L. (2004), 'School Choice and Civic Values in Germany', in P. Wolf & S. Macedo (eds.), 213-237.

Ribolzi, L. (2004), 'Italy: The Impossible Choice', in Wolf & Macedo (eds.), 268-286.

Richards, D.A. (1986), *Toleration and the Constitution*. New York and Oxford: Oxford University Press.

Richardson, H. S. (1990), 'The Problem of Liberalism and the Good', in R. B. Douglass, G. M. Mara et al. (eds.) *Liberalism and the Good*. New York: Routledge, 1-28.

Robbers, G. (1995), 'Staat und Kirche in der Europäischen Union', in Robbers (ed.), 351-362.

— (ed.) 'Staat und Kirche in der Europäischen Union.' Nomos: Baden-Baden. English version (1995), *State and Church in the European Union*. Baden-Baden: Nomos.

— (ed.) (2001), *Church Autonomy*. Frankfurt am Main: Peter Lang.

Robertson, R. (1987), 'General Considerations in the Study of Contemporary Church-State Relationships', in T. Robbins & R. Robertson (eds.), 5-12.

— (1987a), 'Church-State Relations in Comparative Perspective', in T. Robbins & R. Robertson (eds.) *Church-State Relations*. New Brunswick: Transaction Inc., 1987a, 153-160.

— (1993), 'Community, Society, Globality, and the Category of Religion', in E. Barker et al. (eds.), 1-18.

Robbins, T. (1987), 'Church-State Tensions and Marginal Movements', in T. Robbins & R. Robertson (eds.), 135-152.

— (1987a), 'Church-State Tensions in the United States', in T. Robbins & R. Robertson (eds.), 67-76.

— & Robertson, R. (eds.) (1987), *Church-State Relations*. New Brunswick etc.: Transaction Inc.

Rogers, J. & Streeck, W. (1995), *Works Councils*. Chicago: Chicago University Press.

Rooden, P. van (1996), *Religieuze Regimes*. Amsterdam: Bakker.

Rorty, R. (1994), 'Religion as Conversation-Stopper', in *Common Knowledge* 3/1: 1-6.

— (1997), '*Truth, politics and 'post-modernism'*', Spinoza Lecture 2: Is 'post-modernism' relevant to politics? Assen: Van Gorcum.

Rosenblum, N. (1998), *Membership and Morals*. Princeton etc.: Princeton University Press.

— (2000a), '*Amos*: Religious Autonomy and the Moral Uses of Pluralism', in N. Rosenblum (ed.), 165-195.

— (2000a), 'Introduction: Pluralism Integralism, and Political Theories of Religious Accommodation', in N. Rosenblum (ed.), 3-31.

— (2002), 'Pluralism and Democratic Education', in S. Macedo & Y. Tamir (eds.), 147-169.

— (2003), 'Institutionalizing Religion: Religious Parties and Political Identity in Contemporary Democracies', in *Ethical Theory and Moral Practice* 6: 23-54.

— (ed.) (2000), *Obligations of Citizenship and Demands of Faith*. Princeton etc.: Princeton University Press.

Roy, O. (2002), *Globalised Islam*. London: Hurst.

Rudolph, S.H. & Rudolph, L. (2000), 'Living with Difference in India', in D.. Marquand & R. Nettler (eds.), 19-37.

Sabel, C. (2004), 'Beyond Principal-Agent Governance', in E. Engelen & M. Sie (eds.) *De staat van de democratie*. Amsterdam: Amsterdam University Press, 173-196.

Saeed, A. (2005), 'Muslims in the West and their Attitudes to Full Participation in Western Societies'. Forthcoming in G. Levey & T. Modood (eds.) (2007).

Safran, W. (2003), 'Pluralism and Multiculturalism in France', in *Political Science Quarterly* 188: 3, 437-463.

— (2004), 'Ethnoreligious Politics in France: Jews and Muslims', in *West European Politics* 27: 3, 423-451.

Saharso, S. (1999), 'Female Autonomy and Cultural Imperative: Two Hearts Beating Together', in W. Kymlicka & W. Norman (eds.) *Citizenship in Diverse Societies*. Oxford: Oxford University Press, 224-244.

— (2006), 'Is Freedom of the Will but a Western Illusion?' Forthcoming in B. Arneil et al. (eds.) *Sexual Justice/Cultural Justice*. Routledge.

— & and Verhaar, O. (2004), 'The Weight of Context: Headscarves in Holland', in *ETMP* 7/2, 179-195.

Salvatore, A. (2004), 'Making Public Space', in *Journal of Ethnic and Migration Studies* 30/5, 1013-1031.

Saunders, D. (2005), 'France on the Knife-Edge of Religion', in G. Levey & T. Modood (eds.) (2007).

Schacht, J. (1982), *An Introduction to Islamic Law*. Oxford: Clarendon Press.

Scheffler, S. (2001), *Boundaries and Allegiances*. Oxford: Oxford University Press.

Schermerhorn, R. (1970), *Comparative Ethnic Relations*. New York: Random House.

Schiffauer, W. et al. (eds.) (2004), *Civil Enculturation*. New York and Oxford: Berghahn Press.

Schmidt, V. (2006), *Democracy in Europe*. Oxford: Oxford University Press.

Schmitter, P. (2000), *How to Democratize the European Union – and Why Bother?* Oxford: Rowman & Littlefield.

— (2001), 'What is there to legitimize the European Union'. Working Paper EUI.

Schön, D. (1983), *The Reflective Practitioner*. New York: Basic Books.

Schött. R (1995), 'Staat und Kirche in Schweden', in G. Robbers (ed.), 319-332.

Scott, J. (1998), *Seeing like a state*. New Haven and London: Yale University Press.

Segers, M. & Jelen, T. (1998), A Wall of Separation? Lenham etc.: Rowman + Littlefield.

Selznick, P. (1992), *The Moral Commonwealth*. University of California Press.

Sen, A. (1995), 'Secularism and Its Discontents.' in K. Basu & S. Subrahmanyam (eds.) *Unraveling the Nation*. New Delhi: Penguin.

— (2004), 'Elements of a Theory of Human Rights', in *PPA* 32/4, 315-356.

— (2005), *The Argumentative Indian*. Harmondsworth: Penguin.

Shachar, A. (2001), *Multicultural Jurisdictions*. Cambridge: Cambridge University Press.

— (2005), 'Religion, State and the Problem of Gender', in *McGill Law Journal* 50, 49-88.

Shah, T. S. (2000), 'Making the Christian World Safe for Liberalism', in D. Marquand & R. Nettler (eds.) *Religion and Democracy*. Oxford: Blackwell, 121-139.

Shahid, W. & Koningsveld, P. (eds.) (2002), *Religious freedom and the neutrality of the state: the position of Islam in the European Union*. Leuven: Peeters.

— (2006), 'Islamic Religious Education in the Netherlands', in *European Education*, 38/2, 76-88.

Shapiro, I. (1999). *Democratic Justice*. New Haven and London: Yale University Press.

Shaw, B. (1999), 'Habermas and Religious Inclusion', in *Political Theory* 27/5, 634-666.

Sheleff, L. (2000), *The Future of Tradition*. London and Portland: Frank Cass.

Shklar, J. (1990), 'The Liberalism of Fear', in N. Rosenblum (ed.) *Liberalism and the Moral Life*. Cambridge, MA.: Harvard University Press, 1989, 21-38.

Shue, H. (1980), *Basic Rights*. Princeton: Princeton University Press.

— (1995), 'Thickening Convergence: Human Rights and Cultural Diversity'. Amnesty Lectures, Oxford, 6 November.

Sisk, T. (1996), *Power Sharing and International Mediation in Ethnic Conflicts*. New York: Carnegie Corporation of New York.

Skillen, J. (1996), 'From covenant of grace to equitable public pluralism', in *Calvin Theological Journal* 31/1, 67ff.

Smith, A. (1981), *The Ethnic Revival*. Cambridge and London: Cambridge University Press.

Smith, D. E. (1998), 'India as a Secular State', in R. Bhargava (ed.), 177-233.

Smith, G. (2000), 'Sustainable Federalism, Democratization, and Distributive Justice', in W. Kymlicka & W. Norman (eds.), 345-365.

Smith, R. (2003), *Stories of Peopleshood*. Cambridge University Press

Soifer, A. (2000), 'The Fullness of Time', in Rosenblum, N. (ed.), 245-279.

Solinge, H. & Vries, M. van de (eds.) (2001), *De Joden in Nederland Anno 2000*. Amsterdam: Aksant.

Soper, C. & Fetzer, J. (2007), 'Religious Institutions, Church-State History, and Muslim Mobilization in Britain, France, and Germany'. Forthcoming in *JEMS* 33/6.

Soroka, S., Johnston, R., Banting, K. (2004), 'Ethnicity, trust, and the welfare state', in P. Parijs (ed.), 33-57.

Spinner-Halev, J. (2000), *Surviving Diversity*. Baltimore etc.: John Hopkins University Press.

— (2001), 'Feminism, Multiculturalism, Oppression, and the State', in *Ethics* 112: 84-113.

— (2005), 'Autonomy, association and pluralism', in A. Eisenberg & J. Spinner-Halev (eds.), 157-171.

— (2005a), 'Hinduism, Christianity, and Liberal Religious Toleration', in *Political Theory* 33/1, 28-57.

Spohn, W. (2003), 'Nationalismus und Religion', in M. Minkenberg & U. Willems (eds.), 323-345.

— (2003a), 'Multiple Modernity, Nationalism and Religion', in *Current Sociology* 51: 3/4, 265-286.

Stepan, A. (2000), 'Religion, Democracy, and the "Twin Tolerations"', in *Journal of Democracy* 11, 37-57.

Stoep, J. van den (2004), 'Towards a Sociological Turn in Contextualist Moral Philosophy', in *Ethical Theory and Moral Practice* 7, 133-146.

Stoltenberg, N.M. (1993), 'He Drew a Circle That Shut Me Out' in *Harvard Law Review* 106, 581-667.

Strätz, H. (2004), 'Säkularisation, Säkularisierung', in *Geschichtliche Grundbegriffe*. Stuttgart: Klett-Cotta, *Bd. 5*, 792-809.

Swaine, L. (1996), 'Principled Separation', in *Journal of Church and State* 38: 595-617.

— (2001), 'How Ought Liberal Democracies to Treat Theocratic Communities?', in *Ethics* 111: 302-343.

— (2003), 'Institutions of Conscience', in *Ethical Theory and Moral Practice*, 6/1: 93-118.

— (2003a), 'A Liberalism of Conscience', in *The Journal of Political Philosophy* 11 (4): 369-391.

— (2005), 'Advancing Liberalism: Progressing Beyond Autonomy'. APSA paper, 1-4 September.

— (2006), *The Liberal Conscience*. New York: Columbia University Press.

Tamir, Y. (1993), *Liberal Nationalism*. Princeton: Princeton University Press.

Tasioulas, J. (2002), 'Human rights, Universality and the Values of Personhood', in *European Journal of Philosophy* 10/1, 79-100.

Taylor, C. (1998), 'Modes of Secularism', in R. Bhargava (ed.) *Secularism and its Critics*. Delhi: Oxford University Press.
— (2002), *Varieties of Religion Today*. Cambridge: Harvard University Press.
Teubner, G. (2002), 'Idiosyncratic Production Regimes: Co-evolution of Economic and Legal Institutions in the Varieties of Capitalism', in *Proceedings of the British Academy* 112: 161-181.
Thiemann, R.F. (1996), *Religion in Public Life*. Washington, DC: Georgetown University Press.
Tomasi, J. (2001), *Liberalism Beyond Justice*. Princeton and Oxford: Princeton University Press.
— (2002), 'Civic Education and Ethical Subservience', in S. Macedo & Y. Tamir (eds.), 193-220.
— (2004), Should Political Liberals be compassionate conservatives? *Social Philosophy & Policy Foundation*, 322-345.
Torfs, R. (1995), 'Staat und Kirche in Belgien', in G. Robbers (ed.), 15-38.
Tully, J. (1995), *Strange Multiplicity*. Cambridge: Cambridge University Press.
— (1999), 'The Agonic Freedom of Citizens', in *Economy and Society* 28: 2 May, 161-182.
— (2003), 'Struggles of Indigenous Peoples for and of Freedom', in Walkem, A. et al. (eds.) *Box of Treasures of Empty Box*. Theytus Books: Vancouver, 272-308.
— (2004), 'Political Philosophy as a Critical Activity', in S. White & D. Moon (eds.) *What is Political Theory?* London: Sage Publications, 80-102.
— (2005), 'Exclusion and Assimilation: two forms of domination', in M. Williams & S. Macedo (eds.) *Domination and Exclusion*. Princeton: Princeton University Press, 191-229.
Tushnet, M. (1986), 'The Constitution of Religion', in *Connecticut Law Review* 18: 701-738.

Unger, R. M. (1983), *Critical Legal Studies Movement*. Cambridge, MA: Harvard University Press.
— (1987), *Politics*. Cambridge: Cambridge University Press.

Valadez, J. (2001), 'Deliberative Democracy, Political Legitimacy, and Selfdetermination', in *Multicultural Societies*. Boulder, CO: Westview Press.
Valauri, J. T. (1986), 'The Concept of Neutrality in Establishment Clause Doctrine', in *University of Pittsburgh Law Review*, 48: 1, 83-151.
Veer, P. van der (1997), 'Religion, Secularity, and Tolerance in India and Europe', in *The Eastern Anthropologist*, 50: 3-4, 381-393.
Verba, S. et al. (1995), *Voice and Equality*. Cambridge: Harvard University Press.
Vermeulen, B. (2004), 'Regulating School Choice to Promote Civic Values: Constitutional and Political Issues in the Netherlands', in P. Wolf & S. Macedo (eds.), 31-66.
Vermeulen, H. & Penninx, R. (eds.) (1995), *Het democratisch ongeduld*. Amsterdam: Het Spinhuis.
Vertovec, S. & Peach, C. (eds.) (1997), *Islam in Europe: The Politics of Religion and Community*. Houndsmill and London: MacMillan.
Vries, H. de & Sullivan, L. (eds.) (2006), *Political Theologies*. Fordham University Press.

Waldron, J. (1993), 'Religious Contributions in Public Deliberation', in *San Diego Law Review* 30: 817-848.
Wallis, R. & Bruce, S. (1992), 'Secularization', in Bruce, S. (ed.) *Religion and Modernization*. Oxford: ClarendonPress, 8-30.
Walzer, M. (1994), *Thick and Thin*. Notre Dame: University of Notre Dame Press.
— (1995), 'Response' in D. Miller & M. Walzer (eds.) *Pluralism, Justice, and Equality*. Oxford: Oxford University Press.
— (1997), *On Toleration*. New Haven and London: Yale University Press.

Wasserstein, B. (1996), *Het einde van een diaspora*. Baarn: Ambo.

Warren, M. (2001), *Democracy and Association*. Princeton and Oxford: Princeton University Press.

Weber, M. (1972), *Wirtschaft und Gesellschaft*. Tübingen: Mohr.

Weil, P. (2004), 7 February, e-mail to J. Carens.

Weinstock, D. (2002), 'Group Rights: Reframing the Debate'. Paper, Minorities Within Minorities Conference: Lincoln, Nebraska, 4-5 October.

Weithman, P. (1997), 'Introduction: Religion and the Liberalism of Reasoned Respect', in Weithman, P. (ed.) 1997, 1-38.

— (ed.) (1997), *Religion and Contemporary Liberalism*. Notre Dame: University of Notre Dame Press.

Whitehouse, L. (2005), 'The Global Compact: Corporate Citizenship in Action, but is it Enough?', in Eade, J. & O'Byrne, D. (eds.) *Global Ethics and Civil Society*, Ashgate: Aldershot, 108-120.

Wilkins, B. T. (1997), 'A Third Principle of Justice', in *The Journal of Ethics* 1: 355-374.

Willaime, J. (1996), 'Laïcité et religion en France', in G. Davie et al. (eds.), 153-174.

— (2004), *Europe et religions*. Fayard: Paris.

— (ed.) (2005), *Des Maîtres et des Dieux*. Berlin.

— (2006), 'L'enseignement au sujet des religions à l'école publique en France'. Unpublished manuscript.

Willems, U. (2003), 'Moralskepsis, Interessenreduktionismus und Strategien der Förderung von Demokratie und Gemeinwohl', in id. (ed.) *Interesse und Moral als Orientierungen politischen Handelns*. Baden-Baden: Nomos, 9-98.

— (2004), 'Weltanschaulich neutraler Staat, christlich-abendländische Kultur und Säkularismus', in Walther, M. (ed.) *Religion und Politik*. Baden-Baden: Nomos, 303-328.

Williams, M. (1998), *Voice, Trust, and Memory*. New Haven etc.: Yale University Press.

— (2000), 'The Uneasy Alliance of Group Representation and Deliberative Democracy', in W. Kymlicka & W. Norman (eds.), 124-153.

— (2001), Toward a Deliberative Understanding of Justice Toward Groups. Unpublished manuscript.

— (2003), 'Citizenship as Identity, Citizenship as Shared Fate, and the Functions of Multicultural Education', in Feinberg, W. & McDonough, K. (eds.) *Collective Identity and Cosmopolitan Values'*. Oxford: Oxford University Press.

— (2005), 'Tolerable Liberalism', in A. Eisenberg & J. Spinner (eds.) *Minorities Within Minorities*. Cambridge: Cambridge University Press, 19-40.

Wilson, B. (1992), 'Reflections on a Manysided Controversy', in S. Bruce (ed.), 195-210.

Witte, J. (2004), 'Regulation in Public and Private Schools in the United States', in P. Wolf & S. Macedo (eds.), 355-367.

Wolf, P. & Macedo, S. et al. (eds.) (2004), *Educating Citizens*. Washington D.C.: Brookings Institution Press.

Wolterstorff, N. (1997), 'Why we would reject what liberalism tells us etc.?' in P. Weithman (ed.) *Religion and contemporary liberalism*. Notre Dame: University of Notre Dame Press, 162-181.

WRR (Wetenschappelijke Raad voor het Regeringsbeleid) (2004), *De Europese Unie, Turkije en de Islam*. Amsterdam: Amsterdam University Press.

— (2006), *Dynamiek in islamitisch activisme*. Amsterdam: Amsterdam University Press.

Yack, B. (1986), *The Longing for Total Revolution*. Berkeley etc.: University of California Press.

— Young, I. (1996), 'Communication and the Other', in S. Benhabib (ed.) *Democracy and Difference*. Princeton: Princeton University Press.

Zabel, H. (2004), 'Säkularisation, Säkularisierung' in *Geschichtliche Grundbegriffe*. Band 5, 809-829. Stuttgart: Klett-Cotta.

Zeitlin, J. (2003), 'Introduction', in J. Zeitlin et al. (eds.) *Governing Work and Welfare in a New Economy*. Oxford: Oxford University Press.

— (2005), Social Europe and Experimentalist Governance. *European Governance Papers* C-05-04.

Zinterer, T. (2000), 'For Seven Generations': The Royal Canadian Commission on Aboriginal Peoples and Canada's Public Philosophy'. Paper, ENCS Conference, May 2000, Bremen.

Zolberg, A. (1997), 'Modes of Incorporation', in V. Bader (ed.) *Citizenship and Exclusion*. Houndsmill etc.: MacMillan.

— and Woon, L. (1998), 'Why Islam is like Spanish?' in *Politics and Society* 27/1: 5-38.

Zürcher, E. & Linden, H. van der (2004), *Zoeken naar de breuklijn*. Den Haag: WRR.

Index of names

Index of subjects

accommodation 19, 26, 28, 67, 76, 84, 87, 89, 100, 105, 129, 140, 150-151, 153-154, 157-161, 163-167, 172, 177, 206-207, 220, 230, 250, 260, 291, 297-298, 304-305, 312-313, 319, 323-324, 326-327, 335-336
– maximum accommodation 20, 22, 25, 27, 125, 129, 221, 292, 311
– of religious diversity 13, 18, 20, 23, 25-26, 29, 35, 39, 42, 49-50, 67, 83, 93, 164, 171, 204, 210, 291, 306-307, 313, 337
– of religious practices 25, 38, 57, 160, 177, 192
– practical accommodation 18, 28, 178, 206
Afghanistan 97
Africa 36, 236, 331, 340
Alberta 282, 342
Algeria 98, 315, 319, 337
Alsace-Lorraine 305
Alsace-Moselle 59
Amish 137, 323, 334
Anabaptism 192, 211
Anglo-Saxon 19, 58, 112, 169, 201
Asia 236
associative democracy 15, 19-21, 25, 29-31, 63, 77, 86, 130, 177-179, 183, 185, 187-188, 194, 198, 201, 203, 208, 213, 217, 248, 261, 284, 286, 293, 296, 311, 316, 336
– agonistic democracy 49, 108, 179
– American denominationalism 20, 30, 193, 214, 237, 291, 295, 338

– democratic institutional pluralism 19, 141, 178, 188, 194-195, 198, 203, 208, 220-222, 330
– institutional design 22, 70, 117, 187-188, 201, 213, 216, 218, 220, 237, 245, 247, 259-260, 289, 292, 294, 329, 332
– non-constitutional pluralism 168, 203, 208, 326
– political representation 137, 252, 259
– practical democratic experimentalism 288
– regime pluralism 77, 287
autonomy 18, 28-30, 46-47, 51, 56-58, 61, 67, 72-79, 81, 93-94, 98-99, 102-103, 114, 125, 138-142, 145, 149, 151, 154, 177, 186, 191, 196, 198-199, 208-210, 213, 219-220, 227, 230-231, 237-238, 249, 252, 257, 259, 266-267, 276, 279-282, 287, 292-295, 308-311, 331-337, 339, 344-345
– agency 72, 75-76, 78, 103, 211-212, 267, 292, 296, 339
– associational autonomy 30, 132, 138, 140, 143, 145, 148, 209, 213, 221-222, 238, 292-294
– autonomy dilemma 227, 237, 295
– Church autonomy 30, 57-58,142, 177-178, 237-238, 333, 337, 339
– formal autonomy 57, 226, 285
– individual autonomy 30, 75, 77-78, 139-140, 198, 201, 208-210, 214, 293, 331-332